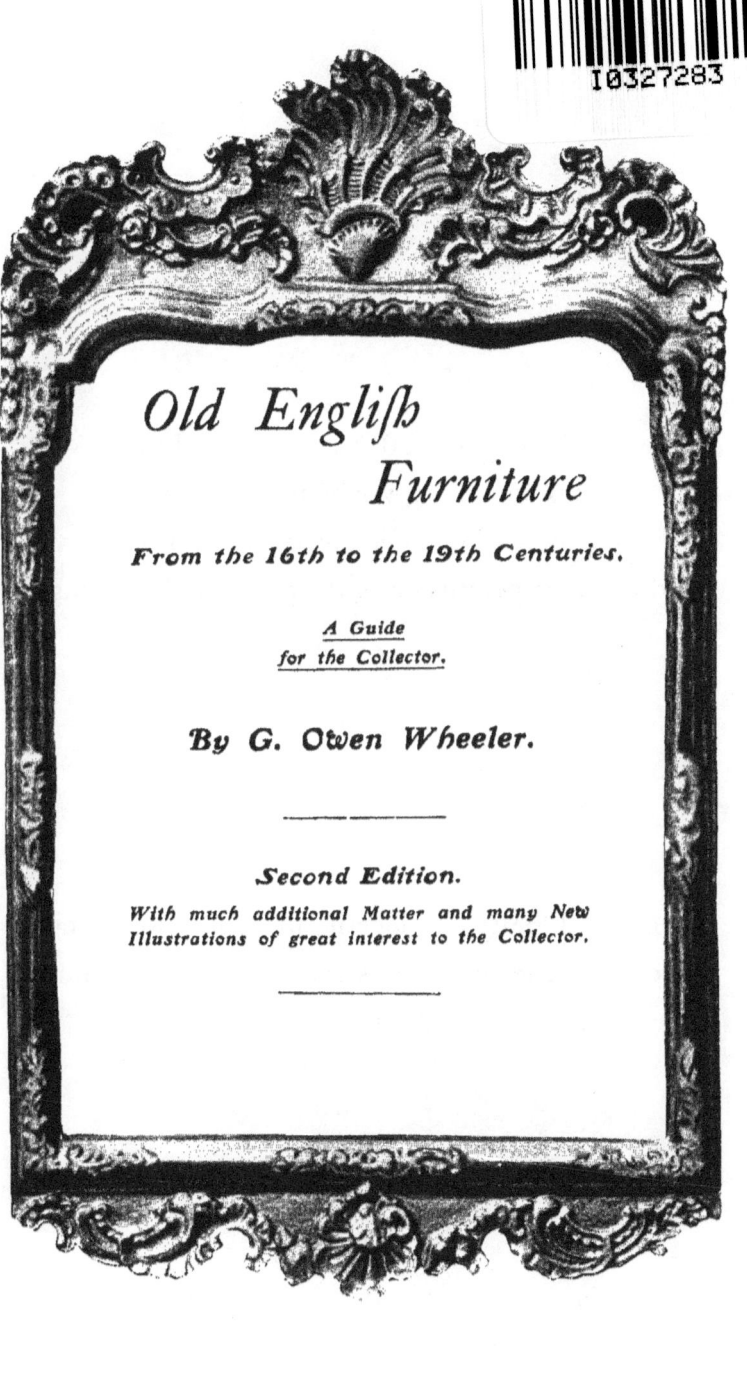

Old English Furniture

From the 16th to the 19th Centuries.

A Guide
for the Collector.

By G. Owen Wheeler.

Second Edition.

With much additional Matter and many New
Illustrations of great interest to the Collector.

Copyright © 2013 Read Books Ltd.
This book is copyright and may not be
reproduced or copied in any way without
the express permission of the publisher in writing

British Library Cataloguing-in-Publication Data
A catalogue record for this book is available from the
British Library

A History of Furniture

Furniture is the mass noun for the movable objects intended to support various human activities, such as seating, storing, working and sleeping. Most often, at least in the present day - furniture is the product of a lengthy design process and considered a form of decorative art. In addition to furniture's functional role, it can also serve a symbolic or religious purpose, for instance in churches, temples or shrines. It can be made from many materials, including metal, plastic, and wood - using a variety of techniques, joins and decoration, reflecting the local culture from which it originated.

Furniture has been a part of the human experience since the development of non-nomadic cultures, and even before this in its crudest form. Evidence of furniture survives from the Neolithic Period and later in antiquity in the form of paintings, such as the wall Murals discovered at Pompeii; sculpture, and examples have been excavated in Egypt and found in tombs in Ghiordes, in modern-day Turkey. Perhaps one of the most interesting archaeological sites is Skara Brae, a Neolithic village located in Orkney (an archipelago in northern Scotland). The site dates from 3100–2500 BC and due to a shortage of wood in Orkney, the people of Skara Brae were forced to build with stone, a readily available material that could be worked easily and turned into household items. Each house shows a high degree of sophistication and was equipped with an extensive assortment of stone furniture, ranging from cupboards, dressers and beds to shelves, stone seats, and limpet tanks. The stone dresser was regarded as the most important item, as it symbolically faced the entrance in each house and was therefore the first item seen when entering.

The furniture of the Middle Ages was usually heavy, oak, and ornamented with carved designs. Along with the other arts, the Italian Renaissance of the fourteenth and fifteenth century marked a rebirth in design, often inspired by the Greco-Roman tradition. A similar explosion of design, and renaissance of culture in general, occurred in Northern Europe, starting in the fifteenth century. The seventeenth century, in both Southern and Northern Europe, was characterized by opulent, often gilded Baroque designs that frequently incorporated a profusion of vegetal and scrolling ornament. Starting in the eighteenth century, furniture designs began to develop more rapidly. Although there were some styles that belonged primarily to one nation, such as 'Palladianism' in Great Britain (derived from and inspired by the designs of the Venetian architect Andrea Palladio) or 'Louis Quinze' in French furniture (characterised by supreme craftsmanship and the integration of the arts of cabinet-making, painting, and sculpture), others, such as 'Rococo' and 'Neoclassicism' were perpetuated throughout Western Europe.

The nineteenth century is usually defined by concurrent revival styles, including Gothic, Neoclassicism, and Roccoco. The design reforms of the late century introduced the 'Aesthetic movement' (essentially promoting the beauty of objects above any other social or political themes) and the 'Arts and Crafts movement' (An international design movement that flourished between 1860-1910, led by William Morris. It stood for traditional craftsmanship using simple form, often applying medieval, romantic or folk styles of decoration). Art Nouveau, in turn was influenced by both of these movements. This latter development was perhaps the most influential of all, inspired by natural forms and structures; evident primarily in architecture, but also the beautiful objects crafted to fill such spaces. Noted furniture designers in this style included William H. Bradley; the 'Dean of American Designers', Goerges de Feure, the Parisian designer who famously produced the theatre designs for *Le Chat Noir* cabaret, and Hermann Obrist, a German sculptor of the Jugendstil (the German branch of Art Nouveaux) movement.

The first three-quarters of the twentieth century are often seen as the march towards Modernism in furniture design. Modernism, in general, includes the activities and creations of those who felt traditional forms of art, architecture, literature, religious faith and social activities were becoming outdated in the new economic, social, and political environment of an emergent industrialized world. Art Deco, De Stijl, Bauhaus, Wiener Werkstätte, and Vienna Secession designers all worked to some degree within the Modernist idiom. Born from the Bauhaus and Art Deco/Streamline styles came the post WWII 'Mid-Century Modern' style using materials developed during the war including laminated plywood, plastics and fibreglass. Prime examples include furniture designed by George Nelson Associates, Charles and Ray Eames, Paul McCobb and Danish modern designers including Finn Juhl and Arne Jacobsen. Post-modern design, intersecting the Pop art movement, gained steam in the 1960s and 70s, promoted in the 1980s by groups such as the Italy-based Memphis movement. The latter group worked with ephemeral designs, featuring colourful decoration and asymmetrical shapes.

As is evident from this short history, the history of artistic developments is inextricably linked with the progression of furniture design. This is hardly surprising, as after all, many artists, thinkers and designers would stringently resist any artificial separation between traditional fine art and functional design. Both respond to their wider context and environment, both, perhaps in differing ways, seeking to impact on reality and society.

Today, British professional furniture makers have self organised into a strong and vibrant community, largely under the organisation 'The Worshipful Company of Furniture Makers', commonly referred to as the Furniture Makers or the Furniture Makers Company. Its motto is 'Straight and Strong'! Members of the Company come from many professions and disciplines, but the common link is that all members on joining must be engaged in or with the UK furnishing industry. Thus the work of the Company is delivered by members with wide ranging professional knowledge and skills in manufacturing, retailing, education, journalism; in fact any aspect of the industry. There are many similar organisations across the globe, as well as in the UK, all seeking to integrate and promote the valuable art that is furniture making. Education is a key factor in such endeavours, and maintaining strong links between professional practitioners, didactic colleges and the amateur maker/restorer is crucial. We hope the reader enjoys this book.

Prefatory & Introductory.

THE welcomes extended to the subscription and ordinary impressions of the First Edition lead the Author to hope that the work in its enlarged form, with its very considerably-increased volume of information and its numerous additional illustrations, may be found to be of use to collectors. The Jacobean section has undergone considerable revision and much amplification, more especially in regard to Charles II. furniture. Extended treatment has been accorded to "Lacquered Furniture," which now forms a separate chapter, and the same may be said of "Georgian." The chapters on Chippendale and the brothers Adam have been materially revised and added to, while "Heppelwhite," "Sheraton," and the "Lesser English Cabinet-makers" have been partially remodelled. "Grinling Gibbons," "The Seddons," "Upholstery," and "Prices" are four additional chapters, and the matter relating to "Musical Instruments" provides an entirely fresh section.

It may be well to lay down that when writing one can only generalise as to dates in the case of many pieces of country-made furniture. Centres such as those of Canterbury, Winchester, Salisbury, Bath, Norwich, Lincoln, and York once possessed an importance as compared with old London quite out of proportion to that which, in these days of rapid transit, they now hold. These seats of craftsmanship, amenable as they were to varying influences owing to their geographical situation, usually supplied the wants of the nobility and gentry of their respective country sides, and a spirit of conservatism or well-balanced taste frequently led to the local retention of commendable detail or outline which had unfortunately become obsolete elsewhere.

An apprentice trained under a clever master at York in 1575 may well have handled a Renaissance bulb with the vigour of the true Tudor school in his later work of the period 1630, and, just as he rose above the level of his contemporaries, so he would be the more likely to have persevered with the spirit of the older vogue and to have despised the degenerate renderings of the same theme obtaining in Jacobean days. It is therefore palpable that furniture made in the decade 1620-1630 may have approximated so nearly to the Elizabethan type as to lead to its being diagnosed as of a date thirty to forty years older than that which in reality it is. Again, the survival of the Puritan feeling accounted for the creation of models during the decade 1690-1700 so plain and unostentatious as to lead to the assumption that they were made during the Commonwealth, whilst the discernment of a craftsman at Winchester who declined to prostitute leg-contour in conformity with Sheraton's latter-day suggestions may quite conceivably have engendered mistakes as between the best and worst periods of that designer's influence.

Having noted these points, it is well to remember that the relationships between our great eighteenth-century masters were far more involved than has been generally supposed. Thus the first Chippendale lived in an atmosphere permeated by Queen Anne ideas, while his famous son broke away from this influence to evolve his own renderings of French, Gothic, and Chinese matter before blending his work with the classicism of the brothers Adam. The third Chippendale doubtless produced many of the examples which rest in collections to-day as " Heppelwhite," " Adams," or " Sheraton." The Seddons, we

Prefatory and Introductory.

know, gave us admirable suggestions sympathetic with the popularly-conceived notions of "Sheraton." George Seddon doubtless gave us skilled expositions of the recognised Chippendale orders. Both the Seddons and the Gillows produced "Chippendale," "Adams," "Heppelwhite," and "Sheraton," as it is now loosely termed, whilst Sheraton probably essayed models on Chippendale lines during his novitiate. Ince and Mayhew, when once the public was satiated with fretwork, must have created pieces based on the patterns identified with the designers of 1770 and onwards, whilst fretwork schemes which would until recently have been associated with Chambers types of 1760 are now shown as belonging to Batty Langley in 1739. Adam furniture would seem to have been built by the Chippendales, Gillows, Seddons, Heppelwhites, Sheraton, and hosts of unnamed lesser craftsmen, and we have also to reckon with the hybrid creations resulting from this complex state of affairs.

The plates published with the works of various designers were often misleading—some showed suggestions which never bore fruit, others were plagiarisms pure and simple, whilst we never find in them a faithful portrayal of *the whole* of a master's life-work, the link which is missing, as fate would have it, being usually of the utmost importance. It is therefore obvious that both dates and generic terms should be used with a certain diffidence, since we have no definite data to guide us, as often as not.

Occasionally we find a piece of furniture with landmarks, so to speak, at either end of it, the decadent application of an idea and the incipient appearance of some fresh *motif*. The natural beauty of Grinling Gibbons's carving, the unorthodox brilliancy of Chippendale, the simple charm of Shearer, or the cult of the brothers Adam, may be recognisable, but far more often than not we have to use a generic term to the best of our ability.

Art is a mountain raised above the plains of mediocrity, and since few men are born mountaineers, guides have to be requisitioned by the majority of would-be climbers. It is the same with the applied arts, even if the peaks attainable are lower. One is apt to run in a groove and to appreciate best those views which are opened up at the heels of him whom we follow. Many people will admire pictures by Rembrandt and Constable, yet argue that if "Chippendale" is good "Sheraton" must be bad, or *vice versa*. All our great masters gave us good designs and divergence of treatment followed as they struck out in an endeavour to leave the beaten track the while they aimed at the summit of the hill.

The Author is particularly indebted to Mr. E. C. Lister-Kay, who allowed him to illustrate the beautiful interiors at Godmersham Park; to Mr. R. S. Clouston, for much information culled from his invaluable writings on Eighteenth-Century Furniture; to Miss Constance Simon, for dates, addresses, &c., which that lady unravelled from various sources and published in her "English Furniture Designers of the Eighteenth Century"; to Mr. F. W. Phillips especially for his help in approving the chapter on Upholstery; to Mr. Alfred Hardcastle for his recipes for exterminating the "worm" pest, &c.; and to that body of gentlemen who readily lent their homes and pieces for illustration and facilitated by every means in their power that which has proved to the Author to be a labour of love.

G. OWEN WHEELER.

Table of Contents.

CHAPTER		PAGE
I.	ON BUYING OLD FURNITURE: SOME METHODS OF THE "FAKER"	1
II.	THE EVOLUTION OF THE CABINET-MAKER'S ART IN BRITAIN	29
III.	JACOBEAN, CROMWELLIAN, CHARLES II., AND WILLIAM AND MARY FURNITURE	59
IV.	LACQUERED FURNITURE.	134
V.	QUEEN ANNE	154
VI.	GRINLING GIBBONS.	177
VII.	GEORGIAN	184
VIII.	CHIPPENDALE.	217
IX.	THOMAS CHIPPENDALE	234
X.	CHINESE CHIPPENDALE	272
XI.	THOMAS CHIPPENDALE (*continued*)	293
XII.	THOMAS CHIPPENDALE (*continued*)	307
XIII.	THOMAS CHIPPENDALE (*continued*)	354
XIV.	IRISH CHIPPENDALE	386
XV.	THE BROTHERS ADAM	400
XVI.	THE BROTHERS ADAM (*continued*)	425
XVII.	THE BROTHERS ADAM (*continued*)	449

CHAPTER		PAGE
XVIII.	HEPPELWHITE	479
XIX.	"GILLOWS"	519
XX.	SHERATON	528
XXI.	THE SEDDONS	601
XXII.	THE "LESSER" ENGLISH CABINET-MAKERS	609
XXIII.	BRACKET CLOCKS AND MUSICAL INSTRUMENTS	630
XXIV.	NOTES CONCERNING MIRRORS	640
XXV.	UPHOLSTERY	662
XXVI.	SPINDLE AND TURNED-LEG FURNITURE	669
XXVII.	MISCELLANEA	680
XXVIII.	ON PRICES	687
	GLOSSARY OF TERMS	710
	INDEX	725

Table of Separate Plates.

	FACE PAGE
WILLIAM AND MARY AND QUEEN ANNE BRASS FURNITURE	19
CHIPPENDALE AND ADAM HANDLES, ESCUTCHEONS AND CURTAIN HOLDERS	21
ADAM, HEPPELWHITE, AND SHERATON HANDLES, ETC.	22
CHIPPENDALE BEDSTEAD IN THE LOUIS QUINZE STYLE	374

Old English Furniture

From the 16th to the 19th Centuries.

CHAPTER I.
On Buying Old Furniture: Some Methods of the "Faker."

Introductory.

It is to the rapidly-increasing value of fine examples of eighteenth-century furniture that we owe so many of the delicate attentions paid to the collector, sometimes even to the dealer, by that enterprising and predatory gentleman usually known as the "faker." As a knowledge of this class of artiste, and of his versatile accomplishments, should be an essential portion of our outfit when starting a collection, if we are to avoid subsequent and vain regrets, we shall do well to put up a notice, "Beware of the Seller," at the outset of this Chapter. Young collectors should invariably decline to purchase from any dealer failing to give a guarantee with his wares; they should never buy a second time from anyone who is shown to have "made a mistake" in selling them something "not quite right," and who then declines to make restitution; and they should study undoubted examples whenever possible, paying due regard to the smallest details, subsequently applying the knowledge so gained. Detailed descriptions should be given with every invoice or account, and where intuition gives rise to doubt at first sight, trust it, broadly speaking, against a subsequent judgment which may have been over-persuaded.

If the intending purchaser hesitates between buying a small but really first-class piece, and something more important but not quite first-rate, let him buy the former; he will derive more pleasure from its acquisition, whilst undoubtedly making a better investment.

Condition.

Before describing some of the many traps which are set for the unwary or inexperienced collector, we may premise that in what is known as "condition" we have the master-key to the difficulties presented. In early days, woodwork, though sometimes painted, was not polished, and this lack of a necessary protection engendered a species of decay, closely bordering on dry-rot, frequently met with in English furniture of the Gothic and Tudor periods. Oak, the timber mostly employed in those days, always prone as it was to outside wastage, suffered badly from surface-poverty as a result of this neglect.

Waxing, Oiling, and Polishing.

As time wore on, waxing and polishing by friction, and waxing, oiling, and polishing came into favour. Wood subjected to waxing alone is generally found lighter in hue than that which was subjected to waxing and oiling. It should be noted that the liberal allowance of " elbow-grease " meted out in these processes accounts for the excellent surface-condition found on some of the specimens handed down to us. From a collector's point of view, it is doubtful whether any better process could have been devised than this oiling and waxing, alike for improving surface beauty and protecting the wood against the ravages of Time. During Tudor times varnish blended with oil—not as nowadays with spirit—came into somewhat fitful use, gradually getting a grip on the public fancy. The secret of its manufacture was brought over from the Continent by journeymen artificers; but, probably owing to lack of attention in its preparation over here, its quality did not compare well with that of the varnish employed in Southern Europe. We can but surmise that our own craftsmen, still struggling with the rudiments of carving and marquetry, lost sight of the importance of a process which they considered to be of doubtful value.

Introduction of French Polishing.

With the eighteenth century came further strides and advancement. The process known as french polishing came to us from over the Channel, and exactly fitted the need for some medium to show up the full beauties of the newly-discovered mahogany. We should not confuse this french polishing with that now generally in use. In the olden times, little polish and much polishing were the order of the day. Wood was polished gingerly, rubbed down, and polished again and again, the grain never being obscured by the process, and this of course entailed considerable expense. The polish itself formed a small item; but repeated polishings proved expensive.

Nowadays, unfortunately, owing to the prevailing craze for cheapness, thorough polishing is stinted, and a heavy, noxious polish which hides the beauties (or defects) of the grain lavishly applied instead. Did the mischief end with the decadence in modern polishing, a casual mention of these facts would suffice, but unfortunately this is not the case. For over a hundred years the old masterpieces have been subjected to acts of the greatest vandalism, and we can safely say that in the last fifteen years as much eighteenth-century furniture has been robbed of its beauty, its interest to the advanced collector, and of its commercial value, by ignorant treatment, as was ever produced in a similar period. There are few dealers even now who thoroughly understand the correct methods of treating damaged examples needing attention; there are practically no first-class collectors or dealers who will look at furniture which has received attention in the unfortunate and misguided interpretation of the process.

It is quite a common experience to walk into a gallery and find that all the examples on view have been brought up to one gorgeous and resplendent level by the addition of a heavy coating of polish closely resembling treacle, with the result that they are irretrievably ruined, although *some modern work may have been hidden thereby.*

On the other hand, one meets the unhappy enthusiast with his " Isn't it a beauty? I got it for £10, *and it has just been repolished";* or, *"I told him I would give him his price if he would scrape and varnish it, and now you cannot see a mark on it anywhere."*

"Patina."

We will now consider the effect produced on old furniture by the original treatment we have been discussing. The wood will be well preserved, and a hard and glossy surface presented; exposed edges and relief carving will exhibit a rich, glowing, and almost metallic brilliance, and

in this condition are said to be "patinated." The term
"patina" was originally employed to describe the rich
hues found on early bronzes, as a result of much dusting
and polishing, assisted by the mellowing hand of Time.
The surface-condition found on genuine and unspoilt
examples of well-kept old oak, chestnut, walnut, and
mahogany closely resembles that to be met with on these
old bronzes, and owes its existence to similar causes.

This "patina" is the first thing a sound collector or
a high-class dealer looks for in eighteenth-century furniture, and its absence should be enough, not only to
engender suspicion, but to exclude examples lacking it
from a well-chosen collection. The novice should become thoroughly conversant with the characteristics of this
sine quâ non, visiting any available private collections or
museums until he can readily discriminate between the
genuine thing and its pernicious substitute by this simple
and unfailing test.

Many thoroughly genuine pieces of furniture of course
exist which are devoid of this most desirable surface-condition, but the wise collector leaves these alone, whilst the
less critical man will do well to eschew them until he is
an advanced judge. The patinated condition, in fact,
constitutes not only a hall-mark, but an added beauty,
just as an old-fashioned lawn excels all those of modern
creation, given similar conditions and surroundings.

This falling short may be due to one or more of a host
of reasons. The example may have been neglected or have
stood in a damp or an exposed position, such as a stable, a
barn, or an outhouse, and in mentioning this it is curious
how old Jacobean chests, for instance, are frequently
found in stables acting as corn-bins. The chair, table,
or chest may have been handed over to the tender mercies

of the village blacksmith to be subsequently varnished by the local coachbuilder. It may have been scraped and polished up "as good as new" by the nearest cabinet-maker, or have been painted by someone with inflated ideas as to his powers of improving on the inspiration of a Chippendale or a Sheraton. A common cause of trouble has been the attempt to wash off dirt or foreign substances with some preparation which, in addition to performing its intended task, has bleached the wood or deadened the beautiful characteristics of the grain. Specimens in this condition, although they may even possess a pedigree, or satisfy the holder on the score of authenticity, lose much of their interest to the collector—more of their commercial value. Within the last year or so a Kentish furniture dealer was commissioned to paint an old serpentine Sheraton chest of drawers green, to match the shade of a "new art" bedroom wall-paper!

As an instance of the importance which should be attached to this condition, the writer was once shown a fine old Chippendale bracket in process of repair; some new fretwork had to be inserted, and he bought the piece with the understanding that the few new pieces should be brought to the tone of the old carcase, or, rather, as near as possible to the correct shade and condition, and he was greatly horrified to find that instead of bringing the new towards the old, the old had been reduced to the level of the new, forming one brilliant and resplendent example of latter-day polishing. Being useless in this condition, it was offered to, and purchased by, a London dealer, and it was not until some long time afterwards that it leaked out that the original bracket remained in a semi-repaired condition in that particular workshop—where it may still repose—and had been sold to seven other individuals (four of whom were dealers), and on each of whom a similar fraud had been perpetrated.

The rogue has not yet found a good substitute for the true patina, and it still stands as a saving clause to those who will be wise in time. If one examines a genuine old carved example of mahogany furniture, the interstices between the raised portion of the carving, and a fringe al' round the outside of it, will be found to be dark in colour The fringe resembles in formation the sand round the sea shore, and the solution is found in the fact that these partly-protected surfaces have accumulated dust, &c., which, once lodged, has not been completely removed by dusting; this has become rubbed or worn in, and though it is in reality dirt, it is fast, and should be left alone, acting as it does as a foil to throw up more strongly the patinated edges which it surrounds, whilst constituting a feature always to be met with in the genuine and unspoilt antique.

Grain of the Wood.

We may here pay some attention to the grain of the wood employed in old furniture. In olden times the log of oak, for the purpose of securing finer fingering, was cut into four sections—in fact, quarters, and these again into logs or planks running approximately to the centre from the outside of the tree. It was an extremely wasteful process, and has now been discontinued. Wood so treated shows the hard figure and grain in strong relief as its leading feature, the adjoining and softer-fibred portions having perceptibly worn down; this is a sure point in judging much of the furniture up to, say, 1725. Mahogany, too, has a vascular grain; but here the signs are not nearly so pronounced. There will be found streaks of softer-fibred cells, which have sunk with the wear of Time, leaving the harder portions in slight relief. A microscopic examination is almost needed to establish this condition, which in antique oak, however, is patent.

Particular attention should be paid to these details where there is a doubt as to the genuineness of carving. The result of wear should be shown over the whole of the carved surface, a feature which will not be pronounced where a fresh skin has been uncovered by the furniture faker.

These details may seem minute, but they are not without their strong points, affording pleasure and protection in an intelligent application.

Speaking after a banquet at Guildford, a gentleman some years ago stated that " the staple trade of that ancient and interesting town was the manufacture of antique furniture." It is not reported whether anyone protested; but the large majority obviously revelled in the " hit."

The commonest form of washing off is by means of a hot soda bath; by this method paint, varnish, polish, lacquer, &c., may be removed, but the piece of furniture is left in a dull condition, bereft of its correct appearance, is soapy to the touch, and has the grain " raised " by the process. It will take many years of assiduous treatment to bring back something of the glories it has lost.

"About Wormholes."

Wormholes in furniture are *not* desirable, as some few people who write in the silly season would lead us to believe. Fine old mahogany is almost impervious to the ravages of wood-boring beetles, and only sappy pieces are attacked.

Buying Old Furniture. 9

Faked furniture may be made out of old and worm-pierced timber, and those people who rely on wormholes as a guide to the authenticity of any given example of the cabinet-maker's skill almost court disaster.

Needless to say, the wild-cat stories of wormhole production by shot or gimlet are exaggerations or inventions. The "wormer," as he is somewhat euphemistically styled, could only be employed by a clumsy master with singularly innocent customers of extreme gullibility.

Common Forms of Deception.

The commonest cases of deception take the form of the re-carving, re-veneering, or painting of genuine but plain examples of Old English furniture. Where re-carving is the artifice resorted to, tables, chairs, and other examples with massive carcase construction are selected, so that there may be room to "create" a scheme of decoration from the old wood, and yet leave sufficient "body" to fulfil the requirements of taste and stability after its reduction consequent on the process of whittling down to which it has been subjected.

Additions to Existing Decoration.

New carving is applied to plain borders, fretwork is added to chair-legs or to cabinet cornices, the bent of the ingenious artist's mind being strongly creative and imaginative. Until some twenty years ago, the then less experienced "furniture improvers" thought out little original schemes of their own for enhancing existing decoration, and these were applied haphazard. If any method obtained, it generally took the form of Tudor adornment to some specimen by Chippendale, or perhaps of Louis

Quinze detail on a Jacobean chest! Nowadays the matter is taken in hand seriously. The period of the proposed "adaptation" is carefully studied, and only now and then does the clever faker "give himself away" by antedating some detail by the mere matter of a century or so. Our friend obtains a genuine carcase void of all decoration, and then, having in mind a genuine example on similar lines structurally, but handsomely decorated, and to which he has access, or of which he has a sketch or a photo, he proceeds to carve out a little fortune for himself. The growing habit of augmenting or supplementing existing decoration constitutes a deadly pitfall, and is all the more specious when accompanied by such a comment on the part of the vendor as this: "There were one or two missing pieces which I had to have put on; but really my man has done the job so cleverly that I doubt if even I——" &c., &c.

There are many instances where the owner may safely have missing portions of mouldings, carving, or inlay replaced; but when buying pieces he should purchase the example in its untouched condition, and he will then know how much of an old chair, &c., he has secured; he will be enabled to supervise, and in time assist, when repairs are in hand, and last, but not least, he will become versed in the points of divergence between ancient and modern work thus definitely located.

"Made-up" Pieces.

Collectors should beware of "made-up" furniture, especially when buying old oak. Old bedsteads, chests, and panelling that have been taken to pieces are commonly made up into pretentious-looking models, and the would-be purchaser should examine the body or carcase of the chest or cabinet and satisfy himself that the decorated surfaces are gracing an original creation. Sufficient panelling may be procured from an oak chest worth £5 to decorate a Court cupboard commanding perhaps £20 on the market because of its greater rarity and usefulness. Dated oak is commonly found, but only a small proportion of this is original, and the collector should always look askance at it until satisfied of the correctness of all other work, decorative and constructional.

"Picked-out Carving."

Original carving is frequently "picked out" when it has become more or less obliterated by wear and tear. Let us take the case of a taproom tripod table, whose carved knees have become worn down by the feet of successive generations. The old work is again brought into relief by the removal of surrounding timber; a touch is added here and there, and lo! we have something like the original, but yet not the original, awaiting a confiding purchaser.

Re-veneering.

As to the question of re-veneering, we will suppose that a plain old bookcase has been selected for operations. This is then supplied with an overcoat of modern satin-wood veneer, to be subsequently glorified by the insertion of an inlaid design, or by the application of modern painting, occasionally even by the transfer of some old engraving, painting, or design from a genuine example, contemporary or otherwise, which has been stripped to supply the want, or otherwise added advisedly. Quite recently the writer had to point out that the paintings adorning a satinwood bureau bookcase in a dealer's gallery had once done duty on the wooden framework over the keyboard of an early piano or a spinet. Now, the period of the bookcase outline was 1775, that of the transposed decoration 1810! On further examination, the satinwood veneer, too, proved to have been added over a plain mahogany frame; yet £50 had been paid to a small country dealer for this "gem," the purchaser, not wishing to "spoil the market" by appearing too keen, having contented himself with a casual examination of the interior and of the painted surface, by matchlight, for evidence as to "maturity."

Replicas.

Not so very many years ago a collector had a very fine drop-in seat, "two-chair back" Chippendale settee, the framework of which needed attention. Retaining the old needlework seat lest it should get soiled, he consigned the frame to a dealer for repair. On receiving this back some few weeks later in an immaculate condition, he could not understand why the seat would not fit into its bed. His suspicions were aroused, and, on going into the matter, the dealer apologised profusely, saying that "he had taken the liberty of making a reproduction, and that, owing to a stupid mistake, his foreman had inadvertently sent this home in lieu of the original, which he now forwarded," &c. In this instance the accidental retention of the old seat led to the exposure of a type of fraud which few who are "behind the scenes" or "in the know" would venture to describe as being obsolete or extinct, and which was once, at any rate, all too prevalent.

In 1901 the writer was offered a so-called Chippendale armchair, which, though spurious, had been very cleverly

handled. Unfortunately this same chair was sold by two
members of the same tribe to two valued customers (notes
not having been compared) within the space of fifteen
minutes. Rather than disappoint either collector, it was
deemed advisable to produce a replica, and so satisfy
each! This was accordingly done.

Needless to say, had either of the foregoing victims
made of "original patinated condition" an essential
point, such as the wise dealer or collector invariably does,
an impudent fraud would have been nipped in the bud.

Evidences of Wear.

Always examine the base of a chair-leg or a table-leg.
These, when genuine, will be found with a soft and glossy
surface, caused by friction over the floor, although cut
against the grain. Suspect any traces of glue—the
ancients were chary of this when mortising their joints—
and note well that one or two carefully-prepared fractures,
mended even with old iron, &c., confer no better patent of
authenticity than the presence of worm-holes in " convincing " numbers.

Marquetry, Inlay, and Painting.

We have to face a serious difficulty in attempting to
set down in black-and-white the points of divergence
between antique and modern marquetry, inlaid work,
and painting on wood. The old inlay of Elizabethan
times was, generally speaking, thick and clumsy, being
frequently met with $\frac{1}{8}$in. in thickness. It fined down
considerably in the days of William and Mary and Queen
Anne, yet retaining comparatively substantial proportions
in the days of Heppelwhite, Shearer, and Sheraton, when
placed side by side with latter-day reproductions. In

the case of the work turned out by these three masters, it is interesting to note how the high standard of perfection then obtaining was arrived at. Apprentices were allowed yearly so much fine wood—*i.e.*, satinwood, hairwood (fine-grained sycamore, stained), kingwood, tulipwood, amboyna, &c. From this they fashioned small tea-caddies, desks, and knick-knacks in their spare time, their scale of remuneration being fixed as time wore on by the degree of excellence attained in the results handed in. This system, in addition to providing pocket-money for a class of youth none too well paid (many hands received 4s. per week only), fostered sterling work from a constructional point of view, and originality in conception of outline and design.

The shading of satinwood was effected by sand-burning; whilst colouring matter was applied now and then to heighten effect. Modern inlay—generally the thickness of paper only—is altogether too stilted and machine-made in appearance. The "fine" woods employed are of a greatly inferior quality owing to exhausted supply and lack of seasoning; whilst they have not the tone of richness which age alone imparts. The original work was innate with verve and whole-hearted artistic handling: the new is, as a rule, stereotyped and overdone. When colouring matter was employed, the cement or glue at the joints closed the pores of the wood there, and prevented the "evaporation" round the edges, colour remaining there when it had faded elsewhere. Satinwood shut off from the light, or exposed to strong sunlight, retains its old pale colour, something between a straw and lemon hue. Exposed in a normal light, it assumes with age a rich and glowing golden-orange tint, unequalled by any "artificial process." Hairwood, too, gains lustre by the lapse of time, and though the faker uses bichromate of potash to deepen his "effects," these latter fall far short of those glories which the ages alone can confer.

Excellence of joinery, of material employed in carcase construction, and evidences of wear in drawer-frames, &c., are more than *primâ facie* evidence of "the genuine thing" *in so far as the carcase or framework is concerned*, simply because, owing to dearth of first-class labour and timber available, it does not pay to put these into reproductions of plain pieces. If the collector will go further, and make himself conversant with the "points" of undoubted examples, he will be enabled to read inlay like "large print"—forearmed on entering a field in which fraud runs riot because the margin of profit on elaborately decorated examples is on a generous scale.

For some reason, marquetry (Fr. *marqueterie*) is the term applied to inlaid work of the English school up to the end of the reign of Queen Anne. In the days of George III. the term "marquetry," generally speaking, was discontinued for "inlay" or "inlaid work."

In addition to colouring, and shading by burning under the sand process, the effect of old inlaid work was often heightened by hand-engraving, generally with a view to the accentuation of light and shadow. Needless to say, this treatment has its more or less capable exponents in the twentieth century.

Inlay will oftentimes be met with in a "started," "blistered," or "buckled-up" condition, with engrained dirt at the edges, where these blemishes have drawn apart the once perfect weldings. In this condition it may be "relaid," a process calling for experienced and very careful handling. This relaying has its opponents in certain quarters. It is difficult to understand why, when it is *properly* carried out, seeing that nothing is added to the work of the artists of the olden days, and only the ravages of time, use, and sharp changes of temperature are brushed aside. Our forefathers "built in" their urns, vases, &c., bit by bit with great *finesse* and artistic cunning. Nowadays the same are made to order by the hundred, and inserted wholesale in a completed form, but they of course lack the merit of their prototypes.

It is difficult, too, lucidly to emphasise the difference existing between original and imitation painted decoration. In conception, the former was artistic and correct, as it was produced at a time when painters and engravers on every hand attained to a subtle delicacy in this and kindred styles of decoration never equalled before or since. Great artists "stooped" to work now executed by mere copyists and mechanics. In execution, the designs, besides being chaste and correct, carried whole-hearted conviction in a free and artistic treatment. The colours, protected by a fine varnish, are now soft, glowing, and translucent, resembling the opaque schemes arrived at in the finest of old porcelains. The varnish referred to will, on inspection, be found to be covered with a network of fine cracks. Yet it has done its work well, for where treatment has been fair, examples possess an added charm at the hands of Time, whilst preserving their old merits. This network of fine cracks is now most cleverly imitated over modern decoration.

The faker has failed in most of the finer points here dilated on; his work is stilted, cramped, or overwrought, and generally of the "Christmas card" order of merit. In appearance it does not approximate even to the old, lacking translucency and surface-condition. Again we must come to the inevitable conclusion: gain acquaintance with the golden, and you will be discontented with the German silver gilded.

Modern painting carefully applied to old furniture is more dangerous, needless to say, than when added to new pieces. In the former case the unsuspecting may let the undoubted authenticity of the carcase carry presumptive evidence in favour of " right " decoration; whilst a fair substitute for surface-condition is attained by weathering the example and so arriving at a state nearly akin to that of the natural varnish decay to be met with in the genuine ancestor. On modern furniture the efforts of the rogue may be easily detected, the effects arrived at being hopelessly chilly.

Correctness of technique is no guide *for all occasions*, seeing that in the olden times many commissions for plain examples were filled which were destined to receive their embellishment at the hands of the ladies of the house, whose efforts unfortunately were all too often mediocre.

Chair "Conversions."

Unless in sets of six or more, " single " chairs have a comparatively small value. Arm-chairs, on the other hand, in pairs or even singly, have a commercial value out of all proportion to the extra labour originally spent upon them. It follows, therefore, that there are many attempts to impose on the credulous by the conversion of single into arm-chairs. Now the old arm-chairs were made broader in the back and frame than the singles accompanying them, probably as a tribute to the more generous proportions of paterfamilias, for whom they were intended, his offspring being content with singles. Sometimes, however, the mother had an arm-chair of ample proportions allowed her.

The grain, colour, and condition of the wood in the arm should be identical with that in the rest of the chair. Any carving on the arm will show traces of wear, whilst the joints at back and on the side framework, where arm and arm supports were attached, should be of first-class workmanship, and where there is any carving, beading, or moulding on the back, this should cease just above the place where the arm runs into the back, commencing again directly below it, as the old workmen did not carve and then cover up their work, but left a space for the reception of the joining member.

Drawers, Joints, and Fronts.

The drawers in fine eighteenth-century furniture run freely, or if they hang owing to excessive wear on the runners, will act perfectly when these latter have been replaced or adjusted. The best of well-seasoned material was employed, generally oak, mahogany, or cedar, and the workmanship was of the finest order throughout, the corners being beautifully dovetailed together.

Glass-fronted Cabinets.

When examining an old glass-fronted cabinet, see that the joints are separately and properly mitred together. The panes of glass, which when old will show circular marks on them (owing to their having been spun), should be separately quarrelled from behind; this process of quarrelling entails arduous and costly labour.

Faked fronts are seldom made like this; the tracery forming the partitions is sometimes laid *en bloc* over a large pane of glass, and where framed separately the joints are generally surface snick-fitted on the dovetail principle, this being a much less costly means of produc-

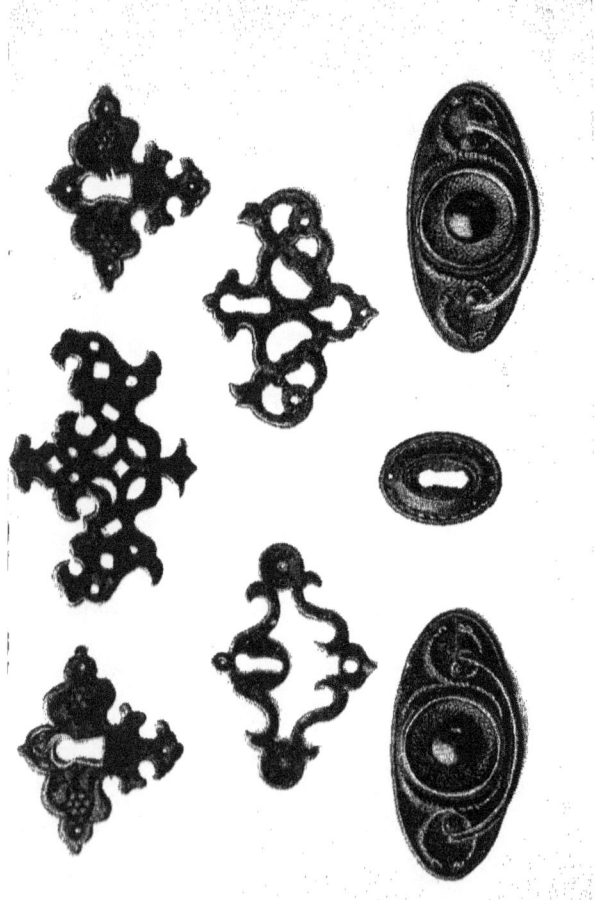

Brass Furniture to Chests, &c. during reigns of William and Mary and Queen Anne. In the country districts some of these models remained in favour until the advent of George II. Author's Collection.

tion. Modern putty at the back of the panes is coloured "old" with brown umber and dragon's-blood powder, &c., being subsequently hardened off with gold size.

Handles, Escutcheons, and other Embellishments.

In the first of these groups we have a fairly representative collection of the styles of brasswork to be met with throughout Queen Anne's reign. Varied in character, it is generally artistic, though lacking in cohesion perhaps if associated with any given vogue, such as that usually implied by " Queen Anne."

The first illustration in the second group shows a pair of handles and escutcheon in the Louis XV. style, of Chippendale character of an early period, probably in the 'thirties, the design being governed by the large shell so favoured at this period. In the second pair we have one of those happy adaptations from the French school of Louis Quinze which Chippendale so frequently gave us. In the centre we see a large typical Adam handle between two Adam curtain-holders, whilst underneath are two curtain-holders and a pair of handles, either in late Chippendale or very early Heppelwhite (*circa* 1760).

When we revert to the third group we are struck by the reappearance of the oval plate and handle. If we refer to the last handles on the first group, we shall see that we have practically a recrudescence of a type in use in the early part of the eighteenth century; yet these are handles in the schools of Heppelwhite and Sheraton from about 1765 onwards. Chippendale having destroyed their popularity for some forty to fifty years, there was a hiatus in their production until his school had practically passed away.

It is important that the collector should pay due and

close attention to the old brass furniture embellishing his antique cabinets, chests, writing-tables, or bookcases, for these add very materially to the beauties of the specimens they adorn, whilst at times establishing the age and source of the furniture to which they are fitted. On such common ground in cabinet-making did Heppelwhite, Shearer, and Sheraton meet at times, that any little inkling, such as the superior daintiness obtaining in the brasswork employed by Heppelwhite when compared with that of Sheraton, affords relief to the collector when in doubt.

From a commercial point of view, the presence of £2 worth of fine Louis Quinze style, original chased handles and escutcheons, may very easily add £100 to the value of one of Thomas Chippendale's masterpieces.

There are two causes which have militated against the preservation of these old fittings, which are seldom to be met with in their entirety. In the olden days when solid brass had a good market-value, hawkers used to call from door to door offering to take all the old brass from furniture in the home, replacing it by wooden knobs (which they explained were much more durable), paying a small monetary consideration in addition as an inducement to lead the owners to " part."

Oftener still the graceful, and in many instances fragile, handles have suffered at the hands of rough usage, one or two having been broken, twisted, or pulled out, and then mislaid, whereupon the remainder of the set has been discarded either in favour of the wooden knob or of some massive brass fittings quite out of character with the specimen to which they are attached. The Early Victorian era saw most vandalism in this as in many other directions; whilst even now glorious old sets are being

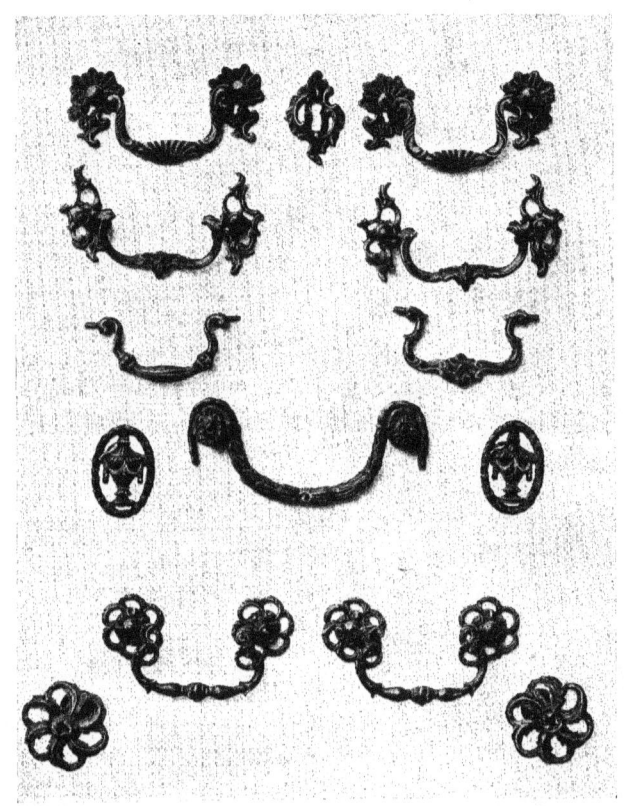

Chippendale and Adam Handles, Escutcheons, and Curtain Holders of the period 1740-1790.
Author's Collection.

ruined by re-lacquering. Old handles and fittings may be carefully washed and cleaned, but should not be re-lacquered; the modern dipping gives a garish appearance in place of the mellow and patinated condition conferred by the ages.

As to the durability of the original fittings, many of those employed during Queen Anne's time used to pull out, being attached only by a wire, bent back inside the drawer to which they were hung.

The fittings beloved by Chippendale combined strength with tasteful grace, those in vogue with Heppelwhite and Sheraton at times lacking the former quality, if possessing the latter in a marked degree. It may be said that most of the work we are reviewing was of adequate strength, when subjected to fair and careful usage, so seldom, alas! meted out to it throughout the course of its existence. Gems passed from the mansion to humbler homes, drawers were overloaded, blocked, or swelled owing to damp, and then the thoughtless and heavy wrench carried destruction in its path.

The hinges, &c., on the old lacquered cabinets at the close of the seventeenth and commencement of the eighteenth centuries were mainly copied from Chinese and Japanese medallions. Outwardly appearing to be of brass, many of them are of silver, which was lacquered brass before mounting. Chippendale gave us the finest if most ornate handles in some of his early adaptations of the rococo school of Louis XV. design, his escutcheons especially being incomparable.

The weakest and least serviceable of all handles came from Thomas Sheraton, when, at his early attempt after light and dainty effects, he employed graceful but ultra-fragile fittings in silver or Sheffield plate; the handle plates have stood, but the handles—mere pieces of silver or copper wire—proved almost ephemeral.

A word should be said concerning the little turned ivory handles freely employed on the small drawers and fittings inside bureaus, bureau bookcases, and so on. These were of refined workmanship; the tone of the ivory has deepened with age, whilst they are frequently to be found in two pieces, the screw or stem unscrewing from the head.

Many collectors will not look at furniture which has lost these original embellishments, considering them as an integral part of the master's scheme.

Turning to the reproduction of fine old handles and escutcheons now extant, these will be found to be of a lighter and inferior metal, weight for weight. The decoration is not so clean and clever as in the case of the genuine ancestor, whilst the condition lacks that soft, mellow and patinated appearance which the centuries should have conferred.

In the original fittings one or two of those handles which have been nearest the door of the room may be found bent down to a fuller swell than is the case with their neighbours in more distant corners, as the result of more constant use (consequent on their more accessible position).

If the handle be raised, the reverse side will show a toned colour and very smooth surface, whilst the woodwork underneath, in the case of handles not fitted to plates, may show an impression of the handle's outline owing to its continual fall and wear.

The interior of the drawer should be carefully examined for traces of other pinholes which may in earlier times have served to attach prior fittings, and the existing pinholes should be the subject of close scrutiny, although

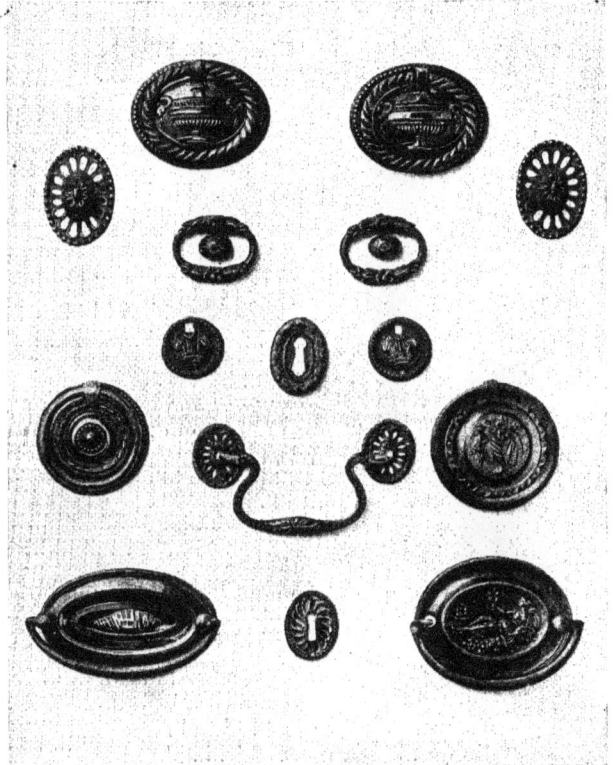

Adam, Heppelwhite, and Sheraton Handles, &c. (of the period 1770-1800). Author's Collection.

they may have been recently disturbed by the tightening of the nuts or by readjustment.

Modern brass is cast or stamped from old models, occasionally in an exceedingly clever manner; in condition it may be found approximating more or less to that of its ancient prototypes, a result due to a course of burning over gas, in a fire or an oven. It is subjected also to pickling in vinegar and acid, or is washed in soda, these processes removing some of its glaring and garish characteristics.

As the different cabinet-makers of the eighteenth century are passed in review, attention will be directed to other phases of the faker's art not touched upon in the necessarily brief survey of a wide subject.

More about Wormholes.

Wormholes are of two kinds—played-out and active—and these may be found side by side on genuine or spurious examples. The played-out hole is clean and empty; its outer edges are slightly rounded and sunken inwards. Active holes display sharper edges: they contain a light-coloured deposit of powder representing the débris consequent on the tunnelling operations of the grubs. Workmen in olden days resorted to many expedients in their efforts to render wood immune from the trouble, but their efforts were not crowned with success. "Worm" follows the sap of wood, and few timbers save hard ones such as mahogany or satinwood resist it. The habit of employing soft-wood inside chair and sofa frames, &c., in order that the upholsterer might the more readily drive in his tacks, was responsible for a considerable volume of mischief. The author has seen the larvæ extracted from Elizabethan models, and he has observed models less than half a century old riddled with extinct borings resembling those to be met with on most of the Queen Anne creations of two hundred years ago.

In dealing with the active mischief, two or three liberal dressings of paraffin may be applied, though this treatment cannot be relied on to effect a radical cure. Some authorities seal up the holes with a sticky composition which quickly hardens, but the pest will almost invariably find fresh outlets. One collector obtained satisfactory results by heating a thin wire and passing it when white hot into each tunnel—an original if somewhat laborious proceeding.

Where the so-called " worms " are present in the unexposed portions of a model, such as in the seat-frame of a chair, the eggs, larvæ, or pupæ of the pest and the perfect insect itself can be destroyed by dressings of carbolic acid and paraffin, but the former of these preparations interferes with wood surfaces and should not be applied in prominent places.

Before any dressings are used the piece of furniture to be treated should be tilted over towards the side which is being dealt with, and sharply rapped to shake out accumulated powder. If this is not done the dust in the active channels coagulates with the liquid entering them and prevents the effective penetration of the dressing.

Varnish.

Although the presence of varnish on old English furniture is an unwelcome feature generally speaking, it is seldom advisable to interfere with it. Varnish contemporary with the model it covers (or practically contemporary) may be found on early oak, just as it may be met with on Sheraton workboxes or other models. Carefully applied, much of this old varnish possessed a peculiar translucency which did not obscure the character of grain, figure, or surface-condition in the underlying model. Time has toned down any aggressive brightness which the process may have originally entailed, and many a specimen has been preserved to us as the result of this " dressing."

Modern or latter-day varnish shows a more opaque consistence, militating against a ready examination of the surface beneath it, whilst conferring an air of gaudy brightness to the specimen bedaubed with it. It would therefore appear that varnish should not invariably be regarded as having a prejudicial effect, provided, of course, we are not considering the more modern products. It is unwise to endeavour to scrape off varnish from carved detail, because it is impossible satisfactorily to search the interstices, and however carefully the work may be done, damage will assuredly accrue to the skin or face of the wood underneath owing to the unevenness of the ground to be gone over. Pickling off of varnish is always undesirable, for the model subjected to this process emerges from the treatment dull in condition, suspiciously weak in hue, and with the grain of the wood raised. In some cases, noticeably in that of such inlaid furniture as Shearer and Sheraton affected, varnish may be scraped off flat surfaces without destroying the skin of the underlying wood.

A clever and painstaking craftsman must be available before this work can be embarked upon. Late eighteenth-century varnish was brittle and comes off readily in a fine powder. When this operation has been completed any veneer or inlay which has " started " or " sprung " should be relaid by ironing, and the specimen of furniture may then be oiled and " bone " or dull-polished, to be subsequently rubbed down again. It is not advisable for the young collector to authorise this scraping on his own authority, for the man entrusted with this delicate process may lack experience or the model may be unsuitable for the treatment. The workman consulted naturally wants a job, and the skin of the wood may very easily be removed with the last of the varnish, with the consequent sacrifice of all old surface beauty.

We have thus a golden rule to guide us. If we must acquire varnished furniture, let us leave such specimens as are carved alone, consulting a man of experience before touching any flat-surfaced varnished woodwork.

Sub-surface Exploration.

Until a few years ago many experts, when called upon to decide as to the authenticity or value of any given piece of furniture, used to scrape some portion of its face or decorative scheme, with a view to determining the age and genuineness of the example. In fact, this process of what we may call " sub-surface exploration " was oftentimes the be-all and end-all of many a professional inquisition. The clever faker began to replace immature timber with fine old wood, and a preparation, the name of which for obvious reasons is withheld, came on the market, and deceived many so-called connoisseurs. The preparation in question, a liquid, soaked into mahogany and other mediums, from one-sixteenth to one-quarter of an inch, according to the porosity of the wood, gave a perfect simulation of antiquity to the medium treated with it.

Of course, now, when wood is beclouded or dirty, it is often necessary to scrape in an obscure corner, to diagnose satinwood, for instance, but it may be generally taken that the expert will not have to carry on " mining operations" when weighing the merits of the untouched specimen. The superior verve and artistic freedom noticeable in genuine models, coupled with original surface-condition, should always suffice as convincing features. Delving with the chisel or knife should only be resorted to in the case of badly-restored work, and here the collector who has his experience to gain should turn to an experienced friend.

Gilding.

In the majority of cases gilding was carried out over soft woods, and it follows therefore that the faker has an easier task in preparing his new model than would be the case if his efforts were of necessity confined to harder mediums. One may reasonably expect to find more "life" in the genuine examples, but as these were painted at the back in a golden-yellow hue right up to the gilt, the safeguard which a knowledge of patina affords is obliterated. The collector has to be soundly versed in a new state of surface-condition, and here again careful study of undoubted examples is the only safe method of gaining knowledge.

Most people are conversant with the subtle charm of old gold in a scheme of decoration, but few collectors are aware that, in the deadliest form of faking in this field, gold or gilding plays no part. The model, duly carved and at times subjected to a preliminary coat of composition, is first silvered and then varnished with a thick mixture in which shellac and gamboge are the principal ingredients. This process, developed as it is by careful experiment and practice, shows wonderful results well calculated to deceive. One has only to look at the clever reproductions of old gilt picture-frames now on the London market to realise the difficulties that exist in sifting the wheat from the chaff.

Many houses possess mediums cleverly compounded, and their preparations are often known to dishonest craftsmen, who will pass off the new gilt as "antique." Burnished gilt, bright and glaring, may be unhesitatingly condemned, and the experienced faker either avoids this feature or dulls it down in smoke or otherwise before issuing it. Many reproductions err in two ways, for in a short while they develop either a greenish or copper-bronze hue foreign to the original work. There are several artists now practising, however, who, in the experience gained over the restoration of old picture-frames, have attained a proficiency dangerous to the most experienced of connoisseurs.

CHAPTER II.
The Evolution of the Cabinet-maker's Art in Britain.

Piecing Together the Unwoven Threads of History.

As we shall be dealing shortly with the handiwork and designs of our great eighteenth-century craftsmen, we shall do well to search for the sources whence they drew their inspiration. There is pleasure as well as interest in this search, and our gems, speaking to us as they do of the epoch-making days so long gone by, have an added charm when once they stand as something more than so much cleverly-conceived furniture. An analysis of the skill possessed by British cabinet-makers during the last five centuries not only gives us an insight into the varying conceptions as to that which is best in applied art for the beautifying of our homes, but also serves to throw into yet stronger relief that excellence which was arrived at between the years 1700 and 1800.

If this research is to be fruitful, the collector must realise how indissolubly connected are the efforts of the architect and the cabinet-maker for interior decorations, and that the controlling element, that of the architect, may almost stand as an historical barometer. Whenever and wherever perfect harmony in household decoration has been arrived at, the productions of the furniture designer have been but a complement of the architect's scheme; so that the question of what we are to collect is oftener than not solved by our environment, unless we are furnishing a museum.

Eastern and Western Influence.

We may premise at the outset of our investigations that artists have ever "heard the East a-calling," and that, just as the sun has risen and journeyed westward, so too has enlightenment travelled the same path. We recall the glories of ancient Greece, and of her artists led captive to Rome, that the Eternal City and the Roman workmen might benefit by their teaching. This in after years was to lead to the Renaissance, destined to govern that which was best in the applied arts of civilised Europe. So, too, the Chinese porcelains inspired the early and best work of such noted factories as, for instance, those of Dresden and Worcester, in addition to transmitting to the world the possibilities of ceramic art. Oriental lacquer found ready imitators in Holland, France, and England. Chinese subjects appealed to such artistic giants as Caffieri of France, and our own great Chippendale, long before the correct drawing but stilted feeling of Sir William Chambers had taught us how mediocre a rendering of Eastern art could be given. Italy, again, gave forth her lore to France, Spain, and Holland; this percolated through, westward, to us, and eventually even guided North American productions. Instances in support of this contention could be easily multiplied, but our purpose is already served.

Reverting to one or two examples of the historical influences bearing on our subject, we shall notice how Henry VIII., Louis Quatorze, and Napoleon, by their strong individualities called into existence fashions symbolic of their leanings towards grandeur and magnificence; whilst Oliver Cromwell, as might have been expected, introduced a leavening of quiet and plain simplicity.

Whilst Italy in the fifteenth century was coming under the influence of the Renaissance, our own country was convulsed with foreign and civil wars, and as a result any development of national taste and culture was retarded. The inception of progress seems to have come with the establishing of a printing press by William Caxton in 1476, an event which nailed down the coffin-lid on mediævalism. Royalty and the aristocracy placed premiums on the diffusion of knowledge, and to a degree encouraged the Arts and Sciences from this time onwards.

Fortunately for us, an expanding intercourse with Italy gave our forefathers new ideas, a consummation largely arrived at through the energy of one man. Born at Canterbury, where he was taught as a boy, Thomas Linacre, after proceeding to Oxford, thirsted for a deeper knowledge of the Arts and Sciences. These he studied in Italy, where he seems to have made the most of his opportunities, for he was considered to be the greatest savant in the kingdom on his return home. Linacre was not only tutor to the king's children, but also trained Erasmus, Cardinal Wolsey, Tonstall of Durham, Latimer, and Sir Thomas More, imbuing them with enlightened ideas. In other words, he had the moulding of the minds and intellects of the rising generation, and incidentally of those men who in after years were to have access to the king's ear. Fortunate, too, in receiving his monarch's support, the seed he had sown speedily fructified, for we find Henry VII. sending to Italy for painters, sculptors, and carvers, not only to embellish the royal palace, but also to instruct native craftsmen.

Henry VIII. and the Advance in Cabinet-making.

With the accession of Henry VIII. came the first great advance in English cabinet-making. Hitherto taste had been monastic in its origin, and for so long as decoration had existed, Gothic feeling of a more or less primitive expression obtained. Henry sought to establish a vogue more majestic and in keeping with his taste for display, goaded thereto largely by the wish to emulate the more magnificent environment of the neighbouring monarch François Premier of France. Much of the success obtained in this direction palpably resulted from workmanship and teaching which had percolated through France to England.

The Waning of the Gothic.

Henry attracted workmen from Burgundy, Flanders, France, Germany, and Italy, offering princely fees as an inducement to the craftsmen of those countries to visit or to settle in England. Following their master's bent, the nobles of England requisitioned the services of such alien artificers as were available, many workmen going straight from the Royal palaces to the homes of the nobility so soon as their original commissions were completed. Although these foreign decorators hailed from divers centres, the fundamental lesson which they brought over was Italian. Each country had its own minor suggestions, its quota of mannerism and modification, yet everything harked back to the main idea of the Renaissance.

Surfeited with Gothicism, Western Europe welcomed

the classic alternative, discarding the old love in favour of a new. Journeymen started out from Italy, gradually penetrating northwards and westwards, moving hither and thither as they were attracted either by specific bids from various princes and nobles, or by the markets for their labour, which opened as culture spread. The course of their wanderings is fairly charted, for we find traces of local influences outcropping in their designs. In their travels they were evidently pleased with novelties peculiar to the temporary homes in which they sojourned, for here and there they stopped by the wayside to embody or to adapt whensoever a touch of local colour caught their eye or appealed to their imagination.

But we as a people were isolated from Italy, from France, Germany, and Flanders; not by the strip of water separating us from the mainland, but by our total lack of artistic enterprise. If Italian art was the hub of progress, the other countries had each a semi-distinctive school of culture with a general regard for taste and progress radiating from it. We in England enjoyed no such advantage as this; no healthy grounding in the rudiments of the new teaching was at the disposal of British workmen, and when, under Henry VIII., the sudden demand went forth English craftsmanship, for all the influence it could assert, was non-existent. To such an extent was this marked that the English people, unversed in decoration save that pertaining to the Gothic of monastic tradition, had yet to learn the desirability of even furnishing their homes on adequate or artistic lines.

If we eliminate such specimens as served to decorate the churches or homes of the clergy, we must realise that even our nobility were satisfied with surroundings at which half a century later the humblest yeoman would have looked askance.

The leaven which came at the close of Henry VII.'s reign worked but slowly; the influence which that monarch's successor, Henry VIII., brought to bear resulted in a scramble—a race for something which the nation, in responding to its King's ukase, was prepared to swallow at the risk of its digestion.

Hither came, as we have seen, craftsmen from all parts; but who was to hold the balance in a country where nobody was versed in the use of the artistic scales? England, whose knowledge of the Renaissance at first hand may be set down as a negligible quantity, found herself suddenly called upon to accept its teachings as seen through the spectacles of many nations. The true objective was lost sight of in a sequence of kaleidoscopic views, each of which, even if it presented some new feature of interest, only served to emphasise the variations and combinations obtainable.

It must not be supposed that Gothic ideas were dropped entirely so soon as the new teaching made appreciable headway, for we find a strongly-marked transitional period showing the meeting of the ways. As the reign of Henry proceeded, more and more of the Italian idea filtered through to England at the expense of the expiring monastic fashion, until, in the reign of Elizabeth, a semi-distinct style of decoration, sometimes known as "Tudor," sometimes as "Elizabethan," had sprung into being.

So meagre were the attempts at furnishing the home in the early phases of the sixteenth century that our ancestors seem to have rested content with the bare necessaries of a semi-barbaric existence—a bed to sleep on, a table to feed from, a bench or stool to sit upon, and chests and cupboards for the reception of clothes and stores, and the inventory was practically complete. The clergy and nobility, in addition to owning good specimens of these articles of furniture, possessed others, such at as buffets, chairs, and canopied benches, whilst their cupboards evolved into decorated hutches for the reception of their wardrobes, or into armoires for their livery rations.

Fifteenth-century Gothic Chest, made in England during the "Monastic" period. French influence is noticeable. The property of Messrs. Gill and Reigate, Ltd.

Perhaps those articles which the owner used regularly to take about with him as he moved from home to home or house to house were deemed to be most important. The bed, with its hangings, the chest, the hutch, the brass-studded leather trunk, and even the chair, destined to play this nomadic part, all had to bear witness to the high estate and position of their owner. Articles which were left in houses vacant during the peregrinations of their owners seem to have been exceedingly plain, and were hardly considered worthy of any serious attempt at decoration.

The early dining-table was, as a rule, plain and devoid of decoration. In trestle formation, its top, long and narrow, rested on two or more supports, the latter being single, or on occasions double, built. When the trestle was double built it usually assumed the shape of a rude cross. The benches made to accompany these tables, though more or less *en suite* with them, were even humbler in appearance. Small side or occasional tables were made showing more or less ambitious garnishment; but so few have come down to us that the collector can scarcely hope to acquire any of them.

The buffet of the times was a low-standing piece, very possibly so designed in order that, like the clothes chest, it could serve as a seat in an emergency. Seldom attaining three feet in height, half of its pitch was allocated to its legs and half to its body. The legs, square and plain, were at times set off by unpretentious mouldings round their edges, whilst they sometimes served to support arch shaping in the overlying carcase. The body of the buffet was freely decorated in a scheme of panelling, each panel on occasion carrying different embellishment. The interior of this model was, as a rule, divided into compartments, access to which was obtained through one or more doors opening outwards from its face.

The hutch, or movable standing cupboard, rectangular in form, was built in one or two storeys, and has accordingly come to be classed as a single or double hutch. A useful model, it was evidently prized in early days, for many of those specimens that have survived show more or less ornate treatment.

The Cabinet-maker's Art in Britain.

Sometimes confounded with the hutch, the armoire or livery cupboard may now and then be met with. Not unlike the hutch in construction, early armoires show pierced decoration permitting of ventilation, but in the majority of instances this piece of furniture was handled in humble manner by English cabinet-makers. From these cupboards the servants' or livery allowances were issued.

Mention should be made of the leather chests designed mainly for the storage of clothes. These models were decorated with brass nails, the initials, armorial bearings, or crest of the owner being cleverly set out. In the corners sprays of flowers and other dainty designs were cunningly introduced, and of such good material were these trunks made that quite a number survive to-day. In shape these old pieces greatly resemble the models now used by ladies for travelling purposes. Smaller specimens in the shape of dressing or jewel cases are not unknown.

When we remember that only two or three chairs were available for use in the larger households, and to this fact add the wastage of centuries, it is easy to account for the rarity of the Late Gothic and Early Tudor models. There seem to have been two main ideas in the cabinetmaker's mind—viz., the fashioning of comparatively light chairs, such as those of the X-shape, and the construction of a far heavier pattern of the box order. The lighter style would seem to have been intended for ladies' use or for the seating of men when clothed as civilians, the heavier to meet the requirements of armed men. The X-chair was Venetian in descent, and would not stand heavy usage. The box-chair, so called because the portion below the seat was panelled in, was of very great strength and rigidity; its back and arms, sometimes closed in, sometimes left open, resembled in shape the corner-chairs and tub, or grandfather chairs of the eighteenth century. There were, in addition, armchairs, massive in construction and strictly rectilinear in form, with low square backs and closed-in square arms, and to these we must add varieties in turned

English turned wood Chair in the Byzantine style. Period of Henry VIII. The property of F. W. Phillips, Esq.

wood; and lighter models with high backs and seats, showing the half of an octagon over light legs connected by primitive stretchers.

The chest seems to have been common to every home, and more specimens of this particular article of furniture have been preserved than of any other. In homes of any importance the chest seems always to have been decorated, even when other models have been left comparatively plain. Tudor chests, however, are rare, and authentic examples are always desirable.

Decoration.

During this reign England never shook herself free from Gothic *motif*. Our horizon was broadening, new ideas were percolating through to us, but ever and anon the idea ecclesiastical outcropped. Linenfold panels, at first plain, then rather more elaborate, and finally of ornate portrayal, obtained throughout the country. Portraits of Royalty in medallions, of heroic heads in strapped and laurelled bands, and armorial designs were freely pressed into service. Trelliswork and the earlier kinds of strapwork came as time wore on, whilst heavy grotesque masks of dogs, dragons, gryphons, leopards, lions, or sea monsters may be found introduced either by themselves or as forming the central feature of coarse, swag-like festoons. Some of our Gothic tracery was excellent, but in execution it was less brilliant than much of that produced by Continental effort in the same direction.

Craftsmen have always endeavoured to vary or to heighten their effects by the introduction of colour or colour-contrasts, but in reviewing this Early Tudor work we have only to notice the most primitive attempts of this nature. Experiments in marquetry were so crude and unimportant that they scarcely deserve comment. The fashion merely obtained of painting the panellings in self-colours and then "decorating" the furniture with the same hues. The author has seen Early Tudor work still bearing the traces of the original paint in hues of soft myrtle-green and in reds ranging to sealing-wax vermilion.

Judged by contemporary European standards, this English work showed good sense of proportion, fair to excellent construction, and a certain dignity, but it lacked brilliancy in conception and in the execution of decorative detail.

Elizabethan.

With the advent of Elizabeth came not only a wave of prosperity, but marked advancement in the applied arts and crafts. All factors at home made for progress when once the lead was given. Elizabeth, by her frequent rounds of visiting, set up a greatly increased demand for artistic decoration and craftsmanship. Whenever it was intimated that the Queen purposed honouring one of her subjects with a visit, the cleverest artist workmen available seem to have been commissioned to prepare and garnish the apartments set aside for the Royal use. This custom, although it doubtless entailed heavy expenses, forming even a severe tax on the means of poorer hosts, yet rendered signal service in the dissemination of cultured and new ideas. Under it many a remote country district received, at the hands of visiting craftsmen, its first insight into the new or classic school of work decades before the seeds of progress might otherwise have arrived.

A woman of education, of some taste and no little vanity, Queen Elizabeth evinced marked pleasure at elaborate preparations for her reception, and so we find that Englishmen all over the country vied with one another in according the Sovereign they hoped to entertain such regal and imposing surroundings as would find favour in her eyes. To-day, scattered over many counties, we find rooms wherein the Queen is supposed to have slept, or bedsteads whereon she once reposed, and although tradition cannot always be relied upon, the fact remains that Elizabeth, in the peregrinations which she took, greatly assisted the cause of decorative craftsmanship.

Although we had no school of native cabinetmakers capable of giving adequate expression to the incoming or classic vogue, we were singularly well placed for obtaining assistance from abroad—Italian workmen were attracted by the high fees offered, and we benefited, too, under the tutelage of Dutch, Flemish, and French craftsmen. The fifteenth century in the Netherlands had been a golden age in art, and Italian artists had even appealed to Dutch painters and artificers for assistance and guidance. During the succeeding century, although the art of the painter was less pronounced, the " applied " arts were making great strides, and history shows us how events favoured our reaping a rich harvest therefrom.

It will be remembered that the northern provinces revolted from the tyranny of Philip II. of Spain, and, uniting with Protestant Holland, defied that monarch and Alva, the Bloody Duke. As a result of this coalition an artistic and cultured race found their country a storm centre of war, wherein the prosecution of peaceful callings met with the ever-recurring handicaps of siege, battery, and pillage. In England the Dutch painter, goldsmith, weaver, or cabinetmaker was welcomed with open arms, and, naturally, many craftsmen left their battle-swept territory for the quiet and Protestant haven of England. So close indeed were the ties joining the two nations that it will be remembered that on the assassination of the Prince of Orange through the instrumentality of the Jesuits the throne of Holland was offered to Queen Elizabeth.

In addition, therefore, to the assistance which we were enabled to obtain direct from the fountain-head of the

Renaissance, fortuitous circumstances placed at our disposal the best talent of Holland. To these advantages we have to add those which we derived in 1572 when, after the massacres of St. Bartholomew, Huguenot craftsmen came by hundreds to these shores.

Elizabeth, practically engaged to the Duc d'Alençon, brother of the French King, for a decade, kept open an intercourse with our Latin neighbours, whilst by temporising with Spain she enabled England, for a period at any rate, to assimilate certain features of culture and mannerism characteristic of that Southern school. Ushered in under such favourable auspices—if by varying channels—the classic idea came to England, to take deep root. In an age when increased knowledge, refinement, and progress were very generally sought after and desired, everything favoured the successful development of the new *motif*. Shakespeare, Bacon, and Spenser all saw the light whilst rapid strides towards artistic advancement were happening around them.

Until the later phases of the sixteenth century no style of work based on the classic could rightly be described as " English "—it had not, in fact, evolved from the plethora of alien interpretations placed at our disposal. In late Tudor days came that semi-distinct method of handling the Renaissance teachings which has now come to be classed as " Elizabethan." The demand for furniture seems to have spread by leaps and bounds. Noblemen, successful merchants, the yeoman class, and the ordinary citizen doubled and trebled their demands upon the cabinetmaker, and, as national wealth increased, the craftsman's business must have shown wonderful returns. Midway through the reign of Queen Bess the merchant would have looked askance at models which half a century earlier had delighted, or at any rate satisfied, the nobility; whilst the models and decoration now favoured by the yeoman were more varied and elaborate than were those affected by the upper classes during the preceding reigns.

Elizabethan furniture possessed a certain rugged dignity of its own. English craftsmen were on the whole masters of proportion, whilst the carved decoration they employed, if lacking in finish, was deep and showed breadth of treatment. An analysis of many of the old decorative schemes, however, reveals inconsequent grouping of matter, many items which would not fuse or blend happily being brought into close juxtaposition. Vulgar overcrowding of detail is too often apparent, with a resultant loss of balance and relief. In quality the carving on English work of the period was inferior to that produced in the classic schools of the Continent, and its arrangement showed what hazy ideas of the Renaissance obtained in this country. As time wore on the abovementioned faults became emphasised and the general run of work decadent, whilst these unfortunate features were all the more apparent in that our carving lost its sharpness, and with this its power of carrying off other defects.

Elizabethan craftsmen evinced a strong partiality for marquetry, a style of decoration which gradually superseded the earlier and primitive essays in plain painting and gilding. A short transitional phase should perhaps be recorded during which a little inlaid work may be found side by side with a modicum of unimportant painting. The study of woods, especially in small strips or sections, such as those built into schemes of marquetry, is a complex one, rendered all the more difficult when, as under the custom then obtaining, these minute pieces were subjected to staining and varnishing. In Elizabeth's reign apple, ash, beech, box, cherry, deal, ebony, holly, limewood, oak, pear, rosewood, sycamore, yew, and walnut all played their parts, and the collector cannot diagnose the constituent parts of some fields of complicated inlay.

The range of subjects covered by the Elizabethan carver was an exceedingly wide one, though most of the detail affected was more or less closely allied with that of the Renaissance. Thus we find specimens with purely architectural garnishment and others showing guilloche bandings, fluting and stopped fluting, gadrooning, nulling or echinus carving. Strapwork was one of the most frequently employed items of embellishment. Grotesque and arabesque work was commonly introduced, whilst wholelength figures, sometimes nude to the waist, stood out as caryatides, usually dividing arched compartments. These figures may be met with sufficiently refined in appearance to suggest their being representations of angels or sacred characters, whilst on other examples of equal importance their portrayal may be so coarse and grotesque as to constitute caricatures of male or female South Sea Islanders. The human figure may be shown to the waist only, or again only the head may appear in mask form. Grotesque masks seem to have been very popular, for we find many of them, and they are commonly framed in strapwork.

Fruit and floral work embellished many pieces, and a rough representation of the " Tree of the Knowledge of Good and Evil," with the serpent's head showing *en profile*, usually from the left side, was a fairly common feature—in recessed panels within archwork especially. The tree has a certain resemblance at times to the pomegranate, and this latter fruit is freely shown on Elizabethan models. The acanthus, coarsely portrayed, was

Elizabethan Buffet Sideboard or Dinner Waggon, showing the typical Renaissance bulbs. The cornice is covered with a network of fine marquetry. These models are of great rarity. Author's Collection.

often inserted, and rosacing was happily introduced. Heraldic devices were greatly in demand, especially so in the case of bed and chair backs. One also finds a pendant resembling in shape a split cannon or mace as a complementary finish to strapwork.

Sprays or bouquets of flowers issued gracefully in shower formation from vases or baskets in the typical marquetry of the day; the blooms spread outwards with a droop on curved stems, and from the fact that the effect conveyed resembles the coloured lights which fall on the explosion of a rocket, this special arrangement of floral detail is commonly referred to as being of the shower or rocket pattern.

Hunting scenes or landscapes were now and again presented, but as perspective was at fault the results achieved were not satisfactory, and the pieces so decorated are prized mainly on account of their rarity and quaintness.

There was little realism in the work relieved by carved or inlaid representations of the animal world, for birds, beasts, and fishes were portrayed as so many mythical or allegorical monsters in the vast majority of instances, and our ancestors seem to have appreciated the beauty of extreme ugliness in common with their Teutonic neighbours, the acknowledged champions of exaggerated grotesquerie.

We find a considerable volume of geometrical and stereotyped detail in the carved and inlaid furniture of the period, chequered or diaper-work being most prevalent as matter subsidiary to more important garnishment.

There is one feature common to nearly all furniture of this period where either legs or supports have been introduced into the model, and this consists of a bold bulbous swell, which has been likened to an old cup with cover. Reference to our illustration on page 45 will show four typical examples of this modelling arranged in two pairs. At first comparatively light in proportion, this detail attained its greatest value from an artistic point of view on buffets, tables, Court cupboards, and bedsteads of the period 1575, or thereabouts. As time progressed the bulb became unduly heavy, and in conjunction with this phase the carving, too, showed signs of decadence. From 1600 and onwards the bulbous swell tended to fade away and to show less and less embellishment, until it grew into the cylindrical turned garnishment of Jacobean days. No other feature of Elizabethan work is so characteristic of the period, few other traits so surely enable us to date the examples to which they have been applied.

Owing to a vagueness in the generic term " Court cupboard," confusion has taken place when young collectors have sought to differentiate between armoires, double hutches, and the models now generally known as Court cupboards. The two first-named are earlier conveniences, usually showing continuity of face-surface throughout their course. In the vast majority of the Court cupboards the upper storey, containing three small compartments, stands back from the under storey and occupies a smaller area.

Livery rations used to be served from the armoire, and the practice was continued in the case of the plainer Court cupboards. From Elizabethan days, however, we find handsome Court cupboards evidently created for the living-rooms of the owners of important houses, and these give one the idea of their being glorified buffets with added cupboard accommodation.

The Cabinet-maker's Art in Britain.

The three-storeyed Court cupboard, or " three-decker " as it is often styled, is supposed to have first emanated from Wales, where it was locally known as a tridarn. Generally speaking, the armoire and hutch proper ceased to exist, or became obsolete, with the sixteenth century. The Court cupboards which largely took their place were popular throughout the Stuart period.

The Court cupboard (French short cupboard) of the period shows two of these bulbs, one at each corner, supporting the canopy; or, in the event of the piece being a " three-decker," as in our illustration on page 61, there may be two pairs of these supports. When the third tier is not supported by these swells a turned ornament is suspended at the corners of the top canopy at the spot where the capitals of the swelled supports would have joined the second and third storeys. The buffet proper shows two pairs of these bulbs, and another variety of the buffet, with its upper section closed in to form a cupboard or cupboards, is usually adorned in similar fashion.

In the case of the four-post bedstead each of the front bed-poles will as a rule be found to taper upwards towards the canopy from one of the bulbous excrescences, the latter capping square and decorated pedestal feet or legs of massive proportion, which rise above the plane of the mattress.

Tables show this common feature, the bulb constituting the main decoration of each leg. Joint-stools or coffin-stools, too, show similar treatment in a lighter and less pronounced form.

The four-poster, the buffet, the Court cupboard, and the dining-table were the most highly-prized and freely-decorated models of importance during the reign of Queen

Bess. No time or money seems to have been stinted in their creation, and their average of excellence witnesses the advance made in the cabinet-maker's art during the second half of the sixteenth century.

The trestle-supported dining-table made way for a handsome and more useful type known as the draw-table—a rectilinear model this, with its legs linked together with stretchers, the top pulled out in rather ingenious fashion. Two leaves, each half the length of a normal top, rested on the table carcase, and above them was a full-length top; the underlying leaves were made so that they could be pulled out at either end of the table, supported by bracket-arms working to and fro within the main framework. When so pulled out the top or main leaf sank down between the shorter leaves, so that the table-top could be extended to double its length when occasion required.

Some early tables have their legs or trestles built into a wooden platform in area and shape practically identical with their table-top; other specimens have a single raised rail uniting the supports and running down the course of the table. The majority of these fittings have been replaced or restored, whilst additions foreign to the original plan are by no means uncommonly met with.

Ordinary long tables, too, with fixed tops, were created, many of them being handsome in design. Small occasional tables, some of them almost purely classic, others with hybrid embellishment, were affected. All tables were liable to more or less elaborate schemes of inlaid decoration in addition to bold and rather rugged carving of the impressionistic type.

Chairs were still comparatively rare articles of furniture, but the designs of the day showed greater variety.

In this Bedstead we see the exaggeration of the Renaissance bulbous swell characteristic of late Elizabethan and early Jacobean work. Photograph kindly lent by Messrs. Gill and Reigate.

Noticeable amongst the principal patterns were those showing pierced archwork with rather squat backs. This balustered style showed the arching in the back, with at times a modified repetition of the same theme in the underframing. In time the backs became higher and the arches within them narrower, higher, and plainer. Tall, narrow-back armchairs known as "cacqueteuse" chairs came into vogue. These talking or conversational chairs were of comparatively slender construction, and were intended for the use of the fair sex. The tall and narrow back-splats were at times covered with fine carving, and their arms and seats opened outwards in horn formation to increase the seating area, which would otherwise have been too limited for the reception of the farthingale.

As in the case of the panelled chairs, the decoration on the arm supports of the cacqueteuse chairs was merely a repetition of that meted out to the underlying front legs. The panelled chairs, surmounted by a scrolled cresting which now became popular, were of far heavier build, and were obviously designed for the use of the sterner sex. Somewhat squat in appearance, many of these models were constructed with a view to supporting knights encumbered with armour, and, as there is a marked resemblance between the English and French chairs of the times, we may have returned from some field of chivalry to repeat patterns which we had appreciated in France.

The X-shaped chair lasted throughout the period, and, with its simple scheme of upholstery on a shaped seat, must have been one of the most comfortable models of the time.

Writing-cabinets in marquetry, with a fall-down front on the principle of the later and well-known Queen Anne model, were not unknown. Other pieces of furniture conformed more or less closely to the general outline and decoration of the Elizabethan school just touched upon.

The background behind carved detail in early oak furniture was frequently decorated with minute and unimportant punched work. Each descent of the punch left four or five indentations, which may resemble asterisks, on the secondary surface.

Renaissance.

We have had to mention, and shall constantly have to refer to, the Renaissance (literally New Birth), and it is perhaps essential as well as advisable that the intelligent collector of English furniture should know something of the inception and progress of the great movement. It will be remembered that in Greece some 500 years B.C. the standard of culture and art was exceptional. Incomparably in advance of other nations, the Grecians gave us in succession the Doric, Ionic, and Corinthian orders in architecture. Nothing to equal these orders had ever been achieved, and nothing since they were conceived has seriously vied wtih them. After the conquest of the country by the Romans, the latter carried home as captives artists and craftsmen of all descriptions, not only to beautify their capital but to train and educate Roman talent.

In Italy, conquerors and conquered, working side by side, besides giving renderings of Grecian art, gave modified interpretations of it showing local colour, and finally evolved two new orders, the Tuscan and Composite, as warrant of their joint endeavour. Of the five orders so introduced, the Doric, Ionic, and Corinthian are known to-day as the Grecian, the Tuscan and Composite, though adapted from the preceding styles, being known as

The Cabinet-maker's Art in Britain. 55

Roman. The two groups combined compose the Classic or Antique period in art, which faded away about A.D. 250.

By A.D. 300 a new vogue, known as the Byzantine order, was establishing itself : it was of a debased classic nature, governed by Eastern expression, and if we examine the art represented by the ikons or sacred pictures of the Greek Church of to-day we shall be able to form a shrewd opinion as to its value. Unreal and garish, if glittering and catchy, it catered for the ignorant and superstitious palate in a symbolic and non-naturalistic manner. This decadent style was superseded by the Mediæval or Gothic order, of which we have so many beautiful examples in our parish churches. The Gothic style governed our cabinet-making until the end of the reign of Henry VII. ; its influence was strong during the period Henry VIII. to Elizabeth, and it is traceable in much of our seventeenth-century furniture. In the eighteenth century our best masters, such as Chippendale and Sheraton, came under its influence, seldom with satisfactory results. With the exception of the triangular-shaped armchairs in turned wood built during the fifteenth and sixteenth centuries there are few English models governed by the Byzantine school of decoration.

Towards the end of the fifteenth century an artistic brotherhood, dissatisfied with the poor results achieved under the Byzantine and Gothic styles, reverted to the antique or classic period for teaching and inspiration. This coterie, which included amongst its members such men as Michael Angelo, Raphael, and Palladio, was so influential that it succeeded in carrying popular opinion with it, and in so doing established the Renaissance in Italy. This movement was coincident with the new thought and letters of the General Renaissance, the doctrines of which were widely disseminated through the agency of the newly-born printing-press.

The new teaching spread rapidly, and was generally accepted by Germany, Holland, Flanders, France, Spain, and finally by ourselves in a more or less literal translation. Transitional phases in which Gothic or even Byzantine feeling was blended with the new Italian work, occurred in each country that favoured the new idea. Subsequently, when the Classic revival was at its height, each country embracing it adapted or modified its interpretation to suit its especial case.

English Renaissance.

There were three channels, broadly speaking, through which the lessons of the Renaissance came home to us in England. The earliest and most obvious facilities coming through the direct importation of Italian craftsmen, Henry VII., Henry VIII., and Elizabeth all adopted this specific for the raising of the standard of British art and craftsmanship. Probably the best illustration of this kind of influence is to be found in the Henry VII. Chapel in Westminster Abbey, a wonderful and beautiful memorial raised by Henry VIII. in memory of his father and commissioned to Torrigiano.

The second source of progress was largely fortuitous, and came with the influx of Continental workmen, who, in following an opening market, led by nomadic tendencies, or driven here by persecution at the hands of Rome, brought over as their main stock-in-trade the principles and practice of the Renaissance movement. These craftsmen, many of whom settled in the country, carried the new idea into every corner of the kingdom.

The Cabinet-maker's Art in Britain.

Under the third heading advancement came through the instrumentality of Englishmen, who left the country with the specific intention of Classic research in Italy at first hand—a practice growing more and more common as the seventeenth century progressed—instances of such artistic enterprise being furnished by the Italian training of such eminent men as Inigo Jones, William Kent, and Robert Adam.

It has already been stated that interior decoration, if it is to be successful and pleasing in its result, must be in harmony with the architect's general scheme—to which, indeed, it should play the complementary part. In the light of this axiom it is important to remember that all our greatest architects of the seventeenth and eighteenth centuries were influenced in their work by the Italian Renaissance. It matters not whether we weigh the genius of Inigo Jones, the masterpieces of Christopher Wren, the " rough jewels " (as Adam described them) of Vanbrugh, the free conceptions of Kent, or the refined decoration of the brothers Adam, they all go back to the same fountain-head, and it follows as a corollary that the best craftsmen of the olden times ordered their designs and decorative detail on corresponding lines.

Now and then we happen on models which have lost something of their possibilities owing to an undue effort on the part of their creators to conform with the idea architectural; more often, as in the case of Charles II. or Chippendale furniture, artistic licence has beclouded the Classic theme, but in all the phases of the work which lies before us the influence of the Renaissance will be more or less patent.

In considering the respective merits of the Doric, Ionic, Corinthian, Tuscan, and Composite orders, it is pleasing to see that our forbears rightly gave precedence to the claims of the three former, which, it will be remembered, constitute the Grecian section in the Antique or Classic style. Now and then we find work obviously biased by the Tuscan or Composite (Roman) orders; but, on the whole, Adam's opinion reflects fairly accurately the attitude of the English school towards the rival schools. Adam, dealing with the subject, wrote:—" We acknowledge only three orders: the Doric, the Ionic, and the Corinthian; for, as to the Tuscan, it is, in fact, no more than a bad and imperfect Doric; and the Composite or Roman order, in our opinion, is a very disagreeable and awkward mixture of the Corinthian and Ionic, without either grace or beauty."

CHAPTER III.
Jacobean, Cromwellian, Charles II., and William and Mary Furniture.

James I.

WITH the passing of Queen Elizabeth and the accession of that sensual and uncultivated monarch James I., a very real incentive to artistic effort disappeared. Bereft of encouragement, or, rather, of that encouragement which a discerning patron can accord, the English craftsman drifted away from the paths of taste in an effort to comply with the demand for comfort. The result is seen in a period of work where beauty of outline and decoration gave way to the dictates of luxury. Under these conditions, though the upholsterer's trade advanced, the cabinet-maker, in failing to progress, actually lost ground, rendering old themes with less skill and power as time wore on.

Left to his own resources and to work out the salvation of his craft, the British workman had barely formulated new ideas when wars and rumours of wars came to hinder their true development. The story of the seventeenth century tells, at first, of acquiescence in debased Elizabethan feeling, then of the Jacobean exploitation of panelled work, sometimes treated with foreign and bizarre marquetry, followed by a hiatus consequent on the Civil War. After this we have the rigid simplicity of the Commonwealth, followed by the somewhat florid work of the Restoration.

Meaning of the Term "Jacobean."

Before attempting to analyse Jacobean furniture, it is necessary to come to some understanding as to the scope of this generic term. Unfortunately, the style has been held to extend over the period James I. to William and Mary, and so to include a series of steps in cabinet-making, many of which are distinct from one another, under one common heading. The dynastic use of the term may be obviously correct, but for our purpose it is misleading and inadequate, and it is necessary to subdivide it into a series of phases if an introspect is to be useful. Under these circumstances it will be best to class such furniture as was created during the reign of James I. and Charles I. as Jacobean, dealing with subsequent work, for purposes of differentiation, as Cromwellian, Charles II., or William and Mary. Were this course not adopted the collector would miss all the finesse and interest in a century's evolution, and he would, at the same time, be confused when confronted with a medley of work traceable to the various and conflicting influences obtaining over the period.

Influence of Continental Schools.

With the passing of time variations upon the Classic idea became frequently noticeable in the applied arts of the Continental schools, and we in England, largely influenced by Italian, German, Dutch, Flemish, French, Spanish, or even Portuguese mentors, seem to have played the part of the shuttlecock to the battledore of Western Europe. Still drawing on the Gothic from time

Very fine James I. Oak Court Cupboard, belonging to Messrs. Gill and Reigate, Ltd. These are generally found with only two decks; when, as in the present example, there is an additional storey, they are termed three-deckers. In Welsh oak the latter variety is often met with, and tradition has it that these were made for people of high degree. The decoration of this piece savours partly of Elizabethan times.

to time, labouring, too, under Elizabethan tradition, or even stooping to incorporate an item of Byzantine detail, it is wonderful to record how our craftsmen yet succeeded in stamping on the bulk of their creations a certain individuality of their own. The decadence in carving which had obtained in late Elizabethan times became more pronounced under the Stuarts, and our workmen do not seem to have seriously combated this retrograde feature of their art. It would appear, from a careful study of the craft, that salvation was sought in the development of upholstered furniture, panelling, and new departures in carving and marquetry.

Evolution of Upholstered Furniture.

The gradual introduction of upholstered furniture, whilst making for comfort in the home, largely circumscribed the province of the cabinet-maker proper, who was now called upon to provide the plainest of frames for such models as day-beds, couches, settees, chairs, and stools. The surpassing excellence of contemporary needlework and embroidery and the rich and delicate hues of the velvets and other materials available perhaps warranted the subordination of woodwork to the scheme of upholstery, but now that this latter, ephemeral in character, has passed away, one can but regret the uninteresting character of such skeletons as have survived.

In the case of the larger models, such as bedsteads, couches, settees, or day-beds, the early Jacobean tendency was towards a model showing the minimum of woodwork, but, now that wear and moth have destroyed the beautiful cushions, coverlets, and hangings which these pieces once proudly boasted, no feature remains suggestive of the cabinet-maker's progress.

After the Restoration the positions were reversed, for day-beds, chairs, and stools then exhibited the maximum of carcase decoration, a scanty regard for the essentials of comfort being oftentimes noticeable, whilst drapery once more became, as in Elizabethan days, complementary to woodwork.

In the field of panelling the Jacobean craftsman regained much of the ground which he had lost elsewhere, for he achieved happy results with pleasing frequency. The panel-work of the day, indeed, cunningly conceived and varied, bears eloquent testimony to the taste and ingenuity of designer and joiner. Set off by artistic and cleverly-applied mouldings, these panels, usually arranged in horizontal pairs, enabled their users to compass either simple or important effects. Bad and stilted work there was, it is true, but this is easily accounted for.

It must be remembered that when once a moulding has been run out its application in panel formation may sink to mechanical routine. The craftsman, with good taste, will arrive at successful results whether he aims at simple or imposing achievements. The workman who lacks the essential qualification when embarking on similar enterprise will scarcely stumble on a triumph of simplicity, whilst he will become stilted or laboured in ambitious venture.

Increasing Demand for Furniture.

It has been seen that the demand for furniture was growing by leaps and bounds, and, to cope with the commissions everywhere going a-begging, a class of cabinet-makers, or joiners, of the calibre of carpenters came to the front. Oak was everywhere obtainable, James I. setting an example by sacrificing timber in prodigal fashion to augment his revenue. With plenty of " hands " available—one cannot dub them craftsmen—and with an abundance of the necessary material, it is small wonder that many people essayed the fashionable panelling on rectilinear models requiring in reality the attention of a craftsman. We must learn to discriminate between the productions of the carpenter and those of the cabinet-maker—it is not fair on the latter to strike an average—and then the Jacobean craftsman will be credited with good accomplishments.

Carving.

It has been stated that the carving of the times reached a very low ebb, but the climax was marked with the very general introduction of a new process. Under this new treatment a more or less primitive and inconsequent design was gouged out from the surface of the wood, with the result that the bulk of the decoration lay below the plane of the model's face. Here and there, as part and parcel of the design, portions of the original surface were left, high and dry, given, too, some semblance of relief by the excavation of the surrounding timber. At times this delving conferred no garnishment on the bed so sunk, as, for example, in such cases as those in which the operator wished to present arabesque or strapwork. On these occasions sufficient wood was removed in the interstices of the pattern to give to the remaining surface an appearance of the requisite character. Often, however, within a diamond-shaped panel, marked out by the gouge, a sunk design was perpetrated by gradation in the amount of wood chiselled out. A yet more skimping method, somewhat hazily known as scratch " carving," consisted in the drawing of some geometrical or other design on the model by the cutting out of a shallow channel from the wood.

Inlay.

No real improvement on the finer Elizabethan marquetry can be recorded during Jacobean days, since the floral sprays of the bouquet and rocket order belonging to the older school still yielded the most pleasing results. An innovation, however, consisting of the inlaying of bone, ivory, mother-o'-pearl, or tortoiseshell, yielded striking if usually bizarre effects towards the end of the reign of James, fitful support being accorded it until the close of the century. The fashion is supposed to have been brought over to Kent by Protestant refugees at an early date, and the number of examples unearthed in that county lends some corroboration to the tradition. Many Jacobean pieces have been inlaid with mother-o'-pearl, &c., during the last five-and-twenty years, and the collector should use great care when making his first purchases; he will then learn the necessity for especial watchfulness in this particular field.

Appliqué Decoration.

The Jacobean craftsman showed a strong predilection for appliqué decoration throughout the century—a fact witnessed by the constant setting-out or building-up of panels with applied mouldings. The employment, too, of round, oval, diamond, or lozenge shaped bosses, and the introduction of pendants of the split baluster, mace, or cannon type, furnish further examples of the same method. Pendants and bosses were stuck on to the face of the carcase in segments, and often many of these are missing from the genuine examples they once adorned.

In an age when bold carved detail proved too serious a strain on craftsmen little noted for originality of conception or brilliancy in execution, appliqué garnishment seems to have been welcomed as a happy alternative. In lending itself to repetition, with the saving clause of minor variation, it seems to have afforded just such possibilities as lay within the compass of Jacobean talent.

But if the potentialities of the new order were limited, this panelling phase, together with contemporary turning, possesses other interests, for the very plain and simple results of which they admitted saved them from disrepute in the austere school of the Commonwealth. As a resultant feature of their immunity from desuetude during Puritan times, the course of evolution in their case runs in an almost unbroken line.

Minor Embellishments—*Study of Detail.*

We have noticed the broad principles of decoration during early Jacobean days, but we must give some little attention to the minor methods of embellishment and to the favourite detail introduced by the craftsmen of the times. Channelling, diaper-work, dentil-work, gadrooning, fluting and " stopped " fluting, nulling, ropework, reed-moulding and stopped reed-moulding were all in full favour. Architectural designs and armorial detail, arabesque and grotesque work, were commonly pressed into service, and geometrical work, incised, inlaid, or in raised panel formation, was ever present. Spandrels were decorated, scrolls, crested or otherwise, were popular, whilst the echinus, acanthus, guilloche band, or cartouche, in somewhat stiff forms, were varied by pomegranates, gillyflowers, vine-leaves, with grapes, laurelling, and such-like embellishments of flowers, fruit, or foliage.

The carved figures, representing the human form more or less accurately, so characteristic of Elizabethan work, survived until about 1645, when their use was very generally discontinued. After the Restoration, cherubs, usually in pairs, but rendered in more refined fashion, usurped the place of the semi-barbaric figure-studies discarded before the Commonwealth.

Under Jacobean craftsmen the leg and pillar supports in furniture assumed lighter proportions, while the bulbous swell, so characteristic of the preceding vogue, gave way in favour of one of cylindrical form. The detail carved on the new model at first bore strong resemblance to that which had graced its Elizabethan precursor, though it lacked the brilliancy and sharpness in execution of the earlier school. By degrees the carving faded away, and the cylinder came in for plain turned-work embellishment. The neck over the cylinder was crowned by an Ionic capital in many of the earlier specimens, but in later days this item was generally discarded in favour of a plain turned cap, all too often weak not only in design but in proportion. One comes across variations of this detail, for the collector may happen on pleasing essays in vase formation, just as he may chance on specimens in which the cylinder has been subdivided into two or more sections, with disastrous results from an artistic point of view.

At times we find pilasters in open clusters fulfilling the office hitherto discharged by the bulbous swell of the Elizabethan or of the cylindrical swell of Jacobean days. This feature is most noticeable in the case of buffets with the top storey closed in, and in Court cupboards, where these little groups of pillars support the hood of the model. Now and then this skeleton-like detail was

German Ueberhangs-schrank, the counterpart of our Jacobean Court Cupboard of the mid-seventeenth century. The analogy between these German and English pieces is very marked, but the Continental specimens have the two central drawers over the cupboards, more florid inlay, and less pleasing hood supports. The property of the Rev. G. A. Schneider.

introduced as the foundation whence the columns of a four-poster bedstead sprang, and it has been met with as forming the leg-supports to table-tops.

One useful characteristic of the period consisted in the very general introduction of drawers. These useful adjuncts had been sparingly used hitherto, but their adoption as an essential convenience came under the Stuarts. The rectilinear shaping of chests, cabinets, and so on admitted of the employment of these fitments in the bulk of the models produced, and without taxing the ingenuity of the craftsman too severely. These early drawers ran on cleverly-contrived side-runners, and, although the original grooves and runners are generally the worse for wear, they may be readily adjusted.

The cabinet-makers of the day evinced a partiality for the subdivision of decorated surfaces, and this particular tendency is noticeable throughout seventeenth-century work. In the case of the simpler models, the geometrical arrangement of panelling, assisted by channellings, mouldings, plinths, and bands of carving, conferred he desired effect, but in the more ornate specimens we find decorated archwork, plaques, corbels, or trusses serving to emphasise the series of compartments which the craftsman endeavoured to present.

Curiously inconsistent in their sense of proportion and in the art of placing decorative detail, the workmen and designers of the century may be found to have arrived at veritable triumphs of simplicity and overladen failures when executing their every-day commissions. A study of the leg-work, posts, and pillars of the time at once brings out the fickle character of Jacobean taste; many of the plain turned legs or spiral supports possess commendable points, whilst side by side with these we find contemporary specimens in which the outline has been rendered top-heavy or confused by the introduction of superfluous and ill-chosen matter.

Marked Progress.

Great progress was marked in the production of chairs, stools, sofas, and settees, which now came to be regarded as essentials in the different rooms of well-appointed establishments. Perhaps we should first look at the examples produced in plain wood, afterwards noticing the development of upholstery. The settle may be found in oak, with panelled back and under-framing, showing all the characteristics of the century's evolution both as to proportion and decorative handling. When acquiring these pieces the collector should evince great caution, seeing that so many putative examples have been built up out of old panelling or material, whilst plain and genuine examples have been subjected to modern embellishment. An interesting and rare variation of this model was produced in which the back was so constructed that it would swing over and, resting on the arms, would thus constitute a side table or buffet. This idea was also brought into play in connection with a few armchairs, when the back, which would be round, admitted of the model's use as a round occasional table.

The well beneath the seat of the closed-in settee was sometimes utilised as a chest, access to which was gained by means of a lid opening upwards on S or cock hinges, and set rather far forward in the seat. It is interesting to note that spurious examples almost invariably show this arrangement, whilst we find the conversion of fixed seat to lid as a common occurrence in otherwise original specimens.

"*Jacobean*" *Furniture.* 73

The panelled chairs of the Elizabethan and Jacobean vogues form an interesting study, and should be considered

Table-chair; period 1620-1640. In the Collection of F. W. Phillips, Esq.

in conjunction with the contemporary settles, seeing that the two models possess so many features in common. Obviously influenced at times by the school of the Louis

Treize, the more striking of these chairs are crowned by scrolled cresting, resting on decorated top-rails, which, contained within the back uprights in the case of earlier

Table-bench; period 1620-1640. In the Collection of
F. W. Phillips, Esq.

examples, came to be superimposed on them at the dawn of the century as a fairly general rule. Below the decorated top-rail we find a scheme of marquetry or carving in the more ambitious chairs and settles; a

"Jacobean" Furniture. 75

decorated arch with its concomitant spandrels enclosing a further inlaid or carved bouquet or spray of flowers,

Very fine Jacobean Oak Armchair, with some Elizabethan character. From a photograph kindly supplied by Messrs. Gill and Reigate, owners of the original.

rather stiffly rendered, it is true, was wont to grace the chair-back and a series of such detail the back of the settle.

The uprights of chair and settle backs were crowned at times by small turned knobs, especially in such cases as those in which the scrolled crestings were omitted; in these latter examples the somewhat severe appearance of the strictly rectilinear outline was but emphasised by the precision of the accompanying panelwork. In the case of the settle-back we find these panels arranged either in one, two, or three tiers, the panels in each row conforming with one another in size as a rule, but seldom with those of the neighbouring row or rows. The legs and arm-supports of the chairs were decorated with turned work, and frequently carried reeded or fluted embellishment—a treatment extended to such settles as had not a "carcase well" below the seat. Now and then one happens on a chair with the carcase box, and here, as in the case of the settles similarly designed, the ground storey is relieved by bold if usually plain panelling.

These settle-backs varied considerably in height, and the chair-back displayed a moderate range. One large panel for the chair and two rows of panelling for the settle-back were commonly used.

Throughout the period given over in the main to oak furniture, certain districts favoured various modifications or developments of general fashion, and the local craftsmen, in addition to adding their respective mannerisms, displayed sufficient continuity of theme to enable us to place their handiwork with fair certainty. Thus Welsh and West of England work admits of differentiation, whilst connoisseurs can distinguish between Southern, Eastern Counties, and Yorkshire and Derbyshire productions.

The several traits did not owe their existence to any fundamental differences, seeing that all the information upon which the various counties relied was commonly available, at any rate within a decade. The potential features of various ideas seem to have appealed to certain

Chairs descended from the early Arcaded Yorkshire and Derbyshire Patterns. Mid-seventeenth century.

groups, and the application of detail and merit of execution evinced by their respective cabinet-makers heightened the local colouring in its distinctive bearing as between the districts.

Thus Welsh work, displaying a comprehensive knowledge on the whole, loses caste by reason of its flat portrayal, whilst Yorkshire and Derbyshire, as the result of the attention which they devoted towards the development of open-backed chairs, stood sponsors to a new order even now, after the lapse of over two hundred and fifty years, called by their county names.

These open-backed chairs are interesting for the arcading which they carried between their two back-rails. The back supports culminated in scrolled finials, whilst down their course inverted split mace or cannon balusters were applied; turned knobs crowned each of the rails in the earlier specimens, whilst in the later examples, when the arcading proper was disappearing in favour of meaningless shaping, the knobs came to be pendent instead of upright. The seats to these chairs were wooden, with a sunk rebate for the reception of a squab cushion, whilst the leg-work was turned in typical Mid-Jacobean style.

In the preceding century chairs had been rare; but in the seventeenth century children and retainers alike were provided with them on occasions. We find children's chairs in almost all of the current vogues, many of them being of important design and treatment. The elaborate specimens are quaint and highly prized by collectors.

Joint-stools or coffin-stools, as these little models are generally styled, came to be common in every home, and, apart from their more obvious usefulness as occasional seats or tables, they were employed at each end of the long tables to knit together the seating accommodation, of which the long side-benches formed the principal part. Some beautiful specimens with typical decoration have survived. Their designation as coffin-stools is traditional, for not only were they employed trestlewise in pairs to support coffins indoors on occasions, but in scattered districts, where house and cemetery were wide apart and no conveyance at the service of the poorer classes, or where the way proved rough and unsuitable, two spare bearers with stools accompanied those carrying the body. At intervals during the journey the bearers would halt, when the stools were requisitioned, and the two spare men took the place of two bearers, turn and turn about, after each rest.

Early in the century, upholstered stools and tabourets, as the rather more showy varieties are sometimes described, came into the better-class homes, but as these were generally plain as to their structural parts a passing notice as to their existence suffices.

The upholstered chairs, couches, settees, and lovers' seats of the period 1620-1660 were plain in conception when considered as a class, and any modern show-room might include models such as our forefathers then favoured. The older specimens would have been covered in far finer material; they would have possessed the plain wood-framing characteristic of their period, but would have lacked the comforts conferred by modern springs. In the case of all examples a strictly rectilinear handling is most generally met with, and we find the back upholstery commencing at some little distance above the seat with an open space beneath it. Sometimes the back was so low as to have constituted no support to the back of the person using the chair, whilst other models afforded this help in the region of the shoulder-blades. Armchairs predominated over singles in the earlier days, but were less freely used as the proportions of the farthingale became exaggerated and rendered their discontinuance advisable.

Like the crested chair reminiscent of the Louis Treize style, many of the upholstered chairs savoured of French origin, whilst others were obviously inspired by Italian models. In the pre-Commonwealth varieties of upholstered work, the soft and wonderful materials employed were generally finished off with fine tasselling, but this treatment came to be discontinued in Puritan England in favour of a severe brass-studded or band and studded scheme of leather-work in which pigskin played an important part. At times the leathers were coloured, whilst on occasions foreign stamped leather-work was used in upholstery. We find these somewhat squat rectilinear chairs, and even settees, carried out as to their leg-framing and arm-work in excellent spiral turnery resembling that in use on the Continent, but, whereas foreign masters were apt to crown their arm-supports with a human bust or a mask of the terminal figure order, this feature is seldom found on native examples: this fact should be remembered, seeing that it is very hard to discriminate between English and foreign specimens of pretentious calibre.

The arms of many chairs of the period were covered in tightly-bound materials—a feature particularly noticeable in the case of the leather-covered Cromwellian chairs.

Charles I.

If the want of taste displayed by James I. and his Court militated against progress in the arts and crafts, the culture and discernment of Charles, his successor, might well have furnished compensating features had other conditions proved favourable. Unhappily for the country the incidence of taxation became acute, and a general feeling of unrest throughout the kingdom made itself felt.

"Jacobean" Furniture.

Later a sense of impending disaster hung like a cloud over the nation's head, so that circumstances which had at first seemed propitious for general advancement in the world of art changed, chameleon-like, into sombre hues. The community tightened its purse-strings, and, as many of the articles of furniture which we to-day consider to be essentials were then held to be luxuries, cabinet-making in

Charles I. Chairs in the original covering; period 1635. From a photograph lent by Messrs. Gill and Reigate.

its higher branches received a serious setback. As the trend of affairs pointed to actual hostilities, stagnation in the crafts supervened, save perhaps in such branches as those of needlework and embroidery, where woman reigned supreme.

Charles, himself a collector of all things artistic, possessed taste and discrimination far beyond the ordinary —in fact, he must have been an actual connoisseur. Unfortunately the collection which he is known to have formed, and which would have been priceless to-day, was destroyed by fire.

In the early and happier days of his reign the unfortunate monarch lavished moneys and encouragement in regal fashion on such artists as pleased his critical eye; but with the passing years and as trouble accumulated he had less leisure to devote to and scantier means to support those who, to a large extent, had come to rely upon his patronage.

The country had benefited by an intercourse with Flanders, then enjoying its second Golden Age. Rubens and Van Dyck had each been knighted by Charles, and each had assisted in the dissemination of taste, but with war came only a scanty demand for the bare necessaries of home life—rough, rugged, and strong, suitable only for the parlous times upon which the country had entered.

A deplorable wastage of fine pieces of furniture occurred in all such districts as were wrested from the Loyalists by Roundhead forces, and, indeed, in all those centres which favoured or were suspected of favouring the King's cause, for, in addition to the normal destruction consequent on fire, siege, and battery, the fanaticism of the Puritans led them to deface anything of beauty with which they came in contact. The animosity of the Parliamentarians was naturally directed against the nobility and leading gentry, seeing that these classes placed their lives and homes at the service of the King, and the result was that just such homes as contained the most beautiful garnishments were those selected for the unfortunate vandalism of Cromwell's companies.

The overwhelming preponderance of mediocre over important pre-Commonwealth furniture is very largely

Very fine Welsh Oak Court Cupboard, belonging to Llewelyn Lloyd, Esq., who kindly lends photograph. It was made in 1666 for Mr. Lloyd's ancestress Mary ap Francis ap Hugh ap Gryffydd of Siamber Wen, who married Frederic, younger brother of Sir John Conwy. The original owner saw ten of her brothers in turn take the field in the Royalist cause, all of whom without exception laid down their lives for King Charles.

accounted for by the foregoing facts, and the bulk of ordinary Jacobean furniture which has come down to us came in the main from such middle-class homes as were removed from the storm-centres of war, or were owned by the supporters of the Parliament. The furniture, too, in these humbler homes, comparatively simple in conception as it was, escaped mutilation by the very fact that it failed to excite the frenzy of Puritan zealots.

Cromwellian Furniture.

The Commonwealth ushered in a decade or so of plain, simple, yet dignified furniture, outwardly typical of the times, constructionally bearing witness to the sound and conscientious spirit of the craftsmen of the day. Cromwell's régime served its purpose well from one point of view. Much that had been florid and ill-balanced in decoration was swept clean away, and the talent of the cabinet-maker was centred in an endeavour to get pleasing and harmonious results with the minimum of applied embellishment. Construction gained as study and work hitherto devoted to carving and inlaying were diverted towards its principles.

Restoration.

If the trend of popular opinion during the Commonwealth had called plain and somewhat uninteresting furniture into existence, it had also caused a wholesome use of the pruning-knife. Detail, which even under the clever interpretation of the Elizabethan school had verged on the florid, had become indefensible in its latter-day application, and the elimination of undesirable matter by the Puritans may be regarded as a partial set-off against their narrow-mindedness.

It must not be supposed that the crafts had been altogether weaned from their old ideals, for there was an under-current at work during the closing phases of the Protectorate tending to introduce colour into the home, and with the Restoration came a recrudescence of models verging on the bizarre, such as the cabinets and chests inlaid with bone, ivory, or mother-o'-pearl. Similarly we find some continuity of detail between Jacobean and Charles II. embellishment wherever furniture of the period carries decoration.

During the interregnum a halt had been called, and cabinet-makers, as though feeling that all was not well, were casting about for some new inspiration. With the accession of Charles new ideas came tumbling in so fast that the craft, recently suffering from poverty of imagination, was surfeited and well-nigh lost its balance. Charles, during his many years of exile on the Continent, had become almost a foreigner in taste. His amorous propensities, whilst unfitting him for sterner work, had rendered him conversant with many a dainty boudoir, and the sombre note predominating in English home-life must have ill-accorded with those gay and luxurious surroundings to which he had grown accustomed.

At the Restoration numbers of banished Royalists, who had escaped to Europe and had had to remain overseas, returned to England. Of these men, no inconsiderable a body possessed culture and refinement, and many new ideas, fashions, and suggestions gleaned abroad by the exiles were now carried to the four corners of the kingdom. Trivial in character and devoted to dalliance, Charles was prepared to bestow on his favourites just such concessions as their whims or caprices demanded. Surrounded by aliens or by Englishmen versed in foreign designs, much of the work commissioned at Court could barely be described as English.

Royal mistresses such as Nell Gwyn or Moll Davies, brought to the palace from the stage, had money showered upon them, and it can scarcely be wondered at that they elected to surround themselves by a mass of ornate and glittering matter. This theatrical and ornate phase was very marked, and the volume of gilt and pretentious furniture commissioned was swollen by the plagiarisms of adulators fawning around the favourite of the hour. As Charles drifted through life, his venalities were so apparent that monarchs bidding for his support elected to press their claims through frail and lovely emissaries rather than by the accustomed channels of diplomacy, and the atmosphere which these fair ones brought, the vogues which they established, were un-English almost without exception.

Friendship with William of Orange and obligations to Louis Quatorze paved the way for the introduction of Dutch and French influence on craftsmen enjoying Royal patronage, whilst Monmouth, who enjoyed his father's affection, levied toll on the arts and crafts of Europe in the gratification of taste formed during his wanderings abroad.

Generally speaking, the upper classes seem to have followed the example set by King and Court, and to have requisitioned gay and elaborate furniture. Where purchases were made in fashionable centres, and in such cases as those in which skilled workmen were imported into the country districts for specific commissions, the brilliancy of execution on models has atoned for their questionable conception, but in the majority of instances we find the handiwork of provincial craftsmen who, trained under the school of the Commonwealth, lacked the verve and finesse essential to success. Many of the bourgeoisie frankly followed the same vogue, though, judging by the rarity of complex yet cleverly handled designs, as compared with complicated and poorly-executed examples, the cities seem to have abounded in workmen aiming at elaborate ideals, whose successful materialisation was quite beyond their powers.

But if numbers of the middle classes favoured pretentious themes, no less considerable a body rigidly eschewed them in favour of the plainer modes which had obtained under the Protector. These men saw in the new order a reflection of that worldliness which they resented and abhorred, and so bestowed their patronage somewhat closely on a simple-minded class of workmen catering for their especial requirements, and the resultant work has a double interest. In the first place, these humbler pieces of furniture go to swell the volume of Cromwellian or reputed Cromwellian work which has survived, and to which they are so closely akin, whilst, secondly, they form a connecting link with the plain and reserved work characteristic of the Quakers in the succeeding century.

It is evident that between those who followed the new fashion and those who saw in it only the evidences of a lavish and distasteful mode there existed a moderate party, and it is to this party of men that we owe much of the artistic work of the time. Much of the typically Charles II. furniture errs on the side of over-elaboration of detail, while as showing the catholicity of its extraction, just that leaven of simplicity which the more tolerant Puritans brought to bear, hits off the golden mean. Not wishing to appear singular in their surroundings or deeming it expedient to swim on the edge of the flowing tide, many

Puritans, by the exercise of instinctive restraint and discrimination, fostered truer art than might otherwise have existed. We see the fruit of this somewhat fortuitous influence reflected in many of the late Jacobean models, wherein, unmarred by the extravagances of the cavalier or by the undue severity of the Puritan school, the characteristics of the age are happily portrayed.

Architecture had made immense strides under the genius of Inigo Jones and his disciples; it was benefiting under the teachings of Christopher Wren; and the dominant note which this art always sounds in the field of craftsmanship was all the more welcome and noticeable in that it had at last assumed a national and distinctive garb. Much Jacobean furniture shows questionable or laboured architectural feeling, but, on the other hand, many examples show our craftsmen as possessing a definite ideal to guide them when supplying their quota to the decoration of the home.

A Study of the Arts and Crafts.

In its relation to the development of the arts and crafts, the reign of Charles II. is most interesting as a study, for England, whilst enjoying facilities for progress, yet found herself handicapped by the untoward trend of internal affairs. A readier communication with the Continental schools brought in its train conversancy with the fashions then obtaining in Flanders, France, Germany, Holland, Italy, and Spain. The dowry of Bombay brought to Charles by his wife Catherine, sister to the King of Portugal, opened up the possibilities of Eastern art. Enjoying the advantages of a base from which to trade with China and Japan, we also benefited by constant intercourse with the Portuguese traders then exploiting the produce of those countries in their golden age. War seems to have played but little part in checking our appropriation of European detail, for we seem to have culled most freely from those who were our intermittent foes, and so it may be said that extraneous circumstances generally favoured advancement, in that our horizon was perceptibly widening. Whilst these opportunities were ours, the internal state of the country precluded that steady patronage of the crafts which is an essential feature if progress is to be maintained. When Charles came to the throne many of the chief houses and mansions were occupied by Puritans whom the King was afraid to dispossess in favour of the original Royalist owners; under these circumstances there was a marked paucity of commissions to be obtained from those very sources most fertile to the cabinet-maker under normal conditions. In many neighbourhoods practically the whole of the important seats had been apportioned amongst the Roundheads, and the loss of custom and of incentive to higher effort must have been seriously felt by the local craftsmen. The rise and fall of political cabals, added to the very serious ecclesiastical troubles obtaining, engendered intrigue and persecution, and many Englishmen, who under happier circumstances would have been patrons of the arts and crafts, were more concerned in the saving of their heads.

The peculation which was rampant in high circles, and the squandering of public moneys which prevailed in all public departments, necessitated heavy taxation, and so we find that the spending power of a mulcted community was seriously curtailed. The stop of the Exchequer in 1672 came as a crowning blow to our national credit, and the distress which it caused throughout the country

Charles II. Chair showing typical turned work and the rare feature of turning in the back-splat where we generally find cane work. This interesting specimen has been handed down to Llewelyn Lloyd, Esq., by his Welsh forbears.

rendered general retrenchment inevitable. In the metropolis trade suffered serious checks with the advent of the Plague in 1665 and by reason of the conflagration of the ensuing year; but although business was paralysed for the time and much fine furniture destroyed as the result of these disasters, they cannot be held to have been unmixed evils.

Little furniture seems to have been saved from the area devastated by the Great Fire, although Pepys records how one lighter escaped with a pair of virginals in it. Over 13,000 houses are supposed to have been destroyed by the flames; others were wrecked or blown up to arrest the spread of the disaster; whilst of the churches, many of which were used as temporary warehouses for the stowage of furniture, eighty-nine were consumed. The loss of interesting buildings and furniture caused by the fire is most regrettable, but Wren gave us finer buildings and a better laid-out city than had hitherto existed, whilst the craftsmen of the day were enabled to secure ample commissions at a time when the genius of Inigo Jones and Christopher Wren had raised the standard of architecture governing the complementary crafts. Much of the destroyed furniture must have belonged to the decadent Jacobean or uninteresting Cromwellian vogues, so that it is more than probable that the new work replacing it was of equal value to the collector, if not to the antiquary.

Salient Points.

If the most salient point in connection with Charles II. furniture was the predominating note of foreign influence, the history of craftsmanship at this period possesses other features of great interest. England stood at the parting of the ways, and at this juncture oak furniture *per se* was being generally superseded by that carried out in walnut throughout or by models veneered with the new medium. Walnut had been fitfully employed since Tudor times, and oak had to fulfil its mission until Georgian days, but the very general demand for the change occurred under Charles II. and James II. Easy to turn and work generally as compared with oak, walnut was also lighter, and the new fashion found expression in chairs, sofas, settees, and stools constructed of walnut in their entirety. Possessing also great possibilities in the way of figure, craftsmen now elected to veneer such models as chests of drawers or grandfather clock cases when aiming at important results. In the country districts oak still retained a hold on the public fancy, whilst heavy models, such as chests or Court cupboards, were generally carried out in the older medium.

Chestnut, too, perhaps more often than is generally supposed, came to play an important part, and many pieces of furniture, supposed by their owners to be in oak, are in reality constructed of walnut or chestnut, sometimes, indeed, of a combination of the two timbers. Walnut and chestnut show rich surface condition under favourable usage, and will be found to harmonise with oak quite admirably. Laburnum wood was employed on occasion, and cross-cutting of all timbers for the accentuation of figure beauty in veneers came to be quite a common practice. But the advance marked by the introduction of new materials was no more pronounced than that witnessed by the introduction of new models. The grandfather clock (of which more anon) dates from the period under discussion, whilst the importation of china, bronzes, enamels, ivories, and bijouterie from the East called into

Charles II. Armchair. Circa 1670. The spiral turning as seen here is the most highly prized by collectors.

existence the forerunners of our china cabinets and show-cases.

The most interesting, because the most characteristic, of all Charles II. models are the chairs, day-beds, and stools of the period. All the phases of evolution may be found on these pieces, which show faithful record of the changes in proportion, contour, and garnishment favoured under the " Merry Monarch." To make our study comprehensive, it is necessary that we should for a moment revert to the Cromwellian chair with its shallow leather padded back and its framing of knob-turned work. The early departures from this model showed greater height of back—an innovation becoming more pronounced with the passage of time—the supersession of knob-turning by spiral-turning, and a new system of back decoration.

In the short transitional phase chair-backs may be found almost as squat in outline as were those of the Commonwealth, and we may also happen on chair-frames in which the knob and spiral turnery are compounded; but the backs quickly assumed different characteristics. The padded back-support gave way to one in open-work, showing either turned decoration in one or two tiers, a series of plain or turned uprights, or caned work. The early caned work was coarse and showed an open mesh, the cane being pegged down at each hole in the receiving framework. Gradually caning came to be closer and finer.

Incidentally, it may be remarked, most Stuart chairs show defective caning to their backs and seats; many have had the cane altogether removed and have been treated to a scheme of padded upholstery. Where repairs or restorations have necessarily to be made the services of an expert caner should be requisitioned. Many recipes exist for toning the new cane, and the following will be found invaluable :—Select sound cane, then stain with bichromate and vandyke brown; oil cane, and then re-seat model. When seat is made up, polish with added colouring matter should the latter be necessary. Latter-day caned seats are attached to a cane beading running round the edge of the seat (or back frame) and plugged at alternate holes, or even at wider intervals.

Reverting to these early chairs, a noticeable innovation came on the scene soon after 1660, when the two horizontal rails uniting the back uprights—the one supporting, the other crowning the back—were deepened and subjected to carving. Simultaneously the two outer perpendicular rails within the uprights of the back were widened and also carved. Within this framing early chairs may exhibit turned or other perpendicular woodwork, as in our illustration on page 91. The vast majority of chairs, however, show caned panelwork. These panels on some of the finer chairs were oval-shaped, but we generally meet with single or double panels of rectilinear shaping. The single-panel chairs, such as that seen on page 95, are the commonest, and where the craftsman has bisected the back by a central rail, so providing two panels, as seen in the chair on page 99, we find the dividing-rail covered with carving. In the more ordinary specimens the decoration is carved out of the solid face of the wood, and stands in fair relief; in the better models the design is in carved and pierced work. The arm-supports were carried out in turned work or, in the case of many of the finer varieties, in a scroll resembling an attenuated S.

In the better-class chairs the seats were carved on their top surface and on their front and side faces, the carving being flat and rather uninteresting in quality. In less

Fine double-panelled Charles II. Chair, showing scrolled legs with the inturned toe or whorl, and S-scroll arm-supports; period 1670. Author's Collection.

pretentious designs the carving made way for shallow, scratched diamond tracery, covering the exposed seat surfaces as with a net. Chairs handsomely treated as to their back-rails present complementary decoration on their front under-stretchers, the latter showing garnishment which is more or less a repetition of that placed on the crest-rail.

Almost invariably the back legs of these Charles II. models are in turned work, the treatment being extended to the front legs in the case of the humbler varieties. In this turnery we find the evolution from plain Cromwellian patterns to those of the later Stuart school. The collector will find elaborate scrolled front legs with the toes turned inwards on some of the finer specimens, whilst now and then he will happen on ornate chairs with front legs scrolled and the front feet pointing outwards in anticipation of the supervening cabriole. At times we find that Stuart craftsmen capped somewhat stumpy scrolled legs by a little turned ornament not unlike a cricket-bail, this mannerism being commonest between the years 1670-1700.

The pierced scroll, cupid, and flower work so universally adopted by our craftsmen for the embellishment of typical Charles II. models has been stigmatised as an inconsequent importation. In reality, it was a perfectly logical adaptation from the realm of architecture. The design came over to us from Holland, where architects employed it in schemes of balustrading, an excellent illustration of which usage is to be found in the staircase of the Brewers' Hall at Antwerp. In England this detail was similarly introduced at Thorpe Hall, Peterborough, and at Eltham House, to quote two instances only; and the collector who studies the excellent illustrations in " Later Renaissance

Architecture in England" (by John Belcher and Mervyn E. Macartney) will at once realise how accurately our craftsmen availed themselves of a striking idea.

So delicate were the shaping, piercing, and tracery of the top rails on the finer examples of these chairs that one loses sight of the office which they structurally fulfil in appreciating the dainty presentment of the scrolled cresting which they afford. There was one dominant item of decoration common to the head- or crest-rail and the front-stretcher of these models, the idea finding an echo more often than not on the lower back-rail, and frequently on the side-rails framing the panelling.

These leading items may be found occurring time after time or only twice on the models of the day, and here we may allude to those most generally introduced :—

I. Heraldic crestings, as carrying on the idea prevailing since Tudor days. (Under this style examples are extant showing the Royal arms.) Sometimes a Stuart crown alone.

II. Seraphim supporting a Royal crown, as though in the act of crowning the person sitting in the chair. This device has been held to symbolise (*a*) the Divine character of Kingship, (*b*) a Heaven-sent welcome on the restoration of the monarchy.

III. Winged cherubims, as translated by Grinling Gibbons on the stall-work of St. Paul's or in the library of Trinity College, Cambridge.

IV. A large shell, as exploited during the subsequent school of Queen Anne.

V. Conventional scroll or floral work, flowers being handled somewhat stiffly, scrolls with considerable success. The prominent surfaces of scroll-work to arm-supports or legs may be found showing acanthus or foliated carving,

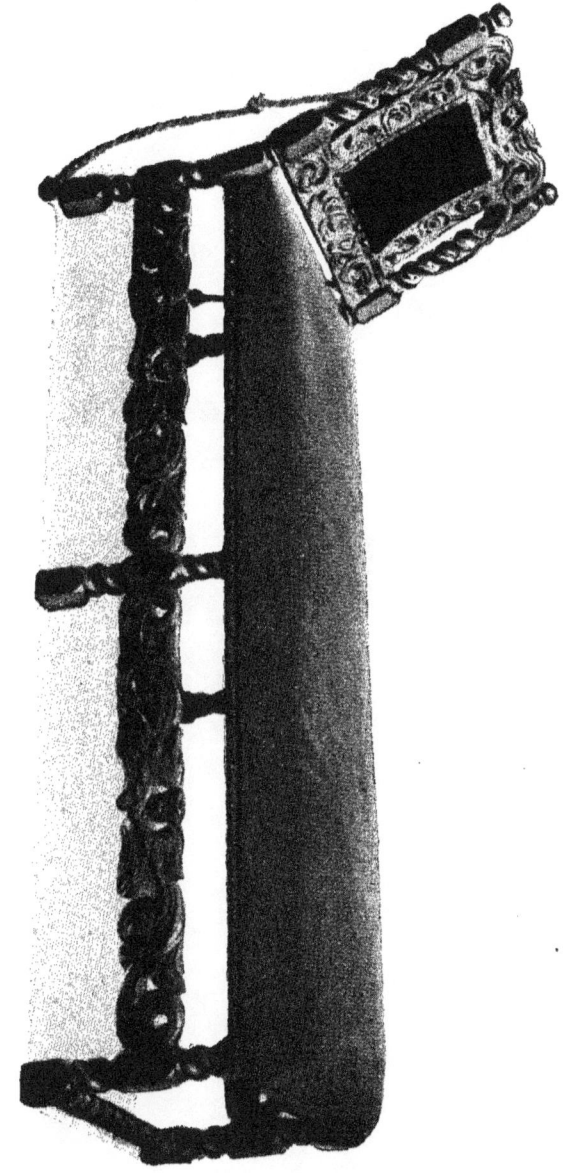

Charles II. Couch or Day-bed, showing decoration of the period 1670. The caned wood to this model has been removed in favour of modern upholstery.

whilst the arms themselves were frequently carved at either end of their sweep.

Day-beds followed closely on the lines of the chairs, but their head-pieces were adjustable through the instrumentality of chains or cords, which permitted the user to increase or to decrease the angle of the head-rest. Some of these were designed to stand against a wall, such examples showing a decorated stretcher on one side only. Other specimens intended to stand out in a room carried carved stretchers on either side, and these latter examples are deservedly prized and sought after.

The stools of the day resembled the contemporary chairs from the level of the seat downwards, with this reservation that they may be found showing two carved stretchers—one on either side—in lieu of the one as situated at the front of the chair.

Between 1680 and 1690 a change which had been coming over Late Jacobean woodwork became very pronounced, and just as we could best follow the evolution from Cromwellian to Charles II. style in the chairwork of the times, so, too, the supervening fashion is most noticeable in the similar field. The old Dutch scroll, cherubim, and floral work which had influenced the backs and stretchers of our Charles II. chairs, stools, and day-beds, began to give way in favour of the hooped scroll-work and other detail of Flemish extraction. The S-scroll became more popular for arm-supports, whilst the heavy scrolled legs began to approximate more closely to a bold, if somewhat confused, portrayal of the cabriole. Now and then we find legs terminating in the claw-and-ball, but as yet our craftsmen were not attaining to that eminence which they subsequently gained in the handling of this detail. Chair-backs became weaker, owing to an accentuation of their backward rake, whilst we find many examples in which the craftsmen of the day tried to improve upon the limited comfort to be derived from the upright back-work of the Charles II. models proper.

The fine spiral turnery so popular during the period showed to especial advantage on the later Jacobean side- and occasional-tables, but at its best, perhaps, in the case of the gate-table. The pattern introduced for leg embellishment was frequently repeated on the connecting stretchers, with the result that one sees almost a maze of delicate spiral work on examining the under-framing of these models. In the case of humbler designs plain stretchers were employed, and we even find plain pivot-legs surrounded by six in turnery on some of the less pretentious gate-tables. All the phases of the turner's art are recorded on these pieces, for we see the plain knob or columnar handling of earlier times gradually making way for the graceful twist which came to displace them.

Although the table-top was generally fitted in round or oval form, the shape of the supporting under-frame may be found showing angular facets. This conjunction was most favoured during Cromwellian days, when side-tables with one half of the top rigid and the other half hanging down behind against the wall, but ready to lift up and rest on a supporting pivot-leg, gained popularity. Tables fitted with angular top under-framing show repetition of the theme in the supporting stretcher-work. They are rare as compared with those showing round or plain rectilinear handling, and are highly prized. The angular framing usually takes the form of the half of a hexagon, and often contains a drawer on the front facet. Sections of octagons are also found on these interesting models.

The long side- or serving-tables and the dining-tables

of the day were almost invariably fitted with fixed tops. The adjustable draw-table had lapsed into desuetude, and the patterns now in favour showed poverty of outline and pettiness in decoration as compared with the earlier examples and when studied as a general class.

The knob finial, plain or with decorative variations, was a pronounced feature of Charles II. models. It may be found crowning the back-uprights of chairs or day-beds; or, again, in an inverted position, fulfilling the duties of a foot whereon reposed tables, cabinets, &c.

The chests and cabinets of the day followed closely on the lines of those constructed before the Civil War, embodying just such little innovations as the different phases of foreign or local influence were accountable for. The mouldings marking out the patterns of applied Jacobean panelling lend themselves to ready reproduction, and many country craftsmen have planes made with which they to-day repeat the standard patterns. London houses supply these reproduced mouldings at so much per 100ft., and enterprising tradesmen are now engaged in purchasing plain chests of drawers, &c., for the express purpose of turning them into Jacobeans. The author has seen deal or even walnut furniture which, having first been stained to a more or less satisfactory semblance of old oak, has then been embellished with applied panels of these modern mouldings; whilst, on occasion, one or two sections have been left out, and the surface which they should have occupied has been " treated " with a view to conveying the impression that the missing members have been absent for many a long day.

The C-shaped scroll so prevalent during the initial stages of the eighteenth century and so generally associated with its leading exponent, Chippendale, emerged from its chrysalis form during the reign of Charles II. At first its portrayal was hazy, but the genuine C came before James II. was seated on the throne, and remained as a characteristic item of English decoration until the Chippendale school of work was on the wane. In the earlier work the second terminal of the C was not completed, but between 1680 and 1690 a rather blunt yet perfect presentment of the letter was commonly used.

1. S-scroll. 2. C-scroll. 3. C-scroll plus half reverse C-scroll, in contour reminiscent of the S-scroll.

During the latter part of Charles II.'s reign the S-scroll and C-scroll were often employed on the same model, whilst now and then, at the period when the latter was gaining the ascendency in popular favour, the top half of a C, turned backwards, was superimposed on a perfect C, thus forming a suggestion of the declining S. This S, C, and, if we may so style it, compounded scroll-work, often governed the contour of arm-supports and legs, and it was also the dominant feature of back-work and stretcher-work in chairs and day-beds, and of stretcher-work in stools and other models.

During the seventeenth century these letter-scrolls, if bluntly drawn, were always portrayed on a generous scale ; but with the advent of the eighteenth century the C-scroll, which retained its popularity, was oftentimes depicted with relative meanness. A reference to the chair shown on page 117 will show the S-scroll figuring to right and left in the chair's cresting, and again at the base of the back immediately below each of the side-rails, just over the plane of the seat. In the next illustration (page 118) the C-scroll is similarly introduced, and also supplies the *motif* of the back-work garnishment.

Although prior to 1680 we find isolated cases of decorative stretcher-shaping, the main progress in this direction took place under James II., William and Mary, and Queen Anne. The uninteresting turnery of the Commonwealth gave way to the livelier handling of the Charles II. style; but, as we have seen, the main feature of this latter school of work was to be found in an important and freely-decorated front-stretcher. Now this deep and imposing rail practically obliterated the posterior scheme of stretcher-work when the model carrying it was viewed from the front, and so long as it was deemed advisable to concentrate the effort of the craftsmen on this central item the potentialities of the other work were overlooked.

In Flanders and at the Court of Louis Quatorze, to cite the case of two European schools only, it was held that good results were obtainable by making the mission of each section of stretcher-work complementary to the other. Under this idea, stretchers were shaped or decorated in unison, and, as a very common feature, pointed inwards to meet in the centre, there to be crowned by some light form of ornament known as a tie. So soon, then, as the typical stretcher of the Charles II. type and the succeeding stretchers of Flemish or hooped scroll-work had enjoyed their run, designers commenced to work out well-balanced schemes of stretcher-work, carrying the art to a high state of perfection. Instances of this unobtrusive yet well-balanced effort will be noticed in our illustrations on pages 117, 118, and 119.

From this time onwards the practice of inserting one heavily-embellished stretcher to the impoverishment of the general scheme was discontinued. The single-stretcher theory predominated under Charles II., enjoyed much favour under James II., and in the earlier days of William and Mary was still resorted to on occasion. Under William and Mary the benefits of a logical scheme asserted themselves absolutely, enabling the new order to find happy expression from that period onwards.

Our craftsmen now very generally ceased to employ the single preponderating front-stretcher, and in such models as those illustrated on pages 284, 512, and 575 we notice Chippendale, Heppelwhite, and Sheraton employing the Continental idea much as it was interpreted by their late Jacobean predecessors.

About the period 1680 a renewed demand for marquetry sprang up, the public being surfeited with the barren and geometrical designs of the earlier Jacobean vogues. Our craftsmen, influenced by Continental workmen imported into England, but, above all, by exponents of the Dutch and Italian schools, rose handsomely to the occasion. Two distinct methods were adopted in the former, of which our inlayers, by the insertion of stained segments of wood and by the employment of ivory or bone, sought to build up realistic pictures such as those of bouquets of flowers or presentments of birds, beasts, or fishes. Time has caused the coloured matter to fade or to evaporate, and although the ages have mellowed the general schemes, there is an absence of naturalistic colouring in the bulk of the surviving examples.

The second and simpler practice consisted in the building-in of light wood on a dark background, or *vice versa*, and in the employment of shaded segments of two different colours only. These colours were generally speaking dark, rich or grey-toned browns, foiled by yellow, orange, or yellowish-browns. The general results achieved were often pleasing, and, as compared with the first-mentioned style of work, low-toned. Conventional patterns of the seaweed, spider's-web, or arabesque type were generally portrayed under the second method.

Collectors should very carefully examine the stands whereon the inlaid cabinets of the period 1680-1720 repose, as for some reason, in addition to that attributable to the perishable qualities of the walnut which was used in its construction, genuine under-framing is rare. These stands were created in four distinct styles, for we find the scrolled leg-work, twisted spiral, turned baluster or columnar work, and the pure cabriole. In addition, we find frank adaptations from the Louis Quatorze school, and on the lacquered and contemporary cabinets or mounted chests pure plagiarism of the idea Oriental.

As in the case of much of the James I. and Charles I. work, the cabinet-maker's art was often subordinated to that of the upholsterer. Bedsteads furnish perhaps the strongest evidence of this particular phase. Many important four-posters were enveloped in costly and beautiful hangings, showing only the minimum of carved or other decoration to their woodwork. We find the feet of the front poles peeping out from under the valance and displaying a little characteristic embellishment, whilst on many occasions no portion of the carcase is visible amidst the drapery.

Evelyn, in his Diary under date January 24th, 1686, tells us: " I saw the Queene's new apartment at Whitehall, with her new bed, the embrodery [sic] of which cost £3000." From this it is pretty evident that the craftsmen's scheme of woodwork was not restricted with a view to economy, but rather supplanted by a fashion entailing lavish expenditure. Again we have to bewail the ephemeral character of the work, in which so much money was spent, to the displacement of the more permanent woodwork. Many Elizabethan four-posters exist in all their glory, but the hangings to Late Stuart bedsteads have vanished, and as few bedsteads carried fine post or cornice decoration, the skeletons which have survived are for the most part uninteresting.

During the period 1680-1690 we find fixed padded upholstery playing an increasing part in chair-work and so on. Hitherto loose squab seats destined to lie over caned work or to fit into rebated wooden seat-frames had been very popular, but the tendency towards a permanent and comparatively luxurious scheme of the upholsterer's creation became very marked. The backs of chairs, instead of being in caned work, were frequently carried out in padded upholstery to match their seats; whilst we find numerous examples wherein the seats are padded and the backs are in decorated woodwork.

Frail, high-backed chairs with cane seats and backs, and wherein the spiral twist has been dropped in favour of turned legs and back-supports in pseudo balustrading, are characteristic of this period. On examination, such decoration as they carry will be found to be mainly Flemish in the earlier and less satisfactory types, whilst later they breathe Dutch teaching. Some of these light chairs of the period 1790 and onwards, with their spoon-shaped backs and light cabriole legs joined by shaped stretcher-work, are distinctly artistic.

We are sometimes confronted with furniture covered in a rich scheme of upholstery in which the feeling may be, for instance, French, Flemish, or Italian, and the suggestion so conveyed leads the collector to doubt whether the model so covered is English or foreign. A certain amount of material for upholstery was imported after the Restoration, but the bulk of that used in England was woven by refugees who had settled in England to escape persecution on the Continent. These European weavers established a prosperous industry in our country, but finding no distinctive or national processes or designs to wean them from their old love, they continued to produce materials reminiscent of the schools wherein they themselves had been trained.

The collector will find many examples of the period 1665-1700 which savour of foreign origin because the woodwork and upholstery which they display are more or less literal translations of Continental patterns made either by settlers in England or by Englishmen who have not imparted marked national characteristics.

Walnut.

Besides our own native walnut, which was sometimes pollarded, and under such treatment yielded handsome effects, there were two American varieties used, known as the white and black, both of which came over from Virginia. The former of these ranks as a hickory; the latter, hard and heavy, attained to a fine-surfaced condition, equal to perhaps second-grade mahogany. In the days of William and Mary, chairs, sofas, &c., were still commonly executed in oak, chestnut, or even soft wood; but the fine work put into important clock-cases, cabinets, or picquet-tables, for instance, was faced with walnut for decorative effect, though olive and laburnum woods were sometimes employed as alternatives.

Tradition has it that mahogany—first brought to England by Sir Walter Raleigh in the reign of Queen Elizabeth, A.D. 1595—was employed in the building of a chair ordered for the personal use of William of Orange. The story is not authenticated, and this, the finest of all woods from the point of view of the cabinet-maker, and with the introduction of which we shall shortly be dealing, did not come into general use until the early part of the reign of George II.

Other Woods Used.

Apple, pear, cherry, pine, yew, box, ebony, sycamore, and holly were woods frequently employed in the marquetry of those days, and these were stained or burnt to the requisite shades, as demanded by the general composition of the designer's scheme. The cabinet-maker's effects were heightened by engraving on the inlay, usually after this had found its home in the bed of the piece to which it was attached, or by the arrangement of a " grain scheme," showing the figuring of the wood at its best.

Woods were cross-cut in order that the full beauties of their figure or flower might stand out on the veneers of the day, whilst many timbers introduced, noticeably those of the walnut varieties, show the fine burr of pollarding.

Lignum vitæ was requisitioned on occasions, and may

be found inlaid on cabinets and chests of drawers of the late Jacobean times, whilst sections of small walnut branches were built in veneers, and presented an appearance akin to this lignum vitæ, resembling also oyster-shells, and, owing to this latter similarity, this particular work has come to be classed as " oyster veneer."

William and Mary—Sources of Inspiration.

Turning to the sources of inspiration governing the creations during the times of William and Mary, we find that these were mainly Flemish interpretations of Italian Renaissance, with French and Spanish mannerisms and detail interwoven. Dutch William and his Queen brought with them Dutch ideas, and, finding nothing in England to wean them from their old love, speedily set to work surrounding themselves with household penates such as they were accustomed to. Dutch furniture and workmen were imported wholesale, and English craftsmen found their talents perforce diverted into an interpretation of foreign ideas. It is not to be wondered at then that experts to-day disagree in " placing " certain early examples, which may have been (1) Flemish, (2) made by Flemish hands in England, (3) made by English craftsmen under Dutch influence. The word " early " was used advisedly, for at this time the sterling work of the British workman was just beginning to assert itself, and the undoubted superiority of his productions henceforward enables us to differentiate between native and alien work with comparative certainty.

A Retrospect.

Let us look back. In earlier days we rather more than held our own in matters constructional, but were hopelessly outclassed in carving by, for instance, Italian artists. In Cromwellian times our ancestors were thoroughly grounded in the rudiments of their profession. Always acquisitive, we now began to beat the foreigner at his own game. Marquetry, the chief form of decoration from 1680 to 1715, showed possibilities at the hands of English masters to which no Dutchmen ever attained. Turning in our country was brought to a pitch of excellence undreamed of on the Continent. The cabriole, coming to us from the East *viâ* Holland, instead of being a wooden curve, assumed graceful and dignified lines of strength—instinct with life—a poem in place of a rhyme. Relief-carving began to be naturalistic where our Dutch mentors produced but engine-turned and expressionless knife exercises.

Perhaps the art of chair-making improved out of proportion to kindred branches of cabinet-making. Chairs not only assumed lighter and more dignified proportions, but they became more comfortable and inviting for use. The Flemish chair, as imported from 1680, was weak in construction — and is generally to be met with in a "sprung" condition as to its back—at the plane of the seat; the badly-chosen woods in which it was all too often executed have perished at the hand of Time and ravages of "worm." In character it was ambitious, but painfully hybrid. Let us examine one. Portuguese scroll-turned pillars at back; legs, and possibly stretchers, of the same feeling; Spanish feet; brace of under-frame and back-splat Flemish, with Louis Quatorze under-framing, the whole upholstered in some brilliant Flemish wool-work.

Replicas of this style of chair were produced in England by the imported Flemish artisan, but a change came over the scene when our workmen began to assert themselves. Portuguese turning below the seat and the

"Jacobean" Furniture.

Spanish foot disappeared, together with the Flemish brace, in favour of well-ordered turning, built up more on the lines in vogue in France. Native upholstery took the place of foreign, and construction received more attention.

Chair made under Flemish influence during the reign of William and Mary—probably of English origin.

Experts differ in fixing the absolute time at which the transition took place, but the more chaste the leg and stretcher, the better the building, and the more homely the upholstered scheme, so much the more likely that we have before us an example of English handiwork. The two exquisite examples of William and Mary chairs which are here illustrated come from the collection of Mr. Grylls, so well known as an authority on stained

Chair made under Flemish influence during the reign of William and Mary—probably of English origin.

glass. Connected and well-ordered stretcher-work, such as we see in these examples, is suggestive of Louis Quatorze influence, and the scheme, with its central ornament, is generally known as tied work or tied stretcher-work. It formed the basis of cabinet-stands, dressers, and table-framing until well into the reign of Queen Anne, when it was usually superseded by the cabriole formation. A glance at the backs of these chairs shows strong Flemish influence, and in turning to the next illustration of a small card-table, of rather later date, we find that the whole

Small Card-Table of English manufacture, dating from the closing phase of the William and Mary period, showing a refined interpretation of the legs supporting the Chairs in preceding illustrations. From Author's Collection.

specimen has become anglicised. In life it is an exquisitely chaste specimen, with finely-banded top, veneered in panels of figured walnut; the legs are of the pleasing style to which our own countrymen elevated the "turned" school, and it is built with an oak carcase. The little gem is as sound to-day as on its first birthday over 200 years ago. It is shown open and shut in order that the gate action of the legs when open may be observed, together with the little fittings which the conscientious workmen of those days so frequently introduced.

The same Table when opened, showing Candle-slide and Card-drawer.

Popularity of the "Grandfather" Clock.

With the advent of William the popularity of the long-case or grandfather clock, introduced at the close of the reign of Charles II., had become assured. Fine examples are to be met with of commanding height, surmounted by gilded and pointed balls; the framework of oak was veneered with fine walnut, which, in the case of the finest specimens, is again almost obliterated by an intricate and finely-executed maze of seaweed or "spider's-web" marquetry. These clocks were divided into three divisions—hood, waist, and base—all of which were treated to separate panels of decoration in veneer and marquetry, though the scheme was co-ordinated throughout. In form they were perhaps the most graceful of any of the long-cased clocks, whose vogue ran for over a century. The floral and bird design in marquetry was a pure adaptation of the style then obtaining in Holland, but it was at the same time an immense improvement thereon, being light, graceful, and cleverly executed, instead of hopelessly coarse in conception and treatment as in the case of its Dutch prototype.

Towards the close of the seventeenth century came the development of the East India Company, which, making as it did for an interchange of ideas between East and West, had much to do with the introduction of lacquered furniture, and, incidentally, with the inception of that appreciative striving after Oriental artistic effect which was to be a feature of decorative schemes throughout Holland, France, and England.

Applied Art in Cabinet-making.

Hardly had the cry for improved outline and decoration gone forth, when our native craftsmen responded nobly to the occasion. In 1685 few cabinet-makers or designers ventured beyond geometrical schemes of marquetry, which, bizarre in conception and execution as they all too often were, marked decadence rather than improvement on the "rocket" design of flowers and leaves so dearly beloved by the inlayers of Elizabethan times. After one decade— in 1695 in fact—a large school of artist-workmen had arisen, capable of diffusing applied art of an enlightened form over the whole kingdom, its work witnessing quite a wonderful standard of ability.

We had cast off old fallacies with oak furniture: the idea that weight and strength were inseparable had crumbled away, and as a result possibilities of grace in outline and design opened out to us, demanding that embellishment should rise to the occasion and march in harmony. The old ideas outcropped from time to time, but in what different garb! We had culled widely; but when learning was once assimilated, the harvest found expression in the finest of cabinet-making and greatly-improved decoration, which latter, if not perhaps in consonance with present-day views on good taste, at any rate easily distanced the best efforts of foreign inlayers competing for British patronage.

All periods or phases seem to give a particularly happy rendering of some one or more articles of domestic furniture: thus for instance, Chippendale's tripod gallery show tables, Adam's side-tables, with accompanying urn pedestals, Sheraton's adaptations of the bonheur-du-jour, and the clocks of the period we are now discussing, stand out in strong relief as examples of distinct and surpassing merit.

English Marquetry.

We are fortunate in being able to follow the rapid strides made in native marquetry—or indeed its evolution—in the series of illustrations here appearing. These are of examples in the famous Wetherfield collection—by far the finest extant.

Interesting, and withal artistic, the two examples illustrated at page 123 are characteristic of the finest work put into long-case clocks at the inception of the vogue. At this

Charles II. Grandfather Clock, by Edward East, English Marquetry, showing maximum length of pendulum.

Charles II. Grandfather Clock, by Thomas Tompion, English Marquetry, with abbreviated pendulum.

stage the inlayer's ideas were purely reminiscent of the oak age, and though conventional and geometrical patterns, such as wheels or stars, were faithfully reproduced, better schemes were not attempted to any extent, probably owing to lack of ambition on the part of the craftsmen. Decoration was applied in the angles of woodwork and in panels; but this extended as time wore on, until in later years the whole face of the woodwork was covered with a network of marquetry.

The first clock (page 123) is interesting, as showing the extreme length of pendulum (the latter beats $1\frac{1}{4}$ seconds); it is by Edward East. The second represents a rather taller clock by Thomas Tompion. Both run for a month.

In the third, the eight-day clock by Charles Gretton (page 127), we have a William and Mary piece, showing the immense advance native marquetry had made. The design of the inlayer is a glorified translation of Dutch feeling of the bird and bouquet order. It will be noticed that the columns at front of hood are still of the spiral twist character; whilst in the fourth example (page 127), a slightly later specimen, this latter feature disappears in favour of the more classic column. The marquetry on these two examples was of the more fashionable and approved kind, and is commoner than the intricate maze appearing on the fifth and sixth (page 131), which collectors now prefer to all other types.

If we revert to our first clock we shall notice the prototype of the artist's idea in the marquetry on the fifth and sixth, which is usually described as being of the "cobweb" or "seaweed" pattern (this style is closely identified with the arabesque type of decoration); it is seldom met with of poor quality, and was discontinued just after Queen Anne's reign. The circles of glass opposite the pendulums served a double purpose, showing the level of the clock—a most important feature in the timekeeping of the grandfather, on the plumb-bob system—whilst indicating whether the works were in action or repose.

Lantern or Birdcage Clocks.

The precursors of the grandfather clock were the old lantern or birdcage clocks in brass, so called from their general appearance. The pendulum and weights, on cord or chain, swung loose some considerable distance below, through a slit in the bracket upon which they rested. The early examples have a short or "bob" pendulum, which tended to grow longer as years rolled on. They had one hand only, on a dial whose diameter was generally 6in., and which projected over the framework of the clock at each side. They were surmounted by a handsome dome, containing the bell or gong, and had pierced brass fret decoration, resting as a crown on the body of the structure. The date, or even maker, of the clock can be approximated by the nature of the fret in question, which varied with different makers and as fashion changed.

Needless to say, these clocks gathered dust and dirt at an alarming rate, and the necessity for protecting the movements, &c., against foreign bodies quickly asserted itself; hence the covers, which, coming into existence about 1675, took the form of the case to the grandfather clock. It is interesting to note that inventories of these times speak of a clock *and case*, showing that they were held as two separate parts, though acting in conjunction.

It is strange that such happy results should have been so quickly arrived at in the decoration of these long-cased clocks, for it is a fact that within twenty years of their introduction they attained to an average of artistic

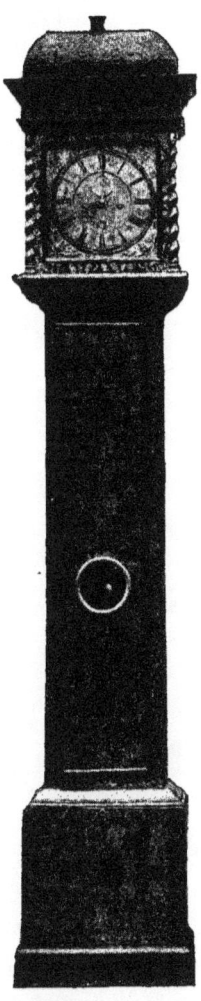 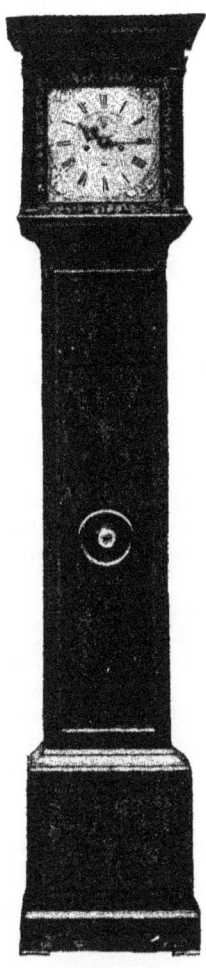

Eight-day William and Mary domed Grandfather Clock, with bird and bouquet or floral marquetry; English, by Charles Gretton.

William and Mary Grandfather Clock, with English bird and bouquet marquetry. In this clock the columns at front of hood instead of being spiral as in the Gretton example are of a more classic order.

excellence in advance of that arrived at in any succeeding period.

Frances Clary Morse tells of an American—Hancock by name—who, in ordering one of these pieces of furniture in 1738, wrote to a friend in London: " The newest fashion with a good black walnut tree case veneered work, with dark, lively branches; on the top, instead of balls, let there be three handsome carved figures. Gilt with burnished gold. I'd have the case without the figure to be 10ft. long, the price 15, not to exceed 20, guineas," &c. From this order it would appear that intending purchasers had a good deal to say as to the decoration of their clock-cases.

The grandfathers of the pre-Chippendale period varied greatly in height and form. The pitch of many rooms was so low that only short or small clocks would fit into available niches. Even now, in some houses, a hole has been cut in the floor to allow the clock to clear the ceiling overhead. Far oftener one finds, alas! the dome, the base, or half the base cut away in order that some fine example may fit into the inhospitable home.

The hands of early clocks of this school were works of art pure and simple, with exquisitely-pierced outlines, finely finished and engraved. Early dials have the hours blackened on a silvered brass " hour circle "; later ones show the dial-face engraved.

The ornaments which fill in the spandrels or corners of the clock's face are of great assistance in determining the date of the example in question. The earliest form of decoration to these spandrels consists of a cherub, whose head and wings are visible, flying toward one from the clock-face. This idea permeated the designer's mind until 1690 or thereabouts, when the cherub was surrounded by

K

rococo scroll-work, as though issuing from a nest. Early in the eighteenth century two cherubs supporting a crown appeared in each corner, holding their own until, roughly speaking, Chippendale's days, when this latter artist rendered popular the rococo work by itself.

Great care should be exercised in buying grandfather clocks which *may have had* new bases or domes put where the originals have been destroyed, as before mentioned. The early hoods were in classical style, with architrave, frieze, and cornice, the first two being modified as time passed; they had supplemented decoration in the form of pinnacles of various shapes or figures, usually three in number, standing up, one at each side, and the third in the middle, at the top of the hood. These are seldom found intact in original condition, having, as a rule, come into too violent collision with a low-pitched ceiling, or suffered decapitation to avoid such a disaster, being subsequently mislaid and lost.

The early dials were in squares of 9in. to 10in., with wooden framework enclosing them; they gradually increased in size to 12in., the framework again of course conforming to the alteration. Later, there was an arch added to the top of the square, and, in sympathy, a moulded and domed arch of woodwork " sets them off." The hoods of early clocks rest on a convex moulding, subsequent types reposing on one of concave form. In addition to the fretwork embellishing the friezes, panels at the sides of the hood are met with in open fret treatment. At first the maker's name, when it appeared, was set forth in Latin under the dial. Subsequently it was shown in English in the domed arch of the dial—these details broadly speaking. Sometimes, moreover, the name on a clock is that of a former owner, and not that of the maker.

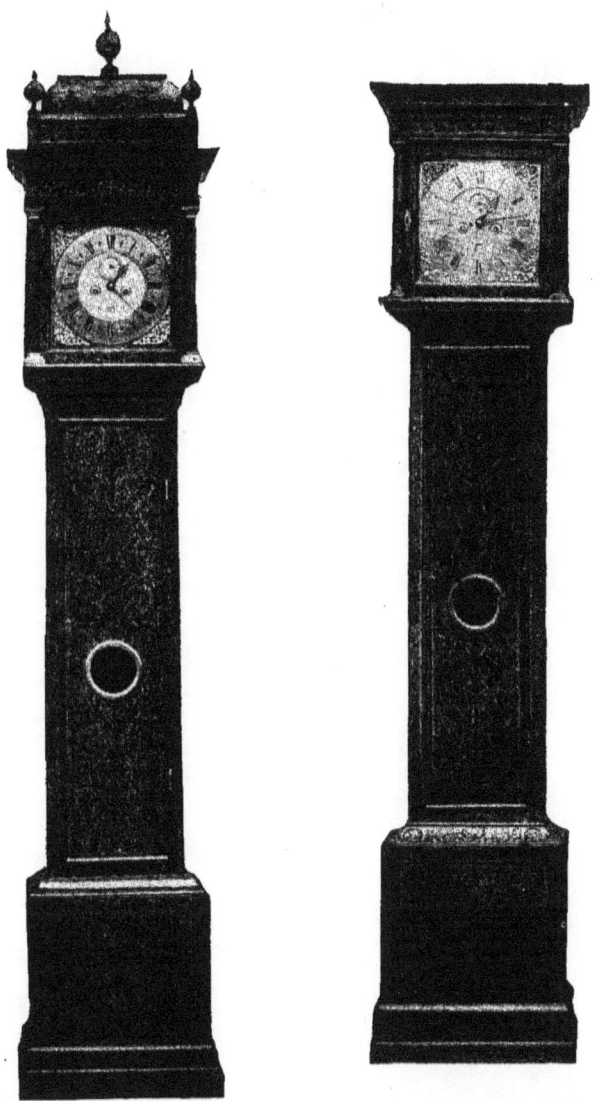

William and Mary to Early Queen Anne Grandfathers, in English marquetry, of the "seaweed," "cobweb," "spiderweb," or "leaf" school; often arabesqued. The clock on the left is by Esoye Fleureau, and that on the right by Jonathan Lowndes.

"Jacobean" Furniture.

Very early "grandfathers" may be found in laburnum and olive wood. Occasionally, too, one may run across them with ivory inlay on Jacobean lines.

Mr. Wetherfield has established that the early clock dials with the concentric minute hands always had the minute divisions at the extreme outer edge of the hour circle in the same line as the Arabic numerals, and that in the later dials the numerals are shown outside the line of the minute division. The change of fashion implied by this distinction dates from the William and Mary period. The same authority points out that the early long pendulums made forty-eight vibrations to the minute, thus beating $1\frac{1}{4}$ seconds. These were quickly superseded by the standard or "seconds" pendulums with their sixty beats.

During the eighteenth century bijou grandfather cased clocks were made from time to time ranging in height from 5ft. to 6ft. These were often known as "grandmother" clocks, probably because their height admitted of their being wound up by the gentler sex.

CHAPTER IV.
Lacquered Furniture.

Periods of Popularity Considered.

LACQUERED furniture enjoyed a somewhat fitful popularity from mid-Jacobean days until the Victorian Era, but the vogue was distinctly on the wane before the middle of the eighteenth century. During the decade 1750-1760 new life was temporarily infused into the fashion by the craze for Chinese matter then sweeping over the country, and the Chambers' teachings may have been partly responsible for the aftermath of bad work characteristic of the English school of the 1770 period. From 1670 until 1760 the designs portrayed in lacquer were almost without exception of Eastern composition and detail, whilst the media wherein European craftsmen sought to present their ideals were compounded more or less roughly after Eastern recipes.

The revival in lacquering, if so we may style the sorry movement of 1770, resulted in the production of much work wherein Eastern designs were discarded and Oriental processes only caricatured.

In the decorative schemes of the East, landscapes, waterscapes, pagodas and buildings, Oriental figures, studies of animal, bird, or fish life, blossom and foliage, were cleverly introduced, and, as detail stood out in some relief, Eastern craftsmen were able to command an

Lacquered Furniture.

amount of perspective usually absent from their drawings on flat surface fields.

In the earlier examples of this japanned work there is a pleasing breadth of conception, and dainty composition is very marked. The East was bidding for the patronage of the West, and traders carefully sent home fine specimens likely to excite a general demand for the ware. As time advanced we often notice a deterioration, partly due to the restrictions imposed on such of the Eastern tradesmen as were catering for the European market.

In filling orders for the supply of Western models, or for panels to "face" European furniture, the field necessary for the happy expression of Oriental ideas was often curtailed or broken up. Composition lacked something of its earlier rhythm, and colour-massing could not be introduced so effectively. Had the workers of Japan and China been allowed to pursue the even tenor of their way, we should have had much less of this work brought to England, but the diminished volume which came would have been far more artistic. Brisk trade with the West led to the production of potboilers and a consequent lack of caste in the lacquer trade.

European Nations Contributing.

The three European nations to take up the study and production of lacquer were those which, during the century of commercial enterprise dating from 1600, were brought most closely into touch with the East. Spain and Portugal had enjoyed a monopoly of trade in Eastern waters since the fifteenth century, and they had introduced odd pieces of lacquer here and there on the Western markets; but they had not embarked upon any ordered or systematic exploitation of a ware the potentialities of which they overlooked or ignored. During the sixteenth century these two countries had marketed goods sent home from the East mainly through Dutch centres, and the Dutch had become conversant with the wares of the East. With the dawn of the seventeenth century came the formation of the Dutch East India Company and the successful struggle of Holland against Portugal and Spain for the command of the Eastern trade. Founded in 1600, our own East India Company did not embark on concerted action until the Dutch had enjoyed a long start on the road to commercial supremacy in the East Indies. In France successive East India Companies were founded in 1604, 1611, 1615, 1642, 1644, and again in 1710. Individual but disconnected enterprise had been characteristic of English, French, and Dutch traders alike; but, whereas Englishmen and Frenchmen had to face dissension and jealousy in their respective trading communities, the Dutch seized on their opportunity and, subordinating petty interests to the weal of the corporation, pressed home their advantage to the full, despite many set-backs. Holland speedily ousted Portugal and Spain from their control in the East, and herself assumed the governing reins, prepared to supply and to stimulate Western demands. Lacquered chests, boxes, and many other models, in completed form, were sent home from the East, and with them assortments of lac panels suitable for the facing of European-made furniture, while the Dutch undertook to have woodwork forwarded to the East for treatment by Oriental lacquerers, and in this manner England, France, and Germany had their main orders for the popular ware fulfilled.

Presently it occurred to the Dutch traders that a new and profitable industry might be established in Holland, and that, in addition to the advantages which would thereby accrue, a vast saving under the head of carriage from the East in the case of the imported ware, or double carriage in the case of woodwork sent out to Japan or China for lacquering to Western order, would be effected. Accordingly Eastern craftsmen were sent to Holland to found the new industry and to train Dutch lacquer-workers. Some good examples created by these Oriental mentors, or by Western pupils under their tutelage, survive, and serve to confuse the collector who is seeking to diagnose the source of seventeenth-century lacquer.

Now, although it is safe to say that the general demand for japanned work sprang up during the reign of Charles II., England had imported examples at a far earlier date. When Portugal held the keys of the East, and when Spain had a footing in the Indies, specimens had come through to us; whilst in the opening phases of the sixteenth century we had conceived a liking for the ware traded to us by the Dutch or brought home as the result of private ventures by English traders.

The student of old needlework will call to mind many fine pieces of early Stuart stump needlework in the original lacquered frames. It is obvious that these lac frames were specifically designed to enclose the work which ladies were employed on prior to the Commonwealth, and the probabilities are that the Dutch acted as the chief middlemen between West and East at this early date.

Lacquer and lacquer panels were brought home in English, French, Dutch, Spanish, or Portuguese ships commissioned by private enterprise throughout the seventeenth century, but our great chance came in 1662 with the cession of Bombay on the marriage of Charles II. with the Infanta Catherine, sister to the King of Portugal. At this date Portuguese trade with the East was a diminishing quantity owing to the aggression of Holland, but the Portuguese were conversant with all the ins and outs of the Eastern markets, and we gained hints and experience on the tightening of the commerical bonds between Portugal and ourselves. Holland doubtless supplied us with the commodity to the close of the reign of Queen Anne, but from the early part of Charles II.'s reign our own traders secured their fair share of lacquer in Eastern waters.

The practical monopoly in lacquer trading remained for some time in the hands of the Dutch. English people had grown accustomed to order panels or to have the face-work of their models treated through the agency of traders in Holland, who passed on commissions to their representatives in the East; but now, when Holland was actually manufacturing the fashionable ware, she herself doubtless filled most of the orders intended for the East. One can well imagine the wily Dutchmen chuckling as they pocketed the extra profit saved under the head of carriage between Holland and the East, but charged for when the little account was sent in.

England's Quota.

During the last quarter of the seventeenth century lacquer works were started in England, but our mentors seem to have been Dutchmen. France cast herself loose from Dutch influence at an early date, and with great success; indeed, so excellent was much of the French

Lacquered Furniture.

work that one suspects that Eastern lacquer hands must have come to France, to find apt pupils amidst the dainty Latins.

Many of our finest models, whether Eastern in origin, Dutch made to English order, or English built but with faces or panels decorated in Japan, China, or Holland, repose on stands of the Louis Quatorze style. It would seem probable that we not only received tuition in the matter of lac handling and mounting from French workers, but also imported a small number of examples completed or mounted by Frenchmen.

The earliest lacquer was traded by the Dutch to our Eastern counties and to London, and it has been urged that English lacquer was first made under Dutch inspiration in Norfolk and Suffolk. This is rather interesting when we remember that one century later the trading of Oriental china by Dutchmen calling at Lowestoft led people to believe that the bulk of the so-called Lowestoft ware was really made in Lowestoft. A large amount of japanned work was produced in South Wales on commercial lines, whilst all over England people were instructed in the art of lacquering much as they would to-day be taught to paint or to play the violin, and books were published explaining the various details for mixing lac varnishes, the methods of their application, and so on.

Lacquer was in fashion all over the country by 1790, but Englishmen only excelled in carcase-construction, and the question often arises, " How can we consider lac furniture as English? " or " Why should we collect in the one field, where our claims to success rest on such slender foundations? " The reply can only be that we cannot ignore this phase of work. Eastern art was at its zenith just when we rubbed shoulders with it, and the merits of Japanese lacquer and of the Chinese porcelain of the seventeenth century brought the æstheticism of the East to the front door of the West.

We must extract such comfort as we can from the facts that our ancestors had the good sense to appreciate and adopt lacquering, securing for their posterity a fair share of Eastern examples of surpassing excellence; that our own cabinet-makers mounted foreign panels conscientiously and gave us good stands for the display of imported models; and that, although our own lac has been termed insignificant, it only appears to be so when placed in juxtaposition with the work of others who, in the pursuit of their craft, enjoyed greater facilities than were vouchsafed to Englishmen.

Difficulty in Repairing

All lacquer work is difficult to repair when once the original surface becomes scratched, chipped, or in any way damaged, and a large proportion of lac being laid over soft woods is peculiarly liable to the ravages of "worm." Collectors should always remember that the decorative value of damaged examples cannot readily be improved upon, and they should also select specimens wherein the chief panelling is in oak.

Literary References.

There are many references to old lacquer-work in books, &c., of the seventeenth and eighteenth centuries, the most pregnant notice being contained in Evelyn's Diary under date July 30th, 1682. Therein Evelyn tells us—" Went to visit our good neighbour Mr. Bohun, whose house is a cabinet of all elegancies, especially

Lacquered Furniture. 141

Indian; in the hall are contrivances of Japan skreens instead of wainscot." Evelyn mixed with the best people of the day, he was a favourite welcomed in every house, and the only entry previous to this in July, 1682, records in two-and-a-half lines how the Duke of Grafton and the Earl of Ossorie came to dine with him on the 17th.

Evelyn had his finger on the pulse of fashion. By nature he was observant, and wont to record any impressions of interest, yet the only description he has left for July, 1682, refers to the "Indian elegancies" and "Japan skreens." We can infer that the Japan skreens and furniture were getting to be known, as the diarist does not specify their peculiarities, but we must also deduce that this ware had not as yet come into general use.

In her interesting book on old American furniture Mrs. Frances Clary Morse records how in 1712 a Bostonian, one Nehemiah Partridge by name, "advertised that he was prepared to do all sorts of Japan work." Limited in size, the American community was then comparatively remote, and the taste for lacquer must have spread quickly to make it worth while for an American so promptly to learn the art and bid for custom as against the established sources of supply.

Eastern and Western Products Compared.

In weighing the relative merits of Eastern and Western lacquer, all factors were in favour of the former school. The Japanese have regarded lacquering as an art for many centuries, and Mr. Percy Macquoid, who is probably the greatest expert living, has traced the process back to the third century B.C., and he moreover tells us that "red and gold lacquer is mentioned in Japanese writings of 380 A.D."

In Vol. 6 of the *Pharmaceutical Journal*, 1875, a Consular Report from Kanagawa gives A.D. 724 as the date when lacquering was introduced, a statement qualified, however, by the fact that other authorities have established the inception of the fashion as having occurred as late as A.D. 889 or 900. This report goes to show how lacquer came from the provinces of Echizen, Yoshinô in Yamato, Aidgu, Yonegawa in Dewa, Saijo in Dewa, Yamagata, Namba, and Fuknoka, so that the discrepancies amongst those who have studied early work may well have arisen from investigation of different local traditions and records.

Having seen how the Orientals had developed the art through centuries of application and practice, it can scarcely be wondered at that they attained absolute proficiency therein. In the gum varnishes to be found in Japan and China the best media for the ware lay ready to the hand of native workmen, whilst the designs and the matter used in these pictures were alike indigenous to the East.

The rhythm and pleasing grace characteristic of Eastern craftsmanship found happy expression in the lacquers of Japan and the porcelains of China. In these countries the artist was daily in touch with the landscapes, the blossoms, the figure-studies, or the bird-life which his profession led him to portray. Enjoying such advantages, and regarding his vocation as an art rather than a commercial undertaking, the workman of Japan or China produced drawings in lacquer or porcelain subtle and free, whose merits were further enhanced by the brilliant delicacy of their colour-treatment.

In England, France, and Holland the designs which

Lacquered Furniture. 143

the lacquerer sought to delineate, the detail which he had to reproduce, were exotic; his media were inferior to those of the East, and he lacked that knowledge of process and technique which came as second nature to the children of Japan.

Eastern designs were conceived amidst the gardens of Japan or China: Western presentments were based on pictures from the Indies, and savoured of the studio or workshop. But although the Oriental lacquer surpassed the work of the European schools, the students at these latter centres fully appreciated its beauties and seriously strove to embody in their own work something of its elusive grace. Lacquering was defined as an art. Exponents of the work were to be met with throughout the country. In consequence of this trend of fashion amateur lacquerers helped to swell the volume of work created for commercial purposes, and perhaps in the case of such creations as were achieved by gifted pupils, to vary the somewhat stilted renderings of the West.

In the East the varnish-bearing trees were scientifically cultivated, and the sap derived therefrom was methodically harvested and formed a staple commodity. Thus we learn from the aforesaid Report how the sap was drawn off from the five-year-old trees, between summer and November, and that that which was tapped at the summer's close was preferable to that which was garnered earlier or later in the harvest-time. A series of incisions was made in the tree, the object being to catch the rising rather than the descending sap, and the habits of plants on varying soils were carefully taken into consideration.

In Japan varnish was extracted from the Urushi, or *Rhus vernicifera,* after cultivation; whilst the Yamo

Urushi (wild variety) and Tsuto Urushi (climbing type) gave their inferior yields. In China the native gum tree was similarly bled, and gave excellent results.

Repeated coats of these lacquer varnishes were applied on wood, but in summer the dressings dried so rapidly that large fields had to be sub-divided into sections in order that the liquid might be duly handled before it solidified.

In the Report already referred to, full details of the process are given, and subsequently summed up as follows :—" Briefly, then, the designing on lac work is done thus : The flower is traced out on paper and imparted to the groundwork. Gold powder is sprinkled over the wood from a bamboo tube, well rubbed with a brush and then dried, afterwards polished (with a special preparation), and a coating of varnish applied. This is repeated several times. The veins, or tracing of foliage, are now marked out with lac varnish. Before this dries gold powder is again sprinkled over and well rubbed in with a brush. When the surface has dried, it is rubbed over with a piece of charcoal so as to tone down irregularities. After this it is polished (with horn dust), when the design will appear in due form."

Although the above description was doubtless compiled most carefully, it fails partially to convey the methods and characteristics of Oriental lacquering. In the early work the relief attained in the main raised design was sharp and the drawing boldly defined. Digital manipulation was mainly resorted to in the modelling of raised surface fields and for the general working in of colour. European relief detail was podgy-looking in comparison with Eastern work, whilst its distribution lacked that verve and freedom which we associate with Japanese or

Lacquered Furniture. 145

Chinese creations. In body and surface the Oriental lac was at once more lustrous and smooth, and if for comparison we examine fine cut glass and moulded kitchen ware, patent leather and the ordinary blacked boots, we can arrive at the relative value of the cutting and sheen characteristic of Eastern and Western productions respectively.

Gold dust, brass dust, bronze or aventurine quartz pounded, silver, and other ingredients, were requisitioned for the embellishment of designs, and here again the original exponents of lacquering excelled their pupils or imitators and achieved results at once mellow and telling.

In the later lacquer, when the Eastern school were producing their ware commercially and mechanically, the manifest superiority of earlier days passed away. English, French, and Dutch workers had gained experience, and the better-class European work almost equalled the ordinary grade sent home from Eastern Asia.

In addition to the foregoing hints on the merits of Eastern work, we have other factors to consider which assist our diagnosis very considerably. Lacquer was applied to models (1) of Eastern type, (2) of Western type, (3) of composite type.

We may infer that *early* examples of Class 1 are Oriental, but between 1740 and 1760 Chinese contour was especially affected in England, and a large volume of furniture, Eastern in contour and style, was made throughout by English craftsmen. When confronted with Class 2 we have a difficult field before us, and it is necessary to apply the process of exhaustion. Many models, such as lovers' seats—*vide* illustration on page 159—exhibit continuity of lacquered treatment over their whole surface. Now these pieces did not become popular

L

until the practice of lacquering was thoroughly established in England. English dignity in form is apparent, and the soundness of their construction points to their British origin. As there is continuity in decoration we may infer that if any part of the model, such as the central splats, were lacquered in the East, the whole model was sent out after being constructed at home. Such a proceeding would have entailed prohibitive cost, for these examples did not lend themselves to ready stowage in a ship's hold, and we may with safety deduce that Englishmen generally treated such models as were unwieldy from a freightage point of view.

Japan, China, and Holland supplied some few completed models on Western lines, but the superior construction seen in English work and the inferior contour of Dutch examples reduce the number of doubtful specimens under this class to a minimum.

Under Class 2 we find therefore (A) English carcase-work and partial lacquering framing one or two prominent panels of Eastern lacquer or Dutch copies of the same; or (B) models created and lacquered in England. Under Section A we get furniture wherein a governing effect could be arrived at by the inclusion of one or more fine foreign panels, lending themselves to low freightage rates on their single or double journeys between the East and West. Corner cupboards, china cupboards, long-case clocks, and so on were commonly set off by these alien panels. Similarly we find escritoires, bureaus, chests of drawers or cabinets English in all save for their drawer faces, which have been lacquered in other centres of the art.

In conjunction with some of these pieces the decoration applied to the framework enclosing foreign panels

Red Lacquer Cabinet on English gilt stand, showing Louis Quatorze influence. Period 1685-1695. Photo kindly lent by Messrs. Gill and Reigate.

amounts to rude painting rather than to lacquering, for our craftsmen seem to have relied on the effects derivable from the main panels, and to have taken but little pains with the finishing of the less prominent surfaces. As time wore on Englishmen came to decorate their own central schemes, and so the later the model the greater are the probabilities that it may be English throughout.

Under the third section, where we find the composite style in outline, early lacquer is easily diagnosed, for we find Eastern examples resting on European bases, or else Western examples in which European craftsmen have essayed Eastern design but owing to their limited knowledge of technique or detail have achieved hybrid results.

In the Lowestoft china made to order by Chinese workmen the Eastern craftsman continually gave himself away when seeking to delineate Western detail. He would treat the rigging of a Western ship, for instance, as though he were dealing with a junk. Similarly, at the Worcester potteries the English worker would omit the typical eyes and eyebrows of an Eastern face when seeking to portray Chinese figures. These tell-tale errors may also be met with on the lacquers, where men unversed in the models and details they were venturing on sought to give renderings of themes beyond their powers.

At the same time, the commonest, and yet the most striking, of the important composite models in lacquer 'or partly in lacquer), the big, square cabinets on stands, such as that shown in our illustration (p. 147), are most interesting.

These cabinets were frequently sent home to Europe filled with tea, spices, or bijouterie, and so possessed a double value, first as packing-cases and secondly as valuable pieces of furniture, readily saleable on the European markets after they had fulfilled their temporary mission. Usually met with in black lacquer, varieties in red, green, or silver may also be happened on, and the most beautiful example which the author has seen was in the silver hue. Adorned with heavy mounts, which on examination may be found to be silver-gilt, these cabinet chests show fine lacquering on the inside of each door panel and a series of small lacquered designs on the drawers contained within the carcase. These mounts are often met with in Dutch or English workmanship, and although the inference might be drawn that models carrying English mounts are English, and so on, it would not be sound, since European mounts were sent out to the East, just as we in England employed our own mounts and hinges for the knitting together of doors or carcase-work lacquered in the East.

The stands upon which these cabinets and various chests are resting afford invaluable assistance to the collector when he is endeavouring to place their date but has not an expert knowledge of lacquer itself. The stand is often later than the overlying carcase, because the original possessors sometimes mounted their pieces—if they mounted them at all—in primitive fashion, and some subsequent owner has commissioned a supporting framework in consonance with a later vogue which has appealed to him. Where, however, the stand is early and original, a knowledge of English outline will help us to place a cabinet to within a decade, for we find modelling characteristic of Charles II., William and Mary, or Queen Anne, just as the French contemporary vogues may have been requisitioned.

On rare occasions typical Oriental stands were imported, and these, light in build, were carried out in lacquer to match the overlying carcase, but usually with plain line decoration only. Important English stands were altogether heavier, more ornate, and gilded all over, except on those occasions wherein our craftsmen were repeating Eastern designs or cabriole patterns.

Studying the Evolution of Lacquering.

It is perhaps easiest to study the evolution of lacquering by a careful examination of the grandfather clocks of the period 1670-1740, for we have reliable data to go by in our research. First, we know approximately the decade in which these were made owing to the size of the hood face framing the dial and by turning up the clockmaker's name in Britten's records. Where the original dial is present the decoration on the spandrels will assist us in dating specimens, whilst the shaping and decoration of the woodwork prove infallible guides where fine cases are concerned. The domed hooding characteristic of the cabinet-maker's art during the closing years of Queen Anne's reign will be constantly met with on the grandfather clocks, the cupboards, cabinets, and bureau-bookcases of the early eighteenth century. A reference to our pages (122-133) dealing mainly with marquetry clocks may assist the reader in his efforts to follow the minutiæ of evolution. In the commoner clock-cases, made for the most part in the provinces, fashion moved slowly, and the contour of any given model cannot be relied upon as affording an absolute criterion.

Certain models, such as hanging-shelves, china-brackets, stands or show-cases, four-post bedsteads, and, to a lesser degree, mirror-frames, were frequently built on Eastern lines by English craftsmen between 1720 and 1760. Such furniture may be found crowned by pagoda-shaped doming.

Rectilinear gallery-tables also exhibit the same influences, but tripod gallery-tables bearing a strong likeness to Chippendale designs have as a rule little handling reminiscent of the East.

A marked resemblance is noticeable between the stands or under-frames of Oriental extraction supporting early lacquered cabinets and the similar outline designs of the Chambers revival. It is more than probable that during the Chambers craze many stands, in European styles, were discarded in favour of new ones made on Oriental lines, in order that models so remounted might be brought into harmony with the stilted Chinese vogue then obtaining.

These details may assist the collector to judge between the lacquer of the East and that of the West: the lacquer varnishes taken fresh from the trees of Japan or China and the substituted compounds heated and blended with coloured powders under numerous European recipes; but experience in this, as in all other matters, is the surest guide.

Lacquered ware abounds all over England, and the tyro can prosecute his study readily from almost any centre. Bedrooms were most frequently furnished in this style, but grandfather clocks, dining- and drawing-room pieces in black lacquer are found easily, and only good specimens in this, the commonest, style should be accepted.

Red lacquer is greatly sought after, but it presents a glaring appearance, offensive to many eyes, and only the connoisseur who takes into consideration its extreme rarity is likely to be duly appreciative of its merits.

The green and low-tone brown lacquers are rare, but they are not strikingly artistic, and are generally wanting in lustre. Silver lacquer, with its leaning to a dove-grey

Lacquered Furniture.

hue, is of the greatest rarity, and possesses a special value artistically. This latter variety is decorative, and may safely be placed in any room without fear of a discordant note.

In closing this chapter it is interesting to recall the remarks of a Japanese statesman, who, after the recent defeats of the Russians, observed : " For upwards of two hundred years we have been supplying Europe with the most beautiful lacquered ware and other objets d'art, and she has styled us barbarians. We have lately immolated some 75,000 Russians, and she remarks how civilised we are becoming."

CHAPTER V.
Queen Anne.

The Cabriole Leg

WHEN Queen Anne came to the throne English cabinetmakers had little to learn in matters constructional, and were, as a class, first-rate exponents of the effects to be derived from fine marquetry. Their carving was good, if not brilliant, whilst their turning was free, artistic, and harmonious withal. What, then, is it that calls to our minds the subtle charm always associated with the vogue known as "Queen Anne"? It is surely the general introduction of the curvilinear into construction and design. In place of laboured and intricate schemes of almost barbaric magnificence, there came undulating lines *and the cabriole leg*, frequently unfettered by other decoration.

It is impossible to trace with certainty the inception of the cabriole leg. The Greeks employed models nearly akin to it for many hundreds of years B.C., whilst the Egyptians and Assyrians favoured leg-contour resembling it some 2000-3000 B.C. The Chinese affected the idea in more or less fantastic form from the earliest days, and just as Greek and Roman mythology was of Oriental parentage, so, too, the idea of the bent leg may well have emanated from the East.

It has been said that the French established the popularity of the cabriole by their efforts in the school of

Queen Anne.

Louis Quinze—in reality the Dutch should be credited with the new suggestion, bringing it from China to flourish in Holland and England during the closing years of the seventeenth century (until about 1760), and to take root in France in the waning years of Louis Quatorze. Thus it was after Dutch and English exploitation of the cabriole that the artistic eye of France, bewildered by the ornate and grandiose schemes of the Louis Quatorze, found welcome and long-searched-for relief in the same haven that we had attained—the cabriole. Having tapped the same fountain-head for *motif* in leg-outline, the foremost craftsmen in France proceeded to decorate the frame in just such dainty and elegant a vein as we should have expected from them, eventually, alas! carrying to extremes the rococo spirit.

Walnut, which entered largely into every composition of importance, had never been used so artistically and scientifically as it was during the Queen Anne period. Craftsmen made the most of figure and flower in wood, they matched sections scrupulously, and relied on the simple beauty of the wood for prominent surface embellishment to an extent hitherto undreamt of. In some models we find the tentative introduction of gilding in conjunction with walnut, and later it came to be laid on in a lavish manner. Carved or moulded detail gilded stood out from fields of finely veneered walnut, the results so arrived at being striking, if not universally popular. Where the gilt was laid over plain or recessed spaces, a coating of sand was now and then applied before the gold was spread, to give the background a less monotonous appearance. Many examples of furniture were gilded all over, but this treatment appeals to but few people of taste, and, if we must have one or more specimens of gilt work, it is best to select those which exhibit a blending of walnut and gold in unaggressive guise.

One is often asked the meaning and derivation of the

Queen Anne Cabinet, and Spoon-backed Chair showing early cabriole legs.

term "cabriole," so generally employed to describe the bent styles of legs in fashion during Stuart and Georgian days, and a reference to Chambers dispels the doubt, for we read therein: "Capriole, *n.* a leap without advancing. (Latin *capra*, a goat.)" Dealing with "*capra*" first, the hoof which we generally find under cabrioles of the William and Mary period is that of a goat, and the whole leg may resemble the extremities of that animal. "Capriole" suggests a stationary position, notwithstanding the accomplished or contemplated spring, and is rather an apt derivative for a model whose legs suggest power and propulsive force rendered impotent by the limitations of their office.

Throughout the last quarter of the seventeenth century the cabriole leg was making headway towards popularity, but its earlier renderings were obscured, its possibilities overlooked, owing to the complexity of its treatment and surroundings. When viewed at its best, the cabriole should be seen in its simplicity, or at most with a modicum of well-placed embellishment. The essence of the design is centred in the strength and beauty of its sweeping curve, and when the eye is diverted from these points, or when the sinuous lines are marred by unnecessary and protuberant detail, the potentialities of this particular leg are diminished.

The period 1660-1690 was one in which exuberance of detail and intricacy of outline ran riot in fashionable circles, and, as we have already seen, leg and stretcher composition during this phase was often at fault. Cabinet-makers seem to have concentrated their efforts on achieving redundancy of matter and to have neglected their opportunities in simple and well-ordered fields.

With the last decade of the century there came glimmerings of a revulsion in feeling, and, as though bearing witness to this change, the cabriole began to emerge from the hazy and primitive renderings which had hitherto prevailed. Under Queen Anne this change in fashion became very pronounced, for whereas the chairs, &c., of the 1665-1690 period usually became more typical of their day as they became more elaborate, by 1705-1710 the plainest of models came to reflect the purest mirage of the new order.

Due, perhaps, to the swing of the pendulum as much as to national regeneration in taste, the evolution of the cabriole is a landmark in the history of the cabinet-maker's craft, for within thirty years of its advent Englishmen had outdistanced all their rivals in its production. The English cabriole of the early eighteenth century stands unchallenged, and this is all the more remarkable when we call to mind the intricacy of the designs from which it so triumphantly emerged.

From the closing days of Charles II. the scrolled legs, the S-legs, and the double C-legs had contained the germs of the new outline, but it was not until the reign of William and Mary that the cabriole came in untrammelled form. Even during the decade 1690-1700 pleasing handling of this leg outline was rare, because there existed a strong tendency to confuse its contour by angular face-work or by unnecessary decoration. In the earlier interpretation we find angular bases or foot-work underlying legs with rounded or angular shaping and also hoof-work resembling the extremities of fauns or of cloven-footed animals. Following immediately after these items of decoration came the plain club or pad feet which we instinctively associate with the true cabriole. Small variations on this design were soon introduced, and towards the end of the reign of Queen Anne the claw-and-ball foot sprang into prominence.

The English cabriole was not so pronouncedly

Queen Anne. 159

curvilinear as were the examples on Oriental chinastands, but the claw-and-ball legs, on the other hand, show a better curve than do their prototypes, the Eastern presentments of a dragon's claw encircling a pearl. In British work the cabriole and claw-and-ball legs were markedly superior to those of the Dutch school, for they

Two-chair-back Settee in walnut. Period 1715-1720.

combined strength and grace in perfect balance. Our mentors from Holland were wont to exaggerate the curve at the knee or the ankle, or to give a hopelessly wooden interpretation, owing to poor shaping and tapering and a faulty conception of proportion.

The cabriole enjoyed a popularity of 100 years, commencing with 1680, but during its later phases it was fast sinking into desuetude, and between 1760 and 1780 only the later exponents of the Chippendale school and Heppelwhite of the rising fraternity employed it satisfactorily. The brothers Adam gave somewhat far-fetched renderings of the idea throughout their period, but Sheraton's exposition of the curvilinear was as foreign to the original outline as was that of the Late Georgian vogue.

From 1720 onwards the cabriole has to be traced, for the main part, in a series of claw-and-ball or French (so-called) legs, but underlying these more pretentious types the backbone of the original pattern exists. From the days of George I. designers were chiefly employed in dressing the cabriole in decoration, and it may assist collectors if we divide the cycle of the bent leg into three sections, A, B, and C, as follow :—

- (A) 1680-1690. When the cabriole was emerging from its chrysalis.
- (B) 1690-1705. The period during which it was being undressed, to emerge in its perfect form.
- (C) 1715 and onwards. The phase wherein successive designers were re-dressing and partially obscuring the outline of the leg's sweep.

Of the furniture under Section A enough has been said, but it should be stated that the Early Georgian masters, and even Chippendale, produced some renderings savouring of pre-Queen Anne days. Of the furniture coming under the heading C, the plain and lighter specimens of the French style, which replaced the claw-and-ball between 1740 and 1755, and the earlier work of George Heppelwhite approximated most closely to the original cabriole in its perfected state. It may be useful to record that the Early Victorian school reverted to the use

Queen Anne.

of the decorated cabriole, and employed it until after the middle of the nineteenth century.

During the periods B and C the cabriole was often stockinged, an unfortunate treatment which broke its outline and carried the eye away from what should have been an unbroken and perfect curve to a piece of inconsequent detail. Chippendale very generally eschewed this error, but exponents of the Irish Chippendale school generally fell into it, and we see an example of the regrettable handling on page 391.

Throughout the period 1680-1725 cabriole and claw-and-ball legs were frequently knit together by light, shaped stretcher-framing, somewhat resembling that applied to the chairs illustrated on pages 117 and 118 (which show the typical "tied" stretcher-work), but without the central ornamentation appearing on these models as a general rule.

This treatment became less noticeable from 1715 and onwards, and Chippendale seems to have practically omitted it from all his designs of the curved leg pattern. The stretchers were employed in consonance with a general love for this detail, rather than from any necessity under the heading of structural stability, and, whilst they rather detracted from than added to the beauties of leg-work, they are interesting because they establish the early period of such models as carry them. Many Queen Anne chairs, settees, cabinets, and so on were constructed with cabriole legs unencumbered by stretcher-work.

The introduction of the boldly-carved and hairy lion's paw followed closely on that of the dragon's claw-and-pearl variety of foot decoration, but, as it is seldom met with in conjunction with stretcher-work, we are enabled to place its real advent as taking place during the reign of George I. Generally speaking, when we are face to face with chairs, &c., showing cabriole legs in front, but with plain back legs, the examples are of earlier date than are those models carrying cabriole or claw-and-ball extremities all the way round. There is this reservation, however, that in the cheaper furniture craftsmen oftentimes refrained from shaping back legs because the treatment taxed their skill and entailed wasteful use of timber, and it was therefore desirable to save both labour and wood where rigid economy in cost of production had to be observed.

If we eliminate the scheme of the cabriole from the leg-work of "Queen Anne," the styles which remain are nearly akin to those of the preceding vogues. Spiral-turned work and balustrading still retained a large measure of popularity, whilst bold scrolls, often with square edges, were favoured for stands to cabinets and mounted chests of drawers. The legs seen in our illustrations on pages 117 and 119 were subjected to but slight modifications, although the substitution of inverted cupping for the bold turned swell, as seen below the knees of the chair in the former of these illustrations, was a characteristic feature under Queen Anne. Occasionally we meet with square-shaped legs or tapered octagonal specimens in which the treatment is distinctly reminiscent of the earlier Louis Quatorze handling. Underneath the majority of these legs the foot is furnished by a round or bun-shaped knob in turnery.

It will be remembered that our craftsmen under Charles II., James II., and William and Mary favoured repetition of the cardinal points in outline and decoration as between those parts of the chair which rose above the plane of the seat and those which lay beneath it. During

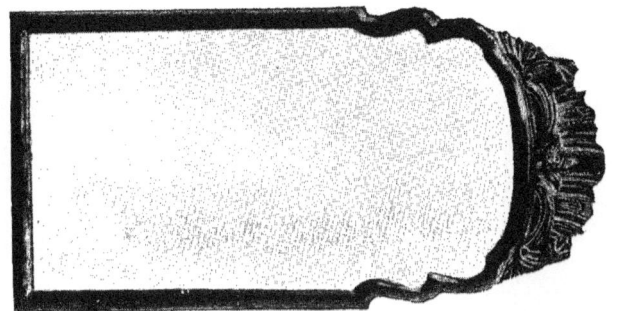

1.

2.

3.

1 and 2. Mirrors showing typical Queen Anne shaping.

Details and outline losing this characteristic feeling.

Queen Anne. 165

Queen Anne's reign this mannerism was still adhered to, but, as decoration was often applied in scanty fashion, the chances of repetition of matter were minimised.

The chair which is truly "Queen Anne" in style generally possesses a hooped back, and if we refer to our illustrations on pages 159, 166, and 170, we see this characteristic back-shaping, and with it the repetition between back uprights and legs. In each of these illustrations it will be noticed that the sweeping curve of the leg is duplicated in the back upright above and behind it. In the early examples where this treatment of contour has been followed, the curve in each of the back uprights describes that of the attenuated S-scroll, but it so happens that each of these examples shows the lower point of the S cut off before it is returned on its upward fish-hook course, and so the letter remains incomplete.

Chair Decoration.

Reverting now to the repetition of decorated matter on the overseat and underseat structure, the common employment of the large escalloped shell immediately strikes us. On many examples the item in question was introduced on the top of the back over the main splat, and in the position where the main cresting in earlier examples was placed. It was also applied to the middle of the seat-rail, midway between the front legs, and again on the knee of each leg. Our illustration on page 166 shows the employment of the shell in the two latter positions.

The C-scroll was often pressed into service in similar fashion by weaving the C into the design of the backsplat and echoing it again on each side of the top of the leg, or on the bracket-swells in the case of the later varieties. Variations of shell-work were peculiarly characteristic of the Queen Anne craftsmen, just as plays on the letter C were typical of Chippendale at a later date.

Rare style of Hogarth Chair in walnut. Circa 1715.

We also find chairs and two-chair-back settees with the head of an eagle or a vulture carved in profile at the top and on either side of the back-splat and on the accompanying leg-work, whilst the eagle or vulture mask acts as a terminal decoration to the arms of the model.

Spoon-backs.

The height of chair-backs, which during the preceding reign had assumed exaggerated proportions, was now modified, and in our illustration on page 156 we see one of those transitional specimens with cane panels and the spoon-back, which gives us an approximate knowledge of the proportion favoured on Queen Anne's accession. On this model the cresting is diminished, but the back has not yet assumed the typical hoop of the new order. Within this hoop the Queen Anne chair proper shows one bold, solid central splat, as seen on the settee on page 159, and although this example dates from about 1720, it is fitted with back-splats which might have been affixed in 1710. Following after this type of splat came another, such as we see in our illustration, page 166, wherein the central splat does not run down the full course of the back, but is suspended on a secondary rail connecting the uprights below the upper part of the hooping.

This particular vogue enjoyed great favour in the last years of Queen Anne's reign and in the earlier days of George I., when it was very generally supplanted by another type, wherein the back-splat was pierced and decorated, as in the case of the chair shown on page 170. This style is chiefly noticeable because it formed a connecting link between the walnut and mahogany ages, in both of which periods it was produced. Chippendale was either employed in the development of this treatment or became struck with its possibilities, for it furnished the governing principle in all his earlier open-backed creations.

In addition to the carved and lacquered chairs of the hooped order which have come down to us, we find specimens from time to time decorated in marquetry, and many of these, with delicate seaweed inlay over spoon or fiddle backs and with their elegant fine cabriole legs, are extremely effective. Collectors should beware of these marquetry chairs until they have a sound knowledge of English work, for the Dutch supplied England freely with the inferior productions of Holland, and are even now sending over reproductions, duly weathered in order to give them a semblance of age, for sale through certain well-known sources and to the discomfiture of the unwary.

Upholstered Furniture.

Upholstered chairs, settees, and couches resting on the various schemes of leg-work already noticed followed in the wake of open-backed models, in that their height was diminished and their back crest-shaping curtailed as time wore on. Chair-backs and seats were covered in beautiful needlework, damask, or other materials, mainly of native creation. In the earlier models the arms were turned over in heavily-padded C-scrolls, but with the progress of time outline lightened and the C nature of the scroll faded away.

Chairs of the Early Queen Anne style may be found with caned seats, but these generally disappeared in favour of upholstered ones on the " drop-in " principle, whilst the outline of the seat-frames opened out from the back in a variety of contours.

The side-framing and the front rail may be met with showing rectilinear handling, but this phase does not portray the typical treatment of the day. Characteristic chairs show their seat-frames rounded at the front—at the front and sides, hooped or bell-shaped, with the convex face pointing forwards. The lower edge of the front

Queen Anne.

seat-frame was oftentimes shaped, and this treatment was extended to the side-framing on many occasions.

High-backed Chairs.

Mention should be made of the plain quality high-backed, turned (or thrown) chairs which came into fashion about this time, for they are extremely interesting as constituting an exception to the general evolutionary rule. In form they resemble the well-known hooped Windsor types of the George III. period, but in the outline of their backs we find rectilinear crowning. Thus when hooped crests were prevailing we find a flat top rail on the bulk of these models, whilst, when a hundred years later Sheraton was exploiting the rectilinear back, they, in inverse fashion, harked back to the curvilinear shaping of Queen Anne in the majority of instances. The early types are pleasing, and the more artistic varieties repose on light cabriole legs.

A Progressive Period.

It has been urged that the Queen Anne period was devoid of interest, save for evolution of the cabriole proper. In reality it is open to question whether any preceding or succeeding phase since the Elizabethan witnessed such progress. The wing-ear or grandfather chairs, the writing-chairs, the writing-tables, kneehole-tables, bureaus, bureau-bookcases, card-tables, china-cabinets, settees, and two-chair-backed settees, to cite some models only of those brought near to perfection between 1700 and 1720, show the wonderful strides which craftsmen were making in their work. Of the pieces of furniture just mentioned, all came to be accepted as standard models for the guidance of posterity, whilst the mirror-frames, toilet-glasses, and side- or carving-tables of the day have since been varied rather than improved upon.

The wing-chair, with its ear-guards against draughts, had been taking definite shape gradually, but the perfected article, as we now know it, must be assigned to the Queen Anne period. The kneehole-tables were too

Chair showing Late Queen Anne influence and early pierced splat-work.

small for practical use when taken as a class and in the light of the more commodious specimens which Chippendale taught us to appreciate, but still, they were dainty-looking and well suited for occasional use or for small rooms. Card-tables were now built on lines suitable for four-handed games, and our present-day whist-tables

Queen Anne.

retain the proportions which the larger Queen Anne models assumed. In their proportion and in the internal fittings built into their body-work the bureau and bureau-bookcase of the time were well conceived. The early bureau has its upper storey overhanging, and is thus suggestive of the large desks on stands which preceded it. The bureau as evolved by 1710 has remained the standard pattern, save for minor variation of internal conveniences.

Glass-fronted bookcases and china cabinets were treated in a rather primitive and severe manner, for within rectilinear framework we find small panes framed in square-shaped lattice-work, the whole being suggestive of cage-work. Occasionally we happen on specimens treated in lighter vein, but as a class the lattice designs of 1700-1720 are uninteresting.

The two-chair-backed settee, such as that shown in our illustration on page 159, came into fashion about 1710, and it is doubtful whether the contour of the earliest examples has ever been improved upon. Plain specimens showing the early hooped backs and cabriole legs are met with pretty frequently, but the later examples, with their lower and wider-backed frames more ornately decorated and with claw-and-ball legs, are becoming very scarce.

Perhaps the large rectilinear marquetry cabinets on stands are the most striking of Queen Anne models, but they exhibit only minor variations on their prototypes of the preceding reign. Under Queen Anne, inlaid work became very generally quieter, the redundancy of detail found on William and Mary furniture lost its popularity, and the framework supporting raised cabinets or chests became well ordered, dignified, and restrained.

Low-toned feather-edging, herring-boning, and cross-banding came to the front, whilst well-shaped panels of floral or arabesque marquetry were cleverly introduced. As in the case of the inlaid designs of the late seventeenth century, the most successful results were achieved when inlayers employed seaweed or spider-web patterns in inlay to show off their models.

A reference to the grandfather clocks on pages 127 and 131 will show the types of marquetry still current, but whereas the somewhat florid taste of the preceding vogue had favoured fields of continuous decoration, the improved perception of 1700-1720 led more and more to the development of finely-shaped panels of marquetry on a plain walnut background. Under this latter treatment, which had been inadequately appreciated since the days of Charles II., the foil of the background at once rested the eye and heightened the effects of the marquetry. Experts will always differ in placing the exact period of given examples where outline is indefinite, as in the case of square-shaped cabinets whose stands may or may not be contemporary with their superstructures, but there is a distinct tendency nowadays to ascribe to the Queen Anne period work which a decade ago would have been attributed to the more sober-minded exponents of the preceding order.

A Period of Plain Furniture.

Although it is difficult, or impossible, to name a model which was not on an occasion treated in marquetry, an increasing demand for plain furniture made itself strongly felt and was responsible for the main artistic successes which we associate with typical Queen Anne furniture. Relying on the figure which walnut afforded and on the outlines which they had developed or refined, craftsmen now built chests of drawers or cabinets

Queen Anne.

on raised stands in perfect taste—simple in conception, yet strikingly effective. No marked departure may have been effected in the matter of detail, but a process of sifting and elimination had been going on, and the surviving matter, well selected, was co-ordinated. Thus it is hard to find a line in the rectilinear handling of the day which may not have been culled from, or suggested by, earlier designs, but whereas the item of 1680 or 1690 suffered loss in value owing to the juxtaposition of unsuitable surroundings, the same item in 1710, in happier environment, harmonised with its adjoining members, and, retaining its own beauties undiminished, contributed its full quota to the success of the general scheme.

The balustered work forming the leg-supports to stands for cabinets or raised chests of drawers and also in table framework was frequently crowned by dainty archwork from which pendent cusps were suspended. This treatment was less regularly applied after 1710, by which date stands of plainer character, but resting on cabriole legs, had become popular. We see the cabriole in slender proportions or in stunted form, according to the pitch of the overlying model, and by 1715 squat and heavy claw-and-ball extremities were commonly introduced under massive examples of furniture.

The turned knob supports of the Stuart period began to lose favour, and ogee or other bracket feet took their place quite commonly. We find small models, such as tea-caddies or toilet-glasses, and heavy furniture alike presenting this new feature in pleasing fashion.

Closed-in bookcases, bureau-bookcases, &c., were at times adorned by sunk, shaped panelling of Queen Anne type, and a reference to the first and second of our little mirrors on page 163 will show us, in the shaping of their upper glass field, the approximate contour favoured for these recessed panels. The edgework setting out the panels was sometimes carved and gilded, whilst, on occasions, the doors of such models as bureau-bookcases were adorned

Late Queen Anne Easy Chair, with typical cabriole leg.

by large, shaped mirrors let in in place of the receding woodwork.

Domed work, more or less reminiscent of the Renaissance, had been fitfully introduced into chests and cabinets since Elizabethan days, but it attained its greatest popularity under Queen Anne. Small recessed domes formed the central feature of the interior fittings of fine

Queen Anne.

cabinets; they were employed to embellish the lower edges of cabinets or double chests, and in this position took the place of the central shell or other ornament so frequently seen there. Corner-cupboards were built showing the doming in their roofs, whilst all models of height and importance were at times capped by domed hooding.

Doming was resorted to by Dutch cabinet-makers in their various cupboards, and we probably turned our attention to this handling at their instigation, for at about the same time the North American colonists borrowed the idea from Holland, exploiting it for half a century.

The broken pediment frequently crowned tall double chests, cabinets, and other upstanding pieces of furniture, but it was generally arched, in sympathy with so many of the contemporary architectural translations of this detail. Bearing in mind the strong popularity of the domed hooding of Queen Anne's day, it is probable that the pediment was arched in order that the curvilinear element might be retained and the transition from doming rendered less abrupt.

Shaped finials rose from the outer wings of domed or pedimented hoods and from the space or spaces between the domes where two or three of these figured in the design. In the cornice an ovolo was often inserted as a face to a shallow and pseudo-secret drawer. Secret drawers were commonly introduced into all manner of cabinet-work, but they were scarcely calculated to resist the attentions of dishonest explorers.

Armorial decoration was applied in a good number of instances, chairs and tables being the chief models selected for the display of heraldic devices. We find such matter inlaid on the central splats of chairs or two-chair-back settees, and now and then it figures in carved relief almost as a cresting to the model. On side-tables this carved detail may be found at the centre of the framework and immediately underlying the table-top.

We often notice examples which show how strongly architectural influence was at work amongst the craftsmen of the day, and small hanging mirrors or heavy bookcases may be found showing pure and distinct inspiration from the Renaissance.

Dutch Weakness.

In addition to the weakness of the Dutch cabriole, their hooping of backs was decidedly feeble, and the curvilinear element was generally stilted or exaggerated. Pronouncedly weak in quality, the bulk of Dutch marquetry showed the leaves much narrower and more pointed than those of English creation, facts which should be borne in mind by the young collector in quest of " Queen Anne."

CHAPTER VI.
Grinling Gibbons.

Position as a Craftsman.

THIS craftsman stands in a position which can best be described as unique—to him it was given to stamp the outlines of his personality on all work which he took in hand, and this at an age when fashion was constantly changing, and when no other artist had risen above the level of his peers. Of foreign origin, he yet gave distinctly English translations of exotic matter. A natural genius, he was self-taught, and improved on the rendering of any British or European detail which his fancy led him to essay. Inigo Jones had removed the reproach which, prior to his day, had rested on British architecture; Grinling Gibbons accomplished the same service in the field of carved or interior decoration. His carving was natural, his composition complementary, in the best interpretation of the word, to the designs of the architect with whom he was collaborating. Alive, he exerted a good influence on the crafts during the reigns of Charles II., James II., William and Mary, Queen Anne, and George I.; whilst his posthumous power may be traced throughout the Georgian period. He welded together the schemes of the architect and the mission of the craftsman, and, in furnishing the connecting-link between the two, usually supplied the most striking feature to the allied scheme.

Biography.

Grinling Gibbon, or Gibbons—for his name may be found recorded in either style—was born in 1648, and was of Dutch descent. His birthplace is obscure, but historians have endeavoured to convince us that he was born in Rotterdam, arguing on somewhat nebulous grounds. Evelyn, the main chronicler of the artist, refers to him as Gibbon, on 18th January, 1671, and on the ensuing 1st March, but in his later references he uses the concluding " s," and after the latter date does not again employ the name as originally spelt. Evelyn may have caught the word incorrectly, Gibbon may have adopted a word hastily, and have subsequently used a final " s " with a view to anglicising his name more completely, but we may correctly use either style in speaking of this brilliant master.

In January, 1671, we find Gibbons admitting to Evelyn that he was but a beginner, and the latter's diary contains a long report of the first interview between these two—a meeting fraught with such import to the young carver. Evelyn, in addition to admiring the artist's work, found him " likewise musical and very civil, sober, and discreete in his discourse." The diarist goes on to tell us : " Of this young artist, together with my manner of finding him out, I acquainted the King, & begg'd that he would give me leave to bring him & his worke to Whitehall, for that I would adventure my reputation with his Ma^{ty} that he had never seene anything to approch it, & that he would be exceedingly pleased, & employ him. The King said he would himself go see him. This was the first notice his Majestie ever had of Mr. Gibbon."

The promised interview was not long delayed, for on

the ensuing 1st March Evelyn records :—" I caused Mr. Gibbon to bring to Whitehall his excellent piece of carving, where being come I advertised his Majestie, who ask'd me where it was; I told him . . . & that if it pleas'd his Ma^{ty} to appoint whither it should be brought, being large & tho' of wood heavy, I wo^d take care for it; ' No,' says the King, ' shew me ye way, I'll go.' . . . which he immediately did.

" No sooner was he enter'd & cast his eye on the work but he was astonish'd at the curiositie of it, & having consider'd it a long time & discours'd with Mr. Gibbon, whom I brought to kisse his hand, he commanded it should be immediately carried to the Queenes side to shew her. It was carried up into her bedchamber, where she & the King looked on & admir'd it againe."

From Evelyn we glean that the carving was eventually sold to Sir George Viner for £80, the Queen being somewhat biased against the work by one Madame de Boord, " who us'd to bring petticoates & fanns, & baubles out of France to the Ladys," and who " began to find fault with several things in the worke, which she understood no more than an asse or a monkey."

The long association between Christopher Wren and Gibbons, which resulted in so many pleasing and historic productions, commenced shortly after this, for Evelyn introduced the latter to Wren, and obtained promises of commissions from him for his protégé.

On 2nd March Evelyn asked Charles to employ young Gibbons on the decorations of Windsor, and succeeded in interesting May, the architect, and Sir Peter Lely, the Court painter, in the career of his protégé. On 28th June, 1677, Evelyn states : " I went to Windsor with my Lord Chamberlaine (the Castle now repairing with exceeding cost) to see the rare work of Verrio, and incomparable carving of Gibbons."

Evelyn seems to have conceived an affection for this clever carver, who owed so much to his patronage, for he kept a watchful eye on his career, and we find him writing of " our " Gibbons on 16th June, 1683, " who is beyond controversie the greatest master, both for invention & rareness of worke, that the world ever had in any age; nor doubt I at all that he will prove as greate a master in the statuary art." This eulogium was scarcely disinterested; but Henry Colburn's 1827 edition of " Evelyn " quotes as an editorial note an appreciation of Gibbons appearing in Walpole's " Catalogue of Painters and Notes on Artists ":—" An original genius, a citizen of nature. There is no instance before him of a man who gave to wood the loose and airy lightness of flowers, and chained together the various productions of the elements with the free disorder natural to each species."

As an All-round Craftsman.

Gibbons not only proved himself on the whole a good designer, a sound composer, and a brilliant carver, but he attained distinction as a sculptor. His favourite medium was limewood, which permitted him to show that delicacy of carving which first and last was characteristic of his work. Other soft or white woods were now and then employed by him, and he occasionally worked in box-wood, cedar, pear-wood, and walnut, and often in oak. Mahogany was just coming into favour as he died, and although he is doubtless to be credited with some early work in this hard, and from a carver's point of view treacherous, timber, the bulk of mahogany decoration in his style should rightly be attributed to his disciples.

Grinling Gibbons.

It would have been manifestly impossible for Gibbons to have carved all the interior decorations with which his name is, rightly or wrongly, associated. He must have trained a considerable number of craftsmen in the class of work which he loved to introduce, and, working in their midst, have supervised their productions, whilst himself carving the central and more intricate designs intended to govern the whole.

The softer mediums which the master favoured were ill-calculated to resist the ravages of Time, and many examples of his work have come down in fragmentary form. Carving which may have been applied in remote positions, and so have escaped wear and tear or other devastating forces, was often the production of his pupils. Gibbons is oftentimes judged on the merits of such carving, which naturally lacked the verve and finesse of the master's touch to a more or less marked extent. Where designs fell from the hand of the man himself, they were, in the words of Evelyn, incomparable.

Gibbons chiefly carved swags, garlands, or festoons of flowers, fruit, and foliage, looped up at their extremities by carved ribbons, below which fell pendant strings of similar detail. His love of music led him to introduce violins, reeds, and other instruments emblematical of Harmony. Trophies and emblems in consonance with the apartments under decoration were inserted in his schemes, whilst his facile handling of cupids and animal life reflected the sculptural leanings and power of this genius.

We are forced to take into consideration the last-mentioned side of Gibbons's talent by the fact that so many of his compositions needed a crowning touch of sculptured detail to render the design complete. At one time a carved and winged cupid, savouring more of the sculptor than of the craftsman, would figure as a central cresting. At another the central plinth in a broken pediment seemed to demand a crowning bust, whilst Gibbons's schemes in plaster often cry aloud for heroic heads or busts as complementary items of decoration. Gibbons seems to have been an accomplished sculptor, for on 16th November, 1686, we find Evelyn thus recording his impressions of the New Catholic Chapel at Whitehall: " Nothing can be finer than the marble work & architecture at the end where are four statues . . . in white marble the work of Mr. Gibbons, with all the carving & pillars of exquisite art." The statue of James II. erected by Gibbons at Whitehall in 1686 was contemporary with the work in the New Chapel, and is to-day considered to be a most excellent work.

Grinling Gibbons's carvings at such places as St. Paul's Cathedral, Blenheim, Burghley, Oxford, and Cambridge, to cite a few cases only, are rightly considered as classics; but within reach of most collectors there are other mansions or buildings wherein the brilliancy of his execution stands exemplified. Thus, Petworth and Belton House, Grantham, have each in turn been held to show the master at his best.

Gibbons was responsible for much fine plasterwork in ceiling and mural decorations; but collectors naturally prefer his creations in wood. In his treatment of a frieze, a cornice, a capital or other detail in classic style, he showed to great advantage, for he rose superior to the caprice of the hour, and in so doing avoided the anomalies and complexities of the period 1665-1700. Always in advance of his day in execution and technique, he used an ennobling influence on the arts and crafts in an unostentatious way. In declining to embody extravagant fashions, or in seeking to better current practices, he led rather than dróve his less talented brethren, and so we have it that his work, although superior to, seldom clashed with, that of contemporary craftsmen. Gibbons raised the standard of craftsmanship without treading on the toes of the craft, and he demonstrated the full and potential value of a perfect understanding between architect and craftsman.

From 1714 until 1721, when Gibbons died, he held the position of master carver to George I. at 1s. 6d. a day; but this small emolument was probably given as a retaining fee rather than as an inclusive payment for the discharge of such duties as the appointment entailed. The highest price which Evelyn hints at as having been given for one movable example of Gibbons's carving, was the £200 said to have been paid by Sir Robert Greere for a pelican with young at her breast. But recently part of an interior by him changed hands at 30,000 guineas!

As Gibbons traditions faded away and became remote, swags, festoons, pendants, and detail, such as he had employed, became lighter and more attenuated. Gibbons had been responsible for no volume of actual furniture, and the bolder surfaces which he had embellished had called for comparative massing of detail and breadth of treatment. In the Georgian endeavour to transplant the master's designs on to the restricted surface which pieces of furniture present, schemes and proportions had to be curtailed, and so the designs came eventually to lose their character and scale, and detail its sharpness and relief.

If there was a redeeming feature in the massive and ornate Late Georgian furniture, it is seen on those examples showing fruit and floral designs in bold relief, somewhat reminiscent of Gibbons's work in palmier days.

CHAPTER VII.
Georgian.

Meaning of the Term.

CONSIDERABLE confusion exists amongst collectors and students as to the precise meaning of the term "Georgian" in its relation to the applied arts, and we must consider the various uses to which the term is put. The most obvious interpretation of the word would be that in its generic sense it embraced such work as saw the light under the Georges; but although the broad definition might be defended, it would altogether fail to convey the generally accepted meanings of the expression. During the reign of George I. Queen Anne fashions largely obtained, and there is little evidence of marked changes such as one would look for on the incoming of a new and distinct vogue. Under George II. the genius and ability of Thomas Chippendale the Second led to the creation of a distinct school of work, and when designs are in consonance with the thought and modelling of that king of craftsmen, or even when they bear more or less resemblance to his masterpieces, we talk of them as being "Chippendale" or "after Chippendale." Previous cabinet-makers had existed as units who were engaged in furthering, more or less successfully, the fashions of the hour: they had contributed their quota towards the success of the Elizabethan, the Jacobean, the William and Mary, and the Queen Anne vogues; but individual achievements were merged in the fortunes of the prevailing style. Chippendale, on the other hand, made history, and his name, like that of Grinling Gibbons, has come down to us as that of a master—not as that of an adherent of some subordinating order. The position has been accepted tacitly by those who have admired and by those who have sought to disparage Chippendale, and posterity, in associating the name of the subject rather than that of his Sovereign with the best work of the earlier George II. period, has paid the great designer and adapter the sincerest of tributes.

We are now primarily engaged in studying the early phases of Georgian craftsmanship, when Chippendale was, so to speak, bearing the brunt of battle and laying the foundations of his subsequent success, and it is obvious that a large volume of work, emanating from minor or obscure sources quite or partially out of touch with his influence or style, awaits classification. The productions of these lesser lights were interesting, and frequently meritorious. We know less perhaps of this page of history than of many another far more remote in period. We know that during the transitional phase (1715-1735) the doctrines of the Queen Anne school were seldom lost sight of; we meet with expositions of the idea architectural which may be traced to the influence of Inigo Jones, of Christopher Wren, or of William Kent, and others. Obvious emulation of Grinling Gibbons is apparent, and the resultant work has, for want of precise information as to its parentage, to be styled "Early Georgian."

Towards the middle of the century the success which had attended Chippendale's career had attracted numerous disciples, and between 1745-1760 well-known craftsmen whose style was modelled more or less closely on that of their acknowledged leader were catering for the public. From 1765-1805 the latter-day designers—R. and J. Adam, Heppelwhite, Shearer, and Sheraton—had evolved semi-distinctive fashions from sources common in the main to one and all of them. The merits of their styles, the advertisements which they issued in book form, brought within their several folds an ever-increasing proportion of the less important craftsmen. Despite this process of absorption, cabinet-makers there were who, owing to their independent views or catholic fancies, failed to attach themselves to the school of any one given master or to bring their work into line with specific fashions. These free lances, contemporaries as they were of the better-known designers, were responsible for no mean volume of work, and for want of a more definite term their production can be classed as being of the "Mid-Georgian" order.

During the closing phases of the reign of George III. taste was markedly decadent, and a race of cabinet-makers then began to pander to the depraved fashion of the day. These workmen ignored the lessons taught by their illustrious predecessors, and correctly interpreted the heavy, vulgar, and ornate spirit obsessing popular opinion. We turn with an instinctive shudder from such work, which we class as "Late Georgian" in no half-measure of reproach.

Summarising, then, the various characteristics of Georgian furniture, we find that much good work was produced during the somewhat nebulous period known as Early Georgian. The Mid-Georgian models emerge from our scrutiny as being somewhat invertebrate, and with a leaning towards mediocrity, whilst the claims of

Domed Niche and Frieze at Godmersham. The frame enclosing the niche, door, window, or chimney-piece in this Classic style was known as a Tabernacle frame.

the Late Georgian style cannot be recognised by people of taste.

The Queen Anne style is clearly defined, but the inception of the Chippendale régime is shrouded in a haze. The slow process of evolution was steadily at work; it linked up the two styles in many directions, but motive, which governs production, was rigidly distinct in others. The objective aimed at and achieved under Queen Anne had been comparative simplicity, and this had been arrived at after the elimination of superfluous matter. The Queen Anne craftsmen handed down dignified yet simple designs which they had evolved from chaos. Under George I. came the swing of the pendulum, and craftsmen relied again on the elaboration of matter whilst persevering more or less closely with the salient points of the meritorious outline bequeathed to them. Under these circumstances a study of the Early Georgian transition largely resolves itself into an analysis of the origin and methods of application of its extended embellishment.

Early Georgian Work.

The reign of George I. was so short in duration that evolution is not strongly marked, and it might almost be studied in conjunction with that of Queen Anne from the furniture-lovers' point of view. The chairs called after Hogarth now made their appearance, and owe their designation to the fact that their advent synchronised with the days which we associate with that artist. The armchair shown on page 166 exhibits the main characteristics of the new model save that its back is scarcely high enough to be typical.

The love of gilded furniture, which was growing in

the preceding reign, reached its unhappy climax between 1715 and 1730, and is traceable partly to slavish emulation of contemporary French vogues. Models so embellished generally carried vulgar to grotesque carving, and were, in comparison with their predecessors, heavily built and clumsy in proportion.

It is in the reign of George II. that we look for and find the motif which governed the better-class productions of the Early Georgian school. Queen Anne principles in decoration ceased to appeal to the Georgian palate, which demanded something at once solid and impressive-looking. Legs had to be more stoutly built, chair-backs became lower and more powerfully framed, and decoration which would have been considered superfluous in Queen Anne's time was now freely resorted to.

Designers whose main aim lay in the achieving of harmony between the architectural and interior decoration of the home had been faced by a new problem on the advent of the Queen Anne building. The Queen Anne style of architecture is so called because it reached its climax in that reign, and because early in the eighteenth century a definite and homogeneous style to which all the arts and crafts supplied their quota had been evolved. In reality the conception of the Queen Anne house dates back to the days of James II., and the Great Fire of London was very largely responsible for the impregnation of the new idea. London had been all but demolished, and Christopher Wren was mainly responsible for the remodelling and rebuilding of the new city. That Wren improved on the earlier laying out of London is generally admitted; whether he gave London more artistic effects is a disputed point. In common with the chief architects of the later Renaissance, he relied largely for

Corinthian Doorway at Godmersham.

Georgian.

his results on that balance of outline and proportion which we instinctively associate with the classic orders. In Grinling Gibbons he found a collaborator of extreme power, and one well fitted to supply the complementary embellishment to designs such as he favoured. The volume of work called for bore such marked resemblance to the ensuing Queen Anne that it may be said to have contained the embryo of that vogue; the large scope of Wren's work influenced fashion in the heart of the country, and that influence flowed from the metropolis through the main arteries of the kingdom.

Influence of Architecture.

In the Early English Renaissance period the true significance of classic teaching was submerged, for it was subordinated to the whim or the licence of the hour: thus houses were primarily Elizabethan or Jacobean, and incidentally savoured more or less of the Italian revival. Furniture followed in the wake of architecture, and the modifications, adaptations, and variations introduced by artists and craftsmen took the eye away from what should have been the central scheme.

In the Later English Renaissance, Inigo Jones's influence was marked, and his pupils Webb and Carter, with Wren, Hawksmoor, Sir John Vanbrugh, Gibbs, Ripley, Wood, and Kent, to cite some leading names only, aimed at a pure interpretation of the classic style and a truly national school of architecture. Under such influence designs came to be regularly ordered and well balanced, and harmony and proportion were carefully studied. Interiors were decorated as nearly as possible with the correct and concomitant mouldings and detail, and a conscientious regard for the minutiæ of garnishment was apparent on every hand. The day of casual and haphazard embellishment had passed; we had ceased to embody in our schemes items culled from itinerant artificers, because our architects were at pains to learn Roman art at Rome and to eschew second-hand goods.

The Queen Anne and Georgian styles were born from this methodical and systematic rendering of the Renaissance, and although there were minor dissimilarities of treatment, due to the varying conception and power of successive architects, the classic orders governed English work for the main part throughout the eighteenth century. The Brobdingnagian work of Vanbrugh and the Lilliputian detail of Robert Adam show two aspects of the same theme as seen by architects practising at the end of the seventeenth and eighteenth centuries respectively.

Classic Treatment.

The precedent set by our architects was followed by the interior decorators, then by the craftsmen, and by 1700 the home was co-ordinated and the public passed a favourable verdict on the result. From that time onward the lay mind paid more attention to sympathetic decoration, and artists catered for its requirements. Cabinet-makers prefaced their books by dissertations on the five antique orders; they justified their works on the ground of their classic treatment, and the Georgian furniture was conceived in this particular vein.

Chippendale, it is true, with his sublime unorthodoxy, broke away from the limitations of the classic style, but even he preached the doctrines of the Doric, the Ionic, and the Corinthian orders, and we seldom meet with an example of his work which fails to show Renaissance detail; whilst just as much work with which he had nothing to do is attributed to him, so, too, many fine examples in the classic style of the period 1725-40 at present unfathered should doubtless be placed to his credit. Temporary influences, such as the Chinese craze or the Gothic revival of the mid-eighteenth century, only placed Renaissance matter temporarily in the shade, and, if we add the exception brought about by Chippendale's wanderings from the straight path, we can say that the classic idea in one form or another outweighed all others during the finest period of British craftsmanship.

In the broad and casual handling of the earlier Renaissance house, where little heed was paid to external orthodoxy, our forefathers achieved picturesque and pleasing results, and it is only when we analyse their buildings piecemeal that faults become transparent. Such homes were eminently suitable for furniture whose leading features were in reality hybrid and cosmopolitan. In the succeeding " Late " Renaissance period the general results achieved at times conveyed a chilly or laboured effect, although the detail and proportions embodied in the structure may have been faultless. These facts may seem to point towards the superiority of the earlier types of house, but whether this is the case or not, the analogy between house and household furniture would not hold good. Faults which passed unnoticed or were overlooked in long, straggling, and picturesque homes became patent when compressed into a smaller compass, and the debased Elizabethan, the Jacobean, and the early Restoration furniture shows inconsistencies and incongruities which are wholly indefensible.

Even if the classic school of work was in reality exotic, it was balanced and correct, and mistakes in its interpretation or materialisation were due to the limitations of the exponent rather than to any inherent weakness in the themes it bred. Stilted or overladen much of the eighteenth-century work undoubtedly is, but where design marched with the Renaissance there was a welcome absence of vulgar blundering.

It is improbable that people of taste will ever agree on the question of the respective merits of the various types of English domestic architecture, and we are not concerned in advancing the merits of the one style or in belittling the value of another. Ours it is to understand the basis of the complementary parts played by successive generations of cabinet-makers, and, having laid out the lines of our own collections, to show them off to the best advantage.

Few collectors can hope to live in pure Elizabethan or Jacobean homes, but for those who are so happily placed the furniture of the day contemporary with their house will surely commend itself. If it is difficult to obtain a true and typical building, there are at any rate many old nondescript and rambling houses which have been added to and adapted by many generations. Such buildings possess a general air of artistic abandon and an indescribable charm. They are pre-eminently the places in which general collections of oak, walnut, and mahogany should repose, and we instinctively look for mixed treasures when we cross their thresholds. Whenever we find oak panelling half the difficulty of showing off oak furniture passes away, but when we have to repair, restore, or replace panelled work we are faced by what may prove to be a herculean task.

The majority of houses at the disposal of collectors date back less than two hundred years; they were probably

Early Georgian Doorway and Decoration at Godmersham.

Georgian.

papered inside or fitted partially with painted soft wood panelling. The judicious selection of a wall-paper restores their original character, and they in their turn demand the complementary furniture of their day. In the modern home new panelling and oak-work are apt to confer a governing sense of modernity on the interiors to which they are fitted, but the lately-built house can be readily adapted for the display of eighteenth-century furniture—an old fireplace and chimney-piece, and, if possible, an old door, and the reproduced paper will not prove aggressive. If the old fittings are not available clever replicas are readily obtainable, and these, as compared with the more ambitious reproductions demanded, if we are venturing on oak rooms, will prove singularly inoffensive. Common sense will tell us that Elizabethan or Jacobean interiors should not be selected to show off dainty pieces of satinwood, or that eighteenth-century homes with decorations by Pergolesi or Adam must not contain cumbrous oak.

A Taste for Oak.

For some reason most collectors commence with a strong penchant for oak, and it is usually observable that they give it up in favour of eighteenth-century furniture as they gain experience. From a sentimental point of view there is something essentially British about oak, and one can make quite an imposing display with it at moderate cost. As one grows older and wiser one realises that not one piece of oak furniture out of twenty is worthy of a place in a well-chosen collection. Incomparable in large halls, dignified in library or dining-room, oak is unsuitable for boudoir or drawing-room use. Rugged, bold, and sometimes picturesque, our English examples possess artistic values, but we cannot compare them with early Italian creations.

One of the most pathetic of sights is to see a group of old oak devotees discussing a fine specimen of Italian work, and trying to convince themselves and one another against their better judgment that it may be English, or at any rate may represent the work of an Italian who was living in England. We instinctively train our eye to appreciate English oak because it is English, allowing patriotic principles to blind us to its manifold shortcomings. These facts are borne in on the collector of some standing, and he, moreover, realises that in the mahogany age our work stands *facile princeps*. He finds that "Chippendale," "Heppelwhite," or "Sheraton" will readily fulfil the duties of oak, and will answer well in positions where oak is unsuitable (as, for instance, in the drawing-room). The probabilities are that the house in which the collector lives will look better with eighteenth-century than with sixteenth-century furniture, on account of its period, and so he transfers his allegiance to the later school of work.

William Kent.

Mr. T. A. Strange, in his valuable "English Furniture, Woodwork, Decoration, &c., during the Eighteenth Century," tells us that "William Kent was born in the North Riding of Yorkshire in 1684," but Messrs. Belcher and Macartney give the date of his birth as 1688 in their work on "Later Renaissance Architecture in England." Kent, with the assistance of patrons, was enabled to study in Rome, whither he went in 1710. On his return to England in 1719 he was welcomed by society with open arms, and enjoyed considerable popularity as an architect,

Early Georgian Mirrors and Detail at Godmersham.

sculptor, ceiling and staircase painter, mural decorator, silver-worker, and furniture designer. Possessed of all-round talent, he shone in no particular rôle, and his reputation has suffered in consequence of the many ornate, heavy, and pretentious designs which he produced. His greatest and staunchest friend seems to have been Lord Burlington, and the evidence adduced by Messrs. Belcher and Macartney points to there having been a considerable amount of collaboration between the two. In their "Later Renaissance Architecture in England" these authorities tell us that "Kent was at first employed in painting portraits and decorations (in colour and in monochrome) for the houses of Houghton, Wanstead, Rainham, and Stowe. Subsequently he began to practise as an architect. Amongst the works of his designing may be mentioned the Royal residence at Kew; Holkham, Norfolk, for the Earl of Leicester; and the Horse Guards, London." Kent therefore had most exceptional opportunities, seeing that he was accustomed to suggest furniture designs for the houses which he built or for the interiors which he treated; but we are unable to associate with his name any one piece of cabinet or chair work showing outstanding merit. His compositions were hybrid, and showed a superficial knowledge of Louis Quatorze, Regence, and early rococo detail, with classic or pseudo-classic matter thrown in; they lacked dignity, grace, and proportion, and, as in the case of the majority of his chimney-pieces, a laboured striving after effect is observable.

The author once owned two chairs of the Hogarth style carrying decoration identical with that on chimney-pieces known to have been designed by Kent, and it is probable that this designer achieved some little success in his modifications of Queen Anne work. Kent seemed unable to curb the pompous vein running through his temperament, and, though he enjoyed exceptional advantages, it is questionable whether he contributed anything to the better side of Early Georgian art. Messrs. Belcher and Macartney tell us that he edited and published at Lord Burlington's expense "Designs of Inigo Jones," with added suggestions or designs by his lordship and himself, in 1727; and Mr. Benn adds that he further published in 1744 "Some Designs of Mr. Inigo Jones and Mr. Wm. Kent." Kent died in 1748, and his reputation was eclipsed by those of contemporary artist-craftsmen.

Minor Masters.

Throughout the period 1650-1750 many people were quietly and unostentatiously furthering the development of the later Renaissance; and, if they were not self-advertising, and consequently easily traceable, their work was meritorious and fulfilled a useful mission. Clare College, Cambridge, contains many beautiful features of Renaissance proportion and detail, and we learn from Messrs. Belcher and Macartney that these were largely due to the efforts of one "Thomas Grumbold, *a Cambridge mason.* . . . It is to him that we are indebted for its supreme charm and excellence. . . . He succeeded in giving to the whole a valuable scale and a solid effect." That which the mason of Cambridge achieved in the field of architecture had its counterpart in the work accomplished by the humbler exponents of the allied arts and crafts, and if it were possible to identify the furniture of the times with the rightful designers we should certainly find that a large proportion of the truly artistic examples

Fireplace, Overmantel, and Frieze Decoration at Godmersham.

fell from the hands and pencils of obscure craftsmen whose names have not been handed down to us.

In Burke's "Landed Gentry," 1875, we read: "Thomas Brodnax of Godmersham, who relinquished his patronymic and assumed the surname of May. In 1729 this gentleman kept his shrievalty for the co. of Kent and rebuilt three years after the mansion of Godmersham." The beautiful decorations at Godmersham were created at about the most interesting period in the century; they are in perfect preservation and are thoroughly typical of their day. Added zest is given to the study of the mansion owing to the fact that it was further embellished in the style of the brothers Adam in 1793, and so includes very early and late examples of good Georgian handiwork. As it so happens, the work was commenced before Chippendale had established his position, and the later work was added just one year after the Adelphi partnership had been broken up by the death of Robert Adam. The work therefore from first to last just covers the period rendered celebrated by our line of master cabinet-makers. The mural decorations are in plaster, and they have this great distinction, that whereas they exhibit the rich and handsome characteristics of their day, their artistic value is not marred by that unfortunate tendency to excess which so often pervades Georgian schemes. The doors are in fine mahogany, with well-grouped panels, and these latter are in some instances set off by sharply-cut egg-and-tongue or echinus carving. Thoroughly typical of good Early Georgian work, the general scheme is most pleasing, and it not only shows the complementary part to the architect's work subscribed by the decorator, but the individual items, such as the domed niche, the doorways, the mirror frames, and overmantel embellishment on pages 187, 191, 197, 201, and 205 respectively exhibit the modelling and detail which guided the cabinet-maker when supplying his quota to the whole.

The illustrations on pages 187 and 205 show how strongly Grinling Gibbons influence was still at work in the realm of frieze handling; whilst in the illustrations on pages 191, 197, and 201 the same characteristic is observable, only that in these cases the massing of festoons has become rather lighter.

In the projection of the central features shown on pages 187, 191, and 197 we find the suggestion which influenced Early Georgian craftsmen in their designs for wardrobes, bookcases, bureau-bookcases, and china cabinets, whilst the bulk of such smaller detail shown on pages 187, 191, 197, 201, and 205 as is not reminiscent of Gibbons resembled that which our chief designers incorporated in their various creations.

Our illustrations on pages 187, 197, and 205 show the tabernacle frame crowned by the broken pediment, whilst on page 191 we see the pediment complete.

Chippendale usually employed the former of these styles, varying it after the turn of the century by the swan-necked pediment. Early and Late Georgian bookcases, &c., may be found showing the plain pediment, but this feature is usually met with in conjunction with heavy and uninteresting examples.

As a contrast to the Early Georgian handling of mural decoration our illustration on page 209 furnishes an instructive and excellent example. In this instance the work is some sixty to sixty-five years later in date, and, in sympathy with the influence of the Adam and later Italian school, detail has become lighter and far more sketchy. The cornice covered with delicate acanthus

Fireplace, Cornice and Frieze Decoration with mural paintings by Angelica Kauffman in another mansion. Period 1770-1775.

leaves, dentil work, and echinus now overshadows the frieze, and this latter occupies a secondary rather than a primary position in the crowning scheme.

As in the case of the five earlier illustrations, the treatment of decorative detail again resembles that applied to contemporary furniture. The bold and massive handling of architectural outline and detail typical of Early Georgian day has been swept away, to be replaced by a more airy rendering of the classic.

Turning to our illustration on page 213, we are confronted with an example exhibiting the late characteristics of Adam influence. This bookcase, one of three in the library at Godmersham, dates from the period 1798, and is therefore a posthumous example of this architect's work. Designers had now gone from one extreme to the other, and in their efforts to avoid ponderous effects had become finicking and unimpressive. The frieze is the one redeeming feature in this model, and even this carries sketchiness to the extreme. The attenuated renderings of the pseudo-Ionic pilasters, the insignificance of their capitals and bases, conduce to a feeling of poverty of the general scheme, and show the ultra-refining influence of Robert Adam in an unfortunate light.

The heavy, pompous, and frequently vulgar furniture and embellishment of the Late Georgian vogue were bred of a dislike and contempt for this thin type of Mid-Georgian garnishment, and the revulsion was all the more pronounced because no genius arose to stay the swing of the pendulum.

By the middle of the eighteenth century many houses showed interiors decorated in consonance with the rococo spirit of the Louis Quinze, and for such mansions the furniture of Chippendale and Heppelwhite was available and suitable. Later, when the Louis Seize teachings were influencing taste in England, the complementary finish was yielded by Heppelwhite, Shearer, Sheraton, and their numerous disciples.

The Gothic revival, with which Horace Walpole had so much to do, bred a certain amount of sympathetic interior garnishment, and most of our great cabinet-makers essayed corresponding designs. Many houses after the turn of the century were governed by Chinese *motif* as expressed by Sir William Chambers and his following, and here again the creations of Chippendale or Ince and Mayhew in this particular field gave a singularly appropriate finish to the Eastern scheme. Thus we find that throughout the eighteenth century our master cabinet-makers carefully studied the ordinances of architect and decorator in their efforts to strike notes of harmony.

During the Early Georgian period literature bearing on furniture was distinctly limited; indeed, authors seem to have been content with embodying a few hints to craftsmen, with more or less prosy dissertations on architectural matter. " The Gentleman's or Builder's Companion," by William Jones, published in 1739, shows some Georgian work which is passable, and furniture designs of a quasi-French character which are generally execrable. The " City and Country Builder's and Workman's Treasury of Designs," published for Thomas Langley in Meard's Court, Dean Street, in 1740, price 16s., is comparatively interesting, and calls for special comment.

The work was prepared in 1739, and comprised upwards of 180 designs by Batty Langley and Thomas Langley, and dealt, amongst other things, with designs for pier-tables, chimney-pieces, frets, pedestals, and book-

Columbian press of the eighteenth century.

cases, and was intended "for the use of workmen." Of cabinet-makers Langley had but sorry opinion, for he remarks: "The Evil Genius that so presides over Cabinet-makers . . . I am at a loss to discover; except Murcea, the Goddess of Sloth, acts that Part, and has influenced them, to conceal their dronish, low Life, incapacities; and prompt them with the Fox in the Fable; to pronounce Grapes, sower, that ripen out of their Reach. Cabinet-makers, originally were no more, than Spurious Indocible Chips, expelled by Joiners, for the Superfluity of their Sap. . . . But to prevent this Infection from diffusing its poisonous effluvia any further . . . . I have compiled this Work."

We have here a very sorry picture of the cabinet-makers of the day, but it is only fair to add that the taste exhibited in the designs for furniture which the Langleys submitted was mediocre in the extreme. The authors naturally wished to make out a good case to warrant the production of their book, and in doing so may have unfairly misrepresented the standard of the craft; added to this, there is little in the Langleys' book to warrant their having constituted themselves as critics of the arts.

If the book under discussion fairly represented the limitations of contemporary craftsmanship, Chippendale may well have risen to its leadership without serious rivalry, but the strides made by cabinet-makers under his guidance during the decades 1740-1750 and 1750-1760 then testify all the more strongly to his generalship.

Amongst the subscribers to Langleys' book one James Chipendell, joiner, appears, and collectors may see more than a coincidence in the similarity between this and the now generally accepted name and style of Thomas

Chippendale, joiner. Mr. Edwards, a cabinet-maker, also figures in the list, and was probably he of Edwards and Darly fame.

Turning for a moment to the designs in the " Builder's and Workman's Treasury," &c., the earlier plates show the Langleys as possessing fair knowledge of the classic. Plates 61-93 contain moderately good expositions of items of interior decoration in the Early Georgian style, pervaded at times by Grinling Gibbons influence. Plates 97 to 102 reveal fretwork somewhat anticipatory of the ensuing 1755 vogue as expressed by Chippendale, Ince and Mayhew, and Chambers, whilst the designs for tables as introduced on Plates 141-147 would, after a cursory examination, be very generally attributed to Chippendale by those who are not conversant with Langley draughtsmanship. The leg-contour throughout the book shows indiscriminate filching of French matter without taste or restraint, and at the same time the more vulgar and ornate characteristics of the Georgian order are here and there presented in complex and ill-balanced vein.

CHAPTER VIII.
Chippendale.

Influences on the Cabinet-maker's Art.

IN the days of George II., when we first pick up the evidence of Chippendale's influence, architectural feeling governed the cabinet-maker's craft in a manner unprecedented since the Gothic phase of English work. French influence of an unfortunate type was making itself felt, and Queen Anne teachings still carried weight. In sympathy with the spirit of the hour, designs were heavy and pretentious, and models which under clever handling should have been massive, all too often came to be ponderous. Craftsmen, in their somewhat laboured renderings of a part, were apt to overlook its function in relation to the whole, and furniture oftentimes had its weighty aspect accentuated because designers did not realise the limitations of their restricted field when embodying outline and detail culled from the broader sphere of architecture.

Classic or Renaissance detail was conscientiously incorporated on many occasions, and the carving was at times so sharp that nobody could carp at it; but, just when success seemed assured, the contour of a member, or a lapse from orthodoxy, would discount the whole performance.

A craving after grotesqueries found its expression on much of the Early Georgian furniture, and we not uncommonly find masks of mythological or unnatural character introduced on the furniture of the day. The decorative value of such matter is at best hypothetical, but when we see its exaggerated application in conjunction with a foil of pure and correct detail the contrast is too

Early Georgian Mahogany Chair; circa 1735. Probably by Chippendale.

abrupt. Legs crowned by hideous masks supported entablatures graced by classic friezes, and whereas our handling of the latter showed a stolid interpretation of Italian matter, our portrayal of the former savoured of earlier Teutonic or contemporary Irish effort.

Chippendale.

A study of the first five illustrations in our Georgian chapter will show the general run of the purer type of embellishment and outline affected during the times, and it will also be apparent that their general rhythm and dignity would speedily lose caste if the scheme under which they stand ordered and balanced were varied to permit of the introduction of detached extravagances. Fortunately we had the correct side to our national character, and this it was which gave us the sterling Georgian models. Unfortunately the seductions of debased French work proved oftentimes fatal, and when once the door was opened hybrid variations crept in. The classic theme became more or less obscured, English types gave way to Continental abortions, and for some fifteen years the national character of British craftsmanship was again jeopardised. Chippendale was therefore faced in his rise to power by a national problem rather than with individual competition. Considered by the standard of the almost pedantic late eighteenth-century styles, his work was heavy and at times ill-balanced, yet we pick out this earlier work because it stands out from the productions of the other craftsmen of the day, light and homogeneous. He dignified leg-work, he improved on existing patterns of back-shaping, and, with a pretty taste in detail, welded together a definite and English translation of exotic matter. Finding French influence a retrograde factor in his craft, he seized on the daintiest features which it afforded and presented them to Englishmen anglicised under his pencil.

Everything is a matter of degree, and the public which appreciated designs such as that shown on page 197, would have felt an aching void had it been offered an alternative suggestion of the nature of that shown on page 213.

No master presented such an all-round and comprehensive bill of fare as did Chippendale: no designer showed so great a range of massive to dainty outline. There was nothing inconsistent in this latter feature, for models such as those shown on pages 218 and 246 only reflect the changes in fashion which were taking place.

Early Georgian Mahogany Stool; circa 1735. Probably by Chippendale.

The former of these illustrations shows the strength and dignity which massive proportions permit of when properly treated, and the latter shows a blending of power and grace with the minimum of material.

There is nothing so misleading as a matter-of-fact perusal of the works of Chippendale, Robert and James Adam, Heppelwhite, and Sheraton. One leaves Chippendale's "Director" amazed to find that he has ignored the claw-and-ball masterpieces with which his reputation

Chippendale.

is so largely bound up, and wondering whether we shall ever find in materialised form the suggestions issued for purely commercial reasons and on which he is sometimes hastily judged; R. and J. Adam leave the reader with the impression that they were responsible for no mahogany furniture; Heppelwhite's book conveys the mistaken impression that he was lost to all sense of perspective and proportion; whilst Sheraton would seem to indicate that his finest drawing-room chairs were those in white and gilt.

The fact is that these literary ventures were scarcely more than glorified catalogues, and as such convey little authentic evidence on general achievement. It is far safer to judge the craftsman by his deeds than by his words, and, in the pages that follow, the various books will be treated as being of secondary importance only.

Early Models.

We usually find Chippendale models in mahogany, but many of the earlier pieces by this master are in walnut, whilst now and then rosewood entered into his schemes. It has been suggested that Chippendale's early efforts synchronised with the general introduction of mahogany, but this contention has only been urged tentatively, and must not be accepted literally. The author has recently added to his collection a mahogany gate-leg table of the period 1695-1705 which may well have been constructed before Chippendale was born.

Very few of the all-gilt models which were so common from the end of Queen Anne days can be definitely ascribed to Chippendale, and in view of this fortunate fact it is interesting to note that Chippendale's " Director " would lead us to believe that he favoured gilding above all other methods in decoration. The salient point which emerges from an examination of the early and doubtful run of designs is that Chippendale's leg-work combined grace, grip, and dignity when compared with that of his more ordinary contemporaries. Having learnt to

Very early pair of Mahogany Brackets by Thomas Chippendale, carved out of the solid block. Dating from the early inception of the rococo inspiration. When designing these Chippendale obviously had in mind the office of the Corbel in Architecture, and of its application as favoured in the Caryatides treatment of the Louis Quatorze School; circa 1735. Author's Collection.

appreciate this distinction, the collector will find the trend of evolution best traceable in the chair-backs of the day.

Chippendale was first employed in anglicising the surviving Dutch element bequeathed by the Queen Anne vogue. This he accomplished by reducing the hooped scroll-work to a minimum and by enlivening the splat-work. Within the hooped backs we sometimes find interlaced ovals in strap-work, whilst now and then the back-work was divided into compartments by pendent looped strap-work contained within a frame rather resembling a blunt heart in outline. With their hooping cut down, chairs emerged squarer, lower, and more sturdy-looking, though not yet typical of the recognised Chippendale order of later days. The top corners of backs were slightly rounded, and a series of experiments was carried out with a view to the production of a satisfactory cresting-rail.

With the exception of the upholstered chairs such as that illustrated on page 218, we seldom meet with plain straight lines crowning chair-backs by Chippendale, for the master was wont to break the line at the centre and at either end with projecting curls or rolled-over decoration. The nearest approach to the dead straight line came just before 1740, by which date the Dutch feeling had as often as not completely disappeared. At about the same period designers sometimes favoured top-rails describing a concave sweep, and with their ends as a rule scrolled over backwards.

After 1740 the majority of cresting-rails were convex in outline, and they described a more or less perfect serpentine swell. The chair shown on page 248 is representative of this phase of work, and it is, moreover, interesting as showing the survival of the inner scrolls of the earlier Dutch hooping which descend to right and left of the upper portion of the back-splat. Chippendale persevered with the development of this particular sweep until he brought it to perfection in designs such as that shown on page 246. The outline here resembles that of a cupid's bow, and this term as used to describe the consummated design owes its application to R. S. Clouston.

In the earlier designs armchairs showed a terminal decoration projecting beyond the point where the arm

Massive early Mahogany Tripod Table by Chippendale; circa 1735.

was met by its upright. An eagle's or a vulture's mask often figured in this position, but it must have proved ruinous to the clothes of the fair sex at any rate, and it was generally superseded by a less pronounced knob

Chippendale.

or finial scroll, which was again reduced as the French fashion came to be closely portrayed. Our illustration on page 245 shows an example of this modified arm finish. In the country-made furniture the projecting arm finials

Lighter early Mahogany Tripod Table by Chippendale; circa 1740.
Author's Collection.

were employed right through the fifties. The French finish showed a knuckle, with a taper below it at the top of the support, and running away from it towards the back-upright. The arm-support raked or swept backwards, and the curved arm was frequently padded to within two or three inches of the knuckle-end when the chair-back was upholstered. Such models were thoroughly practical, and gracefully decorated with carved acanthus foliage or similar detail they presented a refined appearance.

Hints for the Collector.

These few points may help the collector to follow the progress of craftsmanship during the years in which Chippendale was forcing his way to the front, and the individual who renders himself conversant with the best compositions in the chair-work of the period 1735-1750 will soon possess a good general idea of Chippendale technique in the other paths of cabinet-making.

Careful study, comparisons, and examinations of authentic and doubtful pieces, and, above all, instinct, enable us to recognise those factors which point towards Chippendale parentage of early designs. The manner in which the master's leg-work gripped the floor, his control over the members in a combination, and his brilliant placing of well-cut detail are at times unmistakable, and so it follows that we can sometimes identify his pure, if prehistoric, efforts as certainly as we can place his later and recorded work.

And now, having dwelt on the somewhat obscure phase of work from which Chippendale so successfully emerged, we enter on a more definite field, and are enabled to pursue our studies with certain data to guide us.

Biographical.

There were three Thomas Chippendales—father, son, and grandson—all of whom in succession were employed in one form or another of decorative art. Of Worcestershire origin, the first Chippendale earned a considerable local reputation, and, encouraged thereby, decided to remove to London, there to adventure his career in the wider sphere which the metropolis afforded. A carver, and doubtless a joiner too, Chippendale senior is reputed to have been a first-rate hand in picture-frame work, whilst some evidence which R. S. Clouston has adduced points almost conclusively to his having produced good furniture in Worcestershire before he left that county on his new enterprise. It is probable that the second Chippendale, who subsequently rendered the name famous, was born during the reign of Queen Anne, and that he was brought to London by his father between 1720-1725.

It may be urged that his influence would hardly have been felt during the fourth decade of the century if his house had been of such recent establishment, but the Chippendales brought no mean reputation with them, and the state of the craft, if we are to believe what Langley wrote in 1739, was so parlous that new workers would have been welcomed and at once assured of a fair field.

The second Chippendale was reared amidst surroundings well calculated to develop latent talent. His father was a skilled craftsman, and doubtless inculcated the theory and practice of design and execution in the boy's mind, and if we look at our illustration on page 229 both the outline and detail which would have appealed to young Chippendale lay ready to hand. The pair of carved wood frames, of which one is here depicted, date from the closing phases of the seventeenth century, and might well have fallen from the hand of the elder Chippendale. The decoration resembles much of that seen later on Chippendale's cabinet-work, whilst the outer contour is suggestive of the crowning rail to Chippendale chairs.

We lose touch with Chippendale père after his arrival in London, but we see the fruits of his training in young Chippendale's achievements between 1735-1750.

In her "English Furniture Designers of the Eighteenth Century" Miss Constance Simon has told us that "on 19th May, 1748, a marriage is recorded in the parish register of St. George's Chapel, Mayfair, between Thomas Chippendale and Catherine Redshaw, of St. Martin-in-the-Fields," and also that "at Christmas, 1749, Chippendale (II.) took a shop in Conduit Street, Long Acre, and in 1753 removed to the larger premises, No. 60, St. Martin's Lane." Chippendale would assumedly have been between thirty and forty years of age at his marriage, and the prosperity which warranted his settling down and opening larger premises was probably also leading him to collect material for the preparation of his book.

Miss Constance Simon quotes the *Gentleman's Magazine* for 5th April, 1755, as follows:—"A fire broke out in the workshop of Mr. Chippendale, a cabinet-maker, near St. Martin's Lane, which consumed the same, wherein were the chests of twenty-two workmen." We do not know whether these craftsmen were carvers or upholsterers, or whether a number of workmen saved their belongings, but it is evident that the designer had an important establishment by this date, for a good proportion of the commissions entrusted to eighteenth-century designers were "put out" as a general practice, and Chippendale had quite conceivably as much work under his supervision outside his workshop as within it.

One of a pair of Carved Wood Frames, circa 1775, of English make, either by Chippendale's Father or by one of his school. Author's Collection.

Chippendale.   231

Miss Constance Simon further quotes the *Public Advertiser* for 10th Feb., 1766, as follows :—" Whereas by the Death of Mr. James Rannie, late of St. Martin's Lane, Cabinet Maker and Upholder, the partnership between him and Mr. Thomas Chippendale dissolved at his death, and the Trade will for the future be carried on by Mr. Chippendale on his own account."

There is nothing to lead us to suppose that Rannie had other than a sleeping interest in the business, and the fact that Chippendale now began to lose touch with his patrons is probably due to several causes. In the first place, competition had now become acute, and Chippendale had already exploited most available schemes; secondly, Adam influence was at work, and the public were being enticed by the new teachings; and, thirdly, Chippendale was probably taking life more easily, resting on his laurels, and gradually leaving the helm at St. Martin's Lane. The writer considers that the last of these reasons largely accounts for the decline in designs entirely characteristic of the second Chippendale.

To those who have studied the man, our designer appears as an artist; to those who have studied his book he emerges as an enterprising man of business; and both aspects are correct, for to taste he added commercial acumen. In whatever vein he found the public he met it half-way, catering for the wants, anticipating the requirements, of the nation. He handled Queen Anne memories cleverly, he culled with taste from the classic or the Louis Quatorze, eliminated the baneful teachings of the Style Regence, and made his name largely through pleasing translations of the Louis Quinze. He excelled Sir William Chambers, fresh home from the East, in the interpretation of Chinese embellishment, and, lastly, gave expression to the best Gothic work produced by our mahogany school.

Between the years 1765-1770 a style quite foreign to anything Chippendale had accomplished or attempted was being introduced by Robert Adam to the delight of the public. Keen business man that he had been, Chippendale, had he still been actively engaged in *designing*, would certainly have published fresh suggestions to feed the new taste. As he failed to do this and "Chippendale" furniture lost its individuality in the sixties, it would appear that Chippendale *and Co.*, Chippendale and Haig, and Haig and Chippendale were content to build furniture to the order of such designers as the Adams, Seddon, Sons and Shackleton, or Sheraton.

In her "English Furniture Designers of the Eighteenth Century" Miss Constance Simon tells us: "The exact year of the death of Chippendale (II.) has been ascertained for the first time from the following entry in the burial register of St. Martin's Church—' 1779, November 13, Thomas Chippendale'; and again, ' On the death of Thomas Chippendale (II.) his eldest son succeeded to the business.' The third Thomas Chippendale entered into partnership with Thomas Haig, a Scotsman, who had been bookkeeper to James Rannie, and also one of his executors." Again Miss Constance Simon writes: "According to the directories the firm from 1779-1784 was styled Chippendale and Haig, but in 1785 Haig appears as the senior partner. Haig withdrew from the firm in 1796. . . . In 1814 Chippendale opened a shop in the Haymarket, No. 57, and for four years carried on the old St. Martin's Lane business simultaneously with the new venture. In 1821 he removed to 42, Jermyn Street. . . . The will [Chippendale

Chippendale.

III.'s] was proved by Sarah Wheatley on 28th January, 1823."

The third Thomas Chippendale did not possess the power and business ability which his father had evinced; he did little to add to the reputation of Chippendale furniture, and in no sense can he be treated as one of the great eighteenth-century *designers*. When " Chippendale " is used as a generic term to signify a certain style in furniture we refer to the distinctive creations of the second, or great, Thomas Chippendale. As the second Thomas Chippendale relaxed his hold on the helm, the business became more and more akin to that of the cabinet-maker who is not self-reliant in matters of design.

Chippendale's Status.

There have been such varying conceptions of Chippendale's early status in the arts and crafts that we have to consider under what branch of the applied arts he launched himself on the road to fame. He might have been a carver, a cabinet-maker, a joiner, or a journeyman jack of all trades but master of none. The last-named may be swept aside, for, in the words of R. S. Clouston, " We have only to carefully compare Thomas Chippendale's work with that which was going on around him to see that in furniture he was the master-mind of his time."

In Redgrave's " Dictionary of Artists " Chippendale was described as a joiner; but R. S. Clouston, in commenting on this, thinks his designation should have been that of a carver. Redgrave was probably quite correct, for the position in which joiners, carvers, and cabinet-makers then stood to one another has materially changed. The term carver rather implies a man who decorates a given design, but although Chippendale and his father could both doubtless carve brilliantly, they were artist-craftsmen of a more comprehensive order. If Chippendale had been classified as a cabinet-maker nobody would have raised the point, but on looking into the matter we find joiners were held to be superior to cabinet-makers. On 20th May, 1740, B. Langley wrote of cabinet-makers that they " were no more than spurious Indocible Chips; *expelled by Joiners*. . . . 'tis a very great Difficulty to find one in Fifty of them; that can make a Book-Case, &c., indispensably true . . . *without being obliged to a Joiner, for to set out the work;* and make his Templets to work by." The soundness of Chippendale's work points to his having studied his theory of construction and composition under the joiner, who was apparently the most trustworthy fountain of knowledge at that time. Again, if Langley's report on the merits of the cabinet-makers and joiners of his day was correct—and we have no reason to suppose that it was otherwise—Chippendale would have elected to identify himself with the latter branch of craftsmen, for his dicta would have carried greater weight with practical workmen. The reproach which Langley had hurled at craftsmen in the cabinet-making branch was swept aside by 1750, and it was Chippendale who chiefly brought about this happy consummation.

The great designer added carving to the other accomplishments making up his stock-in-trade, but he was grounded in all branches of cabinet-making and design under his father, and he would have preferred the comprehensive style of " joiner," with its implied mastery over the technique of composition and construction, to the less weighty designation of a mere carver. Chippendale set a very high standard of knife and chisel work to his employees; but had he restricted himself to this particular

Chippendale.

line of work he would have been glorifying existing patterns rather than regenerating the whole spirit and essence of English design.

Chippendale furniture is always characterised by the best of carving, it is true, but many craftsmen would have been competent to produce such work under the designer's tuition and superintendence. Where Chippendale made history was in the realm of constructive outline.

CHAPTER IX.
Thomas Chippendale.

The Artist-Craftsman.

So much for the family history in brief, and we can readily understand why, when "Chippendale" is spoken of, the reference is to the furniture of 1735-1770, when the great Chippendale held sway. Chippendale's galleries became the rendezvous of men of art and letters. The fashionable world used to foregather there and pass the time of day, seeking advice in matters pertaining to decoration, giving commissions, or gleaning new ideas from the masterpieces, which they were shown in finished or semi-finished condition.

In the year 1760, Chippendale was elected a member of the Society of Arts, and if the reader will but visit the headquarters of this institution in John Street, Adelphi, and examine the original autograph album, he will find our designer's signature side by side with those of such giants as Sir Joshua Reynolds, Edward Gibbon, Richardson, Dr. Johnson, David Garrick, Horace Walpole, the Earl of Bute, and John Wilkes (Miss Constance Simon), eloquent testimony of the esteem in which the erstwhile joiner was held by the most cultured in the land.

By reason of the advertisement it afforded him, Chippendale's book was an undoubted success commercially, though in our time he suffers heavily by having the work of incompetent copyists fathered upon him by those

Octagonal Fret-top Gallery Table, by Thomas Chippendale, showing down-turned shell border. These gallery tables, which are shown tilted and fixed in ordinary position, were intended for the display of knick-knacks, such as enamels, miniatures, and small pieces of silver, &c., the gallery keeping them within bounds. Finest period, circa 1745. Author's Collection.

who will not, or cannot, eliminate the chaff from the wheat. Judged by an artistic standard, the results achieved were perhaps but moderate. The designer could only devote odd intervals of leisure to his stupendous task, and, as we shall see, he was under great disadvantage, having a large and happy field of design at any rate partly barred to him.

In olden days, as now, a craftsman's patrons would raise objections to the reproduction of models which they had acquired, and Chippendale, in deference to this very natural feeling, refrained from publishing drawings of his greatest achievements. In these circumstances the very creations which had established our designer's reputation were those which from fear of indiscriminate reproduction he dared not embody in his book.

Chippendale was voyaging into new seas, and he had perforce to trim his sails, remembering the interests of his old customers while bidding for the patronage of a wider circle whose custom he coveted but whose tastes he did not necessarily respect.

Hedged in by these limitations, and egged on by a desire to satisfy those whose ambitions or predilections favoured the quest for novelty, Chippendale failed to do himself justice in this direction, and it is worthy of note that his volume seldom if ever gives an exact counterpart of any of his early and more sterling works. Chippendale's venture was, it must be owned, a purely commercial one, in which he strove to cater for the multitude, and we can safely say that of the designs included in his work many were but catch-pennies and did not receive his artistic endorsement. Listen, for example, to what he says when introducing some Chinese chair designs: " Nine chairs in the present Chinese manner, which I hope will improve that taste, or manner of work, it having yet never arrived to any perfection. Doubtless it might be lost without seeing its beauty. *As*

The conjunction of Gothic and claw-and-ball as seen here is rare, for when Chippendale was embracing the Gothic he had very generally discontinued the use of the earlier footwork; period 1750-1760.

it admits of the greatest variety, I think it the most useful of any other." Of a " sopha," he tells us : " If well executed by an ingenious workman, it can't fail of giving content." Of some tables : " Will look neat if well executed." Again, in referring to tables from his designs: "If made by a skilful workman, and of fine wood, will give great satisfaction." Of a cabinet, he tells us: "The design is perhaps one of the best *of its kind*, and would give me great pleasure to see it executed, as I doubt not of its making an exceeding genteel and grand appearance." Referring to a bookcase: "This, properly made, will look well."

We can easily read between the lines here: the tradesman is commending that which the artist is damning with faint praise.

Chippendale, as we shall see later on, always referred to his vocation as an art, and he constantly strove to elevate the profession he adorned. A large amount of the success he achieved must be attributed to his realising the exalted position which the decoration of the home should occupy, and to the common sense he displayed in borrowing and adapting from the many sources which his erudition enabled him to tap.

There were over 300 subscribers to Chippendale's book, and we can well imagine the reputation which this great artist had won when we scan the list of their names, amongst which we find those of the Dukes of Beaufort, Hamilton, Kingston, Norfolk, Portland, the Duchess of Norfolk, the Marquis of Lothian, the Earls of Chesterfield, Hopton, Halifax, Morton, Northumberland, the Countess of Shaftesbury, and Lords Clifford, Delawar, Elphinston, Faversham, Guildford, Guernsey, Montford, &c. Besides these, baronets, knights, and gentle folk galore; but—and it is a large "but"—the fact which strikes us most is the wide circle from which subscribers to this expensive work were drawn—upholsterers, or "upholders," cabinet-makers, carpenters, watchmakers, carvers, booksellers, joiners, surgeons, painters, architects, plasterers, jewellers, engravers, enamellers, bricklayers, chemists, founders, frame-makers, merchants, organ-makers, and professors of philosophy, figure amongst the original units making up the subscription, and they hailed from all parts of England, from Scotland, Ireland, and Wales.

For some reason, York seems to have given the best provincial support; whilst in the booksellers' trade we find Francis Swan taking twelve copies of the work. These facts speak for themselves, and whatever verdict or criticism we in our poor judgment pass, it is evident that by 1750 Chippendale was recognised by high and low alike as an inimitable genius, and this at a time when true artistic perception was at a vastly higher level than we can claim for it to-day.

The early illustrations have been selected to show the varying phases of Chippendale's work leading up to and during the so-called "Louis Quinze" period; that is to say, whilst the designer was building and setting the seal on his reputation. Some of the gallery-tables are shown in two positions, as they were destined to fulfil a double function—primarily to house bric-à-brac when open, secondarily to furnish a corner when tilted. In this latter position they look very handsome, facing the room from the angle they stand in. The bulk of the finer examples had tops that tilted or revolved at the owner's will.

Grades in Eighteenth-Century Furniture.

There were approximately three grades of furniture made by the eighteenth-century masters, and, broadly speaking, these were (1) for the aristocracy and a few of

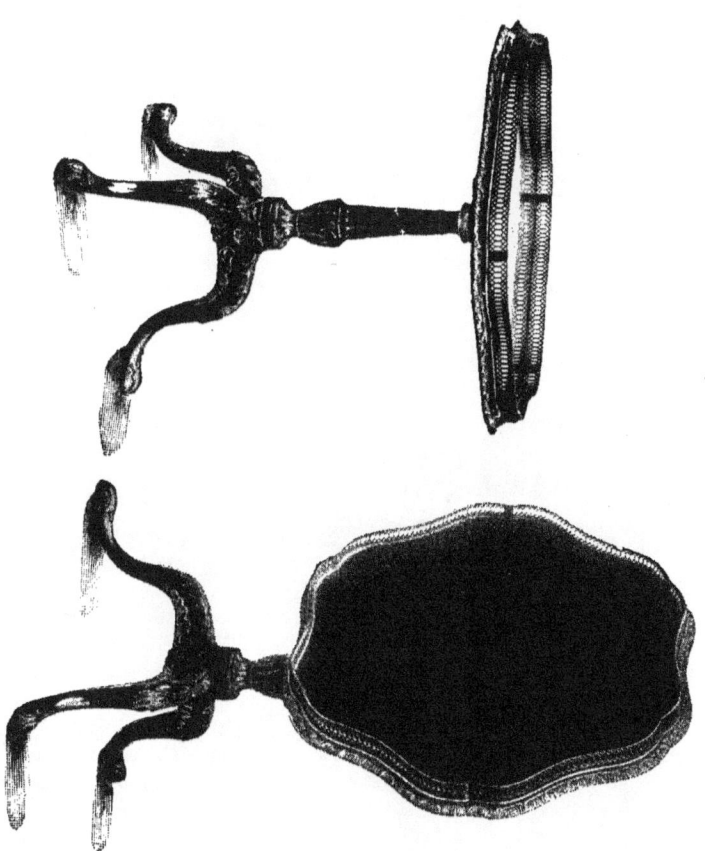

Chippendale Carved and Shaped Gallery-Table: period 1755. Author's Collection.

the merchant princes; (2) for the well-to-do upper middle classes; and (3) for those less favoured in this world's goods—a yeoman's quality we may call the last-named in the country districts. The chairs illustrated on this

Class I.—Exceptional Armchair by Thomas Chippendale; early period of the Louis Quinze inspiration. Period, about 1745. Author's Collection.

and the three following pages convey a fair, if approximate, idea of the calibre and treatment to be found in these different grades. The first class united beauty of outline and decoration, which latter it must be owned was sometimes overdone; the second relied on outline with plainer decoration; whilst the third possessed more rugged qualifications.

Now, the upper classes had homes already filled with oak or walnut furniture, and when new penates had to be acquired, they frequently placed their orders in France, the fashionable home of elegant taste. The middle

Class II.—Light Drawing-room Chair, relying mainly on beauty of outline for its effect; period, 1750-5. One of three in Author's Collection.

classes, on the other hand, were freely leavened with Quakerism, and, though they could have aspired to the best masterpieces of the cabinet-maker had their views permitted it, they were necessarily content with little or no outside decoration or show when furnishing their homes.

Thomas Chippendale. 247

So we have it the very classes which might have commissioned the best of English work, failed frequently to avail themselves of it: the one from an imperfect appreciation perhaps of what their countrymen could do when given a free hand; the other debarred from enjoying its use in conforming to the dictates of conscience.

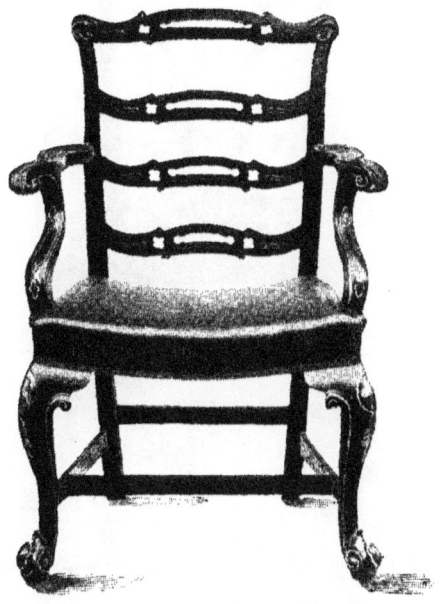

Class III.—Rare conjunction of Ladder-back and Cabriole leg. The front and side stretchers are additions. Period, 1755.

Added to this there was an appalling wastage of such gems as survived during the first three-quarters of the nineteenth century, a period during which vandalism and bad taste ran riot in a country where previously good and artistic feeling had generally obtained. We need look no further than these varying causes when asked to account for the rarity and intrinsic value of such few exquisite specimens as the ages have handed down to us.

Dining-room Chair by Thomas Chippendale, Yeoman's quality. Mahogany; period, 1740.

Chair Detail.

Chippendale discarded stretcher-work from those chairs which showed the French style of leg, but he adhered to it in the case of his early square-legged models and throughout his Chinese and Gothic phases. Chairs such as those shown on pages 245 and 246 would never have had stretcher-work originally; but, as in the case of the model shown on page 247, it may have been subsequently added to strengthen leg-work which had become rickety.

Collectors highly prize such specimens as that seen on page 246, on account of the decorated shaping to the front and sides of the seat-frame. Where this embellishment was employed the model was generally of exceptional, even if of plain, quality.

Designs of other Schools.

There were cases, though these are seldom met with, where Chippendale adopted designs clearly reminiscent of other schools or vogues, without stamping them with any distinguishing mark of his own personality in the shape of characteristic decoration. A case in point is found in the little "wig"- or basin-stand shown at page 250. This, though it harks back to the Late Queen Anne in its curvilinear treatment and foot-moulding, was published as a model in the designer's book of 1754. Many a time and oft did Chippendale reproduce this dainty little gem, yet only on the rarest occasions does the "hall-mark" of its parentage appear, probably because the artist saw its charms, and realised the doubtful advantage of taking the eye away from outline in favour of clever carving.

Now, these little stands were furnished with basins and ewers that fortunately give us the date of the examples which they grace. The earliest of these porcelains were of the "Famille rose" or late "Famille verte" period, and date back to the Chinese times of Yung-tching, 1723, or a year or two earlier. The vast bulk, however, were made in the succeeding reign—that of Kien-lung (1736-1796)—whilst those of Worcester origin, for instance, saw the light between 1751-1780.

The stands were necessarily light, and often toppled over, when, of course, fresh china of a later date was obtained to replace the shattered original set. Such posthumous

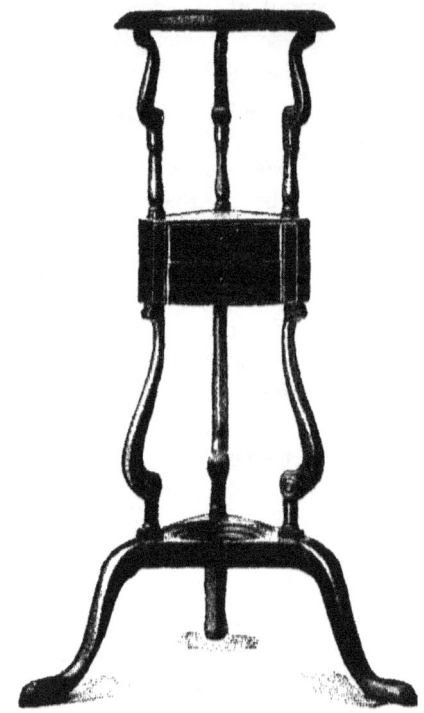

Early "Wig"- or Basin-stand in Mahogany. Author's Collection.

specimens are, comparatively speaking, without interest, as they establish nothing as to the age of the furniture enclosing them. Usually of mahogany, these stands may be found in other wood, such as oak and fruit-tree woods;

Thomas Chippendale.

but the better-class examples are almost invariably found in the first-mentioned timber.

Now, we have seen that these stands go back to 1720 or so; in other words, their introduction nearly synchronises

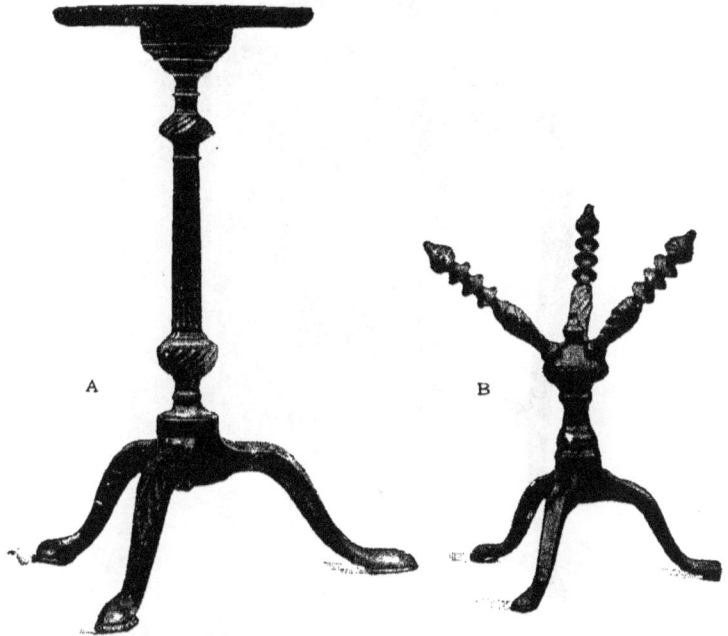

A, Small Tripod Table in Mahogany; circa 1735. B, Revolving Bowl- or Plate-stand in Mahogany; pre-Chippendale; circa 1715.

with the advent of mahogany. This medium, owing to its intense hardness and awkward grain, at first defied the efforts of the carver and his tools—so much so that at the initial stages of work in it absence of ambitious carving is a noticeable feature. Turned work was often met with, but in conjunction only with the minimum of knife or chisel garnishment. One cannot help noticing the peculiar aptness with which the cabinet-makers settled on mahogany for such pieces as these. The daintiness of outline

Lady's Writing-table in Mahogany, by Chippendale, modelled on a Louis Quinze design, and showing bombé outline; period, 1750-1755.

obviated the necessity of carving, their *bête noire*, whilst the strength of the wood served well the tender and frail model destined to be in constant use.

It is obviously correct to describe these little examples as basin-stands; but why "wig-stands"? They used to

The little Table previously illustrated, showing writing-slab pulled out and ready for use, whilst the fire-screen is raised.

stand in some ante-room convenient to the entrance-hall of the mansion; hither the "exquisite" was wont to repair, on arriving at the house, to adjust his periwig, after removing his hat. On the little platform under the basin, or within the drawer, rested powder and puff; on the second platform stood rose-water in a jug or ewer. The wig was dusted with powder, and the wearer, after sprinkling his hands to remove any traces of the process, was ready for entrance to boudoir or drawing-room.

If we turn for a moment to B, the little double tripod shown on page 251, we shall notice a small bowl-stand, with revolving top, of the same early period. Punch or pot-pourri found its home here, and again "turned" decoration prevails, with the material advantage afforded by the little ridges which serve to hold in place the plate or bowl placed on them. Models somewhat similar to this double tripod were used for wool-winding.

On the left of the double tripod, the tripod table A, some twenty years later in date, marks a distinct advance in decoration, and heralds-in the Chippendale era of carving; it might even be a piece from the hands of the great Chippendale when a young man.

In the lady's writing-table (page 252) we see again that Chippendale contents himself with producing a replica of a French model in the Louis Quinze style. It is one of a pair made by the master for a gentleman living in Sussex. The twins were separated, and now rest in different collections. Chaste in execution, this little piece furnishes an object-lesson to those who carp at Chippendale's powers of handling simple subjects. The next illustration (page 253) shows the fire-screen raised, and the little writing-slab pulled out. On the right is a drawer, fitted up for pens, ink, and stationery. It is amusing to note that a recent writer gives Thomas Sheraton the credit for this arrangement, yet Sheraton was certainly under five years of age when this piece saw the light.

Drawing-table in Mahogany, carried out to an architect's order, showing the artist's knowledge of the Early English and Perpendicular styles. Period, about 1755. Author's Collection.

By 1750 Chippendale was a master of practically all the mysteries of what may be called *multum in parvo* furniture; but it never appealed to him as strongly as it did to his successors, Heppelwhite, Shearer, and Sheraton, who developed it often at the expense of art and true usefulness.

The same Table open, showing the ingenious mechanical arrangement whereby the top is adjustable to the draughtsman's requirements.

Chippendale's mechanical knowledge was far-reaching; but, reading between the lines, he thought but lightly of the Jack-in-the-box school of boudoir and bed-sitting-room furniture: he seems to have been satisfied with placing on record his familiarity with what there was worth knowing or introducing in this direction, and there leaving the cult. So it follows that we only find here and there a specimen—always a gem, bearing witness to his power.

In the drawing-table (page 256) we have probably the most beautiful and ingenious example of the "Jack-in-the-box" vogue which has been handed down to us. Built by Chippendale to the order of a London architect, it is of exquisite form and mechanical construction, equally suitable for a draughtsman of 5ft. or 6ft. in height, being readily adjustable, and as sound to-day as when first made in 1755. Doubtless as a compliment to its future owner the designer imparted an architectural feeling to it —viz., Gothic. The legs are formed by a cluster of columns in a quatrefoil group, and may be classed as Perpendicular; the mouldings in the middle and under the entablatures are Early English, as also are those at the base, these latter showing the distinctive water-hollow. The moulding at top, known generally as "gadroon," is Classic; whilst there is a touch of Eastern art imparted by the six brackets of Chinese feeling. Shaped in front, the body all the way round is of graceful pierced work, almost resembling fine lacework.

The next illustration shows the action of the table when ready for use, a triumph of the designer's and the cabinet-maker's skill. Curiously enough, this same contrivance is claimed by the before-mentioned author as another feather in Sheraton's cap, though Sheraton's is an altogether inferior application of the principle. Sheraton, as a matter of fact, was, as already stated, a mere child when this table was being completed.

The Tripod as an Adjunct.

The tripod has been known as an adjunct to furniture from time immemorial. The pagans of old used it, and, in one form or another, most of the masters of the eighteenth century employed it in their designs for small

Early Chippendale Table, showing the secondary columnar swell. The top was inlaid with burr walnut, probably to a specific order, or as an experiment with some fine wood left over from Queen Anne days. Period, 1730. Author's Collection.

tables, candle-stands, flower-stands, or fire-screens. It was not thought much of in England until the end of the Queen Anne period, and only one master—Chippendale—realised its full beauty and possibilities.

In Sheraton's book "The Cabinet-maker and Upholsterer's Drawing Book" we find the following note:—
"Anciently the word tripod used to be applied to a kind of sacred three-footed stool, on which the heathen priests were seated to receive and deliver their oracles; from which we may learn how time alters words."

Gilded tripods were known in Italy, France, England, and other countries in pre-Chippendale days, and they were fairly common in England during Queen Anne's reign. Such models were gaudy, and lacked the delicate symmetry which characterised Chippendale's productions at a later date.

Following an earlier custom greatly favoured in Queen Anne days, Chippendale at first introduced a secondary swell on his tripod column, such as that seen on page 259, but he soon recognised that this treatment diverted the eye from the main bulb, broke the flow of the overlying column, and served no artistic purpose. Under his treatment the superfluous excrescence was reduced, and then altogether done away with.

The main swell retained was usually the tulip-shaped bulb of the Renaissance, or the later vase-shaped variety, and our illustrations on pages 237 and 243 show these typical details underlying the corrected columnar work.

Chippendale designed some beautiful dumb-waiters resting on typical tripods. Three trays of diminishing sizes revolved round a central shaft rising as a column from the tripod, but treated by the carver as three small superimposed columns—one to each tray, and tapered to suit the proportions of the trays which they severally supported.

The fine tripod—and when we say fine, we mean the really high-class and artistic specimen—was a thing peculiar to Chippendale; he seemed never to tire of adding to his list of triumphs in this direction, and if we could examine fifty or even more examples of his

Very fine Tripod Table by Thomas Chippendale, rather later than the specimen shown at page 237. Shell discontinued in favour of foliated work standing up in strong relief. Note lighter appearance of ankles to tripod, and very rare shape of foot. Mahogany; circa 1745. Author's Collection.

little gallery-tables we should find each with some distinctive mark of its own. Nobody entered the lists against Chippendale in this direction, and no other school lent itself to so happy a rendering of the theme as did his.

Heppelwhite, it is true, used a tripod "of sorts" as a foundation for very light and dainty little occasional tables and pole-screens; but here he would never have claimed to vie with Chippendale. The Adam brothers harked back to the rendering in favour with the heathen of old when handling this subject, or to a pseudo-classic interpretation of it, anticipating the vogue which English Empire and late Sheraton would affect in after years. Thomas Sheraton, in his early days, when producing his best effects, was rather less happy than Heppelwhite on the few occasions when he essayed a stilted effort based on the latter's designs.

It is interesting to note that the secondary swell surmounting the main swell or bulb to the column, which was much valued in Queen Anne's time, began to fade away, as a general rule, under Chippendale's influence. When it appears in this master's work we expect to find other features showing the example to be an early one. We give (on page 263) an excellent example as an illustration of such early "points." The claws and feet gripping the ball are those favoured by Chippendale, as an alternative to the lion's claw, when at the beginning of his career. The main swell or bulb is a replica of Italian Renaissance detail, known to Englishmen in Elizabethan times; whilst the carving on the knees is of primitive conception and execution. Usually known as lattice or diamond work, it is mechanical in appearance, though relieved somewhat by a foliated frame. The secondary garnishment breaking the fluted column is beginning to assume less aggressive proportions, to disappear as our later examples are discussed.

Thomas Chippendale.

Here we may note one unfortunate feature of these tables when looked at from a constructional point of view: the legs were of necessity cut so that the grain of the mahogany ran across the curve above the ankle.

Early "Pie-crust," "Raised Ribbon," or "Dish-top" Chippendale Table. Circa 1740.

Sooner or later the majority of tables were put down with a jar on one foot, instead of evenly on the three, and then a split occurred. There seems to have been one common way of dealing with this mischief, which has come to be known as "ironing up." Briefly described, this consisted of strengthening the offending member with an iron strap, which, often let into the wood, followed the curve of the leg, losing itself at the foundation upon which the column rises. It is only

Table showing scrolled acanthus and wheel decoration of gallery, with rose and ribbon carving around the bed of the top. Period, 1750-1755. Author's Collection.

fair to say that this process was so carried out as to be inconspicuous. Sometimes, though the legs remained sound, the purchase of their stride created at their common junction a certain amount of "play"; this was dealt

Thomas Chippendale.

with in a similar manner by the application of short straps crossing one another approximately in X-formation.

The same Foliated Gallery-Table tilted to decorate a corner whilst occupying the minimum of space in the room. Author's Collection.

It is doubtful whether a more suitable home for the little snuffboxes and small articles of fine bijouterie (so popular in the eighteenth century) than the table shown on pp. 264 and 265 could be conjured up by the artistic eye. These little gems had to be picked up and opened for their whole beauty to be appreciated, so that a closed show-case or a cabinet did not do them justice. We can well picture a group of connoisseurs standing round this

"Peg-top" Chippendale Gallery-Table. Rim strengthened by brass band let in, a very rare process until 1795. Circa 1750.

table and examining inlaid, painted, chased, or enamelled boxes of the Louis Quatorze or Louis Quinze school—boxes which are to-day worth a ransom—and incidentally appreciating the table upon which they rested.

Thomas Chippendale.

Faked Table-Tops, &c.

Where carved decoration stands out in relief amidst sunken surface beds, as in the case of the table-tops shown on pages 224 and 225, it is of the utmost importance that the recessed surface should show

Plain-Top Table by Thomas Chippendale. French style of whorled feet. Circa 1755.

"original condition." Many plain and heavy table-tops have had the wood worked down in the centre, and a decorated border added with the old worn wood left in relief in the new edge garnishment. Under this style of manipulation the more prominent surfaces rising from the faked work may present all the appearance of antiquity, but the surrounding bed from which the excavations have been carried out will, of course, have been disturbed. If, therefore, the old skin in the field of flat and sunken work has been removed, collectors will do well carefully to scrutinise the whole of the surrounding embellishment. In the genuine example the underneath parts of the projecting detail on models such as those seen on pages 224 and 225 will show pronounced patination; but where the decoration, as in the table shown on page 261, is carved out of the plain, solid round, this safeguard is wanting.

Wine-Tables and Gouty-Stools.

A suggestion of cause and effect is furnished by the wine-tables and gouty-stools which Chippendale used to create. In the majority of instances wine was taken round the dining-tables of the day, but occasionally we find small models which were specifically designed for the use of one or two cronies who wished to while away an hour by cracking a bottle. Such an example is seen in our illustration on page 269.

The decoration on this little piece is peculiarly sharp and fine, the centre of its top being carved with vine leaves and grapes enclosing a reserved circle for the receipt of the bottle or decanter. Chippendale's love of the C-scroll is again exemplified, for it is introduced around the top edging, and again twice on each of the tripod legs.

Openwork tripod columns such as this table carries are exceedingly rare, and we seldom see them in conjunction with models other than the very best. The coquillage round the outer rim of the top and the general outline and decoration on this specimen are thoroughly typical of

Chippendale's work of the period 1745-1755 in the so-called French style.

In after years the wine-table came to be a larger and plainer model, usually in horseshoe or semi-circular

Tripod Wine-Table; circa 1750. Author's Collection.

shape. Such tables had comparatively narrow tops, and would have accommodated a party of ten or more wine-bibbers, seeing that room was found for some members of the party within the inner curve of the horseshoe or half-moon described by the table-top.

Gouty-stools were adjustable and could be raised, tilted, or lowered at the will of the sufferer. They were generally quite plain, as the afflicted party did not feel inclined to receive company when laid up, and even if the invalid had cared about display, the decoration would have been obscured or hidden by the cushions or wraps which rested over the framework.

The Use of the C- and S-Scrolls.

Chippendale was peculiarly devoted to the C-scroll and used to introduce it in large, medium, or small-sized form on the prominent surfaces of his designs. This foible was so strongly marked that collectors have come to regard it as a conceit, thinking that the master may have employed the first initial of his name as a semi-signature.

An early instance of this work is seen on the brackets shown on page 222. It will be noticed again in the decorated edge work to the table shown on page 224, throughout the scheme on the chair illustrated on page 281, in the bracket work to the table on page 284, and on the brackets appearing on page 275. It is introduced with great prominence on the chair-back seen on page 309; whilst in our illustration on page 335 we see the C-shaped under-brackets which Chippendale so often employed on tables, stands, cabinet-frames, and to decorate the corner junctions of square chair and settee legs with the overlying seat-framing.

It will be remembered that the prevalence of C- and S-shaped scrolls during the Restoration period was most marked, but the use of the S-scroll proper had been

Thomas Chippendale.

almost discontinued in Chippendale's best period. We now and then find a small decorated bracket crowning a chair- or table-leg which suggests the S contour, but we seldom meet with a specimen in which it figures so pronouncedly as in the bedstead of which a Plate is given. Here the S is introduced twice in the cresting to the head-piece, and in modified form again in the pierced work setting off the cornice.

CHAPTER I.
Chinese Chippendale.

Its Origin and History.

MANY are the amusing remarks which come one's way when showing " Chinese " Chippendale to those whose knowledge of the antique is limited or practically non-existent. More than once the writer has been greeted with : " How clever of them! I thought they only used bamboo," " Did they really make that in China ? " or " I wonder how it got over here." It comes as a disappointment, or even as a personal grievance, when such people hear that the chair or the table was fashioned in England and by Englishmen.

It has been generally accepted that " Chinese " or " Chambers " Chippendale came on the scene when Sir William Chambers (then twenty-nine years of age) landed in England, in 1755, with the glamours of the Celestial Empire permeating his being. Absolutely distinct in reality, " Chinese " and " Chambers " Chippendale have been held to be analogous.

Many years ago the writer combated this erroneous supposition; but it was not until 1903, when he was writing on the subject for the Paris edition of the *New York Herald*, that it was tacitly admitted that Chippendale breathed the spirit of the East in English furniture as no Englishman before or since has ever done, and before he knew that such a young

Chinese Chippendale.

gentleman as William Chambers was in existence. William Chambers was born at Stockholm in 1726, and was educated at Ripon. At the age of eighteen he went out to the East as supercargo on one of the vessels of the Swedish East India Company. In following up this venture he visited and became conversant with various parts of the Chinese Empire, and, being clever with his pencil, he made elaborate and copious drawings of interesting buildings, &c.

The architecture of China burned itself into his soul, and, we may say, stayed with him as the predominant factor throughout his career. Unfortunately, Chambers, in appraising the value of Eastern art, forgot to discount the loss which it would suffer when transplanted into Western environment, and so we have it that many a charming little pagoda which nestled in a Celestial garden seemed commonplace when raised at Kew. Before returning home to settle down in 1755, he found time to study the teachings of the Renaissance in Rome and Paris.

In England, from a material point of view, his career was brilliant, for he was appointed tutor to George III., and subsequently, on his espousing the architect's profession, he was appointed architect to the Royal Family, and honoured with knighthood. In addition to this, he was one of the founders of the Royal Academy in 1768, being elected as Treasurer to that body. Weighed in the balance of the ages—the keenest sifter of wheat from chaff—it would be useless to maintain that he attained to any merit beyond the limits of mediocrity; but he had power, and was a man of many parts, though sadly lacking in discrimination.

Two years after his return from his travels—in 1757, in fact—he published "Designs of Chinese Buildings,

T

Furniture, Dresses, Machines, and Utensils," and this work undoubtedly gave impetus to a fashionable taste, which, as the writer hopes presently to show, was already firmly established. This publication was followed by another, viz., a "Treatise on Civil Architecture," whilst in 1772 he issued "A Dissertation on Oriental Gardening." Perceiving the co-relation between architecture and cabinet-making existing in all well-conceived decorative schemes, he essayed the character of cabinet-maker in order that his decorative efforts in the Chinese school might be pressed home to a logical conclusion. In this phase it is kindest to draw the veil over a series of badly-constructed and stilted plagiarisms of an art which was perhaps better adapted to Eastern climes.

In 1904 a book was written on old English furniture in which the following paragraph appears: "It only remains to state here that a noted English designer, Thomas Chippendale, became greatly interested in Chambers's 'Chinese' extravagances, studied them, and came to the conclusion that, in the proper hands, something might be done in that direction. By its admission to the homes of Royalty, a certain demand seemed to have been created for such work. Chippendale consequently took them in hand."

This statement fairly reflects the views generally obtaining amongst collectors less than a decade ago, but which the present writer has from first to last striven to refute. In the article referred to earlier in this chapter the author adduced evidence in October, 1903, showing that Chambers's influence was perceptible *only after 1755*, when the young architect had returned from the East to practise in England, and that when he settled in this country a clearly defined taste for Chinese outline

Chinese Chippendale.

and detail had existed for a number of years. Chambers was a poor exponent but an ardent champion of Celestial art, and, as we shall presently see, he was mainly responsible for one phase only of this Eastern work in the cabinet-maker's craft.

We have already noticed that the cabriole leg was

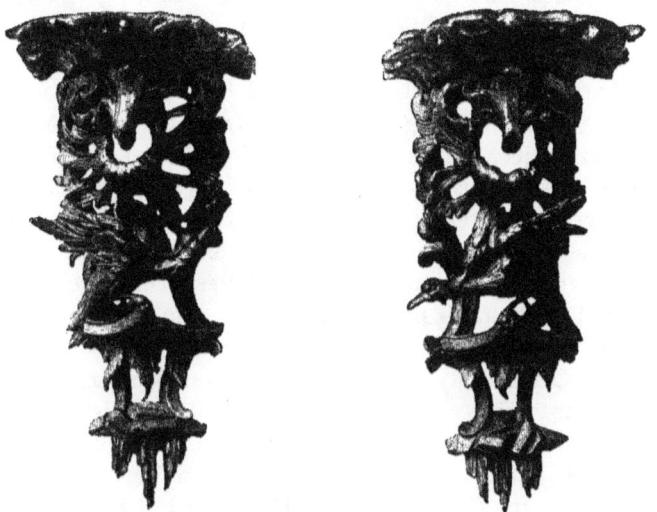

Pair of Brackets by Thomas Chippendale, in white wood, gilt, showing Louis Quinze and Chinese detail compounded; period, 1750.

brought from the East by the Dutch to be perfected under Queen Anne. Similarly, the early Dresden porcelains were governed largely by Chinese influence as to their modelling and decoration, whilst the lacquered ware, which we had first imported and subsequently endeavoured more or less successfully to reproduce, spread the taste for Oriental matter and design. We had been importing carved ivories, enamels, bronzes, porcelain, &c., from the East for a century when Chippendale, in 1754, the year before Chambers came into the arena, in submitting some Chinese chairs, premised "*which I hope will improve that taste or manner of work, it having yet never arrived to any perfection; doubtless it might be lost without seeing its beauty.*" When Chippendale wrote those lines he had evidently been studying Chinese *motif* thoroughly, and endeavouring to give pleasing interpretations of it.

In the 'forties Chippendale had been taking an item here, a detail or suggestion there, from Eastern models such as lacquer panels, and embodying selected matter in one or other of his selected fantasies. If we read between the lines, however, the passage just quoted shows the great designer as approaching the subject with some diffidence, and throughout his career Chinese furniture commended itself to his commercial rather than to his artistic nature. Thus we find Chippendale in 1754 recommending the Oriental style for its "usefulness because of the scope for variety which it affords." The artist shows through the tradesmen here—no words of eulogy as to the taste, but attention drawn to the promise of novelty held out by the Eastern order. The artist in Chippendale damned with faint praise that which the tradesman in him commended.

Prior to 1754 Chippendale had been drawing on the East to an increasing extent. In his earlier essays he contented himself with small detached suggestions, which in no way governed the models upon which he was at work. As time progressed he wove more and more of the exotic matter into his theme, and we find many models in which Chinese and Louis Quinze feeling are practically

Chinese Chippendale.

balanced. Soon after 1750 Chinese detail and contour very commonly *governed* such furniture as was in any way treated in the Eastern manner, and, after 1755 and until 1760, we find plagiarism of the East ousting all other ideas.

Chinese Chippendale Chair with Appliqué Fret Decoration.
Exceptionally fine; period, 1755-1760.

By 1760 the Gothic style was again growing into favour, and here an interesting phase of work meets the collector, who will find hybridised fretwork, &c., partly Gothic and partly Chinese. Chippendale continued to build purely Chinese models until the end of the 'sixties to the order of customers whose predilections pointed that way, but he evolved and pushed the sale of composite designs from approximately 1760, and he seems to have welded the two orders together pretty regularly when given carte blanche in designing. As the Gothic style gained in popularity the Chinese vogue decayed, and by 1765 the former had gained the ascendency. To the close of the 'sixties we find the isolated introduction of Oriental detail, and suggestions of the influence run into the 'seventies.

As we have already seen, Chippendale was not enamoured of the purely Eastern fashion, and he seems always to have been trying to tone down the clash of Eastern and Western styles by a more or less pronounced fusion between them. Thus we find in mahogany furniture alone the following combinations :—

Leading up to the Chinese style pure and simple:
  1. Floral work of Grinling Gibbons type cum Chinese.
  2. Classic architectural type cum Chinese.
  3. Louis Quinze cum Chinese.
  4. Flowing Chinese with exaggerations.
  5. Chinese of the Chambers type.

Receding from the Chinese style:
  6. Chinese cum Gothic.
  7. Gothic with a modicum of Chinese.

To these we must add such complications as those which arose when Chippendale blended Louis Quinze, Chinese, and Gothic together.

Sir William Chambers's Part.

We must now revert to Sir William Chambers, and follow the part which he played in connection with this

Eastern work. In 1744 Chambers left for the East
Indies at the age of eighteen. *But* in 1739 Batty Langley designed six large fretwork schemes, publishing them
in 1740, to meet the requirements of those appreciating
Chinese fashions (Plates 97, 98, 99, 100, 101, and 102,
" City and Country Builder's and Workman's Treasury of
Designs "). These designs were analogous to those
issued by Chambers seventeen years later.

In 1755 Chambers returned from the East to publish
his Oriental designs in 1757. *But* in 1754 Chippendale
published his "improved" Chinese designs in his
" Director," and Edwards and Darly " A New Book of
Chinese Designs." Both of these books showed that
their respective authors had made careful studies of such
Oriental matter as they considered suitable for adoption
in their craft.

Chippendale issued his designs hoping to "improve
the Chinese taste." Edwards and Darly's work speaks
for itself. The evidence that this Chinese phase of work
was existing long before Chambers entered the arena is
therefore complete.

Chambers's book tells us exactly where he took up
the threads of Oriental work, and it must be admitted
that he did not increase its reputation or adequately
represent its value. He gave many doubtless correct
drawings of fretwork, palings, &c., which he had
sketched in the East, but his renderings were laboured,
stilted, and lacking in the necessary rhythm. Obsessed
by Eastern ideas, he could not adapt matter or make
concessions as between Pekin and Kew. Grasping the
potentialities of Eastern design, he failed to materialise
its spirit when essaying to transplant it.

Chippendale, Johnson, Edwards and Darly, and

Ince and Mayhew all erred in giving exaggerated portrayals of Chinese garnishment, but it may be said that whereas the first-named of these designers failed most frequently owing to the freedom which he displayed in his

Chinese Chippendale Chair with Pierced Fret Decoration.
Very scarce; period, 1755-1760.

handling of matter, Chambers courted disaster by the cramped methods which he adopted.

It is more than probable that the life of the Chambers lattice and fret vogue was prolonged owing to fortuitous circumstances, for in 1756 the seven years' war with France commenced, and from that date, for a decade or so, French influence was submerged. It may

Chinese Chippendale.

have been only a coincidence that French teachings were generally overlooked for the currency of the war, but the manner in which we reverted to them shortly after the declaration of peace suggests that they may have been temporarily taboo.

A considerable number of specimens of mid-eighteenth-century furniture, built by our designers on Chinese

Chinese Chippendale Armchair, showing the wings set at a typical angle; circa 1755. Author's Collection.

lines, survive in poor condition. The fretwork has often been damaged or altogether broken away, and this is noticeably the case with the little corner brackets decorating the angles between legs and table-tops or chair-seats.

It must be remembered that this particular work is very readily imitated by the faker, and the collector who elects to have deficiencies made good should carefully see that the new work is brought as nearly as possible to the old and the latter left untouched. If left to their own devices workmen will often fill in the missing links, and then go over the whole model, reducing it to one resplendent level of uniformity. Quite recently the author was shown a gallery-table which would have commanded £200 in its broken condition, but which, after "treatment," was not distinguishable from the modern fakes, and would scarcely have drawn an offer of £20.

Warning Note to Prospective Buyers.

"Surface-condition" is often missing from Chinese Chippendale, this necessary adjunct having disappeared when the lacquer with which the model was originally covered was washed off. Lacquered furniture was considered to be especially suitable for bedrooms, where it met with heavy and somewhat bad usage, and, as a result of this, the collector will find many chairs and other specimens which have been scraped or washed and then repolished. The majority of renovated pieces bear a strong resemblance to the clever imitations which exist, and intending purchasers will be well-advised to bear in mind the facts laid down in our early chapter on faking.

The Fret- and Lattice-work Craze.

There can be little doubt that the craze for fret- and lattice-work obtaining in the 'fifties was fostered by a general demand for lightness. Between 1740 and 1755 Chippendale had reduced the weight of models by leaps and bounds, and the open work, which came so promi-

Chinese Chippendale.

nently on the scene after 1755 admitted of light and sketchy effects. Surface areas of plain wood were reduced and brightened at times by fretwork, which was rightly introduced on models intended primarily for the display of china. Similarly, applied frets livened up fields of mahogany which would otherwise have been left plain, and the treatment, when well ordered and restrained, showed satisfactory results. The fretwork on table-galleries, china cases, and hanging shelves, and the applied fret- or lattice-work on tallboys, grandfather clocks, and cornices, were peculiarly successful.

It is a striking fact that Chippendale should have beaten Chambers on the latter's own ground. Chambers had studied Chinese palings, frets, and lattices at first hand, whilst Chippendale had to make up for want of experience by the exercise of artistic imagination. The great designer rose to the occasion, for whereas Chambers frets were laboured if correct, Chippendale often achieved triumphs of rhythm and daintiness.

Chippendale's Chief Competitors.

The main competition which Chippendale had to face in the Chinese furniture of the 'fifties and 'sixties came from Edwards and Darly, Thomas Johnson, and Mayhew and Ince. We have already seen that Edwards and Darly published a book on Chinese Designs in 1754, and they, together with Johnson, were leading exponents of Louis Quinze or rococo cum Oriental work. Johnson published drawings in the late 'fifties, but his main publication came in 1761, when he issued what he was pleased to style his " One Hundred and Fifty New Designs."

R. S. Clouston found out an interesting fact in connection with this latter book, for it seems that one John Weale, at a much later date, reissued the book but little altered, under a different title, ascribing it to Chippendale, after having removed Johnson's name from the plates and substituted that of the more famous designer.

Small Fretwork Table, showing pierced tie surmounted by a flame. Chippendale, 1755-1760 (possibly Ince and Mayhew).

Johnson's numerous creations included as typical examples mirrors, pier and console tables, brackets, lanthorns, and candle-stands. His work can best be described as eccentric; the element of repose was lacking

Chinese Chippendale.

from it, and his suggestions were weird and exaggerated. Chippendale's power showed to least advantage in this particular phase of design, and he, together with Edwards and Darly, and Johnson, seems to have expected the public to condone the shortcomings of the designer in admiring the brilliancy of the carver.

Chippendale showed a certain amount of restraint at times, and his composition was more subtle and fluent. Johnson, on the other hand, favoured meaningless excess on almost every occasion. Edwards and Darly were not so ordered in their drawings as Chippendale, but they were scarcely so extravagant as Johnson.

If the truth were known, not one of these designers would be found to have been responsible for the whole of the designs they severally uttered. There is such a strong resemblance running through the drawings for certain articles of furniture that one sees the handiwork of hack draughtsmen, whilst engravers are known to have assisted one cabinet-maker after another.

The only possible defence open to the exponents of this unfortunate work lies in the fact that the public craved for it, and they as tradesmen had to meet the demand. However satisfactory such an excuse might prove to be in the case of Edwards and Darly, and Johnson, we might have expected Chippendale to have used his influence against the obnoxious style, and we can only imagine that the impending production of Edwards and Darly's designs drove him into a corner, and that, finding himself faced by the possible alienation of custom, he elected from commercial reasons to follow the trend of fashion.

If the craftsmen who were associated with Chippendale in filling orders for this hybrid work were his competitors, Ince and Mayhew, or, as they were sometimes styled, Mayhew and Ince, rose to be dangerous rivals. These cabinet-makers subscribed for the second edition of Chippendale's "Director" in 1759, and we can follow the hand of the great designer in much of their work and in their published designs. It is obvious that Ince and Mayhew also studied the drawings which Chambers had issued in 1757, and their style may be said to have been founded on the French and Chinese renderings of Chippendale, supplemented by the Oriental suggestions of Chambers.

Further than this, these cabinet-makers were, after Chippendale, the best exponents of the Gothic order in our mahogany school. As luck would have it their lot was cast in days of kaleidoscopic transitions, for, having appropriated the leg-contour and rococo detail of Chippendale, they had also to turn their attention to the Chinese vogue, as expressed by Chippendale and Chambers. With these materials they had barely evolved a partially-defined style of their own when the Gothic order claimed their attention. Under these conditions we find Ince and Mayhew furniture in (1) Louis Quinze, (2) Louis Quinze cum Chinese, (3) Chinese, (4) Chinese cum Gothic, (5) Gothic, (6) Louis Quinze, Chinese, and Gothic compounded, within the space of one decade.

Such types were submitted to the public in 1762, when Ince and Mayhew issued "The Universal System of Household Furniture," which contained between 300 and 400 designs. The designers doubtless suffered owing to the fact that their suggestions *re* the French and Chinese vogues came when the demand for such furniture had slackened.

Ince and Mayhew helped to popularise the Gothic

Chinese Chippendale.

order, and, to a lesser degree, they were again beholden to Chippendale in this particular direction. They were most successful when approximately conforming to Chip-

Fret Card-table by Mayhew and Ince. Finest period; circa 1760. This table is serpentine-shaped and shuts up on the concertina principle. In the collection of R. R. P. Hilton, Esq.

pendale outline, but introducing their characteristic frets and tracery for the embellishment of the designs. The similarity between the work of Ince and Mayhew and that of their mentor was at times very marked, and many little gallery and occasional tables, chairs and cabinets, &c., produced by his disciples are to-day attributed to Chippendale.

When endeavouring to depart from recognised contour Ince and Mayhew were less successful, but they evolved some danty schemes of pierced and cluster-leg work of a semi-distinctive character, whilst, like Chippendale, they designed many meritorious patterns of pierced and decorated stretcher work to set off chairs, small tables, and other models of the period 1755-1765.

One feature of their work is apt to be misleading to those who are seeking to diagnose furniture standing on the borderland of Chippendale, for they repeatedly embodied bold C-scrolls as angle brackets and elsewhere in their designs. The C was so popular with Chippendale that its presence on a chair or a table in prominent position has ere this been erroneously held to constitute a determining factor in favour of Chippendale authenticity.

In their " Universal System of Household [sic] Furniture " Ince and Mayhew described themselves as "Cabinet-makers and Upholders," 2. Broad Street, Golden Square, London; but in 1778 Causton gave them as "Cab Makers, Upholders, and Dealers in Plate Glass, Broad Street, Carnaby Market." In the same year Loundes described them as of Broad Street, Soho; whilst three years later Causton placed them at 20, Marshall Street, Carnaby Market. Baldwin's 1783 Directory mentioned them as occupying premises at Broad Street, Soho; whilst Loundes from 1784-1791 and Kent from 1792-1800 placed them at Marshall Street, Carnaby Market. In 1806 Kent recorded Mayhew's name alone,

Very fine Cluster-leg Chinese Chair, probably the work of Mayhew and Ince.

but in the Post Office Annual for 1807 Ince's name reappeared; and in 1810 the firm's address was given as at 47, Marshall Street, Carnaby Market.

Résumé.

Summarising the main points to be remembered in connection with mid-eighteenth-century work in the Chinese style, we must credit Batty Langley with early influence on the craft in the matter of fret- or lattice-work, but attribute the exaggerated application of this matter mainly to the influence of Chambers. Chippendale was the best blender of Oriental *motif* with models showing Louis Quatorze, architectural, or Louis Quinze feeling. Ince and Mayhew challenged his superiority in the last of these fields. Edwards and Darly achieved mediocre, and Johnson poor, because exaggerated and restless, results in the same direction.

A diagnosis of this rococo cum Chinese fashion is complicated because Darly, as an engraver, collaborated with the other designers in advancing the merits of this vogue.

Of the fret- and lattice-work applied to models showing more or less of Eastern contour, Chippendale was again the most successful exponent, with Ince and Mayhew as his runners up, and Chambers as his most soulless competitor.

In excluding Ince and Mayhew's claim to such models as that shown on page 284, we very possibly do them an injustice, but the pieces shown on pages 287 and 289 are almost undoubtedly theirs.

The pair of brackets shown on page 275 point to the authorship of Chippendale, owing to the comparative restraint which the designer has brought to bear as contrasted with the general run of Johnson's suggestions in the same realm. The bird which underlies the Louis Quinze portion of the work, and crowns the quota of Eastern matter, somewhat resembles the Hoo Hoo bird (held sacred in the East), which was supposed to take a particular interest in human affairs. Although generally described as " a sort of an eagle," it would bear more likeness to a hybrid between that bird and a stork. This ornithological freak was commonly portrayed in carving as a cresting to mirrors, &c., and there may have been some significance in its introduction over glasses, seeing that a watchful curiosity over mankind was held to be its leading attribute. By the end of the century the hybrid bird had disappeared in favour of a thoroughbred eagle.

The chairs seen on pages 277 and 280 are extremely interesting, for they show Chippendale outline enclosing mainly Eastern detail. In the back-splat of the specimen on page 280 we can trace the dawning of the Gothic. In the chair illustrated on page 281 Chippendale has made a concession to Chinese outline, but he has introduced considerable licence into his decoration of the backwork and wings.

CHAPTER XI.
Thomas Chippendale
(continued).

Card-Tables.

IN eighteenth-century homes the card-table seems to have been an indispensable adjunct, and all the cabinet-makers who come under our notice revelled in its production. Gambling was universal, and whether it was in the castle or the mansion games of chance were equally in favour as afternoon or evening pastimes.

In the days of Charles II. we know that charming little piquet tables were fashioned, but though whist was coming into popularity, the larger card-table, such as we now use, was of great rarity. Our forefathers seem to have used ordinary square or round dining-tables draped with heavy cloths, and if we refer to the woodcut illustrating Whist in " The Compleat Gamester " (published in 1674) we see a party playing the game round a table at which twelve people might well have dined.

Queen Anne's reign saw a great development in the matter of card-tables, which then very generally assumed the proportions now in fashion, and it is worthy of note that the card-table of two hundred years ago, in addition to being much more graceful and pleasing in appearance than its descendant of to-day, possessed all the merits which convenience could suggest. In size it resembled the table now most generally approved for practical use.

It stood firm, with a good grip of the floor, and was usually constructed of fine-grained wood which had been well seasoned. At each corner there was a sunken round or square in the wood as a common feature, and in this the old silver or Sheffield candlestick rested secure. When

Early Chippendale Claw-and-Ball Table, showing stands or candlesticks and guinea wells; these features came down from Queen Anne times. Four legs are rigid; the fifth swings out to carry the flap. Circa 1740. Photograph kindly lent by Messrs. Gill and Reigate.

this was missing, we find sometimes a slab which pulled out from the carcase and carried the light. Almost invariably when the candle hollow appears we find an oval well on each of the four sides in front of the players, and these, of course, were intended to hold the guineas or counters of the players. The centre, though sometimes of beautifully figured wood, polished, was as a rule covered with a finely laid cloth, generally green in colour, but on rare occasions fine needlework designs, shaped round the wells, graced the table-tops.

Incidentally, the original covering is often met with to-day, and, as a result of the many years' service which it has seen, it will, as a rule, be found to be badly stained or moth-eaten. When it is advisable to remove this old covering, it may well be replaced by old cloth discarded from a billiard-table; this substitute looks well, wears well, and fits the rebate in the table-top.

There were various devices for holding the cards, &c., in the body of the table, the most primitive consisting of a small drawer let into the face of the table and worked by a single brass handle. Again, the body of the table would be made hollow, and access to the well would be obtained either by raising the flap-top or by screwing the whole of the top round until the cavity was disclosed.

Occasionally one finds very complicated fittings to early card-tables. The author once owned a table with a double top, the first consisting of a card-table, the second of a chess-board, whilst underneath was a well in which reposed a backgammon-board. The body to hold these different parts was, however, so deep that the players' legs could not rest under it with comfort; it was therefore in reality rather a white elephant.

Although the usual allowance of legs was four, tables may be found with five or even six. Needless to say, four only were necessary, as any additional " understandings " only tended to inconvenience people sitting round the table. These legs were arranged, broadly speaking, in three ways. The two hind legs pulled out, with a supporting framework (on which the flap was turned back and rested), in a concertina action; or they were pulled out to fulfil their function one at a time on a pivot situate at the centre of the table (when on the top flap being folded back on this V-shaped support the table was ready for use). Again, three of the legs would be rigid, one only being swung out to carry the top. The concertina action, though liable to get out of order if carelessly handled, was the best, as it did not restrict the knee-room under the table. Unfortunately, it could only be employed with square or serpentine-shaped tables.

Owing to the number of card-tables originally made, genuine examples are, comparatively speaking, common. Small side-tables, on the other hand, are much rarer, doubtless because our ancestors, with their practical minds, realised that the card-table when closed and placed against the wall did duty equally well. The card-table, indeed, in addition to fulfilling its main function, acted as a centre or side-table at will.

Now fashion, proverbially fickle, rules to-day that the side-table is more valuable than the card-table, other things (outline, medium, and decoration) being equal. When we remember the superior usefulness of the card-table, the greater skill demanded of the cabinet-maker in its construction, and the great point that edge-decoration, whether carved or inlaid, is doubled in the card-table, by reason of its second flap (which forms a double top to the table in repose), we may rest assured that common sense will eventually prevail and place the card-table at its proper value.

The original leg to the card-table, as we know it, was a plain cabriole or a claw-and-ball, frequently with a large shell carved in relief on the knee. The early examples show very fine dragon's or lion's claws, later specimens the eagle's claw and ball as terminal decorations. As the Chippendale epoch approached, the knee was handsomely carved with rococo decoration, consisting of coquillage, cabochons, and foliated work. Queen Anne card-tables were executed almost exclusively in walnut. Chippendale,

An exquisite example of Chippendale's refined modelling: note the graceful lines of the legs and classic decoration. Circa 1750. Author's Collection.

on the other hand, used practically nothing but mahogany. There is, however, one salient difference between the two styles, for Chippendale carved the edges of some of his fine tables as an innovation, a treatment which proved to be an unqualified success.

In the illustrations on this and the next page we have two beautiful examples of this work. The pattern on the first is classic, and is known as egg-and-tongue, egg-and anchor, or egg-and-dart; whilst the legs are set off by the moulding known as "pearl-and-lozenge"—another tribute to ancient Greece. The four front and two side brackets show a *soupçon* of Louis XV. handling, to which source, too, the curvilinear element of the top harks back. The second table shows us a rather later example, again drawing on the Renaissance in an exposition of the rose-

Another very fine example of Chippendale's work, showing his knowledge of the classic and Chinese school. Circa 1755. Author's Collection.

and-ribbon border, Chippendale's favourite form for table-edge decoration. The brackets in this instance show palpable Chinese influence, as also do the carved details at each foot.

Card-tables were made, approximately speaking, square, round, oval, serpentine, and broken-fronted. Of these the serpentine are the most graceful and valuable. By broken-fronted we refer to such tables as that shown in the illustration on page 297, where there is a protrusion, round or square, at each corner, caused by the provision of a space whereon candles, &c., might stand. The use of round and oval tables, fitfully seen during the walnut period, was discontinued by Chippendale, to be subsequently revived by the masters of the late eighteenth-century schools.

Chippendale, unlike his precursors and successors, seldom fitted the carcase of his tables with any drawer or well wherein to hold accessories.

Ordinary card-tables are practically a drug on the market, and advanced collectors and dealers will only purchase very fine specimens. Care should be displayed when purchasing early examples of the cabriole order, for there are no inconsiderable number of "Dutchmen" awaiting the unwary.

Introduction of "Foreign" Details.

Rarely, but still now and then, Chippendale would seem to have foreseen the tendency of the next age; but, just as he had built some piece almost in consonance with its demands, he would deliberately go off the rails and introduce foreign matter. This was sometimes noticeable in his outline work, sometimes in the decorative detail which he affected. Such an example is the lady's writing-table illustrated on page 300. The outline is almost suggestive of Louis Seize; the carved rose-and-ribbon and gadroon edges and the quatrefoils on feet are classic; but our artist flew off at a tangent, and gave us Chinese brackets and piercing of the legs.

Turning to page 301, we see a late chair of the style known as ladder-back. Chippendale seldom employed the Anthemion or Grecian honeysuckle as an item of garnishment, but Robert Adam, his successor, popularised it from 1765-1770. The hollowed seat also indicates the lateness of period, but this is not an infallible feature for the collector's guidance, for a reference to our illustrations on pages 309 and 312 will show this shaped seating on comparatively early models.

Lady's Writing-table by Thomas Chippendale; circa 1760-5.

The Anthemion was destined, with other little items culled from the classic orders, to supplant those rococo scrolls and foliations which Chippendale so dearly loved, and it is interesting to find the great master forestalling public taste, as shown by the two illustrations here referred to. It is probable that if a complete enumeration of Chippendale's masterpieces could be made, we should find that, at one time or another, he had given expression to practically everything worth recording in the matter of eighteenth-century carving, and it is certain that no school of carving approached his for all-round merit and interest.

His Cabinet-Maker's "Director."

The student or critic of the eighteenth-century cabinet-makers, in whatsoever directions his predilections may lie,

Ladder-back Chair by Thomas Chippendale;
circa 1770.

cannot but admit that Chippendale was the most comprehensive caterer for the artistic public. His versatility enabled him, too, to approach his subject from so many standpoints, and, as he was a man of very considerable erudition and taste, despite what his few critics may avow, his own pronouncements and writings dealing with the big field which he essayed to cover are of the greatest interest.

When introducing his *magnum opus*, "The Gentleman and Cabinet-Maker's Director," in 1754, the first book of its sort worthy of the name to be published, he spoke of his designs as being "calculated to improve and to refine the present Taste, and suited to the Fancy and circumstances of Persons in all Degrees of Life." This claim was certainly established, and owing to the modest reservations which qualified it, it was not made in blatant or objectionable form. "I hope," he tells us, "the novelty as well as the usefulness of the performance will make some atonement for its faults and imperfections. I am sensible there are too many to be found in it, for I frankly confess that in executing many of the drawings my pencil has but faintly copied out those images that my fancy suggested."

The connoisseur will unhesitatingly confirm what the master asserts, for it is generally recognised that whenever Chippendale produced an example resembling or approximating to one of his published designs, it is infinitely superior to anything we should have expected from a mere perusal of the relative drawing. At the same time, most examples of the great master's work are plainer and less pretentious than the bulk of his drawings would seem to suggest. Master of design, carving, and construction, versed in the orders of Classic and Gothic architecture, Chippendale's literary powers, as we shall presently see, were of no mean order.

Dulcique animos novitate tenebo.—*Ovid*.

Apt as was the quotation by Chippendale, and

breathing as it did the spirit of his work, he cannot claim perhaps to have substantiated it *literally*. Novelty was not his *forte*; but an artistic and novel rendering of old themes was thoroughly characteristic of the man. His knowledge of the mother-tongue was remarkable, and if we consider the dedication contained in his first edition of the " Director " (as it is generally styled), we shall find composition which would satisfy—shall we put it mildly?—the average University examiner of to-day.

> " To the Right Honble. Hugh Earl of Northumberland, Baron Warkworth, of Warkworth Castle, Lord Lieut. and Custos Rotulorum of the County of Northumberland, &c., &c.
>
> " My Lord, your intimate acquaintance with those Arts and Sciences that tend to perfect or adorn life, and your well known disposition to promote them, give the following Designs a natural claim to your protection. They are therefore with great respect laid at your feet by—Yours, &c., Thos. Chippendale."

Possessed of a fund of humour, Chippendale now and then affords us a glimpse of this trait in his character. " I have been encouraged to begin and carry on this work," he tells us, " not only (as the puff in the playbill says) by persons of distinction," &c. Again, when dealing in analytical vein with his own work : " And had they (the designs) not been published till I could have pronounced them perfect, *perhaps* they would never have seen the light. Nevertheless, I was not upon that account afraid to let them go abroad, for I have been told *that the greatest masters of every other art have laboured under the same difficulty.*"

This must not be mistaken for egotism, for our artist continues: "I am persuaded that he who can survey his own works with entire satisfaction and complacency will hardly ever find the world of the same favourable opinion with himself." Underlying these remarks are dry humour and shrewd commonsense. Later on, when tentatively approaching the critics, who, he feels, will be weighing the merits or the demerits of his work, Chippendale affords us a valuable insight into his outside knowledge and attainments. "The corrections *of the judicious and impartial* I shall always receive with diffidence in my own abilities and respect to theirs." There is here a welcome absence of that self-assertion which sometimes mars the utterances of a genius. Continuing, he writes: "But though the following designs were more perfect than my fondness for my own offspring *could* ever suppose them, I should yet be far from expecting the united approbation of all those whose sentiments have an undoubted claim to be regarded, for a thousand accidental circumstances may concur in dividing the opinions of the most improved judges, and the most unprejudiced will find it difficult to disengage himself from a partial affection to some particular beauties of which the general course of his studies or the peculiar cast of his temper may have rendered him most sensible. Thus, for instance . . . the excellency of the Roman masters in painting consists in beauty of design, nobleness of attitude, and delicacy of expression; but the charms of good colouring are wanting. On the contrary, the Venetian school is said to have neglected design a little too much, but at the same time has been more attentive to the grace and harmony of the well-disposed lights and shades. Now, it will be admitted by all admirers *of this noble art* that no composition of the pencil can be perfect where either of these greater qualities is absent; yet the most accomplished judge may be so particularly struck with one or other of these excellencies in preference to the rest as to be influenced in his censure or applause of the whole tablature by the predominancy or deficiency of his favourite beauty."

It is not the mere fact of Chippendale's grasp of the points characterising the Roman and Venetian schools which strikes the student most forcibly. We know that our master had so studied his subject as to make of it an art, and, if he had weighed other material, why not this?

But it is remarkable that any man with the limited advantages which a craftsman enjoys should have been such a master of analogy, and able to cite matter so aptly in pressing home his premises to a logical conclusion. Chippendale, in addition to having an acquisitive and well-balanced mind, must have worked unceasingly in what would otherwise have been his leisure moments.

We get one more view of the man when he was dealing with the calumnies spread against him by trade rivals. " Upon the whole," he wrote, " I have given no design but what may be executed with advantage by the hands of a skilled workman, though some of the *profession* have been diligent enough to represent them (especially those after the Gothic or Chinese manner) as so many specious drawings, impossible to be worked off by any mechanic whatsoever. *I will not scruple to attribute this to malice, ignorance, and inability.*" Very plain speaking, this; but, as we shall see presently, borne out by facts. He continues: " I am confident that every design in the book can be improved both as to beauty and enrichment in the execution of it by their most obedient servant, Thomas Chippendale."

Chippendale's word is again vindicated by his creations, for many examples of his which required yet more careful handling than the questioned designs would have entailed, are handed down to us. This class of work was executed almost exclusively in pine or other soft wood, and was then gilt and burnished. Incidentally, being florid, it was of questionable value from an artistic point of view. The writer regards this phase merely as an exposition of what the advanced carver could accomplish, just as in later years Thomas Sheraton gave opportunities for laboured renderings of the power of the inlayer.

CHAPTER XII.
Thomas Chippendale
(continued).

Comprehensiveness of his Work.

ELSEWHERE reference is made to the comprehensive nature of Chippendale's productions, and it is probable that only one exception can be made or placed on the debtor side of his account. The sideboard as we know it, and as created by R. and J. Adam, Heppelwhite, Shearer, and Sheraton, was a thing almost unknown to our master. He gives designs for four sideboard tables, and the sideboard to him was merely a long side- or carving-table, usually with a marble top, upon which dishes, &c., could be placed during the meal. R. and J. Adam added pedestals to stand at each side of the board, and these were fitted for wines, linen, &c. They next incorporated these pedestals—upon which urns to hold knives, &c., used to stand—with the board.

As we shall presently see, the daintiest of sideboards proper came from William Shearer, whilst the more majestic examples were produced by the brothers R. and J. Adam. The ordinary sideboard usually ascribed to Thomas Sheraton was as often as not the handiwork of Thomas Shearer.

Chippendale announced that his book showed " a great variety of Bookcases, Commodes (drawing-room ' cabinet ' chests of drawers), Library and Writing-tables, Buroes,

Breakfast-tables, Dressing and China tables, China cases, Hanging shelves, Tea-chests (caddies), Trays, Fire-screens, Chairs, Settees, Sophas, Beds, Presses, Cloaths-chests, Pier-glasses, Sconces, Slab-frames, Brackets, Candle-stands (known also as *torchères*), Clock-cases, and Frets." As a matter of fact, it dealt also with lanthorns, organ-cases, chandeliers, wardrobes, commode tables, chimney-pieces, terms (tall pedestals upon which busts, &c., were placed), burjars, wine-coolers, sideboard tables, girandoles, and stands of varying height upon which Oriental china vases could be displayed.

This list will establish the comprehensive character of the great master's work, especially when we remember that he gave numerous designs and suggestions for almost every article mentioned. Our designer had strong views as to the fitness of things in connection with house decoration. Thus, with a view to influencing his *clientèle*, he wrote: " Three designs of chairs. That in the middle is proper for a library; the two others are Gothic, and fit for eating parlours." And again: " Nine designs of chairs after the Chinese manner, and are very proper for a lady's dressing-room, especially if it is hung with India paper." He evinced similar interest when making suggestions for organ-cases, holding that these should be decorated in Gothic taste.

Chair-back Decorations.

There were, approximately speaking, four different methods applied to the decoration of chair-backs under Chippendale, and each of these was again liable to sub-division. The rarest and handsomest perhaps is known as the ribbon-back; and here the carved detail of the type suggested would form a *cross* at times within the back-

Thomas Chippendale.

frame. Then there was the more or less graceful network of decoration extending practically over the whole of the back, seldom employed in chair-backs outside the Chinese or Gothic schools of Chippendale embellishment. Next

Very rare Chair by Thomas Chippendale, with back governed by Louis Quinze handling. From the bottom rail of back downwards the outline is Chinese. Observe the two large C's connecting centre work with back upright, a conceit of the great master's which is frequently introduced. This chair came from the study or consulting-room of Dr. Palmer, the celebrated Rugeley poisoner. Circa 1755. Author's Collection.

we come to the ladder-back, with its three or four rungs running horizontally across the frame.

Finally we have the pierced splat rising from the plane of the seat, and spreading out to join the top or crest-rail of the chair-back. This last-named is the commonest form of construction used by Chippendale, the tracery being often flamboyant in the literal if not in the popular interpretation of the word.

Chippendale Armchair, showing late development of his original type of leg; the cresting rail exhibits traces of Chinese influence, and the back-splat is of flamboyant character. Circa 1760.

Architecturally speaking, flamboyant (French *flambeau*, a torch) is applied to that vitiated decorated work which is characteristic of the French school contemporary with our English Perpendicular. The decoration consisted of an intricate and closely-woven scheme of flame-shaped panes, and defeated its own ends by reason of this very intricacy and elaboration; hence flamboyant has come to be a by-word. Chippendale's schemes, if often following this flame-shaped web, are generally characterised by artistic handling, though now and again he seems to have crowded too much matter into a given space, and so has given grounds for the critical judge to carp.

Contour of Line v. Luxury in Furniture.

It has been urged that our forbears, although they studied elegance and sense of proportion in their furniture, neglected the element of ease. This indictment would hold good during the period when oak was in fashion; but during the walnut era a state of comparative luxury obtained, and so we find many of the upholstered chairs and sofas of the Queen Anne style uniting in happy manner comfort and graceful outline. It cannot be contended that any eighteenth-century furniture was so luxurious or rest-compelling as are, for instance, the modern divan and the easy chair; but these latter would have been taboo in the artistic circles of the days we are considering.

Our ancestors when resting in the sitting-room seem to have studied dignified or graceful poses rather than to have yielded to *abandon* attitudes, and so their furniture conformed with such reasonable comfort only as a pleasing and elegant model could afford. Of course, generally speaking, furniture became more comfortable as padded upholstery superseded woodwork, and the youthful collector, in his effort to obtain comfort in a chair, may be making a bad bargain *as a collector.* We value most highly to-day those old pieces which exhibit the maximum of decorated woodwork with the minimum of padded upholstery. In other words, our sympathies are with the old-time craftsman who interpreted the inimitable tastes of his generation rather than with the workman who may have sacrificed something of this grace in an effort to achieve luxury. The

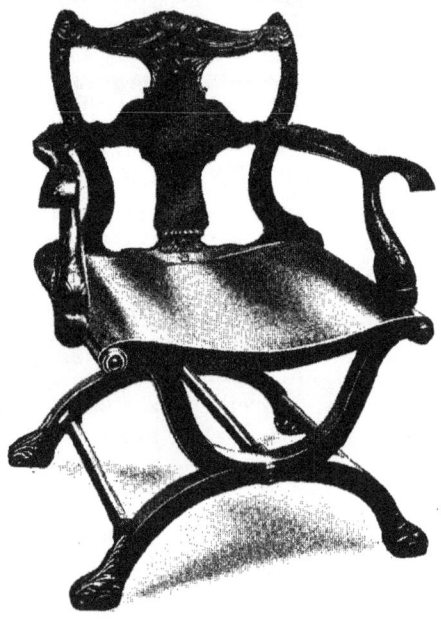

A very rare X Chair by Thomas Chippendale (circa 1755). X stools are far commoner during this period than are the corresponding chairs. From a photograph kindly lent by Messrs. Partridge and Neave.

reason is not far to seek. Our national taste is improving, and we realise that our forefathers eclipsed us in the conception and execution of artistic designs, just as we excel the old-time school in pandering to mere creature comforts. *We* suffer from a surfeit of all the luxuries which machinery can produce and money purchase, and may well revert to those better lines which, fortunately, we are again beginning to appreciate.

The French school relied on the figured silks from Lyons, or the brocades, embroideries, or tapestries of Aubusson, Beauvais, or Gobelins, for the decorative effects of their chairs, couches, &c. Chippendale often reproduced these models of padded-back armchairs, &c. ; but he seldom shone in so doing, because he had at his disposal inferior material for upholstery, whilst his particular *forte*— that of back *woodwork* decoration—was thereby curtailed, if not almost eliminated from the scheme. Chippendale was the greatest chair-maker of the period, and many of his chairs and sofas are comfortable as well as pleasing; but the young collector must not think that comfort rather than design in early furniture is of necessity the goal to aim at. The tendency in the olden time was perhaps to neglect comfort; but the pendulum swung full and, in the nineteenth century, Englishmen rushed to the other extreme.

Types of Chairs, &c.

The ordinary dining-room or hall chair was as comfortable in the eighteenth century as it was possible to make it, and Chippendale was a master in the art of tilting and shaping the back, so that the contour of the body might be supported by its modulated sweep. Our master also gave us armchairs, easy chairs—which he styled burjars (French *bergère*, of which more anon)—"drunkards'" chairs, lovers' seats, couches, settees, sofas, and the chaise-longue.

As we have already seen, the armchair was broader than the single. It had at times a stuffed back and padded arms; but it was usually of carved mahogany, with a "drop-in" or stuff-over seat. The burjar was a development of this; the wings formed by the arm enclosures were padded and upholstered, instead of being left open as in the armchair or fauteuil proper. Literally, the chaise bergère means shepherdess's chair, a distinctive title amongst the old French cabinet-makers difficult to account for.

The ordinary English "wing" or "grandfather" chair furnishes us with an example of this bergère fitting, which was also at times applied to sofas, couches, and settees. When so fitted the example is less sought after than if it had been adorned by a decorated wooden arm.

The "drunkard's" chair resembled an ordinary armchair, with this difference, that it had exaggerated breadth of seat and back. It was so called because the unfortunate tippler of the olden times could collapse within its ample folds, there to sleep off the effects of his carousal.

The lovers' seat was a contracted settee, whose proportions suggested that only two people should use it, and that they should sit in close proximity to one another. The term was rather happily chosen, and some of these seats are dainty and charming little pieces.

The couch proper was made by Chippendale at rare intervals. It was, as a rule, an exceedingly handsome bit of furniture. Its outline was very similar to that of the Flemish or Stuart models so common during the latter half of the seventeenth century; but it was not nearly so comfortable. The early examples had frequently an adjustable head-rest fitted to them to suit the comfort of the person reclining on them; but Chippendale unfortunately made them, as a rule, with a *fixed head-piece*, which, sometimes padded and upholstered, was usually in

Two fine Single Chairs, showing adjusted proportions for varying sizes. Chippendale, circa 1755. From Mr. Dalby Reeve's Collection.

Thomas Chippendale.

the shape of an ordinary chair-back, rising abruptly from the floor—almost at right angles to it, in fact. The frame would rest on six or eight legs, and these were linked

Typical Chippendale Ladder-back Armchair, circa 1755, from Mr. Dalby Reeve's Collection.

together by shaped, carved, or pierced stretchers. The decoration favoured was nearly always Louis Quinze for back, arms, and legs, and in the more elaborate examples the framework would be similarly treated. The canvas seat would be stretched or drawn tight by ropes laced over wooden knobs, and upon this a long squab (flat cushion) was placed. Occasionally the seat would be on the stuff-over system.

Chippendale always wrote of " sophas " and settees as being two separate and distinct articles of furniture. The sofa lent itself to rest perhaps more than the settee, which was a stiffer-looking model. The sofa nearly always had a low and shaped back. The settee-back was higher, generally speaking, and often square, especially when *covered* by upholstery. The former piece had, as a rule, bergère wings; the settee oftener than not had arms resembling those on an ordinary armchair, sometimes with the addition of elbow-pads. *The collector should always choose examples with decorated woodwork at arms and crowning the back whenever he may have the chance of so doing.*

Two- and Three-chair-back Settees—" Fakes."

There was one very interesting development of the settee, known as the two-chair-back or three-chair-back settee, which became popular in the reign of Queen Anne. As the name implies, the back was formed by a scheme resembling connected chair-backs, and we see in the illustrations (pages 159 and 327) interesting examples of this work. Rightly prized by collectors, these settees command high prices, and are accordingly faked by the dishonest.

Fortunately there are one or two cardinal points about these pieces which protect those conversant with them from suffering by such impositions. The commonest fraud on the market consists of a settee made up out of two chairs with a new frame and arms added. Supposing one

Fine Upholstered Chippendale Settee of the Louis Quinze period. Photo kindly lent by Messrs. Partridge and Neave.

could make the genuine article by this process, it would be possible to convert £15 into £100; hence the temptation to essay it. But fortunately there are the stumbling-blocks which the rogue cannot circumvent, and it is necessary to understand these, seeing that to be forewarned is to be forearmed.

If the two-chair settee has

(1) Square,
(2) Chinese, or
(3) Gothic legwork,

it will almost assuredly possess stretcher-work, and as this detail on the chair would not be adaptable for the wider span of the settee, it will have been replaced by new work in the "conversion."

At each corner in the inside of the seat-frame anglebrackets strengthened the frame and served to support the drop-in seat. The two front brackets will have been disturbed and refitted in the fake to enable the "artist" to fix the new front seat-rail.

If the seat-frame is new throughout, scent possible mischief.

If the seat is on the stuff-over principle, and there is room for suspicion, examine under the upholstery at the junction of legs and seat-frame. It is always desirable to tilt these models and examine them from underneath when one has not had much experience.

Just as the armchair is wider in the frame than the single, *so, too, the chair-back in these settees is wider than the armchair.* Hence it follows that a correct imitation cannot be made out of genuine material. If the faker uses two armchairs he cuts into a valuable bit of property, and the inside uprights (at the junction of the two chair-backs) show where the arms once were. This necessitates the substitution of two new inside back uprights. Again, these uprights were probably decorated; and they would certainly have been connected by some carved work, either at the top or half-way down their course, quite possibly in both places, and these details should be examined first of all. If there has been any disturbance or new work suspect the piece at once.

Then there is the question of the frame and of the *centre* legs; the genuine leg starts down from the ground common to both chairs. The front centre leg in the bogey (unless further new work has been put in) would, of course, be a continuation of one or other of the chairs before the "conversion."

A far harder problem confronts the beginner when the fraudulent settee with upholstered frame is offered him. Half the difficulties above mentioned are swept from the path of the deceiver, and a very presentable imitation is often evolved from an old pair of arms, old chair-legs, and quite possibly an old frame, the evidences of conversion being hidden by the subsequent attentions of the upholsterer.

Two-chair-back Settees—Foreign Specimens.

These two-chair-backed settees were often made in both Holland and Portugal, and the collector must keep his eyes open if he wishes to avoid purchasing a foreign example. If experienced, the person to whom such a specimen is offered will note the wooden handling of the Dutch settee, which is greatly inferior to its English contemporary. The Portuguese piece may prove more difficult to diagnose.

In "Furniture of the Olden Times," by Frances Clary

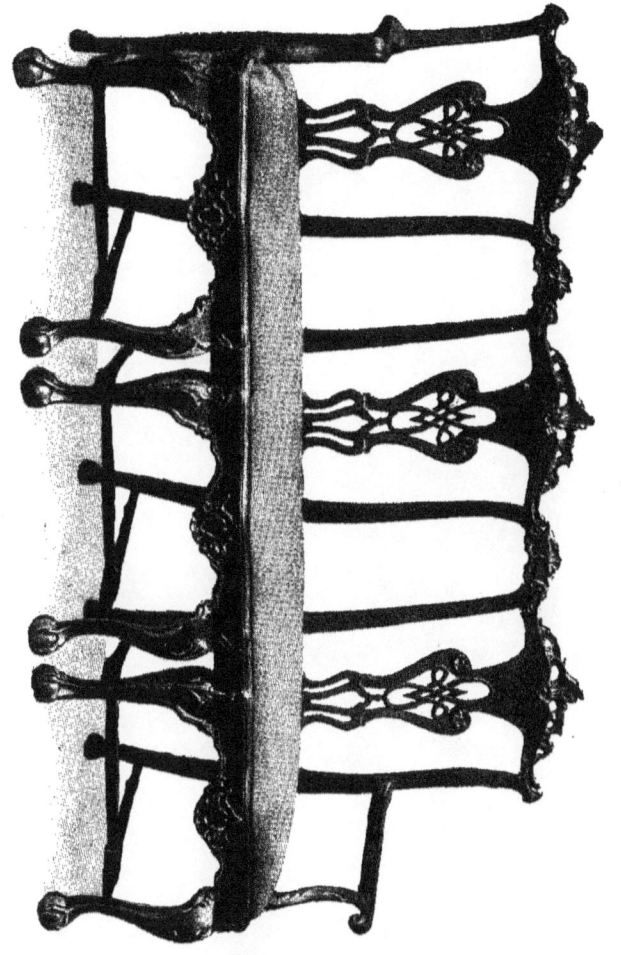

Very fine old Portuguese Three-chair-back Settee of the period 1750. From a photograph kindly lent by Mr. Pinto Leite.

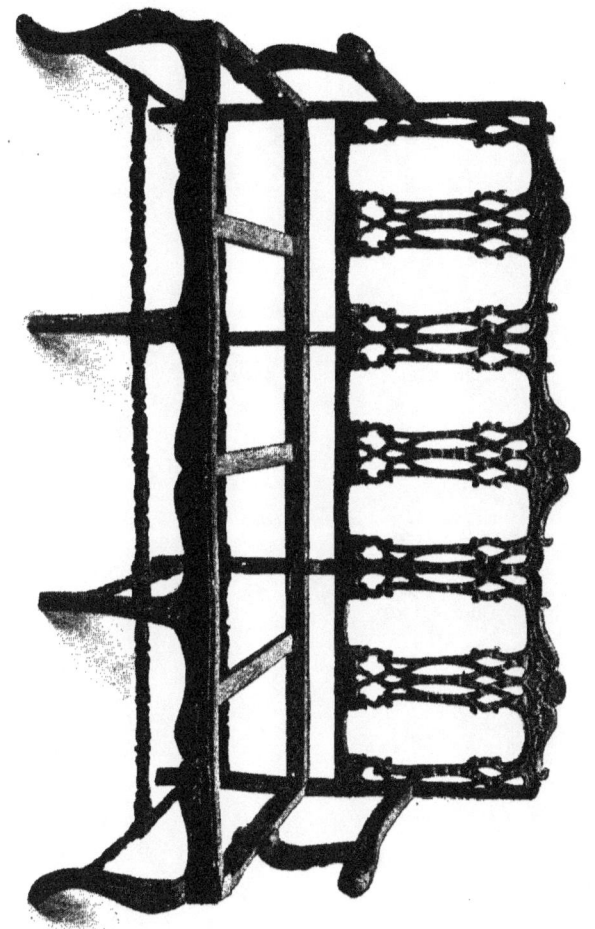

Dutch Three-chair-back Settee after Chippendale, showing ribbon work arranged in flamboyant manner. It will be observed that the leg and arm outlines are inferior to those of English models, whilst the outside back uprights are overweighted by the heavy proportions of the arms. The property of J. G. Stenhouse, Esq.

Morse, illustration No. 167 shows one of these Portuguese "double chairs," *but it is unfortunately mis-described as Chippendale.*

The Dutch settee will have either the cabriole or the claw-and-ball foot in front, with shell decoration, as a rule, on the knee, if there is any carving, and the curves of the leg will be found to be "weak" in conception.

Double Chair Settee, by Chippendale, showing Gothic and Chinese detail contained within his typical outline; period 1760.

The Portuguese specimen will generally have a cabriole leg; but the carving common to leg and back will show florid rococo embellishment not so happily placed as was, for instance, Chippendale's work.

In addition, we shall expect to find its contour marred at the top of each chair-back, and very possibly in front of each chair-seat, by some rococo excrescence, which, intended to improve the decoration, diverts the eye from the general scheme, and does away with the element of artistic rest.

Though the backs in the two-chair-back settees were very broad, those in the three-chair-back settees reverted closely to the dimensions of the single-chair back. It is therefore most important that the beginner should look for original work in the frame at front and back, and also at the junction of the backs themselves, *the safeguard of abnormal back breadth being absent in these models* as a general rule. The necessity for this careful examination stands out very forcibly when once we realise that three single chairs worth collectively £30 would command upwards of £100 if they could be satisfactorily "converted," and that, whereas in the case of the two-chair-back settee a genuine pair of armchairs must be utilised by the faker to bring about a fairly roomy appearance in his creation, *single chairs may be adapted for the three-chair-back fake.* Now a *pair* of armchairs have a good market value at all times, whilst singles, unless in sets of six or more, are hard to "place."

The Chaise-Longue.

During the reign of Louis XV. the chaise-longue came into favour, this consisting of three pieces of furniture which could be used as one. A pair of armchairs and a stool *en suite* formed the complement. The chairs could then be turned inwards towards one another, with the broad stool connecting them, and on this improvised couch one person could recline, or two people could sit with their feet pointing towards one another. This was a very handy arrangement when sofa space was limited, and Chippendale availed himself of the idea.

Large Fitted Writing-Table by Thomas Chippendale. Illustration kindly lent by Messrs. Gill and Reigate. Circa 1750.

Chippendale advised all cabinet-makers to make small models of important pieces before embarking on their construction proper. This plan had obtained in England since Tudor times, and some people go so far as to make collections of these models, which are just too large for use in dolls' houses. The practice began to be generally discontinued at the close of the century, when designers of the Sheraton school published elaborate section and elevation measurements and diagrams for any intricate work.

Writing- or Pedestal-Tables.

Chippendale's large writing-tables were unique, commodious, and dignified; they stand to-day as some of the greatest triumphs of the cabinet-maker's art. These pieces were made in a variety of pleasing and graceful shapes, well calculated to display the telling panels of Louis Quinze, Chinese, or Gothic embellishment distributed over their upright surfaces. Every contrivance calculated to act as a convenience was embodied in the carcase, and the best of them were decorated on all four sides alike, so that they could stand in the centre of the room. Apart from these fine cabinets, Chippendale also made excellent writing-tables on less pretentious lines; but these smaller ones are very rare, and seem to have been made only to special order. Chippendale differed here from the masters who came after him, for they commonly made dainty, if somewhat impracticable, models, whilst seldom launching out into the handsome and commodious examples beloved of their more illustrious brother.

Serving-Tables.

It has been noted that Chippendale made sideboard tables, not sideboards. These tables were of varying type;

the earliest were on Queen Anne lines, and ranged from 4ft. to 7ft. in length. The legs were massive, with claw-and-ball decoration or with Classic terms, and they are often found with bold and most effective carving. The frame supported on these legs was generally plain; but in the more expensive specimens it was set off by typical Classic work deeply carved. The upper edge supporting

Massive and very early Chippendale Side- or Carving-Table. Circa 1725. Author's Collection.

the top was commonly carved with egg-and-tongue or similar classic detail. The top was sometimes of mahogany, but generally consisted of a large slab of finely-figured marble, occasionally of some coarse slate or other medium, with a veneer of fine marble over it. The master eschewed the use of wood, because it was liable to be marked by the hot dishes placed upon it. The bulk of these tables surviving with mahogany tops to-day have

Thomas Chippendale. 333

had the original tops removed. Now and again during this period soft wood coloured to look like mahogany was employed; these pieces are not nearly so valuable as are those executed in mahogany itself.

Chippendale subsequently employed Louis Quinze models with typical rococo decoration, and later he gave us Chinese designs with carved or applied fretwork laid over their carcases. The rarest treatment consisted in the

Very finely carved Chippendale Side- or Carving-Table, showing the master's use of the Vitruvian scroll. Circa 1745. Author's Collection.

piercing of the leg, so that a skeleton effect more or less Chinese in character was arrived at. Whenever possible our master set these latter tables off with large carved C-shaped brackets at the angles where the legs joined the body of the piece.

During the latter phases of his work Chippendale gave us some Gothic renderings of these tables; but they are seldom met with *pure*, being, as a rule, blended with

Louis Quinze or Chinese garnishment. The legs might be Perpendicular or Early English, with corresponding mouldings, whilst the superstructure would be governed by Celestial tradition. Rarely, but still now and then, there would be a low back rail of wood rising on the wall side of the top, and though these are reputed to have been decorated with pierced work, &c., the writer has never seen an authentic specimen of the kind.

Fine Chippendale Side- or Carving-Table, showing gadroon edge and shell. Circa 1750. Author's Collection.

It is quite exceptional to find one of these " boards " with a drawer or other fittings; but now and then one comes across an example with a single drawer, more commonly a slab to pull out and increase the area upon which china, glass, or silver could rest. Of course there was no absolutely hard-and-fast line of distinction between these methods of treatment, Louis Quinze, Chinese, and Gothic, on many occasions, for Chippendale would put one

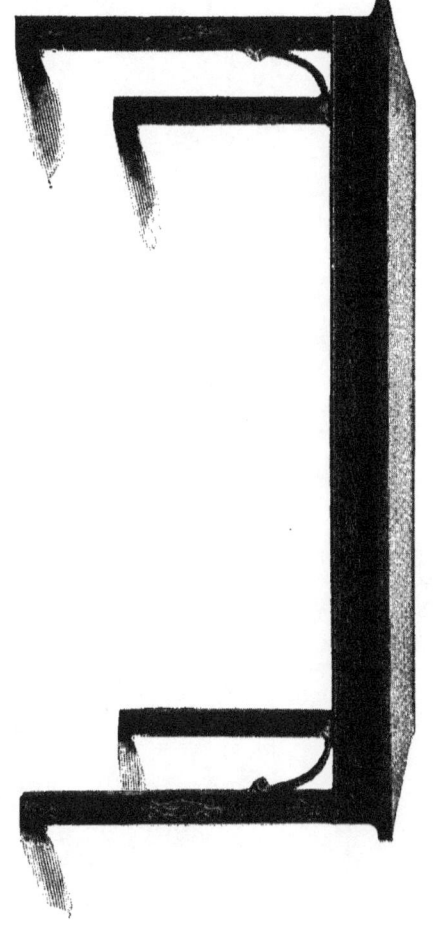

Very large Side- or Serving-Board by Thomas Chippendale, with appliqué fret decoration; circa 1755.

little touch of rococo in an example governed by Chinese or Gothic feeling, just as he would not hesitate to incorporate a trefoil culled from the Gothic in a model otherwise Louis XV.

Extremely fine Chippendale Wine-Cooler (or Cellaret) Stand, decorated in Louis Quinze style; circa 1745-50.

Wine-Coolers.

With these sideboard-tables went wine-coolers, sometimes standing at their side, usually underneath them. Of these coolers there was a great variety; but very few were really well decorated. One type has come down to us in profusion, comparatively speaking; it is an octagonal brass-bound "bucket," with lid, and zinc fitted within. Possessed of four legs, it is in two pieces; the legs are connected with a platform upon which the cooler reposes. The cooler was never carved; the stand was—sometimes.

The legs were nearly always square, and when embellished had plain fluted mouldings running down their course. A good C or Chinese bracket fills the angle where the leg joins the platform in many of those that we now meet with, and the platform on each of its facets will as often as not exhibit some twelve or more short flutes. *Very rarely* the legs were claw-and-ball or cabriole in type, with fine rococo knee garnishment.

Other suggestions for wine-coolers, to many of which Chippendale gave effect, comprised various square, hexagonal, or octagonal caskets—suspiciously resembling sarcophagi—which, squat in form, rested on four clumsy *feet*, usually of the lion's-paw order. There were also oval pails, brass bound and without lids, some on legs, some on feet, others merely made to "sit" on the floor. As this particular article nearly always was tucked away *under* the side-table, people contented themselves doubtless with comparatively humble designs.

The Péché Mortel.

We recently dealt with the chaises-longues as adapted from the French school by Chippendale, and mention should here be made of the Péché Mortel, which, under a different name, was in reality an almost identical model. Chippendale, in describing it, wrote :—" They are sometimes made to take asunder in the middle; one part makes a large easy-chair and the other a stool, and the feet join in the middle, which looks badly. Therefore I would recommend their being made, as in these designs, with a pretty thick mattress. The dimensions are 6ft. in the clear " (reclining space) " and 2ft. 6in.—3ft. broad."

It will be gathered that our master seldom favoured the Péché Mortel, and such specimens as he created were probably made to order. When he had a free hand he made a couch proper with bergère wings or fauteuil arms, carved. The frames were covered with a substantial mattress, whilst on rare occasions a raised footpiece in carved woodwork harmonising with the rest of the scheme was added with rather pleasing results.

In addition to the stools which rested on four claw-and-ball, cabriole, or square legs, Chippendale favoured a variety of other models, the commonest of which perhaps were in the Chinese taste. In these little pieces the legs would be decorated with fretwork, and they are generally found with a pierced stretcher attachment, uniting the " understandings " and emphasising their Eastern characteristics.

The two-angle brackets were sometimes of fretwork, but often of a rococo nature, in which Chippendale's glorified C figured frequently. More ornate and pretentious designs were embodied in the " Director," but the cabinet-maker seems seldom to have given effect to them. Those worthy of our notice were in X-formation, strengthened by rather florid schemes of stretchers. The plane of the seat was sometimes level, but usually more or less shaped.

The X-formation seems to have been used for chairs in this country since the fifteenth century. It was common during Tudor times, and fine specimens of these chairs are preserved in the cathedrals of York and Winchester.

Organ-Cases—Method of Adapting.

When building his wonderful mahogany organ-cases, Chippendale studied fairly closely the dictates of environment. The trend of his mind is easily seen throughout his work, but in addition he wrote:—"As most of the Cathedral churches are of the Gothic architecture, it is a pity that the organs are not better adapted to that style." Consequently, we find him adhering more or less closely to the Gothic in most of his productions in this field, though he could seldom resist the temptation to introduce in his design some little detail of Louis Quinze decoration or Grinling Gibbons festoons.

As might have been expected from one so wedded to the graceful curvilinear element of the French school just mentioned, Chippendale's rendering of the Gothic was extremely " free " on occasions. He handled the lancet-shaped panel with a sublime disregard for hidebound tradition, and yet, artistically speaking, the results he achieved more than justified the liberties he took. Too cumbersome in their entirety for the ordinary-sized house, these organ-cases are easily convertible into useful and effective pieces of interior garnishment. The happiest method of utilising them consists in the adaptation of the larger models for fireplaces and overmantels, the keyboard section being removed to make room for the fireplace proper. The face of the case may also be employed for doorways and overdoors in large halls or galleries.

The smaller models are best adapted as cabinets, wardrobes, &c., and, as they are the only specimens generally available for the collector (coming on the market as they do from the *private* homes for which they were

Thomas Chippendale.

originally intended), there is no reason why they should not be retained practically intact rather than be broken up for panelling, &c.

Console and Pier Tables.

Probably the most indefensible designs which the great master gave the public were for his console tables. It is hardly necessary to premise that these were "lean-to" tables, meant to stand against a wall, usually underneath a large mirror fixed to the wall and decorated *en suite*. Many of these pieces had marble tops, and the frame, carried out in soft wood, was usually gilt and burnished. Florid in character and marked by over-elaboration of design, these tables with the accompanying mirrors embodied a hotch-potch of eccentricities in which cupids gambolled in a maze of Louis Quinze, Chinese, and Gothic embellishment. But was Chippendale entirely to blame? Certainly not. Again we must recall the conclusion long since arrived at, that the artist was merged at times in the trader, and the nation undoubtedly favoured a taste which had its inception in the vulgarly ornate handling of the Italian picture-frame popular here for a while.

Candlestands (Torchères).

The candlestand, or torchère, was a piece of furniture introduced into few old English homes, and fine examples of it are highly prized by collectors to-day. It was a tall and slender model usually resting on a tripod, and was crowned either by branching candelabra fitted to the platform on the top of the column or by a graceful and dainty little gallery-enclosed or other tray, upon which loose candlesticks could be placed. In the latter forms it closely resembled the *tall* vase - stands which

Chippendale created. Its height usually varied from 3ft. 6in. to 4ft. 6in. The tripod was almost without exception Louis Quinze in style. The column may be met with solid and reminiscent of Louis Quatorze or Louis

A very fine pair of Chippendale Candlestands. Circa 1745. These are of great rarity. Author's Collection.

Quinze. The majority of examples show pierced work throughout the space separating the tripod feet and the top itself. These pierced columns are impregnated with the teachings of the Louis Quinze, Chinese, and

Bureau-Bookcase, probably by Chippendale, showing architectural feeling; period 1740.

Gothic schools, sometimes purely translated, oftener compounded.

Bureaus.

In outline the Chippendale bureau differed but little from those of the oak and walnut periods, but it was of far better construction and altogether a finer piece of furniture. The prototype in oak was fitted with a well, which was enclosed by a sliding lid on a plane with the flap when drawn down ready for writing. During the walnut era this device was frequently favoured, but not universally employed. It was conceived with a view to safeguarding private papers, but its general employment did away with its *raison d'être*. In use it was very inconvenient, as the bureau platform had to be cleared every time access to the well was desired, and pens, papers, &c., used to get lost in it. Chippendale very rightly discarded its use.

The oak bureau has a nominal value only, and is now often veneered with finer wood (generally satinwood) by the faker. These points as to the " well " should be remembered. Practically every oak bureau had the well. Scarcely any fine wood bureau had the fitting. An oak bureau can be purchased readily for £2, add another £2 for veneering, and the rogue offers a counterfeit of an example worth, perhaps, £20. Of course the well fitting *may* be eliminated, but it is hard to blot out these conversions if they are *specially* looked for. With experience the collector will of course readily distinguish genuine old satinwood or other veneer from spurious modern work, but in the gaining of his experience he will remember all these details if he be wise.

There are two more points to be borne in mind : (i.)

the bureau after 1730 was much better lined than were the general run of earlier specimens, and (ii.) the collector should look for signs of other handle fittings *inside* the drawers. The oak piece was fitted with brass handles of the pear-drop (single) character, or with the ordinary drop handle, but with a *smaller* span than Chippendale and Sheraton favoured for their productions.

The more expensive bureaus made by Chippendale were veneered in panels of finely-figured mahogany. Their carcases and linings may be found in mahogany, oak, or even cedar. Exquisite handles of the Louis Quinze style grace their exteriors, and they stand on ogee feet. The bulk of plainer mahogany bureaus attributed to this master knew him not. Internally the arrangement of fittings, shelves, drawers, private nooks, &c., is generally varied, but Chippendale decorated the top or cornice drawers in all his best pieces in either the Louis Quinze or the Chinese fret manner, and he almost invariably decorated the classic column (guarding each side of the central door). These columns formed the face of two pseudo-private, tall, narrow, upright drawers running towards the back of the piece, sometimes hiding other private fittings.

The Bureau-Bookcase.

It was the master's custom to fit bookcase tops to many of these pieces, and when so fitted they are in much greater demand than are the less pretentious bureaus proper. These tops were subjected to two different treatments; some had panelled fronts, others glass latticework, showing the contents of the upper part, and therefore available to-day for the display of old china.

Here, then, is a fine field for the faker, for not only

Fine Chippendale Bureau-Bookcase of the period 1750, in the possession of Messrs. Gill and Reigate, Ltd.

does he build us new tops, converting our bureaus into bureau-bookcases, but, if the panelled example be not decorative, as in the example shown herewith, he cuts out the panel, and fits in a glass-fronted, lattice-contained pair of doors, even going so far as to insert one or two old panes of glass perhaps. This old glass will be found to exhibit a streak or ridge running across its face, a result peculiar to the method under which it was spun out.

The collector must examine carefully (1) the lattice woodwork, which should be patinated on its outside edges; (2) the manner in which this lattice-work is built together and into the door-frame (the original joints were rabbeted together on the principle of the male and female joint—a laborious but perfect system of workmanship; the latter-day work is dovetailed or more crudely executed as a labour-saving expedient); (3) the putty round glass edges (a subject we have already discussed); and, lastly, the foundations on the top of the bureau upon which the upper storey is built.

Bureaus were seldom carved externally. Bureau-bookcases, on the other hand, frequently exhibit classical decoration, with a Chinese fretwork frieze thrown in. All carved work on these examples should be subjected to the closest scrutiny.

Clock-Cases.

An author, in dealing with the clock-cases of the Chippendale school, tells us that they displayed hardly any carving at all—a statement which, to say the least of it, is extremely misleading. The ordinary mahogany plain-cased grandfather is frequently, but erroneously, attributed to Chippendale. *As a matter of fact, most of the long clocks which can with certainty be attributed to the great master are freely decorated.*

In outline, Chippendale's more elaborate suggestions were palpably modelled on the lines of the French or Dutch schools (Dutch through Queen Anne descent). They were relieved at first with a wealth of rococo or more chaste Renaissance embellishment, a fashion which in later years gave way to Gothic or Chinese handling. Our designer frequently introduced fine horizontal belts of classic acanthus on his clock-bases at their junction with the " waist."

Clocks were seldom bought from cabinet-makers, but rather from clock-makers, who obtained the cases from small craftsmen or hands specialising in that branch of work. These case-makers could not cope with elaborate carving, but they could mechanically apply fretwork, and so the majority of grandfather cases of the Chippendale period carry little or no decoration other than that of appliqué work. On the, comparatively speaking, rare occasions when Chippendale secured commissions in this particular field, he gave us carved embellishment to the hoods, waists, and bases of long-case clocks, and we only recognise as " Chippendale " that small proportion of specimens which carries his typical and sharply-cut garnishment.

Picture-Frames.

Chippendale picture-frames are not easily distinguished, seeing that there were many frame-makers who were exponents of the school which the great master's father (Thomas Chippendale the First) favoured. Almost invariably the authentic example is decorated with graceful scrolls and foliated work, linked together by the everpresent C.

Very rare style of Bureau-Bookcase, by Thomas Chippendale
Period 1745. Owned by Messrs. Gill and Reigate, Ltd.

The Hanging Bookshelf or Show Shelf.

The little two, three, or four tier hanging bookshelf, now generally used for the display of china, was a piece of furniture which Chippendale first brought to perfection. Generally in the Chinese vogues, little touches of Louis Quinze or Gothic treatment outcrop in it from time to time. It has usually no glass in its composition, but the front was occasionally glazed. The sides were as a rule formed by a Chinese or Gothic fretwork scheme, a treatment which was from time to time extended to the frame at the top. The more elaborate designs show pagoda shaped domes and Chinese or Gothic strips of decoration running along the face of each shelf. Now and then a plain or a shaped protecting fillet rises in front of each shelf to contain the book or article placed thereon. These little " sets of bookshelves," as they are generally known, are very rare, and as they are rightly valued for their appearance and usefulness, they command a high figure in the market. Particular attention should be paid to their condition, as they are frequently reproduced by the faker, seeing that the fretwork phase of Chippendale is the easiest to simulate with any chance of success.

CHAPTER XIII.
Thomas Chippendale
(continued).

The Square Leg.

THE commonest form of leg employed by Chippendale was square approximately, but as often as not with the inside angle chamfered in order that the leg when viewed sideways might appear to be of lighter proportions. The designer was of necessity often bound down to a certain price for his card-table or set of chairs, for instance, and he very rightly elected to introduce just as much *first-class work* (into the chair-back, let us imagine) as the bargain warranted, leaving the legs plain, rather than to employ a more general scheme executed in an inferior manner and entailing the same cost.

Here we have the keynote of " Chippendale " proper (as spoken of to-day), and this was why so many a comparatively plain model by the great master eclipsed the more ambitious production of some one or other of his less gifted contemporaries.

The square leg may be found with its outside angle decorated with an ovolo or sunk beading; it is commonly met with having a fluted moulding running down the course of its two outside faces, whilst these in turn may be further enhanced by a scheme of pearl-and-bead or lozenge-and-bead carving running down the outer edge

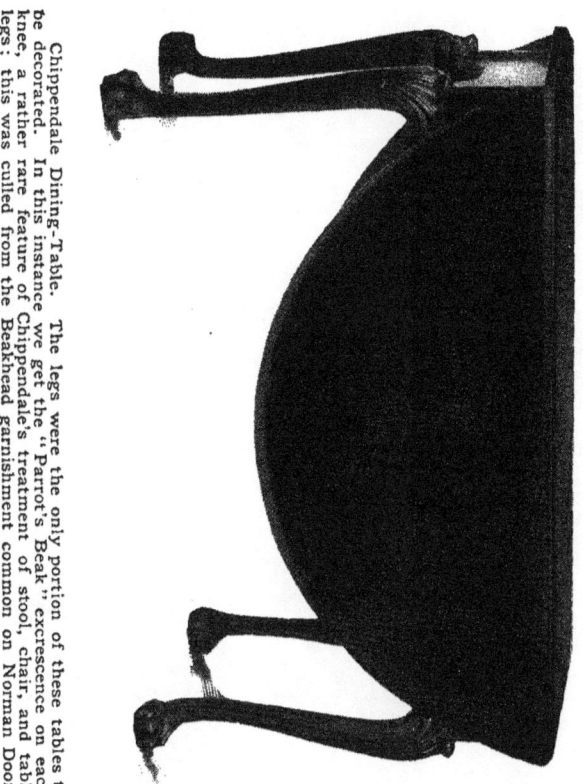

Chippendale Dining-Table. The legs were the only portion of these tables to be decorated. In this instance we get the "Parrot's Beak" excrescence on each knee, a rather rare feature of Chippendale's treatment of stool, chair, and table legs; this was culled from the Beakhead garnishment common on Norman Doorways. Circa 1750. Author's Collection.

of each front leg. Some fine examples show pendent strings of husk nut or other floral character.

Dining-Tables.

Of dining-tables or tables which were suitable, if not exclusively used for, the purposes of meals Chippendale gave some three varieties, broadly speaking. The commonest was a large square or oval model on the lines of the table seen in our illustration (page 355); but only the finest examples were carved on knee and foot. Ordinarily supplied with four legs, two of which were rigid whilst two pulled out, one at each side, to support its relative flap, the collector may now and then come across large specimens with a complement of six or even eight legs. In the case of these six- or eight-legged tables, four legs are usually rigid and support the centre portion of the table. Four-legged claw-and-ball tables of this order are not infrequently met with; but *with finely-carved knee-decoration* they are distinctly rare, and this little addition at once trebles the value of the piece.

The author once owned a fine square-shaped claw-and-ball Chippendale dining-table that opened and closed on the concertina principle to admit of the insertion of a square leaf; this, resting on the supporting framework, had mahogany plugs fitting into female joints on either side—a very rare example.

Miss Constance Simon, in her "English Furniture Designers of the Eighteenth Century," describes fully the dining-table most generally in favour, telling us that it consisted of two centre-pieces, with wide flaps on either side, and two semicircular end-pieces, all four divisions being joined together or separated at will by means of small brass adjustments. Each of the two larger portions stood on four cabriole or other typical legs, and the semi-circular pieces on two legs only; the latter when not in use were pushed up against the wall, and served as side-tables. Some one or other of these sections has generally been separated from its fellows, and so we have it that the complete table has seldom come down to us through the ages. The concertina action freely used for card-tables, &c., is so seldom met with in Chippendale dining-tables that it can perhaps hardly rank as one of the master's stock productions.

Where Chippendale resorted to Chinese decoration of the leg, he now and then carried the treatment round the frieze, a treatment also meted out to Gothic examples on rare occasions.

China Cabinets.

Controversy has raged around the subject of the artistic value of Chippendale china cabinets, and as these pieces of furniture were almost invariably of considerable importance we may well weigh the pros and cons which have been adduced on one side or the other of the case. Broadly speaking, the traducers of Chippendale have based their attacks on two points—(1) his blending of style, and (2) his penchant for the Chinese vogue. Our designer deliberately fused ideas culled from the various schools upon which he drew for inspiration, and he certainly affected the mode *à la Chinois* whenever possible. On the face of it, then, it would appear that the opponents of England's first old master have made good their points; but unfortunately for these gentlemen their arguments on analysis prove to be as shallow as veneer.

Those readers who, in addition to a love for old furniture, have studied the beauties of early porcelains

China Show-Case in the style of Chippendale or Ince and Mayhew.
Author's Collection.

will remember that practically the only china available during the second quarter of the eighteenth century came from China or from Dresden. Now Dresden by 1720 had sent her wares abroad; but what *motif* had governed their creation? Oriental in colour-treatment, the models most in favour were purely Chinese, and it is a remarkable fact that almost every factory in Europe during its best period endeavoured to emulate this Eastern school of work. As an instance, let us take the Worcester factory, first known as the Worcester Tonquin manufactory, which in its infancy copied Chinese models, Chinese colour-scheme, Chinese subjects in matters pertaining to decoration, and then supplemented the whole by forged Chinese factory marks.

We have already seen that Chippendale had a happy intuition when adapting his models to the purpose and surroundings for which they were intended. Citing two instances alone, we remember how the voluptuous lines of the Louis Quinze appealed to him as being most suitable for bed, sofa, and chair, and how as a result his designs were rest-compelling in the extreme. On the other hand, he deemed that organ-cases should be in the Gothic vogue. Why? Because the bulk of English churches would be in consonance with this treatment, and we know that when they breathed other feeling he modified his designs accordingly.

Having noticed Chippendale's common-sense in these directions, we cannot wonder that he elected to follow the Chinese fashion when building his china cabinets or cases, seeing that these were destined to contain and " set-off " either (1) Oriental porcelain itself, or (2) Western porcelain following closely Celestial tradition. In the opinion of many judges the Chinese phase was the weakest of those which our designer gave us; but there can surely be no doubt that it was pre-eminently the best available for the display of contemporary porcelains.

Turning to the other contention, that Chippendale took liberties and blended matter in an unwarrantable manner. He certainly took artistic licence, but we must surely judge him by the results he achieved rather than by the canons he ventured to disregard. It is the rarest possible thing to meet with any china cabinet by Chippendale which is not at once striking and pleasing, even if technical flaws are apparent when the example is analytically dissected.

Now let us examine the question of extraneous influences which may have worked sometimes for purity, sometimes for fusion of styles. The object of the china cabinet is to house and to show off to the greatest advantage the owner's collection of ceramic gems, and it follows, therefore, as a corollary that the show-case should, whenever possible, harmonise with the specimens it contains.

We cannot do better than cite a few facts in matters ceramic, and presently see if they throw any light on the question of the china case. As readers are doubtless aware, the earliest Dresden is held in highest repute, and the early decoration then affected, by artist and modeller alike, was mainly Chinese in character. After 1730, although the same figure or group held the public eye, it would rest on a base distinctly Louis Quinze, besides showing traces of this latter influence in its rococo decoration. One step further and model, base, and decoration became Louis Quinze.

It will be evident that Chippendale furnished a parallel in cabinet-making, seeing that he gave us Chinese designs, Chinese-cum-Louis Quinze, and also Louis Quinze models. Was he to blame for giving his patrons frames to suit their pictures? In justice to him we may safely assert that in his efforts after harmony he followed the trend of public taste and simply provided fitting homes for such phases and transitional phases in china as the fashion of the hour demanded.

Let us for one minute, in support of this, turn again to Dresden, the pioneer factory in Europe. By 1725 practically only Oriental china or " Oriental " Dresden was available for the collector, and what more fitting home for such a collection could be found than a cabinet breathing Chinese inspiration? From 1730-1745 Dresden mandarins and Celestial groups rested on Louis Quinze bases, and here again the hybrid Chinese-cum-Louis XV. would have rendered the china case *en suite* with the gems it was destined to contain. Later again, when, as in the case of mid-eighteenth-century Dresden, or of our Chelsea or Bow groups, the Chinese element had been generally displaced by almost pure Louis Quinze, Chippendale was but creating a harmony when he elected to discard the Oriental tradition in a whole-hearted interpretation of the fashionable and contemporary French school.

There is but one weak spot in these contentions, and that lies in the priority in which these different vogues stand to one another. It might be popularly held that Louis XV., Louis XV.-cum-Chinese, and pure Chinese marked the true sequence in evolution, so that the developments stand in inverse order to the demands of contemporary porcelain. A perusal of Chapter X. will have shown that the public appreciated Eastern work since the days of lacquer ware, and Batty Langley cannot have been alone in suggesting Chinese frets during the late thirties of the century.

Batty Langley had shown Chinese frets in his 1739 design for "Cabinetworks," evidencing an existing taste for such detail. Edwards and Darly, as we have seen, published "A New Book of Chinese Design" in 1754, the very title of which book was significant, as it directly implied pre-existing effort in the same field. Chippendale, when introducing his new suggestions in the Chinese style in 1754, hoped that they might *improve* "that manner of taste," and china cabinets and show-cases, as the most suitable of all models for the display of Eastern embellishment, were certainly decorated with Chinese frets and lattice-work in the 'forties.

The master certainly benefited as a tradesman under the revival, because he was *facile princeps* in the cabinet-making brotherhood of the time, and it follows that there is much of his late work obviously Chinese in character; but at the same time we must remember that his best and most artistic rendering of the idea Celestial antedated the Chambers craze, of which it was in reality entirely independent. Naturally the designer was not always consulted by the intending purchaser; but when his advice was asked for we may rest assured that an artist who ransacked the classics for quotations bearing on his art, who pleaded for the correct tassel to a bedstead, and who indicated the wallpaper which would best show up the beauties of a chair, did not casually design Louis Quinze cases to show off Chinese porcelain, or, on the other hand, Chinese cases to exhibit Louis Quinze china. Gothic ideas were impressed into service now and then; but the show case in this style is very rare, and was probably ordered by somebody asking for "the latest," or to make up the complement of a room carried out in similar style.

Chippendale, in writing of a design of his for a "china case," tells us that it was "not only the richest and most magnificent in the whole country, but perhaps in all Europe. I had a particular pleasure in retouching and finishing this design, *but should have much more in the execution of it,* as I am confident I can make the work more beautiful and striking than the drawing."

There is a grain of comfort contained in this passage. The young collector who first sees Chippendale's book is so disheartened by the bewildering array of pieces there depicted that he is as often as not disinclined to venture on a collection of furniture appearing at first sight to be unobtainable. Many of Chippendale's suggestions were never carried into effect, others were simplified when constructed, and so, after all, nobody who is prepared to devote careful study, reasonable funds, and, above all, patience, need despair of forming a sound and interesting collection of the great master's work.

The quotation we have just been discussing shows again how keen Chippendale was in matters pertaining to his art, and it again affords those who have seen his beautiful cabinets an opportunity of endorsing the designer's contention that black-and-white drawings, however clever, never represented the full charm of the piece "in being."

The china case when carried out in the Chinese taste was usually crowned with a pagoda-shaped dome, a treatment extended to any wings abutting on the main or central portion of the body. The case proper was glazed, the glass being contained in lattice-work of a more or less Eastern character. Generally speaking, these models rested on legs and feet, the decoration to which was in keeping with the rest of the scheme. From the eaves of the pagoda hung little ivory ornaments, and the general effect arrived at suited the china of the period admirably. It would almost seem as though Chippendale had realised that of all the porcelains that had been produced or were to come, none would blend with his productions so happily as did those of the Oriental school.

It is not necessary to describe again the blending of Chinese with Louis Quinze designs, but it is interesting to note that some of the Louis Quinze models were almost exact reproductions of that vogue, and that they may be met with "bombé" in form (having a shaped swell at the sides and front of body), whilst the legs, *very rarely*, were adorned by carved caryatid decoration.

Glazed Bookcases.

Far commoner than the china cabinet or case is the glazed bookcase, and as this article also serves very well for the display of china, it is in great demand. Those specimens which display the serpentine swell in the body are most highly prized by collectors, other things being equal. Some of the cornices and friezes to these important pieces of furniture are exquisitely beautiful, and show the great designer quite at his best, and again some of the decorated lattice-work traceries containing the glass panes in the doors have never been equalled. In the light of this it is only fair to say that many of the later models show laboured tracery where Chippendale was endeavouring faithfully to delineate the precepts of the Chambers school of work.

The broken pediment of Classic days was the commonest garnishment introduced by Chippendale as a crowning feature to his designs for bookcases, and whenever he ventured into this architectural school for inspiration he supplemented such outline teaching with detail culled from the same source; consequently we find carved detail of the dentil or echinus character, for instance, freely introduced on these occasions. The base of the bookcase contained cupboards or drawers, more commonly the former, occasionally tiers of drawers at the wings with cupboards at the centre.

Needless to say, Chinese, Louis Quinze, and Gothic teachings all came in for a turn of popularity, and the designer handled each in turn with his inimitable freedom and breadth.

Collectors should remember that many plain cabinets, bookcases, &c., exist *in old mahogany*, and it should be scarcely necessary to warn them that " carving up " is rife. It is, therefore, advisable to scrutinise relief decoration before making a purchase.

Tea-Caddies.

Chippendale was probably the first master to make a special study of the tea-caddy. To us, with our tea at 1s. 6d. per lb. and upwards, the significance of this little piece of furniture is apt to be lost; but, could we hark back some 150 years, its importance would at once be apparent. Tea was then commonly 7s. 6d. to a guinea a pound, and, as a consequence, had to be jealously guarded under lock and key. This being the case, fashion decreed that a little " strong box " at once graceful and efficacious should form an adjunct of every well-appointed breakfast or other room where tea was partaken of.

We have gathered by now that our ancestors were nothing if not thorough in their artistic perceptions, and so we have it that, with such a small article as the tea-caddy even, harmony had to prevail; thus when we look into the matter we find that there are Queen Anne, Chippendale, and Sheraton caddies, to quote three instances only, each specifically designed to repose on their relative sideboards or tables.

The Chippendale tea-chest or caddy is generally in the Louis XV. style, but has now and then a touch of the Chinese vogue in its composition. Chippendale might perhaps have housed the Eastern leaf in models governed by the Celestial *motif*, but it is only fair to say that no style lends itself so happily to the small casket as does the Louis Quinze. These little tea-chests rested either on ogee feet in mahogany or on finely-chased brass claw-and-ball or French cabriole extremities. They were further set off by exquisite handles and keyhole escutcheons in this metal.

Commodes.

The term " commode " has a corrupt interpretation in our country; in reality it refers to a handsome chest of drawers or low-standing cabinet designed for the drawing-room. The French model which gave rise to English imitations was generally carried out in boule and ormolu, and the panels were often painted, or rather decorated, in the fashion known as Vernis-Martin.

Chippendale obviously had something of the same sort in mind when writing of a commode, for he tells us " The bas-relief in the middle may be carved in wood or cast in brass, or painted on wood." The writer has never seen any of this painted work which can be safely fathered on Chippendale, and it is doubtful whether he or his staff would have had sufficient experience to bring such efforts to a happy conclusion.

Chippendale was seen to great advantage in his handsome but extremely rare mahogany commodes in Louis XV. style. The French feet or fancy brackets which he designed for these models were taller and more elaborately treated than those which were employed for his chests of drawers proper. Chippendale generally decorated the top edge of the piece with a band of classic carving and the lower edge of the carcase with a belt of rococo detail. These two horizontal lines of embellishment were, at times, joined by perpendicular bands of carved matter, rising between the tiers of drawers and dividing the model's face into compartments. Gracefully shaped, the outline of the commode was usually bombé or serpentine, and when the former contour is present we find the upright front edges, showing Louis Quinze decoration complementary to the underlying leg-work. Chippendale is generally credited with the cabinet-work in the best lacquered commodes of his day, but it is probable that the carcases passed from him before the lacquer was applied. The master's Gothic and Chinese designs were not so successful as his French adaptations, and hardly call for especial notice. His later examples may show restrained inlay.

The commode was primarily built low in order that it might display fine porcelains, bronzes, and chased ormolu work at or below the line of vision, and the old-time designer used to give hints as to the equipment of the top. So, too, we find Chippendale telling us "On the top of the commode is a design for a surtout to be made in silver. A candle-stand at each end is very proper."

Fire-screens.

With the fire-screen we come to another of the chief pieces of movable furniture created or designed by Chippendale. This useful and necessary little article was produced in three different forms—the tripod, the folding, and the horse. Each of these could again be sub-divided if we were tracing minor varieties rather than general types.

We sometimes find models purporting to be tripod tables which are in reality conversions from tripod fire-screens. The former articles of furniture are in great demand; the latter are seldom used nowadays save for decorative purposes. The old needlework screens which were fitted to the pole of the so-called banner-stand (the banner proper was a later introduction) are often missing, whilst the poles themselves may be broken, missing, or warped by heat. Upon the tripod accordingly a new column is reared, and this is crowned by a tray, ancient or modern, with the result that a very presentable adaptation is effected.

The converted model possesses these features of merit, that it is useful and that its main decoration is genuine, but the collector naturally seeks to acquire pieces which are authentic and in their original state.

Indications of these alterations and amplifications are to be found in the upper portions of the columnar work immediately underlying the table-top. The similarity between the tripod screen and table ceased just above the swell of the column. In the case of the former it fined down to receive the joining pole; in the case of the latter it was comparatively sturdy to support the table-top. Where the heavier columnar work has been substituted, traces of a joint often appear, and there is generally a difference in the hue and character of the two mahoganies.

The material employed within the frame was usually old silk or woollen needlework, sometimes a combination of the two, with the woolwork predominating. This needlework was as often as not made by some lady of the house, to be subsequently consigned to Chippendale for framing and mounting.

Here it is well to dispel one illusion which is prevalent. It does not follow because the woolwork is of the William and Mary period that therefore the screen is pre-Chippendale, for every household had its examples of home-made needlework, and it may not have occurred to the owner that he could best utilise some piece (which he had on hand) for this particular purpose until he had been pleased, perhaps, by a Chippendale screen, mounting similar work, that someone maybe had shown him.

By far the commonest screens are those with the work enclosed in square or shaped mahogany frames running up and down a pole which rises from a tripod. Usually the frame would be square, and relieved by a shallow moulding; but now and then we come

Chippendale Tripod Fire-screen.
Circa 1745. Author's Collection.

across specimens elaborately shaped, and decorated in the style of the Louis Quinze.

The needlework would be backed by some old self-coloured silken material, or as an alternative by a Chinese picture printed in colour on fairly stout paper, and, although 150 years of age, many of these pictures survive to-day, albeit they are generally more or less dilapidated.

After the tripod-screen comes the folding-screen, and this, though fairly common when plain in character, is distinctly rare if freely decorated. The square-framed folders are generally set off by Chinese fretwork below the needlework, and here we find one evidence of the conscientious work which the old craftsmen used to put in. The dainty fretwork subjected to intense heat would be liable to warp and "draw," and in order that it might be rendered as proof against this disadvantage as possible, it was made up of distinct layers of thick veneer laid crossways and cemented together, so that one "grain" might pull against the other, and thus offer the maximum of resisting power. These frets are styled "three ply."

When the folding-screen was shaped it was also carved, generally in the Louis Quinze style. When so found it proves to be almost an exact duplicate of its French contemporary, though there is more life and sharpness in the carving of the English example. Specimens such as these are very valuable.

The last form of fire-screen which Thomas Chippendale favoured is known as "the horse." This screen rested on two pairs of feet parallel to one another, and the framework resembles that of the single towel-horse with which we are all familiar. The feet would be almost invariably in the Louis Quinze style, and the decoration carried out in character with this school; but Chippendale in the 'fifties often introduced representations of icicles or of Chinese matter within the scheme. A reference to our illustration on page 517 will show one of these little screens by Heppelwhite, who is noted for some of the daintiest of these designs.

Four-Poster Bedsteads.

Chippendale attached quite an unusual importance to his four-poster bedstead, and as a result we find many an example by him which would do justice to a Royal apartment. First let us hear what he has to say when submitting a bed, and we shall then glean at first hand how he approached his subject. He submits the design to the " Judicious and Candid for their approbation. There are found Magnificence, Proportion, and Harmony. If the Pedestals of the Bedstead, the Pillars, Cornice, and Top of the Dome are gilt with burnished Gold, and the Furniture is suitable, the whole will look extremely grand, and be fit for the most stately apartment. The Bedstead should be six or seven feet broad, seven or eight long, and the whole height fourteen or fifteen feet. A Workman of Genius will easily comprehend the Design."

Again, he paid attention to the hangings and drapery. Writing on another occasion of a couch with canopy : " If the curtains and valances are adorned with large gold fringes and tassels, and the ornaments gilt with burnished gold, it will look very grand." Of the carved detail in this instance he further tells us : " The Crane at the top of the Canopy is the emblem of Care and Watchfulness, which is not unbecoming a place of rest." These extracts relate to the more elaborate suggestions put forward by the designer, and, as the reader will have gathered, they refer to that rather garish style of gilded furniture which was somewhat of a blot on Chippendale's artistic reputation.

Our master was in his happiest vein when handling the four-poster in mahogany. There is, and has been for many a long day, a deep-rooted prejudice against this piece of furniture, and as a result it will generally be found to have been broken up. The posts which rose at the foot of the bed and carried the canopy, exhibiting as they did the most exquisite designs and examples of carving, are usually met with cut down and mounted on new or old tripods, with a modern tray crowning the columns; in this form they do duty as lamp or fern stands. Subjected to this treatment, all sense of proportion is lost; a governing air of modernity consequent on the conversion pervades them, whilst the link with the artistic past is swept away. As a matter of fact, the old bedstead *when fitted with the modern spring mattress* is singularly comfortable, yet graceful withal, and the improvement is readily made.

Fortunately the class of vandalism referred to is on the decrease, and a small proportion of these gems will be preserved for posterity in their original beauty. The best examples have pierced-work cornices, exhibiting bold and striking rococo conceptions, carried out by the cleverest of chisels. The bed-hangings used to fall down from *within* the cornice, unless it was a plain one, when they were sometimes fastened on to its exterior.

However plain the rest of the bed might be, the two posts at its foot were always charming. A common feature was the old Renaissance bulb or swell beloved of Chippendale for his little tripod gallery tables, of which we have noticed so many styles. Rococo detail, strings

Bedstead by Chippendale, in the style of the Louis Quinze, probably the finest of its kind extant. Mahogany; circa 1745. Lately owned by Frank Partridge, Esq.

of flowers, husk nuts, or bellflowers fell daintily down gracefully fluted columns, or garlands encircled the tapering pillar. When Louis Quinze work obtains exclusively, the foot will be found to be a massive and handsome claw-and-ball as a general rule. During the decade commencing 1750 our designer trenched on the Gothic and Chinese styles for his bedsteads, and these vogues led to many a good model. The posts in both cases generally rested on a square-shaped foot, decorated with either sunken panes or panels of the Gothic school, or with the fretwork peculiar to the Chinese mode, as the case might be.

The sinuous swells and curves of the Louis Quinze invited rest within their borders. The harder lines of the other fashions did not so readily lend themselves to a sleeping-chamber, and however chaste and beautiful a cluster column of the Early English period might have been to Chippendale's eye, he must have hesitated before introducing it for bedroom garnishment.

Fine Chippendale mahogany four-posters with good cornices are now fetching large prices, and should under no circumstances be dismantled. Occasionally they are to be met with with finely-carved head-pieces, and mutilation here might mean a loss of some hundreds of pounds to the misguided owner.

Other Bedroom Furniture.

Chippendale held that bedroom furniture should be decorative as well as useful, and the pains which he took in the construction of four-post bedsteads, divans, &c., was typical of the man in his treatment of wardrobes, clothes-presses, and kindred articles for upstairs use. Perhaps the wardrobe ranked as the most important piece after the bedstead, and here was a field in which our master had free scope for his abilities. The most eloquent testimony to the excellence attained by Chippendale in this direction lies in the fact that nowadays the true wardrobe attributable to him is deemed worthy of a place in drawing-room or boudoir side by side with other eighteenth-century gems which were specially designed for those apartments.

In the case of the bookcase, Chippendale paid great attention to the cornice, and indeed he placed decorative work there when the rest of the design was almost devoid of garnishment. The wardrobe, on the other hand, showed a cornice plain as a rule, even when the rest of the piece was freely embellished.

If we have, graven on our minds, a fair picture of the various designs which Chippendale conceived for bookcases, we shall be able to form a very fair idea of the treatment meted out to the fine wardrobe in (1) the shaping of carcase construction, (2) the character of carving, and (3) its scheme of application. Two reservations must be made, and then we shall obtain a fairly accurate picture and parallel. First the bookcase would have greater height with the same breadth; and, secondly, the fittings of the wardrobe inside the carcase would, of course, be entirely different.

In contour the wardrobe was sometimes squarely built, and it may be found with a top square built, but resting on a base bombé in form. The whole may be met with showing a graceful serpentine swell from cornice to foot, and now and then the treatment may have been bombé throughout.

Plain French, ogee, or elaborated Louis Quinze feet were chiefly employed, just as the intending purchaser needed a low, medium, or high-priced article, though of course where the *tout ensemble* of the piece demanded it, Gothic or Chinese handling came into evidence. The front angles of the square or serpentine-shaped wardrobe were, as a rule, chamfered or squared off; sometimes the top section of the wardrobe only would be so treated, but on other occasions the base, too, would be similarly dealt with. Upon the surface so prepared, Chippendale was wont to place a long strip of fretwork in the Chinese style, sometimes crowning each strip, top and base, with a classic truss, or with a species of crocket (the crocket hails from Early English moulding crowns, such as those in Lincoln Cathedral, *circ.* 1350).

This method of garnishing the wardrobe was also extended to the double chest, or tallboy (Fr. *haut-bois*), and in this latter piece the fretwork would be extended at the top, underneath the mouldings and dentil work crowning the cornice.

The tallboy commonly, the wardrobe occasionally, are to be found with a slide fitted into the carcase at the waist. Erroneously styled writing-slabs, these were primarily intended for the brushing, folding, or arranging of garments previous to their being placed in the drawers. The base of the wardrobe was rather more than one-third of the whole height of the piece, that of the tallboy approximately one-half of its height. Where the bombé shape of wardrobe was affected the front edges of the base were relieved by sweeping and gracefully-imposed rococo curves. The doors of the wardrobe were sometimes decorated in one scheme, demanding their full field for its display, but they were generally garnished with corresponding and self-contained designs.

At times the relief carving took the form of large

foliated C scrolls, or, again, a Gothic-cum-Louis Quinze rendering may have been selected. Generally we find the wardrobe door showing conventional square-shaped panels decorated with a classic moulding, though this is sometimes broken and relieved by rococo touches at each angle. The best of these wardrobes fetch hundreds of pounds, the finest tallboys, on the other hand, seldom touch fifty. Both are occasionally used for the housing of such delicate articles as miniatures which need protection against strong lights, but, unless really fine, collectors use them for their proper or original purpose.

The clothes-presses which Chippendale gave us are somewhat reminiscent in outline of the old Spanish dower-chests: they were used to store clothes, linen, curtains, and so on; but, judging by their rarity, we may safely assume that they did not come into great favour. They rested on deep feet or short legs approximately resembling those seen on plain commodes. The carcase would be sometimes square, at other times bombé in form, but it seldom displays the amount of garnishment we should expect to find on it after a perusal of Chippendale's book of designs. The feet were linked together by a narrow frame, and upon this the body of the piece reposed.

Where decoration is found it is usually in panel formation on the body, the supporting frame being treated much as a frieze with Chinese or Gothic embellishment. The legs or feet are nearly always found to be well decorated in one or other of the fashions beloved by Chippendale.

The chest of drawers by our great designer is usually serpentine in form, with chamfered ends containing fret work decoration, as often as not crowned by the crockets we have just referred to. It would rest on ogee feet probably, and would invariably display fine brass handles and escutcheons, besides being in construction a master-piece of the cabinet-maker's art.

There are a few fitted dressing-tables by Chippendale still extant, but they are so prized that they are almost invariably brought down to the best room in the house. If we conjure up a fine kneehole writing cabinet such as we have but lately discussed and then add a graceful rococo superstructure containing a glass we shall arrive at the model our designer favoured, only that in this instance the decoration will not be extended to the back, and *may* be only at the front of the table.

As to the Chippendale washstand, we may merely note that the master was quite conversant with all the little devices which went to make up the *multum in parvo* basin and dressing-cabinet, and that he really only excelled other designers in the case of some of the exquisite, if somewhat inefficient, little tripod basin-stands, which he created on the lines of the wig-stand.

Fixed Garnishments.

Chippendale attached more importance to the movable than to the fixed garnishment of a room, and although we now and then find a door, a cornice, or a fireplace with its attendant overmantel, obviously designed by him, he cannot be held to have shone in this direction. His work is always bold and daring, and the carving giving expression to it was sharp and vigorous; but there were contemporary artists making this particular field their especial care who naturally excelled him.

Some of his Louis XV. designs are undoubtedly good, many of his hybrid Louis Quinze and Chinese models show laboured and ornate conception; in fact, the chisel has done wonders where the pencil has been but mediocre.

If there was one form of *fixed* interior garnishment where our master almost held his own, it is to be found amongst some of the less pretentious Louis Quinze window-cornices. Here the gentle swell of the arch, built up of graceful curves, lent itself to that interpretation of the curvilinear in which our master was always a success.

Résumé.

We have noticed how Chippendale was influenced by the teachings of the Renaissance, and how, after giving expression to them chiefly in a rococo manner, he incorporated Eastern and Gothic ideas in his work. There is one point which we must, however, grasp before we can realise the difference between Chippendale and the succeeding masters whose work we shall shortly be studying. Chippendale subordinated classic detail to the idea to which his pencil was giving expression, he drew on old-time teachings just when and where he pleased, and he followed the conventionalities only when it suited his purpose to do so. As a consequence there is no hard-and-fast line apparent in most of his designs showing the point where he ceased to be orthodox, and we find ourselves wondering how an artist can have woven a theme so regardless of the conventionalities referred to, and yet have attained such rhythm and sense of proportion.

Of one thing we may be certain—viz., that Chippendale did not disregard the hitherto conceived proprieties from ignorance; it was rather the daring licence of a great artist which would link together Gothic and Chinese detail with a rococo scroll, and it is futile to endeavour to measure the man's genius by any stereotyped standard or set rule. Wellington did not provide a line of retreat for his army at Waterloo, so that theoretically his plans would be severely criticised by every latter-day exponent of tactics. Rules are of necessity laid down for the guidance of the many, because their framers have to presuppose average ability rather than genius, and so it is that now and then we find some man with exceptional talent who rises superior to their limitations and proves that liberties may be successfully taken.

Inlaid Chippendale.

We so seldom meet with inlaid decoration to authenticated Chippendale furniture that it might be regarded as a negligible quantity were it not for the fact that when found it graces *important* models as often as not.

The tops of some fine writing-tables show banded mahogany veneer set at right-angles to the edges or at a similar angle to the mahogany they contain within their compass. The fronts of serpentine commodes may be found showing inlaid decoration, and we now and then come across cabinet-work showing a modicum of inlay.

The small drawers within bureaus, &c., were sometimes treated with a light rectangular band of insignificant decoration, but not one model in a hundred of those rightly or wrongly attributed to the *great* Chippendale carry inlaid embellishment.

On the rare occasions when this designer departed from his rule his marquetry was dignified and restrained. In colour comparatively quiet, in pattern well ordered, it never approached the bizarre in the same manner as did that of his predecessors and successors of the William and Mary and Sheraton periods respectively.

In some few instances the second Chippendale used inlay to set off his early furniture, the top to the tripod table shown on page 259 furnishing a case in point;

but in the vast majority of cases such decoration spells lateness, and dates from the time when fusion was taking place between the Chippendale and Adam vogues. After Chippendale embarked on marquetry he gave us nothing which reflected the character or glories of his recognised work.

The third Chippendale, and the Gillows, Heppelwhites, Seddons, Sons, and Shackleton, and Sheraton, were all certainly employed by R. and J. Adam, but only the first-named and the Seddons refrained from publishing an independent appeal to the public. Chippendale and Co., Chippendale and Haig, and Haig and Chippendale doubtless retained the more conservative survivors of the old clientèle, and it would appear that the excellence of their execution secured them sufficient supplementary commissions from the Adams and other masters to render further appeals for support unnecessary. It is more than probable that the last of the Chippendales was responsible for a large volume of so-called "Sheraton" furniture.

Résumé of Chippendale Leg-work and Foot-work Decoration.

1735.   Louis Quatorze and Régence influence.
1735-40. Caryatides as supports to side-tables, &c.
1735 &   Architectural.
onwards.   i. Pedestal legs.   ii. Terms or terminal leg-work.
1735-45. Massive claw-and-ball legs, with masks on knees, gradually assuming lighter proportions.
,,   ,,   Massive decorated cabriole, gradually assuming lighter proportions, and with bold whorled feet.

Thomas Chippendale.

1745-55.   Lighter claw-and-ball legs, with cabochons and rococo work to knees, replacing the earlier masked knee-work.

,, ,,   Lighter decorated cabriole legs with cabochons to knees and feet surrounded by acanthus or rococo detail.

1750-60   (but chiefly 1750-1755). Light French cabriole, freely covered by rococo embellishment on many occasions.

,, ,,   Cluster columns in quatrefoil shape.

1745.   Ditto in open pierced work. Commonest after 1755.

Note.—The claw-and-ball and cabriole types lasted fitfully until Chippendale's death.

Supports to Bookcases, Writing-tables, Commodes, and Heavy Cabinet-work.

1735-50.—Short claw-and-ball legs (rarely).
,, ,,   French feet, rococo embellishment.
,, ,,   Scrolled feet, ,,   ,,
,, ,,   Bracket feet,   ,,   ,,
,, ,,   Ogee feet,   ,,   ,,   (commonest of all).

Leg-work Resumed.

1740-55.   Square legs showing floral matter of Grinling Gibbons type.

,, ,,   Square legs showing increasing body of Chinese lattice detail. (In embryonic form until 1750.)

1740-55. Floral-cum-rococo work.
,,   ,,   Floral-cum-fretwork gradually gaining ground.
,,   ,,   Rococo-cum-Chinese decoration gradually gaining ground.
1745 & onwards. Square fluted legs, inner angles chamfered.
,,   ,,   Square fluted legs, inner angles chamfered, with bead or pearl and lozenge decoration to outer front edges of leg-work.

Supports to Heavy Cabinet Models.

1745-55. French feet.
,,   ,,   Brackets, rococo or rococo-cum-lattice decoration.
,,   ,,   Ogee brackets, rococo or rococo-cum-lattice decoration.

Leg-work Resumed.

1755-65. Carved Chinese lattice designs on square legs common.
,,   ,,   Appliqué and pierced lattice designs on square legs common.
1760-65. Appliqué and pierced lattice designs, Chinese-cum-Gothic on square legs.
1765. Square tapered legs and shaped stretcher-work accompanying Gothic models.
,,   Gothic appliqué work showing signs of Chinese influence at times.

Legs and under-frame work reminiscent of the style seen in the illustration on page 118 may be found with Gothic chair-backs, &c., overlying it.

1765. Incipient Classic, uniting Late Chippendale with Early Adam designs.

Thomas Chippendale.

Supports to Heavy Cabinet-work.

1750-65.	French feet.
,, ,,	Louis Quinze-cum-Chinese brackets.
,, ,,	Ogee brackets.
,, ,,	Chinese brackets, sometimes pierced.
,, ,,	Chinese brackets merged with dawning Gothic, sometimes pierced.
1765.	Gothic, or Gothic brackets with a little rococo matter blended. Classic detail may be found on any example.

Plain square legs with a beading running down their outer front edges may be met with through all the phases subsequent to 1740, and the remainder of the models' garnishment may be of the highest workmanship.

Square legs may also carry finely-cut classic detail or twisted garlands of floral matter running spirally up their course.

The foregoing are the *principal* combinations with the approximate dates of their employment by Chippendale. It will be understood that the designer frequently matched or increased sets of chairs, &c., at a date when the patterns in question had become partially or wholly obsolete.

CHAPTER XIV.
Irish Chippendale.

A New School of Cabinet-making.

WHILST Chippendale was picking up the threads of the Queen Anne vogue, a school of cabinet-making and design which had faint points of resemblance to that which he was introducing in England sprang into existence in Ireland. In the absence of definite data as to the fountain-head of this work, it is commonly dubbed "Irish Chippendale," though it is palpable to the student that the great master had no direct connection with its appearance. An examination of its characteristics shows perhaps that a Dutch rather than an English interpretation of the curvilinear permeated it. It is indeed a thing apart, differing from the original and true Chippendale more widely than did the contemporary efforts by French or Portuguese copyists on many occasions.

The evolution of the cabriole progressed in Germany, in England, France, Holland, and Portugal, and workmen from any of these countries would have been available had the inducement to visit Irish shores been sufficiently tempting. We may dismiss from our minds the probability of Ireland's having drawn from England or France. In these two countries continuous employment at fair remuneration awaited the skilled craftsman, who would scarcely have left home for a country where employment was but fitful and pay on a less generous scale. Even had

A fine Example of a Bookcase Writing-Cabinet in Irish Chippendale, owned by Messrs. Gill and Reigate, Ltd. The front legs pull out, when an ingenious arrangement of writing-shelves, &c., is displayed under a writing-slab that automatically rises and is worked by a spring. At the right a fan-shaped drawer holding ink swings out clear of the carcase. Circa 1755.

Irish Chippendale.

these drawbacks been non-existent, we should have observed little French or English mannerisms cropping up here and there; but, as we shall presently see, such handling as is akin to that of the Emerald Isle is reminiscent of Holland rather than of France or England.

The Portuguese school, if clever, was so small that its reputation hardly went outside the Spanish peninsula. Holland, on the other hand, had a plethora of workmen with average ability, some of whom may have welcomed the advantages which Dublin could confer. The stiff and wooden rendering of Louis Quinze emanating from Dutch workshops resembled Irish Chippendale more closely than did any other. Probably some leaders of fashion who knew London brought back the latest taste, or rather a smattering of it, on their return to Ireland, and then native talent, aided by some Dutch carvers, laid the foundation of " Irish Chippendale." We look in vain through the list of subscribers to Chippendale's " Director " for evidence of a body of Irish cabinet-makers even profiting by his designs.

Irish Carving Compared with English.

The great point that strikes us in Chippendale carving is the verve or sharpness which uniformly characterises it. Irish Chippendale, on the other hand, is invariably decorated in comparatively low relief; the edges in the carved detail are rounded off as though the workman, disdaining the beauties of light and shade, had deliberately rubbed them down with emery-paper. Again, in the English school classic detail was freely used when its introduction marched with the dictates of good taste, occasionally even where perhaps it might have been omitted. In Irish work, on the other hand, though an acanthus leaf or a rose may be tentatively put forward in a flat and uninspired rendering, there is a comparative lack of classic teaching. By far the strongest hint we get comes in the handling of the feet supporting Irish tables or bookcases. The graceful dignity imparted to the claw-and-ball foot in England is conspicuous only by its absence; whilst the stilted and expressionless Dutch model stands out unmistakably before us.

Design.

As to the designs, their contour is perhaps suggestive of Queen Anne days rather than of Chippendale's time; but there is nothing to show that a *careful* study of either vogue governed Pat when at his work. There is one cardinal point to be observed by the cabinet-maker—namely, that in every elaborately-decorated piece of furniture some plain line or lines should be left, not only to act as a foil, and so throw up the effect of the carving elsewhere, but to afford the eye a necessary rest. Chippendale realised this, and though he apparently lost sight of it on rare occasions, he observed it as a general rule. In the case of a leg he would taper decoration some little way down its course and up from the ankle again, but he left the central portion of the graceful curve unclouded in its beauty. Pat unfortunately lost sight of this point, and generally defeated his own ends by decorating lines which, if happily treated, would have been left plain. This mistake outcrops continually in the Irish handling of leg-contour, which is frequently marred by an obtrusive gaiter or stocking, enshrouding the outline and grating to the senses.

Generally speaking, the central feature in the Irishman's decorative scheme consisted of a large shell, some-

A very fine Specimen of an Irish Chippendale Side-table; period 1755. From a photograph kindly lent by Mr. Charles, of Brook Street, owner of the table.

what on Queen Anne lines (only more wooden and lifeless), or of a mask, hideous and leering when gazed upon, which was sometimes tilted jauntily to one side. From this central feature the design flowed away, having, it must be owned, a machine-made appearance at times.

The mahogany employed in Ireland was uniformly good, if lacking in character; it appears to have come from one district only. It was hard, uniformly dark, and lending itself to a good polish, patinated readily. The cabinet-making pure and simple was good, though many examples are found having an unnecessarily heavy appearance.

Many triumphs were attained in developing practical convenience, and some of the desk fittings of 150 years ago could scarcely be improved upon in theory or in execution to-day. Veneering was generally eschewed when, as in the case of table-tops, for instance, solid mahogany could be made to serve the same purpose. There is, therefore, an almost entire absence of decoration in the form of panels veneered with fine and fancy grain.

The more we study the work under discussion, the more obvious it becomes that only one or two centres were employed in supplying the Irish demand for good quality furniture.

Staple Pieces.

To digress for a moment. Tables used for side-serving, carving, the exhibition of family plate, &c., were the *pièces de résistance* of the native craftsmen. Sometimes these were made with marble tops, at other times with mahogany ones; whilst occasionally the former were discarded, to be replaced by the latter at some later date. Unlike the English tables, their top edges have, as a rule, only a stereotyped moulding by way of decoration, the classic feeling often imparted by Chippendale in the form of an egg-and-tongue or rose-and-ribbon carving being absent.

Source of Origin.

Now to return to the common source, or possible sources, of this Irish furniture. Each table seems to have been made from the same tree, each design to have emanated from the same brain, and every bit of carving to have been fashioned by the selfsame chisel. It will be remembered that in the early part of the eighteenth century Galway enjoyed perhaps the largest share of Spanish trade in England or Ireland. Readily accessible to ships coming from the West Indies, the natural inference is that mahogany in large quantities found its way into this old seaport from one or other of the many Spanish colonies. But what then? Did it leave Galway for the interior as timber, or as furniture already fashioned? Recalling the ancient prosperity of this old city, one suspects that its citizens did not lose the chance of turning the wood into furniture, and thus securing for themselves a second profit. Be this as it may, during seven visits to the charming old seaport the writer has not been able to obtain anything which can be regarded as conclusive evidence; and so, as Dublin, too, was favourably situated for importing timber, and a fashionable centre withal, the probabilities are that East and West—Dublin and Galway—fed the market.

Irish Chippendale is to be found all over the island, least frequently in the north-west. It has neither the artistic nor the commercial value of its English cousin; hence the necessity for discrimination when purchasing. Roughly, Irish examples might be appraised at thirty-three per cent. of English contemporary work, all things—*i.e.*, importance, size, volume of decoration, &c.—being equal.

When some time ago the supply of Thomas Chippendale's work became practically exhausted, some English dealers, casting about for something to take its place, discovered the field which Ireland afforded to those who wished to re-fill their galleries at reasonable prices. They " got in " with avidity, their " runners " (*i.e.*, men employed in tracking desirable acquisitions, and either purchasing for a given dealer or putting him in touch with the possible vendor) quartering the whole of the island. Then this Irish ware was pushed and exploited on the London market, an operation which only ceased to be legitimate when the furniture was described and sold to the unsuspicious novice as *bonâ-fide* Chippendale. To-day the good-class dealer describes this class of work as *Irish* Chippendale, and does not palm it off on his client as the superior article.

Curiously enough, the Americans have been " landed " with a lot of this produce of the Emerald Isle; in fact, they hold very nearly, if not quite, half of it, often under the delusion that they possess the real thing. If the reader will turn up illustration No. 60 in Francis Clary Morse's interesting little book, " Furniture of the Olden Time," he will there see a table which, though described as Chippendale, distinctly belongs to the Irish school.

Summarised, this Erse work shows good material and carcase construction, but poor outline and inferior, because lifeless, carving.

An Ingenious Fraud.

Another injustice to Ireland was perpetrated when an ingenious fraud was practised by two runners whose names are freely mentioned in the Old Testament. Engaged in writing a history (!), " they visited ancient homes, and noted any particular gem, which we will, for example, suppose to have been a Louis XV. clock or a Dutch master. Then they congratulated the owner on his interesting pedigree, house, and penates, but could not refrain from sighing that the beautiful Louis XVI. furniture in the drawing-room should be marred by a clock obviously Louis XV.; or, again, that the exquisite series of Florentine works should be intruded on by 'one of those coarse artists from Holland.' Having cast their eyes up to the ceiling and sighed adequately, they explained how an estimable man in London—quite irreproachable, you know—would very likely (if the possessor would care for an introduction) take the odd clock or picture, letting him have something else to harmonise better with the room, very likely charging him nothing extra," &c., &c. Supposing the clock, for instance, was an heirloom, and the owner would not part with it, no harm was done, and our two worthies had sighed in vain, probably receiving thanks and the offer of a good day's fishing. Too often, alas! the bait was taken, and then, in a fit of generosity, the kind-hearted gentleman living not very far from Bond Street consented to give a genuine (modern) Louis Seize clock, worth £40, and a material contribution " towards the upkeep " of the two peripatetic historians, in exchange for the antique, time-worn specimen of Louis Quinze, worth perhaps £4000.

For a certain while this ruse worked well in England, too; it is now somewhat over-ripe, and in certain galleries, in an ultra-fashionable street, they pause to shed a tear over the march of education by the countryside.

The grotesque masks found on Irish Chippendale often savour of Oriental influence, and, as the island imported quite a lot of Chinese porcelain, carved ivories, &c., during the early part of the eighteenth century, it is more than probable that Pat worked at times from Eastern models.

The Hibernian craftsmen also treated floral matter in a distinctive style, for, instead of grouping flowers in garlands, festoons, baskets, or bouquets, we generally find that they introduced one large, full-blown blossom, with a long scrolled stalk connecting it with a rather remote portion of the design. Under this treatment compositions came to look thin and more or less detached. Where flowers were in any way massed they were shown in a flat and unnatural manner, and the achievements of Grinling Gibbons seem to have been unknown to the general run of Irish cabinet-makers.

Two models which the designers of the Celtic school produced are worthy of notice, viz., their tall, narrow china cabinets and their heavy clothes-presses. The former of these were in reality lighter than English patterns, yet their ill-chosen garnishment conferred such a semblance of weight that they lack all claim to daintiness. The clothes-presses were more massive than English specimens usually were, but they possessed a rugged grandeur of proportion. Both the narrow showcase and the clothes-press carried ample decoration as to their stands, but were left severely plain in the overlying carcase-work. The better-class show-cases exhibit a carved frieze under a more or less decorated swan-necked pediment of the type seen on page 387.

In the earliest Irish mahogany furniture we seldom find the pediment or plain broken pediment crowning models, but we commonly meet with heavy presentations of the swan-necked pediment; at a later date the severely classic entablature rose quite commonly over cabinet-work.

The chief cabinet-maker in Ireland was one Theophilus Jones, a contemporary of Chippendale, Adam, and Heppelwhite. He advertised that he made all kinds of tallboys, desks, and furniture at the sign of the Reindeer, in Mountrath Street, Dublin, and labels to this effect have been in the possession of Mr. Brady, the antiquarian, of Upper Liffey Street. His work was excellent, though of the solid and typically Hibernian order. An advertisement of his reads :—

Theophilus Jones, Cabinet-maker, takes this method of acquainting his friends and the publick, that he has opened ſhop in Montrath-ſtreet, near Pill Lane, where he intends to carry on his buſineſs in all its branches, and hopes by his conſtant aſſiduity and ſtudy to pleaſe such perſons who ſhall favour him with their cuſtom, to merit their encouragemen [sic] *and intereſt; and flatters himſelf the cheapneſs and quality of his goods, as he is a young beginner, will ſecure to him the continuance of their favour.—N.B. Country commands ſhall be moſt carefully obeyed.*

Dublin Mercury—Numb. 83, 1766-1768.

There was little, if any, Irish furniture made in sympathy with Chippendale's light and dainty French style of the period 1750-5, but in the 'sixties Celtic taste lightened and brightened, and we find many pleasing examples of work created thenceforward until the time of the '98 rebellion.

The influence of Angelica Kauffmann, her disciples and collaborators, had been felt in the Irish arts and crafts, whilst the work of W. and J. Pain had given the Irish people a high standard to live up to. Unlike his predecessor Chippendale, Sheraton had undoubtedly a strong Irish following, for we find in his 1802 edition of the " Drawing Book " the following announcement :—

" Printed by T. Bensley. . . . For W. Baynes, 54, Paternoster Row. *Sold also by J. Archer, Dublin;* and all other Booksellers."

Sheraton therefore only *specified* two shops where his book was on sale, the one in England, the other in Ireland.

Irish " Pembroke " tables in Sheraton's style were broader than English types, having long shallow flaps, and they were usually fitted with five legs instead of four.

Soon after the commencement of the nineteenth century, when things had quieted down, many homes were redecorated, and we find heavy furniture, of the type usually associated with Gillows, scattered all over the island.

CHAPTER XV.
The Brothers Adam.

Mainly Historical.

THE Adam family was Scotch, and the successes which Robert and James Adam achieved were all the more remarkable in that Englishmen looked askance at professional men hailing from north of the Tweed. William Adam, of Maryburgh, near Kirkcaldy, was an eminent Scotch architect and master-mason of Scotland. To him were born four sons, John, Robert, James, and William, of whom John, the eldest, succeeded to his father's practice. Robert came to London, travelled on the Continent, and then returned to town to settle down as an architect and designer; and James, having adopted a similar course, joined his brother under a partnership known as "R. and J. Adam," "Adam Bros.," or colloquially as "The Adelphi." William survived his better-known brothers, but played little if any part in furthering eighteenth-century art.

Robert Adam possessed greater individuality and power than were vouchsafed to James, but we are now learning to attach more and more credit to James for his share in the Adelphi successes of the post-1770 period, and especially is this the case in connection with the interior and cabinet-making designs of the firm.

"Adam," or "Adams," designs in architecture and the applied arts fell from the hand of Robert Adam to commence with, but subsequently the collaboration of James Adam is often traceable. Robert's name carried greater weight than did that of his brother, and we find Robert taking the responsibility and credit in all the early ventures of the partnership. When giving a résumé of the firm's achievements Robert generally used the plural pronoun " we," but we find his signature to the plates throughout the 'sixties. In 1767 the Adams were engaged upon the designs of the mansion of Kenwood to the order of the Earl of Mansfield, and in treating of these Robert subsequently wrote, " There will be occasion to give several examples of each kind, as they have been executed after my own *and my brother's designs*." The building of Kenwood occupied some time, and this passage constitutes the first direct acknowledgment of James's work.

Adam furniture assumed definite form and character whilst Kenwood was building, and if, as seems probable, Robert made architecture his chief calling, we may assume that he oftentimes relegated what he considered to be the less important branch of work, namely, cabinet designs, to the dainty pencil of James. James, who, as we shall presently see, drew his knowledge and experience from the same sources as did Robert, modelled his style on that of his brother, and we shall not err greatly if we place his period of influence as commencing about 1765.

Robert Adam, who was born in 1728 at Kirkcaldy, was educated at Edinburgh University (Clouston), proceeded to London shortly after 1750, and then decided to travel in Italy and France with a view to rendering himself conversant with classic art at first hand. The date of his departure is not exactly known, but it is practically certain that he left England in 1753 or 1754, and we know that he was back in London in

1758. We shall presently be dealing with the influences he experienced whilst on his tour, but it is interesting to note that by 1760 he was well known and was entrusted with the designing of the screen, gateway, and pavilions of the Admiralty at Whitehall, the Earl of Kinnoul then being, in Robert's words, "proprietor of that house." The talent and personality of Robert had therefore, within one or two years of his return from his wanderings, swept aside all prejudices and firmly placed the young architect on the ladder of success.

By 1762 Robert was an acknowledged leader in his profession, for he tells us : " In 1762 the Duke of Northumberland came to the resolution of fitting up the apartments of Sion House in a magnificent manner. He communicated his intentions to me, and having expressed his desire that the whole might be executed entirely in the antique style, he was pleased, in terms very flattering, to signify his confidence in my abilities to follow out his desire."

This extract is pregnant with meaning not only as pointing to the reputation which Robert Adam had already made, but because it clearly indicates that there then existed a taste for the Classic quite independent of Adam's influence, but of that chaste order of which Adam was recognised as a clever exponent. It will be noticed that the Duke had "come to the resolution . . . and having expressed his desire" for the Classic, placed the commission with Robert.

The ultra-rococo, Chinese, and Gothic vogues of the preceding decade had temporarily submerged the Classic theme, and the new renderings of the antique orders which were then gaining ground were distinct from the heavier translations of Georgian days. There is nothing to suggest that the Duke's decision was spontaneous or isolated, and we may therefore assume that the purer fashion was gaining popularity early in the 'sixties at the expense of the kaleidoscopic taste of the 'fifties. When once this

This Adam Grate, of the period 1765-1770, shows the perfected development of the Adam idea.

fact has been appreciated, we have to consider whether Robert Adam originated the Classic revival or whether he read the signs of the times and by study abroad fitted himself to lead a movement the seeds of which were germinating when he was abroad—possibly even before he started on his travels.

After weighing the pros and cons, the writer has come to the conclusion that Robert Adam led forces which had been, so to speak, mobilised before his advent and only awaited a strong and capable leader versed in the new idea to direct their energies. That Adam teachings should not have influenced furniture very strongly during the 'sixties is scarcely to be wondered at, seeing that Robert must have had his hands more than full in the realm of architecture, with but little time to devote to the production of cabinet designs.

The new trend of taste is observable in all Adam's furniture, but in the early or transitional style the line of demarcation between it and the fashions it displaced was not so pronounced as would have been the case had Adam entirely disregarded existing English vogues. Adam left England well grounded in the rudiments of architecture, and it was not until he had been impressed by Italian decorative interiors that he laid the foundations of his comprehensive and complementary theories; his time must have been occupied until the early 'sixties, at any rate, with the pursuit of his profession, and he can have gained no sound knowledge of the craft until the latter portion of his career. His buildings were founded on the antique orders, but in his cabinet designs he grafted Classic matter on the stock of English furniture designs until he had learnt to draw models echoing the theme running through his major creations. That Adam had made a careful and exhaustive study of the works of English furniture designers is clear, for he wrote:

"We by no means presume to find fault with the compositions or to decry the labours of other authors, many

Mahogany Adam Side-table of the period 1770. The weight of the legs and the boldness of the frieze carving suggest that this model may have been executed by an exponent of the Chippendale school.

of whom have much merit and deserve great praise. Our ambition is to share with others, not to appropriate to ourselves, the applause of the public; and if we have any claim to approbation, we found it on this alone : that we flatter ourselves we have been able to seize, with some degree of success, the beautiful spirit of antiquity, *and to transfuse it, with novelty and variety, through all our numerous works.*"

Unfortunately, the Adam brothers also wrote, " We have not trod in the paths of others, nor derived aid from their labours," a statement which was misleading in the extreme. Apart from this appropriation of earlier furniture designs, R. S. Clouston has demonstrated that Robert Adam filched drawings from an Italian architect named Giuseppe Manochi as late as 1768, whilst, more important still, the " Adelphi " were throughout their careers beholden to Italian artists whom they imported to do work which they themselves could scarcely have rendered so satisfactorily.

It is doubtful whether the Adam brothers ever employed a regular staff of cabinet-makers under their direct control, and the probabilities are that, having thrown out suggestions as to the design and measurements, they placed their order with the Chippendales, Seddons, Gillows, or Heppelwhites, or else with smaller cabinet-makers. There is one very strong argument in favour of this, founded on a passage which Adam himself wrote when dwelling on an elaborate harpsichord which he designed for the Empress of Russia : " This design was considerably altered by the person who executed the work." This is very significant, for it implied (1) that a very important model was entrusted to an outside cabinet-maker ; (2) that that craftsman took upon himself to vary Adam's suggestions, either because they were impracticable or because he felt that he could improve upon their decorative value. We should probably find if the truth were known that our designers were as greatly indebted to the English cabinet-makers who collaborated with them in the production of their furniture as they were to the Italian artists upon whom they relied for their mural decorations.

The Adam brothers have therefore been flattered by writers who have overlooked the facts that—

1. There was a revival of the purer Classic style independent of Adam initiative.

2. The Adams's contention that " they had not trod in the paths of others " must be seriously discounted.

3. R. and J. Adam, who claimed that they had not benefited by the works of others, borrowed architectural and cabinet designs without acknowledgment, and were as greatly indebted to Italian collaborators in interior schemes as they were to English cabinet-makers for the execution and correction of their suggestions.

Italian Influence.

Robert Adam during his prolonged absence in the South of Europe concentrated his main studies on the architectural beauties of Italy, paying especial attention to those districts which were rich in ruins of the Antique or Classic orders. If we may judge by the confidence he displayed when writing on Grecian detail and design, it is more than possible that he found time to tour in Greece and to study her art at first hand.

That particular gift, amounting almost to personal charm, which enabled Robert to overcome English prejudice, obtained him also the entrée of artistic coteries abroad, and Adam contracted European friendships which helped to mould his style and generally influenced his career. The art of Italy during the mid-eighteenth century was weak when compared with the work which had gone before, and Italians, always keen critics, proved but indifferent supporters of their modern art-working compatriots. The architects, artists, and engravers to be met with at Florence or Rome catered for English patrons, and Adam doubtless received many a welcome which was tendered with a view to the main chance.

Shortly after Robert Adam returned home from his wanderings there commenced a fresh invasion of England by Italian artists and artist craftsmen, who exploited earlier Grecian and Roman fashions. The hand of the foreigner pervaded the vast majority of interior schemes, and English cabinet-makers began to alter their models and decorative detail in consonance with the demands of the new vogue. Robert Adam has been very generally credited with the introduction of this taste, but an exhaustive study of the question leads the author to class him as the best known champion of the order only. During Adam's sojourn in Italy he had become acquainted with Pergolesi, Angelica Maria Kauffmann, Antonio Zucchi, and other artists whose methods and execution appealed to him. A pupil of Piranesi and a life-long friend of that talented designer, Robert Adam modelled his style more or less successfully on his mentor's suggestions, and then proceeded to link the schemes of the architect and cabinet-maker by decorated interiors executed by Zucchi, Kauffmann, Pergolesi, and others.

The Adams persuaded Zucchi to come to England to collaborate with them in their work, and the Italian artist did much to enhance the reputation of his employers. The Adelphi from time to time acknowledged this assistance, for when treating of their work at Kenwood they wrote : " The paintings are elegantly performed by Mr. Antonio Zucchi, a Venetian painter of great eminence,"

English Mantelpiece showing Classic decoration as seen through French spectacles and independent of Adam influence. Period 1780.

and we find similar allusions in other portions of their book.

Both Robert and James Adam had a rooted dislike to crude whites in schemes of decoration, and at the same time they displayed an almost slavish liking for sympathetic and coloured surfaces commencing with the ceiling and culminating in the smallest article of furniture in the room. By the aid of stuccos and compositions a practically uniform surface was first provided, and upon this the Italian artists worked out their homogeneous schemes. Thus Adam interiors may be found showing governing tints of pinks and greens commencing with the ceilings, descending to the mural decorations, the fireplaces, doorways, &c., and echoed in the cabinet-work, chair-work, and all concomitant detail. Many rooms were so treated that not one jot of natural woodwork presented itself, the beauties of " grain figure " or " flower " being sacrificed in a hard-and-fast endeavour to subordinate the efforts of the cabinet-maker to the brush of the painter. The Adams carried this treatment too far, and as no school of Englishmen had been trained in the new method of decoration, whilst numerous Italians were readily obtainable for the asking, the early 'seventies witnessed a general influx of alien talent. Hitherto the power of Chippendale and others had preserved the character and individuality of the cabinet-maker, the craftsman had been called upon to subscribe his quota of complementary work in oak, walnut, or mahogany, but under the new fashion as often as not the craftsman's productions were so submerged that they played little more than the part of the canvas to the painter.

Adam's justification for this artificial uniformity is found in his writings, and in one passage we read how he introduced these common colour-schemes to " create a harmony between ceiling and the sidewalls, with their hangings, pictures, *and other decorations."* The " harmonies " so brought about may have been very wonderful ; they afforded a Zucchi or a Kauffmann a wide field for the display of his or her talent or vagaries, according to the light in which the collector may regard them, but they dealt a heavy blow at the distinctive and self-contained types of national cabinet-work which they so largely displaced.

Compositions.

The Adams used a variety of stuccos, plasters, and compositions in the preparation of their surfaces, of which "Liardet" and "Carton-pierre" have been held to be the chief and peculiar to them. Liardet was a composition used for the coating of the exterior of buildings, and, to cite two cases only, the Adelphi used it for a house they built for Sir Watkin Williams Wynn in St. James's Square and for Drury Lane Theatre. It was supposed to beautify and preserve buildings, but the Adams themselves wrote of it in the 'seventies that it had been "*introduced into very general use,*" so that we may dismiss their claims to its exclusive employment.

Carton-pierre was an Italian composition which was cast in moulds and applied to shaped or flat surfaces, or else built up round a wire core. It must not be confounded with the earlier plaster work, of which Artari and Bugatti were the cleverest exponents in England, during the last quarter of the seventeenth century. This earlier Italian composition was moulded round a leaden skeleton in the case of delicate and partially detached floral or foliated work, in order that the design might be strengthened by a backbone. The plaster-workers of Italy carried on their experiments with a view to improving on compositions until they had evolved the carton-pierre of the mid-eighteenth century. Adam brought the process over to England and endeavoured to conserve the secret, but he was unsuccessful, for other Italian craftsmen brought recipes over to England and Ireland, and there is a vast amount of similar work still in existence, noticeably

Doorway showing moulded composition decoration and panels painted by Angelica Kauffmann. Circa 1770.

in Ireland, with the production of which R. and J. Adam had nothing whatever to do.

Carton-pierre yielded a fine surface to the painter, and even now experts have sometimes to examine below its surface to distinguish it from wood. Sometimes the design was laid over soft wood, which had a shaped face for its reception; at other times it was applied to flat surfaces, the whole of the relief decoration being supplied during the moulding process. The casts taken from the moulds showed the designs sharp and clear, and so tenacious and hard was the preparation that after the lapse of nearly one hundred and fifty years over-doors treated with it remain intact, whilst numerous little festoons to wall-lights and mirrors, suspended round the light wire cores which it encased, are still in good order. As the Adams resorted to painting in so many cases we sometimes find woodwork decorated *en suite* with carton-pierre, which looks to be identical with the latter. Carved work is rightly prized more than moulded detail because it is less mechanical, and when the collector is at a loss in his diagnosis between the two he can set his mind at rest by using a needle. Having removed the paint from some minute and unobtrusive spot, if the needle will penetrate and remain fixed we know that woodwork underlies the paint, for when carton-pierre is there the needle-point, instead of penetrating, chips off a small portion of the composition and, gaining no hold, falls out. In some cases a chip shows us what we are looking for; in others the presence of a series of superimposed coatings of paint may give the appearance of carton-pierre to woodwork, and will turn the point of the needle much as the composition will do, unless the paint is first removed from the small field of examination. The greatest experts can discriminate between the two mediums by the sound given out when surfaces are tapped, but mistakes often arise from such cursory examinations. But recently an experienced dealer showed the author a beautifully carved fireplace which he had sold for a mere song, imagining it to be in carton-pierre, only to find out his mistake when cleaning off the paint to the order of the purchaser.

The composition served a useful purpose economically, for it admitted of considerable effect at the minimum of cost, and many entablatures, &c., were happily set off by narrow bands of classic moulding applied in carton-pierre at a nominal outlay only.

Many small models in the Adam style, noticeably wall-lights, were executed in papier-mâché. After being moulded these little specimens were gilded or painted, but collectors do not value them highly on account of their mechanical construction.

From these facts it will be seen that Adam designs may be met with in woodwork, woodwork cum composition, or even in papier-mâché, to all of which gilding or painted matter supplied the complementary finish. But what are we to say of plain mahogany furniture, of which R. and J. Adam say nothing? Assuming that Robert Adam was at work for fourteen or fifteen years prior to the publication of his book, in what medium was he first of all commissioning furniture built to his designs? We are faced by questions which appear to be simple when once they are formulated :—

1. What was the readiest available timber or medium at Adam's disposal from 1758 for a decade or more?

2. What were the upper classes accustomed to?

3. What blended best with the furniture of the better class homes?

Double doorway showing moulded composition decoration and the oviform panelling characteristic of English interior decoration and cabinet-work of the period 1775-1800. From Fitzwilliam Street, Dublin.

4. What medium were the skilled craftsmen of the day best able to handle effectively without supervision by Adam?

The answer to all of these questions is "Mahogany."

The "complete" Italian vogue which Adam did so much to foster commenced about 1770, after which date the artists whom the brothers commissioned painted ceilings, walls, doorways, cabinets, commodes, tables, chairs, &c., *en suite*, in a manner novel at any rate to Englishmen. We have therefore a period which is partly blank, and it is safe to say that during this hiatus, dating from the inception of Adam influence to the commencement of his pretentious vogue as exploited in his publications of the 'seventies, he commissioned most of his fine mahogany furniture. If this statement were unsupported by facts, it might be held to be conjectural though probable, but there is circumstantial evidence in support of it.

English and French Styles of Furniture Contrasted.

Adam during his travels had studied in France, and he adduced one fact in connection with furniture which he evidently deemed of great importance, namely, the difference between the English and French styles of decorating dining-rooms. He tells us:—

"To understand thoroughly the art of living it is necessary perhaps to have passed some time amongst the French, and to have studied the customs of that social and conversible people. In one particular, however, our manners prevent us from imitating them. Their eating-rooms seldom or never constitute a piece in their great apartments, but lie out of the suite; and in fitting them up little attention is paid to beauty of decoration. The reason of this is obvious : the French meet there only at meals, when they trust to the display of the table for show and magnificence, not to the decoration of the apartment, and as soon as the entertainment is over they immediately retire to the rooms of company. It is not so with us. . . . The eating-rooms are considered as the apartments of conversation, in which we are to pass a great part of our time. This renders it desirable to have them fitted up with elegance and splendour, but in a style different from that of other apartments." Instead, therefore, of plain garnishment Adam recognised the necessity of having handsome surroundings, and it is curious that the bulk of his finest mahogany pieces were made for the dining-room. Carved mahogany was the very medium which best lent itself to dining-room garnishment, but it did not fuse well with the gayer and more artificial types of furniture which became the rage during the 'seventies.

Sideboards.

In the 'seventies both Heppelwhite and Shearer were producing sideboards with *incorporated* wing-cupboards, drawers, or cellarettes, such as Sheraton adopted at a later date, and which have since come to be recognised as the standard pattern. The Early Adam carved mahogany sideboards were in reality sideboard-tables flanked at times by detached pedestal-cupboards crowned by knife or butler's urns.

The Adam " boards " therefore resembled the models which had obtained under Chippendale in the arrangement of their fittings, and we must assume that at the inception of the Adam vogue the self-contained sideboard was almost unknown. The primitive sideboards, if so we may speak of the earlier creations of the Adelphi, are deemed by many to have been the finest of all Adam productions, and they are interesting because one can

Mantelpiece showing Adam influence—period 1770-1780—in the collection of R. Dalby Reeve, Esq.

follow the increasing tendency towards lightness characteristic of the period leading up to the English Louis Seize in the varied range which they display. They also show dignified and restrained Classic carving unmarred by those whimsicalities and trivialities to which the Adams stood sponsors in the 'seventies. The sideboard improvements evolved by other designers during the 'seventies were not embodied in Adam carved mahogany examples possessing other features of proportion and decoration suggestive of early origin, and the author considers that this Early Adam mahogany had enjoyed its main popularity prior to 1770-1775.

Chippendale, as we have seen, omitted to chronicle his claw-and-ball achievements when issuing his " Director " in 1754, and the Adams in their turn, when publishing their book in 1773, may have felt that urging the merits of mahogany would have resembled the flogging of a dead horse. The alternative vogue which the Adams had up their sleeve possessed greater novelty, and the brothers, in pushing it, advanced the complementary schemes of their Italian collaborators. Late mahogany pieces were, of course, supplied to the order of customers desiring to supplement their earlier furniture in that medium, and, of course, numerous free-lances in the craft appropriated Adam designs, reproducing them in the aforementioned timber because they were accustomed to work in it and it was both serviceable and cheap.

Age and wear may have enhanced the beauty of Adam carved mahogany furniture, but these factors have wrought havoc with the painted and composite types. Each of the fashions has the Classic theme as a backbone running through it, but the processes were distinct. The mahogany period which the author places first in time and order of merit was the more English of the series; the composite types which followed were more glittering and catchy, and frequently the less defensible. The former represented an English view of a dainty Classic theme; the latter represent the same idea portrayed under Italian or French collaboration for the delectation of a public in quest of piquant novelty.

Inlaid decoration was again creeping into favour

Mantelpiece showing outline and decoration characteristic of R. and J. Adam. Period 1770-1780. Drawn from a spoilt photograph lent by Messrs. Gill and Reigate, Ltd.

towards the close of the 'sixties, but it was restrained and usually subordinate to the accompanying chisel-work. It was employed in conjunction with fine mahogany veneer showing handsome figure or flower. From 1770 the tendency of the new taste led to the employment of ampler and more intricate inlays in a diversity of media, at the expense of chisel-work and the now despised mahogany. After 1780 models were oftentimes so treated that the male and female portions of a marquetry field were entirely formed of fine or fancy woods and stained inferior woods.

Early Adam work and Shearer furniture generally follow the quieter and more restrained style of decoration. Heppelwhite examples incline towards the same type, but *important* Late Adam, Seddons, and Sheraton pieces favour the more ornate and glittering vogue in their marquetry fields.

CHAPTER XVI.
The Brothers Adam
(continued).

Influence of Piranesi.

It has been seen that Robert Adam came largely under the influence of Piranesi, and, in the light of this, it is interesting to note what Bryan tells us of that great architect :—" He has been charged, and perhaps justly, with sometimes substituting . . . . the conceptions of his ardent imagination in lieu of the original form. His admirers maintain that if he has not altogether revived the primitive forms, he has exhibited the same genius . . . . as the original designers; and that in his works of imagination it is difficult whether to admire most the fecundity and spirit of the composition or the . . . . brilliancy of the execution. His skill in congregating objects from different localities and arranging them for picturesque effect is admirable." It is well known that Adam found his métier in the classic style which his mentor loved, and we find him repeatedly pleading for that latitude which Piranesi by reason of his genius successfully affected. Thus Adam wrote : " The great masters of antiquity were not so rigidly scrupulous . . . . clearly perceiving that however necessary rules may be . . . . they often cramp the genius." On another occasion we read : " We must beg leave to observe that we can see no reason for assigning to each order its precise entablature. . . . A latitude in this respect under the aid of an ingenious and able artist is often productive of great novelty, variety, and beauty." Again, we find Adam writing: "Corinthian capitals have been injudiciously adopted by Michael Angelo; in order to avoid the irregularity of appearance in this capital when viewed in profile. . . . we are inclined to hazard some defects"; whilst two further instances of Adam variations will suffice to show this foible of theirs. In the first of these they write: "We have formerly mentioned that the ancients used very frequently to indulge themselves in compositions of fancy. . . . A licence of the same kind has been hazarded here"; and in the second case we read: "We do not, however, mean to condemn the composing of capitals. . . . We have exhibited an attempt of our own in this way, and we shall have other opportunities of the same kind."

If, as is only reasonable, we assume that Robert Adam largely based his style on that of Piranesi, it is easy to see how this love of modification and pseudo-novelty crept into Adam's compositions. The power of the mentor's attainments appealed to Adam, but one thing was missing to render the tuition satisfactory, viz., genius on the part of the pupil. Adam was cultivated, he was also dainty and clever, but he never rose to the rank of actual genius, and throughout his career he was intermittently obsessed by a desire to take artistic liberties with olden styles. His criticism of Michael Angelo scarcely calls for comment, but we get a good insight into his mind when he tells us of his improvements (!) on Grecian orders. When commending one of his accomplishments he wrote: "The lion and unicorn support the angles of the abacus, which is adorned with the regal crown, the collar of the Order of the Garter and

This beautiful Cabinet is governed by Adam tradition, but the handling of the lattice-work is so light and dainty that there is a suggestion of Heppelwhite influence; circa 1775-1785. The property of R. W. Partridge, Esq.

acorns in the ovolo. The sceptre and dove and the rose and thistle fill the intermediate space between the leaves of the acanthus. The lion and unicorn are also alternately interwoven in the foliage of the frieze." It is difficult to deal seriously with such suggestions, but the case in point was by no means an isolated one, for we find incongruities in the Adams' designs quite foreign to the orders upon which these architects drew. But if Robert Adam, without realising it, fell lamentably short of Piranesi's originality and power, he possessed a knack of congregating and arranging matter which enabled him to appear as one building new houses with old bricks. Thus, when appropriating Doric, Ionic, Corinthian, or Etruscan matter, he welded it into an individual style of his own. He possessed knowledge, a pretty taste in culling classic detail, and the quality of taking pains with his work; but his construction was at times stilted, and the calibre of his decoration petty and unconvincing. The several items in his schemes were complementary the one to the other, but the units, when disconnected or isolated, not uncommonly appeared to be trivial or finicking. Under these circumstances, though a Chippendale chair or a Sheraton sideboard shows to advantage in almost any home, an Adam mirror may appear inconsequent unless it be supported by other models decorated *en suite*.

When treating of their designs for Sion House, the Adams wrote : " Four of these plates are engraved by Piranesi. . . . This obligation, from so ingenious an artist, we owe to that friendship *we* contracted with him during *our* long residence at Rome, and which he has since taken every occasion to testify in the most handsome manner." This passage not only shows an appreciation of Piranesi, but the double use of the plural pronoun shows that *both Robert and James* came under the Italian's influence on their separate visits to Rome. James Adam left England shortly after Robert had returned to London and traversed much the same ground that the latter had covered, finding an open sesame to the artistic coteries of France and Italy in the numerous friendships that Robert had made.

In 1760 James Adam published a "Design for a Parliament House, executed in Italy, with numerous ceiling designs," so that he had obviously prosecuted his studies to some purpose by that date; and in 1762 he issued a "Design for a British Capital, executed at Rome." After this early period James devoted his attention to pushing the interests of the Adelphi partnership, but in 1789 he found time to bring out his "Practical Essays on Agriculture, &c.," 2 vols. 8vo, and his "Practical Essays on Architecture," 8vo.

Piranesi, "the Rembrandt of architecture," was made an honorary member of the Society of Antiquaries in London, probably owing to Robert's influence, that architect being a Fellow of the Society. If we are to believe what was written a century ago, when Piranesi and his pupils had passed away, the tutor remained not only the friend but *the admirer* of Robert and James throughout his career.

It would require a volume larger than this to inquire into the reciprocal benefits accruing to the Adelphi on the one hand and to the Italian colony in England on the other as the result of their artistic relationships. It is certain, however, that the Adams have been generally credited with successful detail and designs to which they had literally no claim. The Adelphi not only appropriated ideas from such artists as Piranesi, Manochi, and Pergolesi to palm them off as their own architectural suggestions, but they unblushingly availed themselves of decorative schemes and detail evolved by other artists. The Adams were commercial, for they ran up speculative buildings; the Italians whom they employed were commercial too, for they came to England to earn bigger money than they could earn at home. As fashionable architects the English designers were the surest source of income to the alien decorators seeking employment, and, in marshalling the forces at their disposal, the Adelphi did not hesitate to make use of all the grist that came to their mill.

Adam appropriations were so patent that there is little doubt that they were taken honestly with a view to the gaining of employment for the community which contributed ideas, as well as for the architects who stood sponsors to them; thus, although we cannot perhaps impugn the intentions of the Adelphi, we have often to discount their inventive and creative reputation.

It must not be supposed that all the Italian painters and decorators stood in the same position to R. and J. Adam, for we find three semi-distinct classes amongst those who at one time or another added their quota to the Adam schemes:—

1. Independent designers and occasional collaborators.
2. Dependants.
3. Casual and temporary assistants.

In the first of these classes we must place such men as Pergolesi and Columbani, who published books of decoration and design for their own clientèles, and who sometimes inspired, influenced, or assisted the Adams.

Under the second heading were the subordinate artists, engravers, and craftsmen, who practically looked to the Adelphi for their livelihood, and to which body we may attach Zucchi as a trusty henchman always at the beck and call of the Adams.

The third and last class embraces painters who turned aside to glorify interiors and cabinet-work, and amongst these Angelica Kauffmann stands pre-eminent. Angelica had made a certain reputation in the superior branches of her art, and she had shown herself an effective decorator both in England and Ireland before she was attracted by the offers made by the Adams. In her earlier ceiling and mural decoration Angelica was perhaps at her best, and we are fortunately able to see some examples from this, the most interesting of her phases, in the accompanying illustrations. The settings to Angelica's pictures, the accessories such as the fireplaces, &c., during the period preceding her decade of collaboration with the Adams, exhibit a freedom and daintiness altogether missing from some of her later work executed in conjunction with the Adelphi. Detail of the order subsequently identified with Robert and James Adam frames her early work, but it is so pleasing that one is tempted to surmise that when the brothers attached Angelica to their interests they also secured artist-craftsmen who had previously set off the artist's paintings.

One looks in vain through R. and J. Adam's suggestions for ceiling decorations for a specimen half so beautiful as that shown on the opposite page. The relief work framing the painting of Aurora is exquisite, and although the detail it embraces would generally be held to savour of the Adams, its arrangement surpasses that which those architects were wont to achieve. The festoon in the outer

Ceiling showing Painting of Aurora by Angelica Kauffmann and Classic decoration in plaster relief; circa 1770.

circle, of which we catch glimpses in the corners of the picture, the rainceaux of acanthus in the circle enclosing the octagon, the fluting in the outer framework of the octagon itself, the alternate medallions and anthemions, the band of bell-flowers, and other decorative

Marble Mantelpiece in the style of Pergolesi; period 1770-1775. This example stands in the room which possesses the decorated ceiling just shown.

detail all came from the Classic orders independently of the Adams, although they are commonly described as Adamesque owing to the frequency with which they were employed by the Adelphi.

The mantelpiece shown in the above illustration savours strongly of Pergolesi, and here again we find the introduction of detail closely akin to that affected by the Adams in later years, but in a distinctive framing. The medallions seen in these two illustrations are interesting because the Adams were struck by the potentialities of this feature in decoration, and commissioned the Wedgwoods to supply them with plaques to be let into their models. John Flaxman executed these plaques for his employers, and a considerable number were introduced on Adam mantelpieces, cabinets, harpsichords, commodes, writing-tables, candlesticks, and smaller articles of furniture, in the manner shown in our illustration on the next page.

Perhaps the best insight into Angelica's career is seen in "Sir Joshua and His Circle" (Fitzgerald Molloy), where we are told: "She took up her brush to paint languishing, discreetly attired goddesses, and the best-behaved, most emasculated of gods, who had not even sufficient humour to smile at the strangely-proportioned, corpulent cupids by whom they were surrounded."

One gathers from this most interesting work that the artist gained her smattering of classic lore from J. J. Winckleman, librarian to Cardinal Archinio, and the first author to write a comprehensive work on Greek art. Angelica Kauffmann studied in Rome, Milan, Naples, and other centres. Coming to England in 1766, she took rooms in Suffolk Street, Charing Cross, to move into a house on the south side of Golden Square in 1767. In 1769 Angelica began to exhibit at the Academy, where between that date and 1782—when she returned with her second husband, Antonio Zucchi, to Rome—her pictures were annually hung. We learn from Molloy that the Academy accepted eighty-two of her works between the years '69 and '97.

Adam Dressing-Cabinet, inlaid with jasper-ware plaques, probably by John Flaxman; period 1785. The property of R. W. Partridge, Esq.

The fair painter became the fashion, and whatever opinion the reader may hold of her draughtsmanship and vivid colouring, he must own that the best of her compositions blended effectively with the spirit of the hour. Angelica's collaboration with the Adam brothers did not commence until the 'seventies, and prior to this association she, in conjunction with other Italian workers, produced much striking Classic or pseudo-Classic decoration unhampered by the somewhat stilted restrictions of Adelphi technique.

Many of the finer commodes and pieces of cabinet-work of the period 1772-1782 in the Adam style were decorated by means of Angelica's brush, but the vast majority of the pieces attributed to her were embellished by less well-known hands. Numerous reproductions exist, and the collector should seek expert advice before acquiring examples in this particular school.

Angelica Kauffmann, who had, on November 22nd, 1767, married an adventurer masquerading as Count Frederick de Horn, was freed by his death in 1780, and in 1781, on September 8th, she was married to Antonio Zucchi (Fitzgerald Molloy). In 1782 husband and wife returned to Rome. This marriage, therefore, robbed R. and J. Adam of their two most useful collaborators, a fact which the collector should bear in mind, seeing that English interiors and cabinet-work from 1782 onwards were not decorated by Zucchi and Kauffmann, but by their disciples.

As the Adams undoubtedly gave their more independent collaborators carte-blanche at times, it follows that they had little to do with many of the more important creations for which they themselves reaped the entire credit. Enough has been said to show that—

1. The Adams only sought to transplant and slightly modify classic matter.

2. That in carrying this out they were forced to import Italian craftsmen to translate the themes.

3. That the Adelphi appropriated other people's designs, and in palming them off endeavoured to persuade the public that they " had not trod in the paths of others or reaped benefits from the labours of others."

4. Adam masterpieces, as generally accepted, frequently owe their main attractions to the decorations supplied by Italian artists, or in a lesser degree to the incorporation of Flaxman plaques.

Bearing these facts in mind, we have to class Robert and James as clever welders of design rather than as originators. They were thorough-going and painstaking, as witness their introduction of wall-papers and upholstery material *en suite* with their general schemes, and they displayed taste in arrangement and discrimination in borrowing as a very general rule.

French Influence.

When we pass from our study of the relationship between Adam work and that of the Italian school to an investigation of French influence and association in art from the 'sixties onwards, we are at once faced by a problem. Were the Adams mere copyists and adaptors from our neighbours; or did they give as well as receive? The former of these two aspects has been generally accepted, but the more one delves below the surface the greater do the chances appear that in the alternative idea lies the true solution of the case.

When Robert was travelling in the mid-'fifties we know that he studied in France, and we have already noticed

Double Doors showing composition mouldings, and painted decoration by Angelica Kauffman; of the 1770 period.

his remarks on the dissimilarities of decoration between French and English eating-rooms. Adam can scarcely have become conversant with the cult of the Louis Seize when Louis Quinze had yet some twenty years to reign. Even if we make allowance for the evolutionary process which was paving the way for the transition between the two styles in France, it seems impossible to account for the fact that Adam's predilections all favoured a vogue of which he can scarcely have grasped a rudimentary knowledge in Paris. It is, of course, possible that Adam may have paid further visits to France, but as he was in great demand here after 1760 he can scarcely have spared time to study the inception of the new fashion abroad, and it had not sufficiently materialised in the 'sixties for him to have assimilated its features by the perusal of French publications. Yet Adam's designs in the late 'sixties held more than the embryo of the so-called Louis Seize.

The new order in France and Adam's matured style were built up on a basic idea common to both. The detail and designs evolved by French and English masters came from the same sources, and even if their application differed under the two schools, it was but a typical exemplification of the verve and finesse of the Latin artist on the one hand contrasted with the Englishman's more solid methods on the other. Charles Louis Clerisseau, who, according to Bryan, had travelled with Adam and collaborated with his friend, assisted Adam in the preparation of the " Ruins of Spalatro," published in 1764. This work gave the public an insight into those antiquities which Adam and Clerisseau had studied. It was not until some years later that Clerisseau gave his countrymen the benefit of his personal studies in his " Antiquités de France," "Monumens de Nimes," and other publications. Clerisseau was a great power in France in 1783, and he was selected to fill the important post of architect to the Empress of Russia, yet he was the friend and admirer of Adam in the 'fifties.

Are we to suppose that Robert Adam, who during this early phase of his career, when he was associated with Clerisseau, withheld his exploitation of the lighter side of classic work until it had been first developed under the French school of the Louis Seize? Assuredly not. The straight, tapered legs, the graceful serpentine-shaped bodies which crowned them, the festoons of drapery, foliage, or floral matter, and the tapered and pendent strings of bell-flowers to be found on early mahogany furniture of Adam design tell their own tale. Adam combated the decadent rococo work of the English Louis XV. style and its alternatives, the Chinese and Gothic vogues, early in the 'sixties, and the order which he used as his weapon was the light and rectilinear rendering of the antique. The whole-hearted devotion of the French nation was subsequently concentrated on this particular theme, but we must not overlook Adam's part in helping to popularise the foundations upon which the new edifice arose.

There is some very strong circumstantial evidence in favour of the author's contention, for Adam, when bringing out his designs at the end of the reign of Louis Quinze and at the commencement of that of Louis Seize, published his letterpress in parallel columns of English and French in order that it might be equally serviceable to his clientèles in England and France. This undertaking was arduous and costly, and it is inconceivable that Adam would have gone to the labour and expense

Handsome carved Adam Mahogany Bookcase, with hand-worked brass grille; circa 1785. The cornice decoration is carried out in boxwood. In the possession of Messrs. Gill and Reigate, Ltd.

unless he had considered that his designs would have appealed to a substantial body of Frenchmen who already appreciated his efforts. If Adam had been studying réchauffé ideas he would not have obtained a footing amongst the clever French exponents of the incoming Louis Seize style, neither would anglicised French work have appealed to a sufficiently large section in France to warrant the new departure. The probabilities are that the Adelphi had established a sufficient connection over the Channel by 1770 to justify their enterprise, and that they realised that their suggestions had sufficient in common with the latest French style to commend them to would-be furnishers.

The Adelphi kept themselves in touch with fashions over the water, but that they weighed the pros and cons of each style or innovation is evident from their observations, for on one occasion they wrote: " The cornices . . . were intended as an attempt to banish the absurd French compositions of this kind, heretofore so servilely imitated by the upholsterers of this country "; and yet again we read: " The French, *who till of late never adopted the ornaments of the ancients*, and jealous as all mankind are of their national taste, have branded those ornaments with the vague and fantastical appellation of arabesques."

The first of these references shows that the Adams refused to be led by French practices of the earlier type; the latter indicates that the Adelphi were critically watching the dawn of a new movement across the Channel —a movement, be it known, of which they had for fifteen years been giving practical expositions.

It is therefore fair to assume that although the Adelphi drew from time to time on the dainty suggestions of the French school, they more than repaid their obligations by helping in the first place to introduce into England and France that corrective of the exaggerated rococo spirit upon which the style of the Louis Seize was so largely modelled.

Besides the attractive personality which Adam possessed, he owned also the power which a wide education confers. His writings show him to have been well acquainted with history. Like Chippendale, he would quote Latin authors aptly, and would draw parallels between different schools of thought. He believed in the brotherhood of Art, and he doubtless approached his French readers without any misgivings or qualms.

CHAPTER XVII.
The Brothers Adam
(continued).

Their Teachings.

In speaking of a more comprehensive publication on architecture and design which they contemplated issuing at a later date, the Adams wrote that it would " require more time than we can command amidst the multiplied occupations of an active profession. We therefore reserve the subject for some period of greater leisure." Unlike so many of their eighteenth-century brethren, Robert and James Adam did not outlive their popularity, commissions being rained on them to the end, and for them the " period of greater leisure " never came.

The notes and designs which the Adams *did* publish, however, afford ample evidence as to the scope and diligence of their research. They approached all subjects with full confidence in their own powers, and arrogated to themselves the right of posing as censors of art and artists past and present. This latter trait in their character led them to pass criticisms of a wild and unsound nature on Raphael, Michael Angelo, Palladio, Inigo Jones, and others when endeavouring to justify their own variations on the earlier Renaissance designs.

Thus we read : " Variety and gracefulness of form, so particularly courted by the ancients, have not been objects of much attention to modern artists. Raphael and Michael

Angelo, those great restorers of the Arts, almost entirely neglected this pleasing source of beauty. Others made some feeble efforts to revive this (classic) elegant mode, which since their time has been but little cultivated by Palladio, Jones, or any of the celebrated masters of this art."

Towards the end of any great phase of art decadence sets in more or less suddenly, and the brothers Adam were the apostles of the latest of late Renaissance. Posterity, when gauging the merits or otherwise of different interpretations of the Classic order, can judge of the Adelphi conceptions from passages which these designers penned. Robert and James, who had condemned the orthodox methods of the great masters, offered suggestions such as this : " But surely, in light and gay compositions designed merely to amuse, it is not altogether necessary to exclude the *whimsical and the bizarre*."

The earlier masters strove to please and to satisfy, not to amuse, a refinement which the Adams failed to grasp, and there was a consequent polarity between the chaste and dignified handling of the one school and the whimsical and bizarre variations frequently introduced under the other.

It must not be supposed that the lighter side of the Adams' teachings was wholly indefensible, for they realised that such compositions called for "not only fancy and imagination, but taste and judgment in the application." When these necessary qualifications were present Adam designs showed a certain chaste daintiness, and many little models which would have appeared too cold and severe under orthodox treatment bear witness to the happy results of which restrained licence permits. Unfor-

Superlative Adam Side-table. Photograph lent by R. W. Partridge, Esq. Circa 1780-1785.

tunately, as time passed away, the Adelphi showed an ever-increasing tendency to overstep the limits of propriety, and many of their later utterances showed the length to which unchecked licence could be carried when once the thin end of the wedge had been admitted.

In their early work to be met with in mahogany R. and J. Adam gave England dignified yet graceful renderings of up-to-date models bearing Classic embellishment, but so soon as they endeavoured to bring their creations into line with the gayer spirit of Paris their efforts became frequently garish. Mahogany surfaces, comparatively sombre in character, did not call for glittering accessories—the contrast would have been too pronounced; but when these were forsaken in favour of the ornate and variegated fields beloved in the 'seventies the floodgates were opened and excesses poured in.

The Adelphi were appealing to the wealthy and fashionable in England *and France*. Fancy woods were coming into the country from the East and West Indies. Stucco treatment had been popularised by Italian artist-craftsmen. The services of Angelica Kauffmann and other painters were available, and France retained that love of gilding which had characterised her interior schemes for generations. The Adams were faced by a problem, and they took the only course commercially open to them. It would have been obviously impossible to wean Frenchmen to the quieter mahogany style, and mahogany was looked down upon now that fancy grained woods were becoming popularised. It was possible to carry English taste with a glittering and ornate alternative which would also appeal to the foreigner, and this the brothers accordingly essayed. Opportunism therefore carried the day, and it is charitable to suppose that this force was responsible for certain departures not altogether in harmony with Adam convictions.

When once the Adelphi had surrendered themselves to the complex style of embellishment in quest of novelty and as a bid for French patronage, they relegated to the shade models of considerable artistic value, and in their more ambitious schemes frequently descended to trivialities. In frankly plagiarising French ideas they entered upon the pursuit of a will-o'-the-wisp whose dainty spirit proved too elusive, for they never gained such complete grasp of the Louis Seize as did Shearer or Sheraton.

They had early proved themselves masters of outline, and throughout their career they were brilliant exponents of detail. Possessed of a fund of knowledge which placed them in a position of vantage as compared with their contemporaries, they yet neutralised these advantages through over-elaboration, lack of restraint, and fetish-worship on many occasions. Their tables showing soft-wood legs covered with moulded and gilt composition, supporting tops decorated by inlaid and painted schemes in vivid colouring, were more than questionable from an artistic point of view. The outline may have been faultless, the detail introduced may have been in itself irreproachable, but the eye had too many processes presented to it at the same time, and in trying to do too much the creators, by reason of their artificiality, effected too little.

Pateræ and detail, instead of being carved sharply, came to be either mechanically moulded in composition or painted, whilst the central glories of a model passed from the cabinet-maker's domain to that of the artist. English carving had reached the highest pinnacle; the art that replaced it was often indifferent and frequently execrable.

The Adams wrote: " The classical style of ornament, by far the most perfect that has ever appeared for inside decoration, and which has stood the test of many ages, like other works of genius, requires not only fancy and imagination in the composition, but taste and judgment in the application, and when these are happily combined this gay and elegant mode is of inimitable beauty." Yet they at times descended to almost vulgar renderings of it of their own free will and accord.

It is most interesting to note what the Adelphi had to say on the subject of the reintroduction of the Classic style in the latter half of the eighteenth century. " It is only of late," they wrote, " that it has been again introduced into Great Britain with some rays of its ancient splendour." It was the habit of the Adams to claim all, or, rather, more than they were entitled to, and it is therefore significant that they did not associate the reintroduction of Renaissance matter with their own efforts. In another passage the Adelphi suggested that they were *partly* entitled to the credit for the movement, writing: " We have not only met with the approbation of our employers, but even with the imitations of other artists, to such a degree *as in some measure to have brought about, in this country, a kind of revolution* in the whole system of this useful and elegant art." Had it been possible, the Adams would have advanced their claim to the whole credit, and we have in this latter extract from their book direct evidence that their influence was only a partial factor in the new revival.

It was quite another matter when the Adelphi were exploiting their developments of Etruscan art, for they then expatiated at length on the fact that they, and they alone, should rightly be considered as the pioneers of its application or introduction for interior garnishment. "From this number," they wrote, "persons of taste will, no doubt, observe that a mode of decoration has been here attempted which differs from anything hitherto practised in Europe; for, although the style of the ornament and the colouring of the Countess of Derby's dressing-room are both evidently imitated from the vases and urns of the Etruscans, yet we have not been able to discover, either in our researches into antiquity or in the works of modern artists, any idea of applying this taste to the decoration of apartments. . . . The Romans borrowed not only many of their customs, their civil institutions, and religious ceremonies, but also their first knowledge of every art and science, from their ancient and ingenious neighbours, the Etruscans.

"We have mentioned these circumstances with more particular attention in order that if judges shall think any praise due to the discovery of another class of decoration and embellishment *they may know to whom the art is indebted for this improvement.*"

Etruscan Work.

The house which was built for the Earl of Derby in Grosvenor Square contained some of the finest Etruscan work which the Adams designed, and from the 'seventies onwards this particular detail was freely introduced in interior decoration and on furniture by the Adelphi.

In connection with the Etruscan style of Adam decoration one fault is particularly noticeable, for the central scheme was often too sparse and altogether outweighed by a setting of finicking detail. The pictures, so to speak, were overframed, and the artistic poverty of the frames very frequently served to accentuate the inferiority

The Brothers Adam.

of the whole suggestion. This error was not confined to designs in the Etruscan mode, neither was it peculiar to the Adams, for if the reader will turn to designs such as that shown on page 441 he will notice how the meagreness of the central theme is shown up by the maze of surrounding and unconvincing detail. In this latter instance the centres of the panels were treated by Angelica Kauffmann, and the surrounding arabesque work was doubtless supplied by one of her subordinates. To have made the design satisfactory she should have done more or her disciple less, and then the balance would have been perhaps adjusted.

Painted Work.

In all the painted work wherein grotesque or arabesque embellishment contained classic pictures there was a tendency towards this sacrifice of the value of the central or governing unit of decoration. When, at a later date, floral festoons gained greater popularity the fault largely disappeared, for the curves described by the swags and the neat and good proportion of the oval garlands were complementary to the features they connected or enclosed, and, without detracting from the value of these features, offered the artist engaged upon them a better field for the display of his talent. Compositions of floral swags, festoons, or garlands involve a certain amount of reiteration, but it is hard to avoid a mechanical and artificial effect when a painter is commissioned to cover given areas with an arabesque network.

We get a good insight into the various processes which the Adams employed when reading a description of the decorations carried out in the Earl of Derby's house. " The ornaments are all in stucco . . . . the grounds are all picked out in different tints of green. The girandoles are painted (by Zucchi). The frames are carved in wood, and gilt. The chimney-pieces executed with statuary marble, inlaid with various coloured scagliola, and brass ornaments in ormolu. The pannells [sic] of the doors . . . where the ornaments are painted on papier-mâché, and so highly japanned as to appear like glass.''

When one remembers the vast number of houses which the Adams designed, calls to mind the fact that the minutiæ of decoration were everywhere *en suite*, and that, whenever it was deemed necessary, furniture and fittings were specifically designed to fit into given recesses, the magnitude of the Adelphi's creations becomes apparent.

Use of Ormolu.

It will be noticed that the Adams referred to ormolu and japanned work in connection with the Earl of Derby's house, both of which adjuncts to decorative schemes they commonly employed. The use of ormolu or metal mounts was largely a concession to French taste, but although R. and J. Adam at times justified their introduction of such fittings, they lose ground when their efforts in this direction are studied as a whole.

In the first place, the metal work of English craftsmen fell lamentably short of that achieved by their French brethren, for the former exponents were workmen, the latter were artists. Then French cabinet-work generally demanded complementary ormolu fittings, whilst English examples were usually better without them. The Adams displayed a weakness in failing to appreciate these distinctions, and their lack of discrimination perhaps sowed the seeds of those unfortunate abuses which characterised our brass-mounted furniture of the Trafalgar and Waterloo periods.

In their urn- or pineapple-shaped finials, as in some of their restrained, if conventional, bronzed work, the Adelphi were seen to advantage, and their candelabra with rainçeau-shaped branches were exceedingly effective; but the brilliancy of cutting and chasing, and the happy placing of mounts which constituted the main justification in French schemes, were absent from the more pretentious of Adam designs.

Japanned Furniture.

The japanned work, to the rising popularity of which A. Heppelwhite and Co. called attention in 1788, was a decadent survival of lacquer ware. The glutinous mixture was laid over soft woods, composition, or even papier-mâche, and when dry and hard the "japanning" was polished. We usually find it in black or in subdued shades of green or slate, showing gilt or painted decoration overlying it. As in the case of all the late eighteenth-century japanned furniture, Adam creations in this medium are generally much the worse for wear, and the majority of the specimens which appear on a superficial examination to be well preserved have in the past been touched up or redecorated.

Gilt Work.

Many of the mirrors, wall-lights, or girandoles which the brothers Adam designed look well in gilt, but the collector should avoid specimens which have been regilded, and he should, whenever possible, substitute models in carved woodwork for composition or papier-mâché examples already in his collection. It is doubtful whether any English designer produced so satisfactory a range of small pieces for mural decoration as did the Adams, and in the illustrations on this page and the next we see such typical and pure Adelphi suggestions cleverly carried into effect.

Gilt Adam Hanging Lights; period 1770-1775.

Influence of Architecture.

The brothers Adam saw all decorative matters through the spectacles of the architect, but they appealed to a wide circle, in fact to all those "whose professions require taste and elegance," and they emphasised their production of "*every kind* of ornamental furniture" (designs). They aimed, in their own words, "at affording amusement to the connoisseur and instruction to the artist, and although the different editions which they published dealt with the effect of Grecian, Roman, and Etruscan art in the mansions of the rich, they took pains to press home the point that the elegance and delicacy which these antique orders suggest " may be adopted

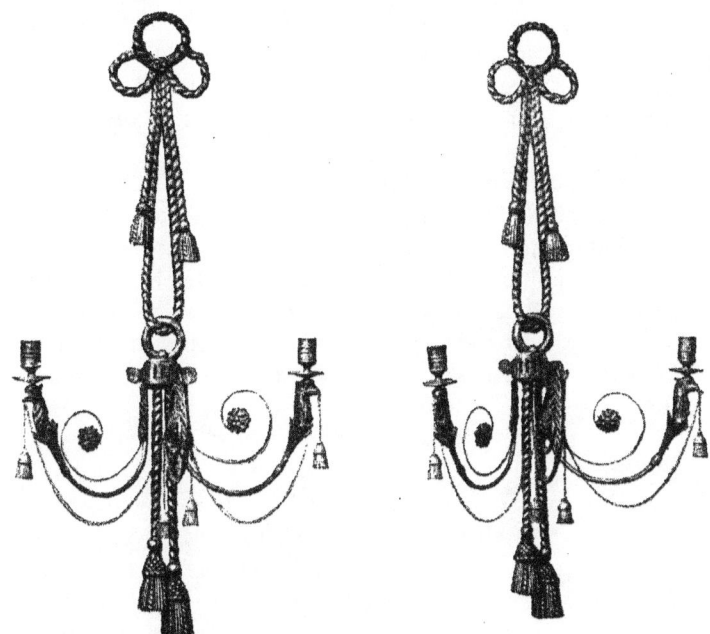

Gilt Adam Hanging Lights; period 1780-1785.

with great propriety *in small rooms and private apartments.*"

Their appeals consequently influenced the middle classes equally with the upper, and although the furniture with the production of which they were directly concerned is, comparatively speaking, scarce, furniture on Adam lines and of genuine age lies spread over England and Ireland.

Did the Adelphi build a house or decorate an interior, design cornices, friezes, doors, chimney-pieces, grates, wall lights, upholstery materials, brass fittings, door-knockers, or wall-papers, we see the evidences of the definite line of thought reflected in their furniture, and when once the collector has grasped the cardinal points of any one branch of Adam suggestion he possesses the key to the whole.

It is certain that the Chippendales, Gillows, and Heppelwhites built furniture on commission for the brothers Adam, and these cabinet-makers, together with Sheraton, imbibed many ideas from the Adelphi. To such an extent was this influence marked that we seldom meet with a model of the 1770-1800 period in English furniture in which detail or outline does not hint of Adam suggestions.

Chairs.

Adam chairs are scarce as compared with other examples of furniture, and they fail to show the craftsmen at their best. It is more than probable that we owe the shield-back and lyre-back patterns to R. and J. Adam, but it would seem that these decorators concentrated their energies on other branches of cabinet designing rather than on chair-work, possibly because craftsmen such as Heppelwhite devoted themselves chiefly to the latter groove. Adam chairs usually have oval or shield-shaped backs in padded upholstery, with padded arms, and straight, square or round, legs, but we find their designs in rectilinear models generally so lacking in merit that we can only compare them with early nineteenth-century creations. Their earlier sofas were exceedingly graceful, and show sinuous outlines relieved by dainty or correct detail. Their later examples were often abominations, and foreshadowed the decadence of late Sheraton days.

Résumé.

It will have been gathered that admirers of the Adelphi are divided into two camps, viz., those who appreciate their sober mahogany style and those who prefer the ornate and composite phases of their work dating from the 'seventies. The author ranges himself with the former class unhesitatingly, and would draw attention to the mahogany side-tables, &c., of early date as constituting the masterpieces of Adam design; but for those who prefer the glitter and colour of the later days the fancy-wood commodes, relieved by japanning, painting, gilding, inlay, and ormolu, possess a peculiar charm. As in the case of *late* Chippendale furniture, Adam examples with overladen embellishment possess a meretricious market value utterly at variance with their artistic worth, and it is quite possible for the collector to acquire dignified, graceful, and characteristic specimens of Adam furniture at reasonable cost if he will but exercise patience and discrimination, whilst resting content with a modicum of first-rate and well-placed decoration.

A word of caution concerning Adam mahogany furniture will not be out of place, and is certainly necessary. In fine examples the entablatures over table-legs, &c., usually carry a central ornament, such as an urn or a swag of drapery, from which to right and left runs fluting divided into compartments by pateræ in strong relief.

These paterae were beautifully cut, *but should always show patination*. In the first place, they were often "applied," not carved out of the framework, and have since been knocked off and replaced by reproductions; and, secondly, plain tables, which were originally designed without fluting, paterae, or central decorations, have since

Painted and inlaid Adam Side-table of the period 1785, suggestive of Louis Seize influence. Photograph lent by Messrs. Partridge and Neave.

been treated by the faker, and now appear as fully-decorated specimens.

The decoration to an Adam table in carved mahogany lies along the underframing, where it is partially in shadow, and the collector *may* let undoubted surface condition of the table-top and legs carry presumptive evidence in favour of the framework decorations connecting the

The Brothers Adam.

two, with disastrous results. This mistake is the more readily made when the individual has learnt, in studying Chippendale, to examine first of all leg-work, and then perhaps the edge carving of a table-top.

In addition to the swags, festoons, urns, and pateræ which we have just noticed, the Adams were brilliant exponents of acanthus and other foliated detail. Their great delight lay in the portrayal of rainçeaux of leaf-

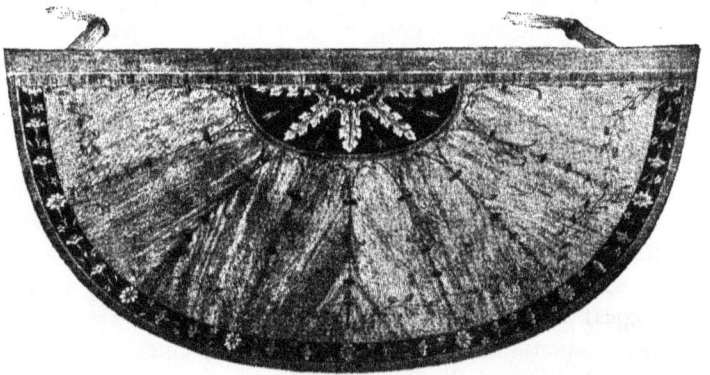

Top of the same Table, showing Painted and Inlaid Decoration.

work similar to those shown on the decorated ceiling illustrated on page 433. The French used this word, derived from "rain," the branch of a tree, "to express the winding and twisting of the stalk or stem of the acanthus plant, which, flowing round in many graceful turnings, spreads its foliage with great beauty and variety" (Adam). The Adelphi constantly exploited this detail, mixing it at times with what they styled a "gay and fanciful diversity of agreeable objects." The acanthus, too, in more conventional form, graced Adam trusses, cornices, and cabinet-work generally in most of their finer creations.

The Adelphi were particularly fond of introducing flutings and stopped flutings, especially on table, chair, or sofa legs, and they were greatly attached to the old Roman key moulding, the Vitruvian scroll or spiral volute, as shown in the upper belt of decoration to the entablature of the Chippendale table on page 333, and strings of the anthemion alternated with other detail, as seen on the side-table illustrated on page 405.

Arabesque or grotesque work was incorporated in many of the Adam designs, and they were past-masters in the use of fine beadings, dentil work, echinus or guilloche mouldings, and similar matter. They introduced military and other trophies in their compositions (an idea which may have come down from Grinling Gibbons or else was drawn from a source common to both designers), but in this phase of effort the Adams, as in the ante-room at Sion, achieved questionable results.

The brothers also drew largely on animal and mythological models, some of their renderings of rams' or goats' heads, lions' heads, sphinxes, centaurs, and so on, being carved in a realistic manner. These creations often fulfilled the functions of caryatides, and, as in the case of earlier English designs, the head of an animal would crown an example whose legs were copied from the extremities of the same beast. Thus we find rams' heads over the relative legs, or lions' masks overlying clumsy presentments of the lion's paw. Occasionally we find human busts on Adam models (as in the case of the supports to the harpsichord which was designed by the brothers for the Empress of Russia), but these seldom yielded happy results.

The chimerical phase of Adam work, if so we may describe it, which led to the embodiment of centaurs, "griffons," sphinxes, and other fabulous monsters, represented that fashion which the Romans had built up largely on Egyptian tradition, and a reference to our illustration on page 471 will enable the reader to draw his own conclusions as to its decorative worth. The French and English Empire styles were partly inspired by this same Roman-cum-Egyptian style, which, when all is said and done, was singularly ill-suited to English homes.

The Adelphi did not neglect the armorial style of decoration, and amongst many instances of such we read of work at Sion House : " The Lyon's head introduced on the abbacus . . . and the claws which whimsically form the bases of the pilasters allude to the Percys' crest," and " the crescent introduced in the entablature is the present crest of the family " ; whilst, when treating of Kenwood, Adam wrote : " The frieze over the columns is enriched with an ornament of lions and the head of a deer, the former being the supporters and the latter the crest of the family " (Lord Mansfield's). These adaptations doubtless accounted for the introduction of animal life, &c., in Adam designs of a character sympathetic with heraldry.

That the Adelphi drew on the mythological element independently of their studies in Rome is shown by work which they did at Shelbourne House in Berkeley Square, where they incorporated a centaur and patera alternately in the frieze of the mural decoration, simply on account of the former being the crest of their employer.

In their selection of outline and relief the brothers Adam paid great attention to " movement," which they stated expressed the " rise and fall, the advance and recess, with other diversity of form" which beautified composition. Those who are conversant with the undulating sweeps of the Adams' serpentine swells will agree

Adam Wall Mirror of the period 1780-1790. These small examples were usually built in pairs.

with these designers, who held that "the rising and falling, advancing and receding, with the convexity and concavity, serve to produce an agreeable and diversified contour . . . and create a variety of light and shade which gives great spirit, beauty, and effect to the composition." This grasp of the principles of contour is particularly noticeable in the mahogany phase of Adelphi work, where the eye was not detracted from curvilinear swells by obtrusive decoration. It assisted many later creations, too, but was not so apparent or effective, in that the vividness of their decoration often relegated outline values to a secondary position.

The benefits accruing from this love of the curvilinear were accentuated at times by liberties which the Adams took in increasing the curves of antique mouldings. The preference which these architects displayed for Grecian as against Roman detail was strongly shown in this direction, for they further bent the curves of the cima-recta, cima-reversa, the ovolo, cavetto, and astragal, so emphasising their departure from the stiffer types of Rome. Aiming at lightness and daintiness, the Adelphi considered that their adaptations blended and mingled themselves " more harmoniously and attained more delicacy and elegance than such as have been commonly used."

In pursuance of the same idea, the brothers very generally discarded the somewhat weighty pediments and broken pediments which had hitherto crowned cabinet-work, and devoted their attentions towards the lightening and brightening of cornice fields. In their pursuit of lightness the Adams carried their theory at times to excess, and as their detail was minute and compactly arranged on many *tall* entablatures, it lost something of its decorative value when viewed from a distance.

How great a revolution had been brought about by the period 1780-1795 can be seen if we contrast the cornices seen on pages 213 and 427 with the entablatures crowning the tabernacle frames shown in the "Georgian" chapter.

Inlaid Designs.

In their inlaid designs exponents of Adam patterns introduced amboyna, hairwood, kingwood, rosewood, satinwood, tulipwood, walnut, and zebrawood, supplemented by such commoner mediums as beech, pear, and holly, which latter were generally stained. The masks of fauns or satyrs, the heads of lions or rams, which we find on carved Adam models were repeated in marquetry, and the festoons of flowers or drapery which these masks or heads supported were characteristic of both these decorative processes. Inlaid oval fans suggestive partly of Adam pateræ, partly of the shaded shellwork chiefly associated with the Sheraton school, were commonly introduced under the Adelphi, the accentuation of colour-contrasts becoming prevalent in the 'seventies.

At the junction of Chippendale with Adam work, when Chippendale in his old age was surrendering his independent style, there exist many examples whose classic friezes suggest Adam influence, but whose heavy, square, fluted legs, possibly with rope or pearl and bead edging on their outer edges, are typical of Chippendale's handling. When we find inlaid decoration on these transitional pieces it is almost invariably quiet and restrained, and not uncommonly it may be met with in diamond or shaped panels of figured mahogany *alone*, such as the earlier master affected on some of his characteristic late cabinet-work.

Where the two styles fused, Adam ideas invariably predominated, and only the expert will grasp those minutiæ which point to Chippendale execution. The collector will find more Adam influence and less suggestion of Chippendale—

1. As the Classic *per se* is present in frieze-work;
2. As leg-work lightens and shows a taper running down to a swelled square toe;

Exceptionally fine Side-table by Robert and James Adam, circa 1780-1790. Photo lent by Messrs. Partridge and Neave. This example is almost at the inception of the "English Empire" vogue, and does not show off the abilities of the designers so well as does their earlier work.

3. As inlaid decoration becomes brighter and more finicking;
4. As the dark, heavy Spanish mahogany tends to disappear in favour of fancy grain.

The Adams at times resorted to designs wherein inlay was carried out in brass, but even the beauties of the designs depicted failed to warrant the procedure. The unfortunate brass inlay of the Trafalgar and Waterloo periods was a development of the Adam idea carried to vulgar and meaningless excess.

Descriptions of Executed Work.

From the early 'seventies the Adelphi brought out descriptions of their better-known works in folio numbers, allotting prefaces and descriptions to each. Thus when Sion House had evoked admiration we read, " Encouraged by this, we now resume our talk, with greater confidence, by publishing the plans, elevations and sections of Kenwood " ; and again : "We proceed to lay before the public *another number of our works*. It contains a part of the designs of Luton House, one of the seats of the Earl of Bute." These publications were collected in batches and again issued in complete form, being sold by Peter Elmsly, opposite Southampton Street, in the Strand. The first complete series, which appeared in 1778, showed :—

    I. The seat of the Duke of Northumberland at Sion (or Syon).
   II. The villa of the Earl of Mansfield at Kenwood.
 III. The seat of the Earl of Bute at Luton Park.
 IV. Public buildings.
   V. Designs for the King and Queen and the Princess Dowager of Wales, &c.

In the following year yet another series of designs appeared, and this comprised :—

    I. The house of the Earl of Derby in Grosvenor Square.
   II. The house of Sir Watkin Williams Wynn, Bart., in St. James's Square.

The Brothers Adam.

   III. The house of the Earl of Shelburne in Berkeley Square.
   IV. The seat of the Duke of Northumberland at Sion, continued.
   V. Various designs of public and private buildings and references to works done for Earl Bathurst, the Duke of Montagu, and others.

The concluding and posthumous volume was issued by Priestley and Weale, No. 5, High Street, Bloomsbury, in 1822, and contained, among other information and designs, a record of R. and J. Adam's further accomplishments at Sion and at Luton, and of their creations at the Admiralty, Edinburgh University, &c. The Adam brothers gave England street upon street in their well-known style, besides numerous public buildings, and their publications give no hint of some of their masterpieces, such as Harewood House, Hanover Square.

Robert and James Adam.

Robert Adam, F.R.S. and F.S.A., was appointed Architect to the King in 1762, and died in 1792 from the bursting of a blood-vessel (Strange). The names of his pallbearers at his funeral in Westminster Abbey as given by Clouston, viz., the Duke of Buccleuch, the Earl of Coventry, the Earl of Lauderdale, Viscount Stormont, Lord Frederick Campbell, and Mr. Pulteney, bear eloquent witness to the esteem in which he was held.

James Adam only survived his brother by two and a half years, dying of apoplexy in 1794, shortly after the publication of the second edition of his " Practical Essays on Architecture," the first edition of which had appeared in 1789.

Résumé.

The Adams were greatly admired in their day, and posterity has come to value many of their buildings. In interior work they were the greatest welders of matter from carpet to ceiling which the English school has produced. Robert's acumen led him to good centres for inspiration; his personality attracted artists and patrons wheresoever he went, and enabled him to take toll of other people's brains whensoever he chose. The Adams were not cabinet-makers, but designers and co-ordinators of designs, and they were singularly fortunate in being able to farm out their suggestions with the Chippendales, Gillows, the Heppelwhites, Seddons, and others, the brilliancy of whose execution added lustre to the Adelphi's suggestions.

William Adam.

There has been much speculation as to the standing of William Adam and as to the part which he played subsequent to the death of his better-known brothers Robert and James. The writer has found the answer in the old Directories issued by Loundes and Kent. Going back to 1770, William Adam and Co. were described by Kent as Merchants, of New Bond Street, Hanover Square, but in 1772 Loundes describes them as of Adam Street, Adelphi, Strand, Kent in 1774 conforming to the same description and address. In 1773 Loundes styled them *Architects*, of Adam Street, Adelphi.

R. and J. Adam doubtless placed the bulk of their orders for building materials with their brother William. William Adam's place of business was in the Adelphi, and it would appear that he received the complimentary title of architect purely on account of his business associations with the senior firm. Be this as it may, William Adam and Co. were in 1781 described by Loundes as Merchants *only*, of Robert Street, Adelphi, whilst in 1782 Kent dropped the " and Co." and spoke of William Adam, Merchant, of Robert Street, Adelphi.

In 1783 or 1784 William appears to have entered into partnership with the " Adelphi," for Loundes then records the business as Robert, James, and William Adam, Merchants, of Adelphi, Strand. By this time the architects, Robert and James, were heavily concerned in speculative building, as well as in the execution of private and public buildings, and they had entered into partnership with their brother William, doubtless with a view to obtaining all materials on favoured-nation terms.

Robert was temporarily dropped from the 1786 records, when Kent tells of James and William Adam, Timber Merchants, Adelphi, and of Pedler's Acre, Lambeth ; Robert and James being described as architects, of the same address. In 1787 Robert, James, and William Adam were set down as Merchants, of 27, Old Bond Street, by Loundes, and Kent followed suit in his Directories of 1788-9, 1790-1-2, by styling them as Timber Merchants at the same place of business.

Here it is noteworthy that, in addition to the description of the business side of the partnership, which Loundes confirmed in 1788-9, 1790-1, Kent allocated specific descriptions to Robert and James Adam and William Adam and Co. as *separate* firms of *architects*, carrying on their profession from the common centre in Bond Street.

William Adam had probably learnt something of the Adelphi's methods and technique, and would appear to have picked up some of the crumbs or unconsidered trifles which fell from the rich men's table.

In 1792 Robert died, and in this, the year of his death, Loundes gave the last record of the triumvirate when he described them as Timber Merchants, of 27, Old Bond Street, and Narrow Wall, Lambeth. In 1793 James and William, the survivors, were still trading at the Bond Street address as timber merchants, James Adam being registered separately as an architect. In 1794 James Adam went the way of all flesh, and Kent's Directory, probably compiled late in the year, notes the fact by omission, for the constitution of the old business is there given as William Adam and Co. alone.

In the following year's Directory by Kent we get the most interesting information, for William had launched out into two establishments, carrying on the timber trade from 2, Old Bond Street and the profession of architect, &c., from 27, Old Bond Street. Loundes, however, persisted in describing William as a Timber Merchant, at 27, Old Bond Street. In 1796-7-9 Kent gave Adam two separate descriptions, the one as Timber Merchant and the other as Merchant and Architect, of 2, Old Bond Street, to which he, in 1800, added the old address of No. 27 in the same street.

In 1802 William Adam was still practising as an architect in addition to carrying on the business, but he had substituted premises at 13, Albemarle Street in place of the establishment at 2, Old Bond Street. By 1806 William had turned from the architectural calling, and had taken two men, A. and D. Robertson, into the business at 27, Old Bond Street, the partnership being still existent in 1810 as " Adam, William, and A. and D. Robertson, Timber Merchants and Builders, 27, Old Bond Street, and 7, Narrow Wall, Lambeth."

These records make it abundantly clear that William

Adam was largely identified with Robert and James during the closing years of their work, and that after the two latter had passed away William continued the profession and business on his own account. It has been seen that Robert and James Adam designed the furniture for the majority of their buildings, and it is only reasonable to conclude that William endeavoured, more or less successfully, to follow out the precedent established by his better-known brethren. For a decade, then, we may expect that there were pieces for which William Adam was in part at any rate responsible. These would, perhaps, have been rechauffé Adelphi types, with concessions towards Sheraton's models and the incoming " Empire " vogue. William Adam's training had been commercial, even if he had gained professional polish by rubbing shoulders with Robert and James, and he would have welcomed the chance of gaining grist for the mill which commissions for furniture would have afforded.

There is a large volume of well-built but somewhat invertebrate furniture of the period 1795-1805 which has been vaguely assigned to disciples of R. and J. Adam, or, in default, to such of Sheraton's partisans as possessed a smattering of Adelphi technique. There is also work bordering on Empire wherein Egypto-Roman work has been rather crudely introduced; but in cleverly-worked mahogany or rosewood savouring of the finest cabinet hands. It would seem probable that many of these examples, which lack the character and finesse of true Adelphi compositions, as they miss the clean lines of Sheraton's pencilling, are in reality the fruits of William Adam's efforts when he was endeavouring single-handed to conserve the family connection and fulfil the firm's traditions.

It is worthy of note that James or William Adam subscribed for a copy of Sheraton's "Drawing Book" after the death of Robert, the backbone of the business. The resemblance between the late Adam and Sheraton furniture of the compounded order may very possibly be accounted for by the theory that William Adam, in default of originality and power, endeavoured to graft Adelphi scions on Sheraton stocks in his efforts to keep abreast of the times.

CHAPTER XVIII.
Heppelwhite.

His Position as a Designer.

PERHAPS no class or style of eighteenth-century furniture is so poorly understood as is "Heppelwhite," or "Hepplewhite," as the name is sometimes spelt. Modern critics are often at variance as to the position which should rightly be assigned to Heppelwhite as a designer, but many criticisms have been obviously based on misconceptions of the man, his methods, aims, and period. R. S. Clouston has shown that Heppelwhite was at one time an apprentice at the Gillows furniture factory in Lancaster, and in her "English Furniture Designers of the Eighteenth Century" Miss Constance Simon has added the date of his death. The passage reads: "By dint of careful research at Somerset House we have found out that administration of the goods, chattels, and credits of George Heppelwhite [*sic*], late of the parish of St. Giles, Cripplegate, London, was granted on 27th June, 1786, to his widow Alice," and that the business was "carried on after his death by his widow Alice and a 'combine' under the style of A. Heppelwhite and Co."

Heppelwhite, as we shall presently see, was influenced in turn by successive designers and styles, but his dainty mannerisms appear on the surface, and usually enable us to identify his creations. An obvious method of penning a criticism on a given designer's work lies in a *résumé* of the suggestions offered in his publications, for it is so very simple to expatiate on the merits or faults which these contain. This elementary process, which proved the undoing of so many of Chippendale's critics, has in the case of Heppelwhite led many writers into a trap.

George Heppelwhite, the founder of the Heppelwhite business, who was certainly engaged on furniture in the late 'fifties, and was influencing the craft in the 'sixties, issued no book of designs. Two years after his death his widow and the " combine " already referred to brought out " The Cabinet-Maker and Upholsterer's Guide, &c.," now commonly known as the " Guide." The work in question tells the collector practically nothing as to early Heppelwhite furniture; it fails to reflect the taste and power of the man who, in the teeth of acute competition, laid the foundations of a prosperous business, whilst the sense of perspective and proportion which its illustrations display is a libel on old George Heppelwhite. Events marched quickly at the close of the 'seventies, and designers or tradesmen who did not move with the times were in danger of having their wares considered as stale by a restless and novelty-seeking public. It was not necessary that ideas should really be new, but it was desirable that they should be re-dressed if they were to be acceptable, and models of ten years' standing were frequently obsolete.

The calibre of A. Heppelwhite and Co.'s " Guide " was mediocre, and one may judge it to have been a hastily-prepared catalogue which lacked the guiding hand of a sound and tasteful helmsman. Bereft of her husband, the main asset in the business, Alice Heppelwhite was doubtless advised by those around her to issue the publication with a view to the retention of her clientèle and as a bid for wider support. In the preparation of this mediocre work the new company sought to avoid the older class of design and to present suggestions which were more up-to-date and yet thoroughly serviceable The venture proved to be a commercial success, for Heppelwhite designs percolated into districts where the name of Heppelwhite had been hitherto unknown. George Heppelwhite

Early Heppelwhite Armchair in the Louis Quinze style; period 1760-5.

therefore enjoyed a certain posthumous recognition and reputation owing to the circulation of A. Heppelwhite and Co.'s book, however imperfectly this publication reflected the early and interesting phases of his designs.

George Heppelwhite had come to the front during the

'sixties, and his daintiness had doubtless attracted a certain number of followers, but the Heppelwhite school in its wider interpretation dates from the close of the 'eighties, when he had been laid to rest, and the doctrines of A. Heppelwhite and Co. were disseminated throughout the kingdom. It follows, therefore, that Heppelwhite furniture should, strictly speaking, be divided into three classes :

    1. George Heppelwhite proper, 1760-1786.
    2. A. Heppelwhite and Co., 1786 and onwards.
    3. The Heppelwhite school as followers of the " Guide's " designs, 1788-1800.

In this classification we take no notice of work carried out by George Heppelwhite or his successors to the order of R. and J. Adam, for it is obvious that when the Heppelwhites, like the Chippendales, dropped their independence in design to become the agents of the Adelphi, they sank to the level of artist-craftsmen.

The valuable and instructive phases of Heppelwhite design are to be found prior to the death of George, the originator of the business. Our designer was primarily a chair manufacturer, and we can best study his initial efforts in an analysis of his chair-work. Lightness and daintiness were his watchwords, and throughout his career he seems to have devoted his main energies to the creation of small models. The Heppelwhite style was transitional, for it began when carved mahogany furniture appealed to the public, and it culminated when the processes of inlaying, composition moulding, japanning, painting, and gilding had been introduced as supplementary or alternative aids to decorative schemes.

Before Heppelwhite came under the spell of Adam influence he had been prosecuting his calling, more or

Heppelwhite.

less closely, on Louis Quinze lines, and he may be said to have picked up the threads of this French style at the point where Chippendale had dropped them. Chippendale had gradually discarded the hooped or rounded back as he lightened the proportions of the curved leg, but as he brought the leg to greater grace he too often imposed excessive decoration. Heppelwhite founded his leg-work on the daintier and simpler examples which Chippendale gave us, and a reference to our illustrations on pages

Window-Seat, thoroughly characteristic of Heppelwhite; period 1770.

481, 483, and 485 will show the similarity which existed between Heppelwhite's chair-legs, &c., and earlier models by Chippendale, as seen on pages 246 and 252.

This development of lightness brought the mid-eighteenth-century pieces more into line with the light and simple cabriole of the "Queen Anne" period, and therein the cardinal difference which we notice between Chippendale and Heppelwhite. Chippendale decorated leg-work freely—sometimes to excess—and, except in the case of such models as wheel-back chairs, resorted to angular back-framing, so emphasising the divergence of his style from that of the pure "Queen Anne." Heppelwhite reduced the decoration of curvilinear leg-work to a minimum, and reverted to hooped or rounded lines for his back-frames, so bringing his designs more into harmony with those of the early eighteenth century.

After a perusal of these points it might be thought that there would be some little difficulty in distinguishing between plain chairs of the early, or Queen Anne, school and those of Heppelwhite; but such is not the case. From William and Mary days chair-backs had been growing lower, and just as Queen Anne models were, as a class, lower than typical specimens of the preceding reign, so Chippendale chairs were, as a class, lower than the Queen Anne. Heppelwhite carried this feature a point further, his models ranging from three to five inches lower than those of his predecessor, and he also exaggerated the curvilinear in back-outline and arm-work.

As he, so to speak, compressed his chair-backs, he accentuated his curves, for these became more pronounced as they were worked into a smaller field. In addition to this, Heppelwhite often imparted saddle-back shaping to his models, so that chairs such as that shown on page 481 consist of a mass of curves. In his arrangement of the curvilinear, matters were sometimes carried to excess, and another unfortunate feature was that this designer came perilously near to weakness when handling some of his individual lines. The curves in the leg-work in our illustration on page 485 are distinctly overdone about the ankle, though the outline of the overlying framework is exceedingly graceful.

When handling the Louis Quinze, Heppelwhite was

Heppelwhite.

lighter and daintier than Chippendale. He lacked the latter's strength, but steered clear of his over-elaboration of rococo detail. Many early Heppelwhite superstructures appear to be stunted, yet they one and all possess individuality and a charm.

After Adam had obtained a footing, in the 'sixties, and was subordinating cabinet-work to his architectural

Heppelwhite Card-table, showing Louis Quinze outline; period 1765-70.

schemes, Heppelwhite forsook the Louis XV. style and became, not only a disciple, but an employee of the Adelphi. With little or no knowledge of the classic, but with a pretty taste in outline and detail, he was just such a man as the Adams would have liked and chosen for giving expression to their designs. As far as we can judge, Heppelwhite shared with Gillows in the chief commissions for Adelphi chair-work and for minor models. From

Adam's suggestions Heppelwhite took various details, such as pateræ, strings of tapered bell-flowers, vases, and festoons of flowers or drapery, which he incorporated with his own models. He was particularly attached to the Anthemion, or Grecian honeysuckle, a pet item of Adam detail, and his collaboration with these great designers opened up new vistas to him. The result is apparent in all of his models subsequent to the Louis Quinze phase, for we seldom happen on a post-1770 Heppelwhite model which looks out of place in an Adam interior. The Adelphi were sometimes too cold, severe, stilted, or finicking when adhering strictly to their ideas of the classic, or when seeking to improve on the antique orders by a blending of members. Heppelwhite did not know enough to essay correct models on such lines, but his knack and intuition enabled him to make dainty changes which relieved the situation and acted as a corrective.

When Heppelwhite's furniture is studied as a whole, one is struck by the pleasing effects which were obtained with a modicum of decoration. In reviewing his creations the collector might almost style him the apostle of simplicity, bearing in mind such other designers as Chippendale, Ince and Mayhew, the Adams, and Sheraton, were it not for another of his contemporaries, William Shearer. Shearer was our finest exponent of restrained embellishment, whether carved or inlaid, yet it is next to impossible to distinguish between his work and some of Heppelwhite's. The love of quiet inlay was common to both masters, and their joint leaning towards a type which came to be known as "Louis Seize Anglaise" points to there having been an artistic association between them.

Heppelwhite, in turn influenced by Chippendale, R. and J. Adam, possibly by Darly, probably by Shearer, and certainly by the Gillows, so co-ordinated his productions that they suit either Louis Quinze or Louis Seize houses and contemporary English interiors. An author recently wrote of Heppelwhite that "he never, under any circumstances, went the length to which his predecessor [Chippendale] went by his ever-present desire to be constantly producing something fresh, and, moreover, something French." It would be difficult to conceive anything more misleading than this passage. Heppelwhite believed that he tendered the latest and most up-to-date models for a novelty-loving public, and it is questionable whether he ever made one piece of furniture to his own designs which was not sympathetic with either the Louis Quinze or the Louis Seize style.

As Heppelwhite's forte was chair-making, it is essential that we should disabuse our minds of one popular fallacy. The author just referred to has laid down that Heppelwhite's chairs, "when really pure and truly characteristic, always have the shield-shape back," a truly amazing statement. The writer went to some little pains to examine a series of Heppelwhite's patterns in various collections and galleries, and found that of fifty-seven Heppelwhite chairs examined, thirty-four specimens were exempt from the shield in any form whatsoever. Ten years ago it was very generally supposed that when a shield-back chair was found it must have been by Heppelwhite, but as the Adams commissioned these models, and the Gillows, with Shearer, Sheraton, and a host of smaller cabinet-makers, created them, the claims on behalf of Heppelwhite must be regarded as shadowy. The Adelphi very possibly introduced both the shield- and lyre-backed patterns, whilst the Gillows' title to their introduction is at least as strong as that of Heppelwhite.

There is one early pattern of chair known as the camel-back, which is supposed to have represented a compromise between Chippendale and Heppelwhite at the parting of their ways, and some colour is lent to this by

Early Heppelwhite Chair, showing low back, which gives it rather a squat appearance. The decoration consists of strings of husks or bell-flowers; the side and front stretchers have been added. Mahogany; circa 1770. Photo kindly lent by Messrs. Gill and Reigate.

the shaping of the cresting-rail (giving rise to the name "camel-back"), and by the pseudo-classic decoration of Heppelwhite style which this usually carries. The contention that these chairs were early departures of Heppelwhite's was stronger a decade ago than it is now, for they often carry a bunch of three or five wheat-ears, and these, like shield-backs, were erroneously held to have been hall-marks of Heppelwhite parentage. To arrive at the camel-back type, take the shield-back chair to the left of the row on page 503, and remove the inner curve of the shield (upon which the splat rests) at its junction with the back uprights, carrying the splat down to the horizontal rail at the plane of the seat. The reader can then realise how small an evolutionary step it was from the camel-back to the shield-back type.

Heppelwhite's wheel-back chair, unlike many of his patterns, may be found with cabriole legs, and later with typical straight tapered ones. These models are striking, and the varieties fitted with the Louis Quinze type of legs are most interesting as showing that Heppelwhite revived this old type of back-work (subject to his variation, of course) at an early date. Our illustration on page 490 shows a peculiarly fine specimen of this class of chair with the later legs. Shearer and other of Heppelwhite's contemporaries also constructed similar models.

The chair shown on the opposite page also possesses interesting features, for it is of a type correctly ascribed to Heppelwhite at an early period of his work. The decoration in relief savours of that which the Adams favoured, and the great resemblance between the front legs of this chair and those shown on the basket-grate in our Adam chapter (page 403) points to its having been made shortly after Heppelwhite had come under the influence of the Adelphi. The squatness of the back is typical of many of George Heppelwhite's early essays.

In the chair A on page 493 we see the most interesting example of Heppelwhite's work shown in our chapters, and it should be studied in conjunction with the armchair illustrated on page 481. The designer has here forsaken the Chippendale placing of arm-supports, and has introduced straight legs *at the front*, with decoration savouring of Adam influence. The back, however, exhibits no traces of improved contour, and the

A typical and beautiful example of one of Heppelwhite's Wheel-back Chairs of the period 1775. In the possession of John Walker, Esq.

rather primitive attempts at lightening the back by the insertion of splats does not remove its somewhat squat appearance, which still remains fully characteristic of *early* Heppelwhite work.

We cannot definitely ascribe the ladder-back chair

Heppelwhite.

shown on page 501 to Heppelwhite, and yet, if we are to attribute camel-back designs to this master, the piece in question might be set down as his. The seat outline, the cresting-rail, and, above all, the proportions of this example are strongly suggestive of Heppelwhite influence.

The chair inscribed B on page 493 shows the perfected model as evolved by Heppelwhite soon after 1770. The camel-back frame has been turned into a shield-back by curving the lower rail, and the splat-work, which resembles that on the neighbouring and earlier specimen, has been appreciably lightened in consonance with the general trend of fashion.

The chair lettered C, of rather later date and with the more pretentious splat-work, is also of interest because the two upper pateræ which crown the splat are inlaid, and so bear witness to that incoming vogue. The reader will notice that at the base of the splat Heppelwhite has utilised the half of a wheel somewhat resembling that seen on the chair-back on the opposite page. This was one of his pet mannerisms.

Characteristics of his Work.

In his early days, when Heppelwhite was feeling his way, he seems to have frequently upholstered his chair-backs saddle-shape in an endeavour to shake off conventional ideas, but with no very definite notion as to alternative suggestions. He carried out shaping to a back and in the upholstering of the seat, and as often as not gave a dainty serpentine swell to the seat-front. The arms and legs were gracefully modelled on the lines of the Louis Quinze or Seize, the former being relieved by slight rococo decoration, the latter by fluting, bead-mouldings, or strings of husks or bell-flowers, for example. At a slightly later date Heppelwhite produced the most glorious chair-backs. Some early ones are wheel-shaped, compounded with Louis Quinze legs, subsequently with those of Louis Seize type; and there were also the shield, lyre, heart, and oval shapes, which rose over a structure otherwise somewhat Louis Seize in character.

If we analyse these creations we cannot with certainty ascribe them to Heppelwhite in their entirety. We have urged that Robert Adam had something to do with the inception of the shield-back, just as we know that he had with that of the lyre-back. Again, the oval back could be claimed by Robert Adam and by the French school of the Louis Seize.

It is when we come to the scheme of garnishment *contained* by these frames that we realise something of the genius of the designer. Sometimes we have the orthodox pierced splat, with its concomitant decoration of classic character, always full of grace and rhythm. Sometimes these splats enclosed a central ornament, such as a large urn, a spray of Grecian honeysuckle, a medallion, or the Prince of Wales's feathers, and pendent from these we may expect festoons of graceful drapery of Adam type.

Now and then we meet with a back reminiscent of the old Queen Anne splat pattern, but by far the handsomest and most striking backs are composed of one bold design, such as the Prince of Wales's feathers, the anthemion, or the lyre, whose outline would stand out boldly a hundred feet away.

Heppelwhite paid great attention to the supports connecting the chair-backs with the underlying legs, shaping them gracefully throughout the course which would be visible above the plane of the seat, and he would occasionally finish them off on their outer edges

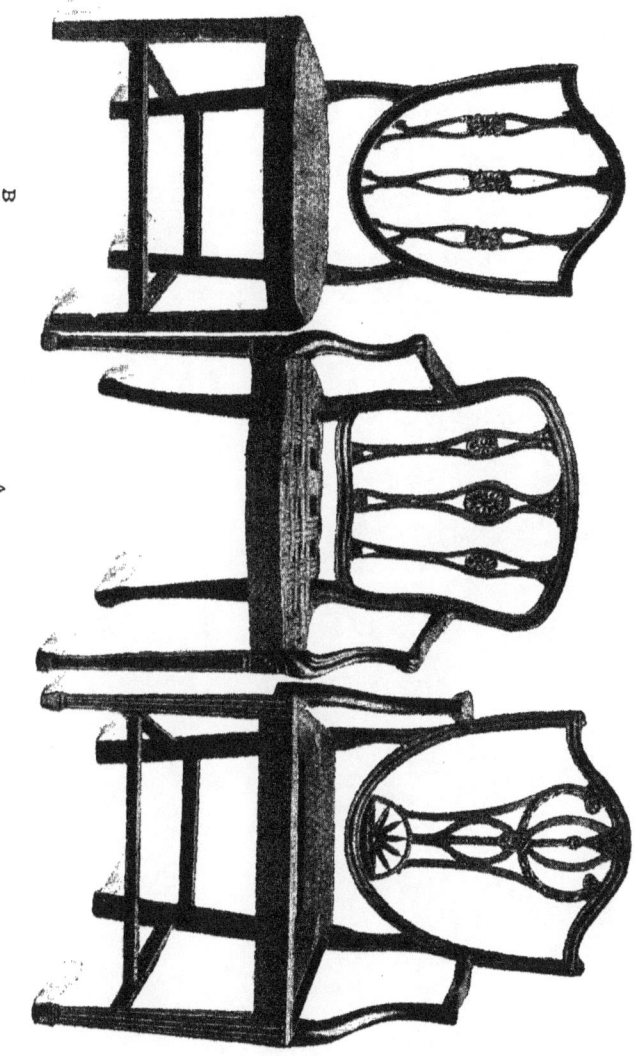

A. Heppelwhite Armchair, showing Adam influence; period 1785-90
B. Single Chair, ,, ,, 1775
C. Armchair, carving supplemented by inlay; period 1780-8

Heppelwhite.

with a scroll head containing a rosette or patera. Sheraton rarely availed himself of this last idea, whilst he made the shield-support rise from a square or an interrupted base standing out in full sight just above the seat. It is also characteristic of Sheraton's work when we find the base of the splat at the apex of the shield complex and lacking in rhythm. Both masters fancied the patera and festoons of drapery which Robert Adam had rendered popular; but Heppelwhite was the less stilted of the two when employing them.

It is doubtful whether any chair of the 1780 period equalled Heppelwhite's oval-back enclosing the Prince of Wales's feathers as one big plume for the splat, and when the feathers made way for a large anthemion the result was also effective. On the other hand, Heppelwhite's models based on the Queen Anne style, but with intricate decoration covering the bold back-splat, were more or less disappointing. There are two distinguishing features which are often present in Heppelwhite's work : (1) The chair-back may be found built up on the two back uprights alone, with no connecting-bar under the design to unite the uprights and stiffen the frame; (2) the complexity of the foot-shaping. Sheraton favoured a plain tapered leg or a plain thimble toe; Heppelwhite used to amplify foot decoration quite commonly—not always with happy results.

Amongst other details characteristic of Heppelwhite the sheaf of leaves stands out pre-eminent. This little item was placed on the chair-back or encircled the tops of legs, both round and square, sometimes even crowning decorated feet.

Whatever preconceived opinion as to the merits or demerits of Heppelwhite furniture the reader may have, one thing is certain, namely, that Heppelwhite was the greatest master in the shaping of an arm which England has so far produced. The chair or sofa arm beloved of Heppelwhite came down from the back in a single curve, sinuous and graceful in character; it was met by another curve, usually concave, with an outward inclination which reached out to the front of the chair-seat, where it capped the front leg (*vide* A, page 493). Upholstered armchairs by Heppelwhite, especially those of early type, in the Louis Quinze style were often fitted with elbow-pads, as in the case of the model shown on page 481.

Heppelwhite's early practice was to build sideboard-tables rather than sideboards, but the latter gradually ousted the former from popularity. The sideboard-tables were flanked at times by pedestals, which were the same height as the major piece and decorated *en suite*. One of these pedestals was used as a cupboard, the other as a plate-warmer, " being provided with racks and a stand for the heater." On these pedestals urns reposed, which were fitted for knives or to hold ice or water for the butler's use. When the sideboard proper became popular, Heppelwhite incorporated wing-cupboards in his designs, flanking the central or linen drawer. The left cupboard, we are told, "has two divisions, the hinder one lined with green cloth to hold plate, &c., under a cover; the front one is lined with lead for the convenience of holding water to wash glasses, &c.; there must be a valve-cock or plug at the bottom to let off the dirty water, and also in the other drawer to change the water necessary to keep the wine, &c., cool " (" The Guide ") The model was, therefore, a wine-cooler and butler's pantry, as well as a repository for linen and plate; but, however generous its proportions, it must have proved inadequate for the butler's use, a fact which quite possibly militated against its earlier introduction. As Heppelwhite did not produce many large pieces of furniture, he probably followed the lead of his employers, the Adams, in the development of the sideboard, incorporating the pedestal accommodation about 1770.

Heppelwhite sideboard-tables were, as a rule, pleasing, and followed more or less closely on Adam patterns; but when he turned his attention to sideboard building. his models approximated more closely to those generally attributed to Shearer and Sheraton.

Although a considerable number of this master's *sideboard-tables* were serpentine in shape, very many were straight-fronted; but in his sideboards he reversed matters. The vast majority of the "boards" proper were freely shaped, sometimes with a single serpentine swell running along the whole face, at other times with this sinuous line in the centre only, between two coved and flanking ends. Sometimes the leg-work was canted; and Heppelwhite often reduced the posterior faces of the leg woodwork with a view to accentuating their appearance of lightness.

It must not be imagined that Heppelwhite confined himself to serpentine or to straight-fronted sideboards. One masterpiece of his in the author's collection is square as to its wings (save for six shaped corners), with a serpentine swell as a connecting-link. The legs in this instance are fluted, and stand on an elaborated variation of the thimble toe, with leaf carving to set them off. The inlay, brasswork, and mahogany in this example are superlative. No other craftsmen excelled Heppelwhite in the production of dainty knife-urns and boxes intended to supplement the usefulness and decorative effect of these sideboards; but, light and pleasing as they were, these models lacked the majestic dignity which was the distinguishing feature of Adam handling.

Now and then we come across painted Heppelwhite sideboards, but the majority are relieved by judiciously

Heppelwhite Chair, showing a back impregnated with Adam teaching. Author's Collection; circa 1775.

applied inlay and exquisite brass fittings. Not so plain as Shearer boards, Heppelwhite's creations are, as a rule, softer, more mellow-looking, and less flamboyant than are many of Sheraton's.

No article of furniture being so useful or decorative

at the price, the sideboard, when genuine *and fine*, is rapidly snapped up, so that the supply is not equal to the demand, since we English like our sideboards. The enterprising faker caters for the demand, and the writer has watched the new creations rising wholesale from old bedsteads, &c., to be subsequently glorified by copious inlay and brass mounts cast or stamped in Birmingham. A more insidious process, too, is rife, for late sideboards of the early nineteenth century have their turned legs replaced by tapered square ones with thimble toes, and their carcases relieved by modern stringing and banding darkened by means of various agents.

The Heppelwhites, in urging the merits of japanning, wrote : " For chairs a new and very elegant fashion has arisen within these few years of finishing them with painted or japanned work, which gives a rich and splendid appearance to the minute parts of the ornaments which are generally *thrown in* by the painter." The treatment, the glories of which A. Heppelwhite and Co. extolled, was rudimentary and in every way inferior to the earlier lacquer. It consisted in the admixture of gelatinous matters which were applied to soft woods and then polished, and upon the surface so provided the artist worked out his design in gold, bronze, or colour. It will be noticed that A. Heppelwhite and Co. do not claim to have originated the idea, which they, however, designate as " new and very elegant," and, as a matter of fact, this japanning was common also to the schools of the brothers Adam, Shearer, and Sheraton.

In the " Guide " the Heppelwhites tell us that knife-urns may be made of copper painted and japanned ; but we may take it that japanning was carried out almost exclusively on what we now style white or inferior woods.

Having coated the chair or table with this japanned work in black or in a neutral colour, such as a slate grey, dull green, or other hue, the less important features of the design were picked out in lines of colour, very much as a carriage-builder is wont to relieve his wheels, and the main portion of the design was then garnished by such painted detail as the artist in question chiefly affected. We get, therefore, Classic detail such as Robert Adam favoured, medallions resembling Wedgwood china plaques, baskets of flowers, or even the Prince of Wales's feathers in strong to bright colours (generally much the worse for the wear and tear of over a hundred years), figuring on these "japanned" models.

Collectors cannot be too careful when acquiring this work. If they put off buying specimens until they have gained knowledge they will purchase but sparingly, seeing that less than ten per cent. of the pieces extant are worth the prices asked when compared with mahogany or fine-wood pieces at a little more money. Again, the "worm" has played havoc with seventy-five per cent. of these examples, whilst the "renovator" and "redecorator" have had many a field-day on what they have come to regard as a happy hunting-ground peculiarly adapted to their enterprise.

Japanned furniture of this period was generally small in size, and erred, as a rule, on the side of lightness. Chairs and settees were produced in this style more frequently than were any other articles of furniture. The seats of these were almost invariably carried out in caned work, and upon this foundation loose cushions were placed for comfort's sake. The settees were, as a rule, of the "three-chair-back" order. Now and then we find models of the two-chair-back or four-chair-back design.

Heppelwhite.

The vogue lasted through the Trafalgar and Waterloo periods, being greatly favoured during the so-called "English Empire" days, and during these late phases some most inartistic models were foisted on a public whose power of discernment had gone awry. It might be safely

A Ladder-back Chair in the Heppelwhite-Sheraton School, the cresting-rail savouring of the Camel-back. In this case the central ornament holds an inlaid shell in lieu of the carved detail which Chippendale would have employed. Period 1780.

asserted that if a representative collection of japanned work (subsequent to 1805) were put on trial to-day, ninety-five per cent. of its constituent parts would be ruthlessly condemned.

Primarily intended for bedroom use, we find many

little examples of early type which admirably fulfil that duty to-day. Here and there we come across a dainty little model worthy of a place in boudoir or drawing-room.

Gold with a copper tinge running through it was freely employed for the decoration of the black japanned work, whilst sometimes we meet with an example which has painted garnishment framed by this copper-gilt treatment.

Heppelwhite Aims.

We get an interesting glimpse of the Heppelwhites in their preface to the " Guide," wherein they say :

" To unite elegance and utility and blend the useful with the agreeable has ever been considered a difficult but an honourable task. How far we have succeeded in the following work it becomes not us to say, but rather to leave it, with all deference, to the determination of the public at large. . . . English taste and workmanship have of late years been much sought for *by surrounding nations* [italics ours], and the mutability of all things, but more especially of fashion, has rendered the labours of our predecessors in this line of little use; nay, at this day they can only tend to mislead those foreigners who seek knowledge of English taste in the various articles of household furniture." Here the Heppelwhites were "having a slap" at Chippendale and his school. To-day " Chippendale " has vindicated and asserted itself.

Sheraton on Heppelwhite.

Now let us turn for one moment to Sheraton's review of the " Guide," for it forms interesting reading after the foregoing introduction. We are told by him :

" In the year 1788 was published ' The Cabinet-Maker's and Upholsterer's Guide,' in which are found no

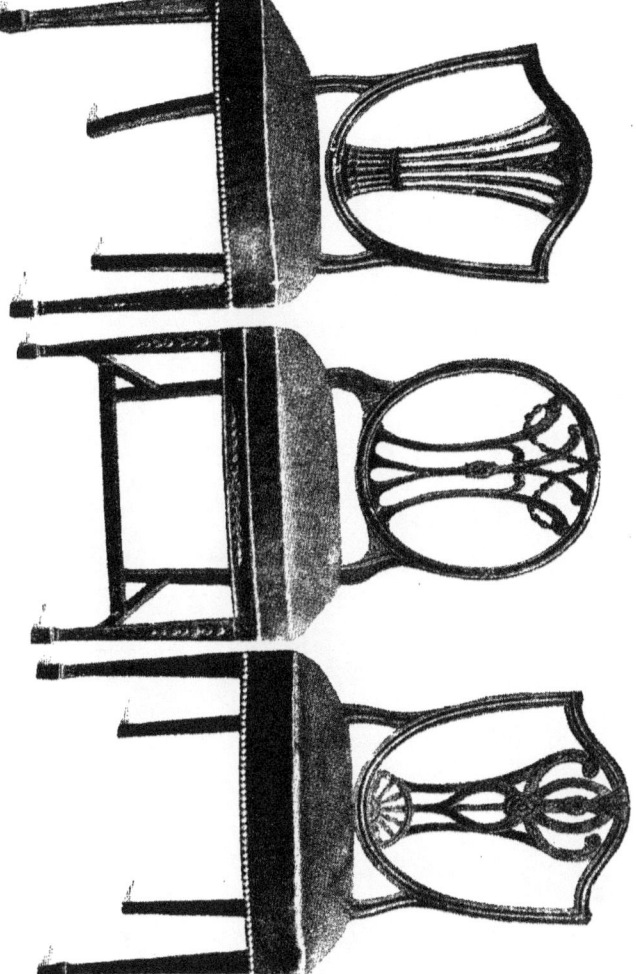

Three typical Heppelwhite Designs of the period 1770-1790. Photograph kindly lent by Messrs. Gill and Reigate, Ltd.

Heppelwhite.

directions for drawing in any form, nor any pretensions to it. The whole merit of the performance rests on design, with a short description to each plate prefixed. *Some of these designs are not without merit*, though it is evident that the perspective is in some instances erroneous. But, notwithstanding the late date of Heppelwhite's book, if we compare some of the designs, particularly the chairs, *with the newest taste*, we shall find that this work has already caught the decline, and perhaps will suddenly die in the disorder. This instance may serve to convince us of that fate which all books of the same kind will ever be subjected to. Yet it must be owned that books of this sort have their usefulness for a time, and when through change of fashions they are become obsolete, they serve to show the taste of former times."

This scathing and withering review was totally unmerited; it was only one of the many examples of that jealousy with which Sheraton looked upon the work of his contemporaries. It must be remembered, too, that Sheraton borrowed many of his best designs from Heppelwhite, unblushingly, without so much as " by your leave," and without any acknowledgment.

Compared with his Compeers.

We have already noticed the strong similarity which existed between the early work of the brothers Adam and that of Heppelwhite, a fact accounted for by Heppelwhite's appreciation of Adam *motif*. As a general rule, this resemblance grew more marked as time wore on, for Adam returned the compliment paid by Heppelwhite, taking a leaf out of the latter's book when handling French models. There is, however, one strongly-marked difference between the two schools, for the brothers Adam, as they advanced in years, produced some extravagant designs, which, when compared with early rococo work, out-heroded Herod; whilst Heppelwhite, as time wore on, tied himself down even more closely to the chaste outline of the Louis Seize.

The brothers Adam would have been much greater artists had they stopped work by 1790, whilst the Heppel-

Mahogany Card-table with carved decoration of the Adam style, but with typical Hepplewhite shaping; circa 1780.

white factory turned out excellent models until some little time after poor George Heppelwhite's death. Reading between the lines, it would almost appear that Robert Adam, in an endeavour to exhibit his knowledge of the arts and crafts of ancient Greece, Rome, and Egypt, became pedantic. Heppelwhite, on the other hand, was less of a *poseur*, and, having found models which suited

Heppelwhite.

his style, rested content with efforts to enhance their beauties by the addition of dainty and well-placed, if less pretentious, garnishment.

Chippendale, as we have seen, erred on the side of extravagance in his late rococo work, and it was left to Heppelwhite to bring this style back to the limits of good taste and simplicity. Adam renderings of Renaissance-cum-Egyptian work, when the country was just commencing to embrace "English Empire," were often indefensible. Sheraton's work after 1800 was so hopeless that we wonder how he can ever have passed as a great craftsman. We can, on the other hand, find no phase of Heppelwhite's work meriting wholesale condemnation such as we have just mentioned, and he shares with Shearer the distinction of standing above resultant criticism. If he was less brilliant, Heppelwhite was more uniformly successful than many of his compeers, for they seem always to have had weak spots in their armour. Possessed of taste and discernment, Heppelwhite automatically rose to be one of the leaders of his craft, and it was a pity that he was not spared to do battle with that latter-day decadence which proved to be the undoing of Sheraton and the Sheraton school.

His Political Convictions Influence his Work.

Heppelwhite was a man with convictions, and did not endeavour to disguise them. The reader will remember that George III. was strongly Tory in his sympathies; whilst his son, on the other hand, was an ardent Whig. In London there was a King's (or Tory) party, and at the same time a Whig faction headed by the Prince, and of this latter body Heppelwhite was a strong partisan. We will not waste time discussing whether our designer had genuine convictions or was something of a time-server, realising that the mental case of the Sovereign was hopeless, and that the Prince's party would sooner or later gain the day; but this we do know, that Heppelwhite symbolised his adhesion to the " young " party by introducing the Prince of Wales's feathers on every possible occasion as an item of decoration. It nay seem extraordinary to find the Classic anthemion and garlands of bell-flowers around this modern detail, but the artist was so happy in his blending of matter that only pleasing effects were arrived at. In later years many other of our cabinet-makers affected the same design, but so far as we know there seems to have been no political significance in their action.

The Heppelwhite School.

A. Heppelwhite and Co. seem to have been responsible for little original work of meritorious character, whilst they certainly identified themselves with some cumbrous and questionable designs for bedroom furniture which cannot fairly be fathered on George. The Heppelwhite school was a force to be reckoned with; it sprang up as a mushroom on the issue of the " Guide," which scored an immediate hit so far as the public were concerned. (An analysis of the " Guide " shows it to have been the work of several craftsmen and draughtsmen of varying calibres.)

We have spoken of the Heppelwhite school as covering the period 1780-1800, but it must not be supposed that Heppelwhite had no followers prior to the first of these two dates. On the other hand, Heppelwhite handling was on the wane by 1795. By 1775 Heppelwhite was influencing his chief contemporaries; thus Shearer learnt much from him, Sheraton plagiarised him, whilst even

Very early Heppelwhite Cabinet in mahogany and satinwood.
Author's Collection.

Heppelwhite.

Robert Adam, who had taught him so much, borrowed something of his finesse when himself essaying dainty models in the vogue of the Louis Seize. Similarly many small cabinet-makers and craftsmen whom he had employed came under Heppelwhite influence, and gave practical effect to his teachings. The large bulk of Heppelwhite's disciples, however, were attracted to his designs when I. and J. Taylor published the "Guide" for A. Heppelwhite and Co.; and so it is convenient and fairly correct to date the work of the school as from the publication of the designs, and we can safely ascribe a decade of healthy life to it. All over the country we come across these productions of the Heppelwhite school, and, taken as a whole, they attain to a wonderful degree of excellence.

The "Guide" Considered.

The first edition of A. Heppelwhite and Co.'s "Guide" was taken up in less than a year, and it was followed by a second in 1789, and by a third in 1794, these successive editions being mainly absorbed by the craft. In the provinces, at any rate, Heppelwhite doctrines remained popular for a long period, and we see their fruits up to the second quarter of the nineteenth century. The shaping of chair- and sofa-arms, and the leg-work and framing of Early Victorian stools, chairs, and sofas, show the decadent application of Heppelwhite's principles as brought about by the evolutionary process, and the author has seen comparatively plain models of the period 1820-1835 openly described and sold as "Heppelwhite."

A perusal of the last (and least artistic) edition of the "Guide" furnishes much useful information on account of the comprehensiveness of its character. Dealing with chairs, we read: "Mahogany chairs should have the seats covered in horsehair, plain, striped, chequered, &c., at pleasure, or cane bottoms with cushions, the cases of which should be covered with the same as the curtains."

Japanned chairs, the Heppelwhites stated, should have

Side view of a Pembroke Table by George Heppelwhite. The top is nicely inlaid, and each of the falling flaps, which are serpentine in shape, has the Greek anthemion inlaid upon it. Made of mahogany and "fine" woods; very rare. Circa 1765. Author's Collection.

cane bottoms, with linen or cotton cushions to match the hue of the model, whilst "saddle checks" or easy chairs might have leather or horsehair coverings. Red or blue morocco, we learn, was employed for the more elegant kinds of chairs, the seats being tied down with tassels of silk. Heppelwhite's stuffed-back chairs were styled

Heppelwhite.

"cabriole chairs," and he described his bergère models as "barjiers."

R. and J. Adam had used vase-shaped decoration for all manner of furniture since the end of the 'sixties, so that it is rather interesting to find the "Guide" in 1794 claiming that the Heppelwhites' chairs with vase-backs were new and had been much approved. This idea was not altogether appropriate for chair-back outline, and it is quite possible that A. Heppelwhite and Co. were the first to venture the suggestion.

The "Duchesse," as advocated in the "Guide," consisted of two arm-chairs which were turned inwards towards one another and connected by a stool decorated *en suite.* By this contrivance three separate pieces of furniture could be temporarily united to form a double sofa, whereon two people could recline their bodies at the different ends.

The confidante, or confidente, as it was frequently styled at an earlier date, was a long settee or sofa, the ends of which were partitioned off by arms to allow one person to sit at either extremity as though in an armchair. The Adelphi models were usually in one piece, but the Heppelwhites sometimes made it in three—two armchairs to flank either end of a sofa, but, of course, identical in decoration and height. Our designers were particularly successful with their dainty window-seats such as that shown on page 483, and they suggested that these should be upholstered in "taberray or morine, of a pea-green, or other light colour."

We glean from the "Guide" how it is that cellarets are so rare, for the Heppelwhites say that these *gardes de vin* " are of general use where sideboards are without drawers." The bulk of the boards made subsequent to

1775 were fitted with lead-lined partitions to hold wine bottles, and so the cellaret was no longer an absolute necessity.

Heppelwhite bookcases, secretaires, and cabinets often show pleasing lattice design, but the proportions of the bases are not infrequently heavy in style. Shearer and Sheraton both displayed a truer eye than the Heppelwhites when handling these larger pieces of furniture, and Clouston calls particular attention to Casement's good work in this direction.

Like most of our late eighteenth-century designers, the Heppelwhites made many small pieces with roll-over tambour fronts. The strips of which the tambour was composed were often mounted on canvas, but when found to-day the mechanism seldom runs smoothly and is often broken. Damaged tambour-fronted cupboards, desks, and so on are extremely difficult to repair, and the collector will be well advised to satisfy himself that defective examples *can* be adjusted at reasonable cost before he decides to acquire them.

In the creation of small tables, urn-stands, &c., the Heppelwhites generally excelled, for these admitted of a full display of their talent in shaping. They said that their models were usually " square, oval, or circular," but we now and then happen on serpentine contour, such as that seen in the flaps of the table on page 512, by far the best which these cabinet-makers employed.

The " Guide " shows a fine range of bedroom furniture, and it gives perhaps the best description extant of " Rudd's table," an article very popular during the last quarter of the century. " The middle drawer," we read, " slides by itself; the two end drawers are framed to the slide . . . and when disengaged each drawer swings

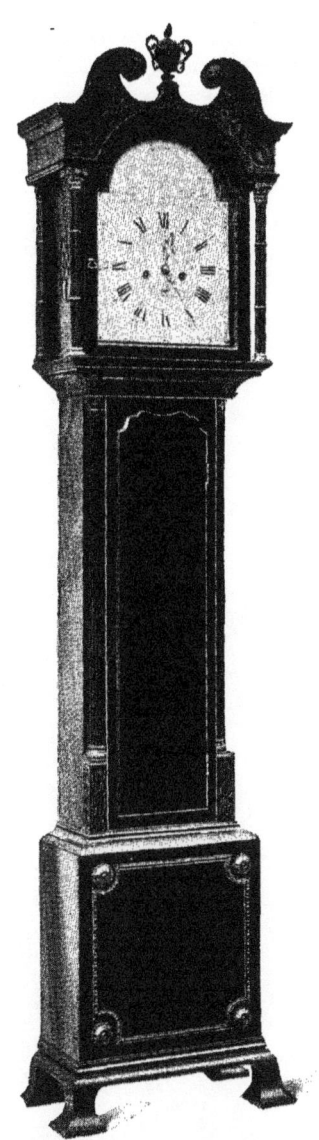

On the left we have a typical Heppelwhite Grandfather Clock, and on the right a Stuart Clock just one hundred years older. The proportions of this old Jacobean specimen are more graceful than are those of the Heppelwhite example, which dates from 1775. Both of these gems come from the collection of D. A. F. Wetherfield, Esq.

Heppelwhite. 517

horizontally on a centre pin." This table was fitted with mirrors which turned upwards but would fall down and slide under the two end drawers; on that account it was sometimes designated a " Reflecting Dressing-Table."

Heppelwhite Horse Fire-Screen, showing Adam influence in the cresting-rail; period 1780. The needlework is about 90 years earlier. Author's Collection.

Sheraton's influence is most noticeable in the 1794 edition of the " Guide," but the Heppelwhites were generally less happy when conforming to the rectilinear outline of the Louis Seize Anglaise at the expense of their own sinuous compositions.

Many Heppelwhite bedsteads showed beautifully-devised poles, the proportion and decoration of which were alike excellent. Wheat-ears and Prince of Wales's feathers were commonly introduced in the region of the main swell to the column. For hangings, Heppelwhite recommended white dimity, plain or corded Manchester stuffs, printed cottons and linens, dove-coloured satin, &c., over green silk linings. The valances to these beds were often tied up in festoons, and the cornices were made low enough to hide the curtain-rods.

Their fire-screens, whether of the pole, folding, or horse type, were good as a class, but Heppelwhite tripods fell short of the standard which Chippendale had set up. The pole varieties, whether resting on round bases or tripods, and their horse models were generally fitted with pulleys in their uprights, enabling the screen to be raised or lowered at discretion.

The " Guide " informed its readers that furniture for the dining-room " should be plain and neat," while that for the drawing-room, " being considered as a state room, should possess all the elegance embellishments can give."

CHAPTER XIX
"Gillows."

Characteristics of the Vogue.

To the large body of collectors and dealers alike the term "Gillows," in its relation to old furniture, stands for a vogue at once heavy and uninteresting, generally supposed to date from 1800 or so and onwards. To such an extent is this delusion prevalent that the majority of would-be purchasers of the antique would not step across the road to look at a specimen which had been described as an example of this firm's work. On the other hand, an individual who was furnishing his house without any regard to artistic effect, but with a strong predilection for solid, substantial, and well-made furniture, would expect to find a bargain to be picked up in the teeth of moderate competition only.

These views are unfair, since the Gillows played an important part amongst eighteenth-century cabinet-makers, displaying considerable acumen in drawing on all that was best, adapting with very considerable precision and taste, whilst embodying consummate craftsmanship in all matters pertaining to construction. Truth to tell, what the Gillows did not know of design between the years 1750-1800 was hardly worth knowing; but they stand in a different category from Chippendale, Adam, Heppelwhite, and Sheraton—to cite four masters whose names are household words. Such craftsmen, by reason of the fact that they published works advertising their wares, and offering suggestions and information to the profession, came to be popularly classed as designers rather than cabinet-makers. The Gillows kept their knowledge to themselves, and earned their living by (1) executing specific commissions entrusted to them by such designers as Robert Adam; (2) working for private clients desiring conscientious expositions of the prevailing vogue; or (3) by carefully watching the trend of Fashion, and placing on the market wares which were well calculated to fulfil the requirements of the moment. They did not bid for notoriety, and were probably better supported in the craft as a consequence, but their mode of procedure did not make for originality.

After the close of the century, when Chippendale, Heppelwhite, Robert Adam, James Adam, and Sheraton had in turn passed away, the house of Gillow came into greater prominence, and it is this phase of Gillow work which the artistic public knows—and avoids. It would be manifestly unfair to condemn Gillows for going with the tide when general taste throughout the country was decadent, and at the same time to withhold from them their meed of praise for yeoman services rendered to their craft when unobtrusive yet sterling merit and endeavour were an exception rather than a rule. It would have been next to impossible for Sheraton, for instance, to have produced anything meritorious without his having forthwith proclaimed it from the housetop, and rather might one have expected him to acknowledge his indebtedness to the various designers whose ideas he so freely appropriated than to rail at them.

To some readers, at any rate, this harking back to the middle of the eighteenth century in the analysis of Gillow work will mean the breaking of fresh soil, yet it is a necessary and an interesting study to all those who believe in according honour where honour is due. Nobody has fought the good fight in the interests of the Gillow business so well as R. S. Clouston, and no writer has collected and given to the public so much interesting matter bearing on the subject.

Opinions differ, vogues change, and verdicts have from time to time to be altered, or at any rate modified, yet no point which Clouston has adduced in regard to early Gillow work has been challenged or confuted. The writer, in common with many other collectors, has received the greatest assistance from a perusal of Clouston's *later* writings, and would commend them to all those who value a sound rather than a superficial knowledge of the subject.

Origin of the Firm.

The name of Gillow has been connected with cabinet-making for over two centuries, and is rightly associated with artistic production until the end of the eighteenth century, or the end of the period in which we are mainly interested. Fortunately, a record of much that the Gillows did is extant, their original cost-books, containing a mine of information and showing the evolution of design as witnessed by their productions, being still preserved.

Amongst other things which Clouston tells us, we find out that the founder of this firm, one Robert Gillow, who was a self-made man, migrated from Great Singleton to Lancaster just over two hundred years ago. Here, after laying the foundations of comparative wealth, he was still content to work on garden palings with his own hands, and, the joiner having become cabinet-maker, next appeared as a general trader and merchant.

Lancaster ranked second only to Bristol as a shipping centre, and Gillow was bent on doing a large export business. Clouston thus writes of him: " As he seems to have accepted payment in kind, he made a double profit by selling the imported goods himself, and one of his chief trading places being the West Indies, he became a licensed dealer in rum. He was a furniture-maker, an undertaker, a jobbing carpenter, and a spirit merchant, besides many other things too numerous to mention. In fact, he put his hand to anything and everything that came in his way, without stopping to consider whether it was either high-class or artistic." This stricture applies to the catholicity of his trades, for it could not be urged against Gillow that he was lacking in taste. He was a great commercial spirit, to whom money-making was the main object, and art had to take a secondary position.

Gillow was a trade rival to Chippendale just at the time when the latter had shaken off the trammels of the Queen Anne and was giving a forecast of the Louis Quinze. Shipping furniture to London, Gillow began seriously to cater for the London market, but he must have conformed more or less to Chippendale's lines, seeing that we can trace no distinctive school of work with which we can associate him. His venture having proved a financial success, Gillow, who had taken his son Richard into partnership, opened a London establishment near the Custom House, Thames Street, under the style of Gillow and Barton, his ledger calling this fresh departure " The Adventure to London."

Clouston further records the subsequent moves and changes in the style and denomination of the firm, some of which are of great interest. Nobody seems to know who Barton was or what part he played in the business;

few writers, if any, have even recorded his name. Probably he was a local manager or agent, with a salary and small share in the profits of the business. Robert Gillow's means were certainly adequate for his cabinet-making branch, and had Barton brought talent or clever designs to the advantage of the partnership, we should have found evidence of them in the perfect records of the firm.

Reconstitution of the Firm.

At about the turn of the century the Gillows moved into Oxford Street, and a new partner, Taylor by name, was admitted, Barton having disappeared. Taylor died shortly after this venture, and the next partnership embraced Robert, Richard, and Thomas Gillow, under the style of " Gillows." In 1790 the designation of the house became Robert Gillow and Co.; whilst on the death of Richard in 1811 the firm was reconstituted as G. and R. Gillow and Co. (Clouston).

It is worthy of note that until the period which this last partnership embraced, the Gillows were responsible for graceful and artistic rather than for cumbrous and dull design. All work seems to have been executed at Lancaster, so that the London premises must have been used to display and act as a distributing centre for Gillow wares. Probably, if the truth were known, clever draughtsmen found places on the London staff whose duty it was to forward suggestions and designs culled from the various workshops of the metropolis.

Clouston, speaking of Richard Gillow, tells us that he was made a full partner at twenty-three, and was a man of just as strong character as his father. Though Robert made a business out of nothing, and even in his old age retained the enthusiasm and business dash of youth, it was Richard who raised it to the front rank. The old joiner had probably felt the want of education, and, being a Roman Catholic, sent his son to the famous college at Douay. That Richard Gillow thus had the education of a gentleman may partly account for the fact that the firm had on its books not only the names of the greater part of the nobility, but of Royalty itself. Richard Gillow was somewhat of a "character," and cared nothing for prince or peer. Several stories are told of him illustrating the independence of his attitude when dealing with the most exalted personages. He was one day showing a table, priced at eighty guineas, to a nobleman. "It's a devil of a price," said his lordship. "It's a devil of a table," replied Richard; and the deal was concluded then and there.

Clouston assumes that Richard Gillow had considerable training as an architect, seeing that the firm after he was admitted did a large business in this direction, and the Lancaster Custom House, which he built, is held to be an excellent illustration of the Adam style. Richard was also the inventor of the telescopic dining-table, and it is stated that he was responsible for the first English billiard-table. The first of these two articles was patented in 1800, and the action has never been materially improved since its creation.

More about the Shield-back Chair.

It is usually considered that Heppelwhite originated the shield-back chair; but many authorities now hold that either Robert Adam or Gillow fathered the design. Clouston tells us that Gillows in their books show the idea in 1782; but if we are to define the parentage of the shield-back we must certainly go back some ten or twelve years prior to this date, and if there is no earlier suggestion in the records of the firm, and these records are as complete as they are credited with being, Gillows' case will not support their claims in this direction.

The author has seen a pair of low, stuffed-backed shield chairs characteristic of the period (1765-70), with arm-

Gillow Shield-back Chair, period 1770. From a set of six in the possession of Messrs. Gill and Reigate, Ltd.

shaping, legs, and carving identical with those obtaining on the earliest authenticated Heppelwhite models, and doubtless produced under the eye of Heppelwhite himself.

Although generally credited to them, the interlaced heart in modified shield-form was not chronicled by the

Heppelwhites in their "Guide"; whilst, on the other hand, it is recorded in the private annals of the Gillows in 1788. These facts would seem at first sight to be remarkable, seeing that the design in question was pleasing, and one which any designer would have liked to claim and hall-mark. Consequently, certain authorities argue that the model is of Gillow rather than of Heppelwhite origin. Too much reliance must not be placed on points such as these, for a reference to Chippendale's "Director" shows that this great designer ignored the claw-and-ball foot in his drawings, although we know that in the twenty years immediately preceding its publication Chippendale had been a brilliant and continuous exponent of this item of decoration.

We must not forget that George Heppelwhite had died some time before the production of the "Guide," and that the prevailing craze in all these books of design was for something "new." We know that the idea in question, one of the best to which the second half of the century gave rise, was freely produced in chisel-work— *i.e.*, at the earlier stages of post-Chippendale creations (ignoring the work of the third Chippendale), and in the light of these facts we are probably faced merely with a coincidence. The Heppelwhites very probably regarded the interlaced heart as a well-worn theme hardly likely to appeal to their patrons as a novelty.

Influence of other Craftsmen on Gillow Work.

There is more Adam influence noticeable in Gillow work than any other, a fact easily accounted for, since Robert Adam placed out much of his work with the Gillows, whilst his architectural style appealed so strongly to Richard Gillow as to have governed the latter's designs.

The Heppelwhites produced their own adaptations, and so we find less evidence of their bias on Gillow work; but still there is a meeting of the ways between the two schools, and the connoisseur is often placed in a quandary when faced with one of these "half-way" models. Sheraton, again, runs into the borderland abutting on Gillows' domains, and here it is well to record that the firm's books show models which they produced, resembling Queen Anne in the case of a card-table, Chippendale work in that of a corner chair, Adam design in that of a commode, Heppelwhite in the case of a chair, whilst Sheraton has actually appropriated *and published as his own* a side-table of Gillow parentage.

It is absolutely impossible to say with certainty who was the maker of many fine-quality models of the period 1765-1795, though Robert Adam's influence may generally be looked for as the dominant factor. It would be useless in the space at our disposal to draw hard-and-fast rules, for the very features to which we may call attention may by their very absence or presence in the next piece to turn up lead to an incorrect diagnosis

Where all the masters met on common ground mistakes as between Adam and Sheraton side-tables of the early 'nineties, or Shearer, Heppelwhite, and Sheraton design of the late 'eighties, *will* occur, and the following story forms an amusing illustration of the case in point: Two experts differed as to the classification of a certain carved, gilt, and painted piece, *circa* 1790, the one holding it to be Heppelwhite, the other Sheraton; they called in a third opinion to settle who was right, withholding their diagnoses from him. The umpire immediately pronounced the example as Adam.

CHAPTER XX.
Sheraton.

His Position as a Craftsman.

WHEN commencing his study of Sheraton, the collector is beset by innumerable difficulties—difficulties, too, which are accentuated rather than solved by the wealth of literature bearing more or less happily on the subject.

Although Sheraton was the most recent of our great cabinet-makers and designers, we know but little of him other than that which may be culled from the pages of his "Drawing-Book." When did he arrive in London from Stockton? What was his status when he came up from the provinces? Was he ever a *master* cabinet-maker? and, if so, did he combine this occupation with the calling of a designer? What proportion of the designs which he uttered were original or partly original, and what proportion of his so-called suggestion should rightly be credited to his contemporaries if the truth were only known? These and a host of other questions face us, and they can only be dealt with circumstantially.

Adam Black has given us a certain insight into Sheraton's *late* home life, but no historian has given us the record of his earlier days; no writer has filled for Sheraton the position which Evelyn filled for Grinling Gibbons as a chronicler of early struggles on the path to recognition. Writers on Sheraton have, therefore, to take Sheraton at his own valuation—as Sheraton would have had us do—or they have to be analytical and sceptical, a course which becomes more obviously a necessity with each hour of study devoted to his claims and pretensions. The former of these two alternatives lies more readily to hand, but it is not expedient; the latter opens up the way to exacting research, and leads in the end to very considerable disillusionment.

In the first place, Sheraton, for all his parade of religion, was not a man whom one could rely on. He was poor, as far as we judge, throughout his career, and he therefore had an incentive to a certain amount of sharp practice. He was bitter to vindictiveness in some cases, whilst generous acknowledgment of others was contrary to his practice almost without exception. He owned, as we shall presently see, that he was in debted to others for designs and ideas; but this was a specious admission, seeing that he told less than half the truth.

It is obvious that poor Sheraton was a clever draughtsman and his contribution to the study of perspective was invaluable, even if it proved to be dry and uninteresting reading. In the craft to-day his first treatise stands almost as a classic, and it evoked only restricted criticism when it appeared. Throughout his main work, "The Cabinet-Maker and Upholsterer's Drawing-Book," which ran into three editions, we find passages tucked away which throw light on debatable points, and in several instances these passages give an inkling of facts which their author had studiously avoided.

Sheraton is generally considered to have come to London as a journeyman worker, and in one line he tells us that his remarks were made not only from his own experience, "*but from that of other good workmen.*" He was obviously well grounded in the craft, and it is probable that even in London he started as a workman.

In the same edition Sheraton set forth: "To assist me in what I have shown, I had the opportunity of seeing the Prince of Wales's, the Duke of York's, and other noblemen's drawing-rooms. I have not, however, followed any one in particular, but have furnished my ideas from

A Sheraton satinwood and fine wood inlaid Corner Commode—circa 1785-90—with decoration of the Adam style. In the possession of Mr. Frank Partridge, who kindly lends photograph.

the whole." It will be noticed that this passage, whilst showing that the workman had risen to a position of privilege, discounts the originality of his compositions.

We are, perhaps, advancing rather by leaps and bounds when we weigh such points at the beginning of our theme; but if we are to study the man we must disabuse our minds of many of the ill-balanced and over-laudatory appreciations of Sheraton which have appeared. If we fail to take this precaution we shall assuredly approach our subject with a blind eye for Sheraton's weak spots; we shall overlook the enormous advantage he possessed in coming on the scene when a host of clever and versatile workmen, trained by his predecessors and contemporaries, were ready to hand; and we may lose sight of the fact that if we eliminate from his designs such of the Louis Seize, Adam, Shearer, and Heppelwhite teachings as he had appropriated, there is hardly an original idea with which we can credit him.

Sheraton the Man.

Thomas Sheraton was born at Stockton-on-Tees either in 1750 (Clouston) or 1751 (Benn). Lowly of birth, he appears to have benefited by no educational advantages. His parents were Church people, but he seems to have become Baptist preacher as a youth, and to have devoted much time to the preparation of tracts. He was responsible for, amongst other productions, " A Scriptural Illustration of the Doctrine of Regeneration," and later he issued from Stockton, in 1782, " A Letter on the Subject of Baptism," in 1794 " Spiritual Subjection to Civil Government " and " Thoughts on the Peaceable and Spiritual Nature of Christ's Kingdom."

The treatise on Baptism which Sheraton issued from Stockton in 1782 has led writers to urge that the author must necessarily have been resident in that town early in the 'eighties. It is, however, possible that he was working in London, but elected to publish this brochure from his old home, where his reputation as a religious man had been early established.

Even in his works on furniture Sheraton eagerly seized

upon opportunities of expressing his religious convictions, and in one instance, when dwelling on one of his own mythological compositions, he found himself constrained thus to explain his scheme: "The subject is a faint moonlight scene, representing Diana on a visit to Endymion; who, as the story goes, having offended Juno, was condemned by Jupiter to a thirty years' sleep. It may not be improper to advertise some, that these, with a thousand other of the same kind of stories, are merely the fabrications of ancient poets and idolaters, forming to themselves innumerable gods according to their vain imaginations, and which now, only serve to try the painter's skill. . . . *And in opposition to these vanities, I cannot well omit whispering into the ear of the reader, that 'To us there is but one God, the Father, of Whom are all things' (1 Cor. viii. 6).*"

As a young man Sheraton applied himself to the study of draughtsmanship, in which direction he attained great proficiency. He was at one time both sound and tasteful in his work, and possessed of a true sense of proportion. During this early stage he was responsible for many fine designs, moulded on the teachings of the Louis Seize; but, unfortunately, decadence in his work was noticeable before he was fifty years of age.

Adam Black, a friend and collaborator of Sheraton's, writes of him: " He (Sheraton) lived in an obscure street, his house half shop, half dwelling-house, and looked himself like a worn-out Methodist minister, with threadbare black coat. I took tea with them one afternoon. There were a cup and saucer for the host, and another for his wife, and a little porringer for their daughter. The wife's cup and saucer were given to me, and she had to put up with another little porringer. My host seemed a good

A Sheraton Writing-Cabinet in satinwood, inlaid with amboyna, showing Shearer influence as to its outline; period 1785-90.

man, *with some talent.* He *had been* a cabinet-maker, was now author and publisher, teacher of drawing, and, I believe, occasional preacher." After a stay of a week in the Sheraton household, Black goes on to tell us: "Not only were all the surroundings exceedingly humble, but also dirty and ill-kept."

Sheraton was unduly self-assertive; he took a warped and narrow view of life and of his profession, was slovenly in his home and person, and cherished a grievance throughout life against everything and everybody. Brilliant to a certain degree, he yet stood an Ishmael in his profession, though spite seems to have emanated from rather than to have been directed against him.

Black, his contemporary, writes of him when surrounded by evidences of poverty and dirt: "We may be ready to ask how comes it to pass that a man with such abilities and resources is in such a state. I believe his abilities and

A Sheraton satinwood and fine wood inlaid Corner Cabinet; circa 1785. Photograph lent by F. Partridge, Esq.

resources are his ruin, in this respect, for by attempting to do everything he does nothing."

It is more than probable that Sheraton lost touch alike with his patrons and the trade by reason of those faults upon which we have just dilated. If we could blind ourselves to the imperfections of the man and of the artist, it would save us much time; but, in justice to his compeers, Sheraton has to be weighed in the balance, and, except in the early phases of his career as a designer, often is to be found wanting. It is difficult to know how to appraise his early work. Excellent in outline and construction, it consists almost exclusively of efforts in the Louis Seize style which might have been designed by Shearer and decorated under the supervision of the Adam brothers, whilst on many occasions we meet with scarcely veiled plagiarism of Heppelwhite. Yet with an almost entire absence of originality, there is generally something distinctive about Sheraton's designs. They lack the architectural character of Adam executions; they fall short of the daintiness to which Heppelwhite at times gave such pleasing expression; not more chaste than Shearer's models, they are often an admixture of grace and austerity, marred, unfortunately, by too mechanical decoration.

The "Drawing-Book" Considered.

In 1791 Sheraton brought out the first edition of his book, "The Cabinet-Maker and Upholsterer's Drawing-Book," now usually styled the "Drawing-Book." This was printed by T. Bensley, of Bolt Court, Fleet Street, and appeared in quarto parts, an appendix and accompaniment being subsequently added to the work as originally conceived. The second edition came out in 1793-4 and a third and enlarged one in 1802. In the

Sheraton. 537

earlier printings, as it was announced that the book was to be had from the author at No. 41, Davies Street, Grosvenor Square, and subsequently from 106, Wardour Street, Soho, we may infer that these were the places

A typical Carved Mahogany Chair in the Sheraton mode, showing the master's eye for proportion. Period 1780; one of a set of six in the Author's Collection.

of Sheraton's abode. In the last edition the work was obtainable from W. Baynes, 54, Paternoster Row, and J. Archer, of Dublin, Sheraton's address being dropped. In this last edition, besides the frontispiece, there were incorporated 14 plates devoted to geometrical lines, 13 to perspective, 39 to furniture, 33 to furniture appendix, 8 from the second edition, and 14 extra as an accompaniment, making up a grand total of 122 plates.

Sheraton tells us of his ambition and aims in the Preface to his work: "I find some have expected such designs as never were seen, heard of, nor conceived in the imagination of man; whilst others have wanted them to suit a broker's shop, to save them the trouble of borrowing a basin-stand to show to a customer. Some have expected it to furnish a country wareroom, to avoid the expense of making up a good bureau, and double chest of drawers with canted corners, &c., and though it is difficult to conceive how these different qualities could be united in a book of so small a compass, yet, according to some reports, the broker himself may find his account in it, and the country master will not be altogether disappointed; whilst others say many of the designs are rather calculated to show what may be done, than to exhibit what is or has been done in the trade. According to this, the designs turn out to be on a more general plan than what I intended them, and answer, beyond my expectation, the above various descriptions of subscribers."

Here, if we may for a moment digress, the master was referring in a spirit of banter to the craze and demand for small articles of furniture of the genus *multum in parvo*. In those days many artists, men of letters, professional and commercial men, occupied bed-sitting rooms, and especially was this the case in fashionable districts where rents were high. Many were the young men about town who preferred this limited accommodation near to the particular club or coffee-house which they affected, to more commodious apartments further afield. To suit the requirements of this often artistic class of customer Shearer, Heppelwhite, and Sheraton devoted much time and thought, and, as a result, we have pretty little tables and cabinets which, on investigation, disclose within their frames washstand, looking-glasses, and dressing-table fittings. In the morning the ablutions were carried out, the wig was fitted on and powedered, and the lace arranged at these little pieces, and then they were shut up, and did duty as sitting-room furniture until the owner retired to rest or wished again to complete his toilet. Similarly the double chest or tallboy (Fr., *hautbois*) would have bureau fittings which pulled out at the top of its lower section—a great convenience where, as oftentimes, room was extremely restricted.

The Adams' doctrines attracted Sheraton to such an extent that he assisted in the evolution of Adelphi fashions during the better phases of his designs. The collaboration which took place between the Adam brothers and Sheraton doubtless accounted for models such as that shown on page 530, but it bore fruit in a far wider sphere of work than that in which these artists were conjointly engaged. When Sheraton, working independently of the Adam brothers, was preparing his own suggestions he subconsciously reflected the composition and detail of his erstwhile preceptors.

The Adams' style, which many writers have described as a gay one, in reality often lent itself to stilted or sombre results, and it was the potentialities of the grey rather than of the rosy side of Adelphi tradition which appealed to the puritanical zealot Sheraton. Shearer, our greatest exponent of the effects derivable from simplicity, evolved outlines so light and correct that they constituted a new departure in design. Refusing to bow down to the fetish of over-elaboration in matters of decoration, he created an alternative style, embodying features well calculated to attract Sheraton.

Sheraton fell captive to this contour handling of Shearer, and many of his plainer models followed so closely on the patterns of his mentor that it is scarcely

Pair of inlaid mahogany Knife Urns, the correct outline and restrained decoration of which suggest Shearer influence; period 1780-90. Author's Collection.
The accompanying tray is typical of Sheraton's early and less pretentious designs.
Although these models may be ascribed to Sheraton, they may well owe their existence to William Shearer.

possible to distinguish between the work of the two craftsmen. In addition to this, when Sheraton was producing more or less elaborate designs with their leavening of Adam or French influence, he frequently resorted to Shearer outlines as a framework. In these circumstances plain Sheraton furniture owes much to the genius of Shearer, whilst elaborate Sheraton may be a picture of Adam or Louis Seize style in a Shearer frame. Had Shearer succumbed to the attractions of ornate embellishment it is more than possible that he would have utilised the same garnishment as Sheraton affected, and in so doing have further complicated the diagnosis which we, as collectors, have to make.

When drawing on the Adams' or Louis Seize suggestions, Sheraton, like the austere Puritan that he was, donned smoked glasses, but he had the good sense to employ the best available settings for his somewhat chilly translations. As a result of this happy faculty one loses sight of his severity in admiring his apt co-ordination.

Possessed of discrimination and, during his early days, of a true sense of proportion, Sheraton was also a master of technique and the most skilled draughtsman of his time. These talents served the designer well so long as he was content to tread the well-beaten tracks which other craftsmen had traversed, but they failed to save Sheraton in later years when he was essaying new departures. His skill with the pencil led him to make a fetish of perspective, and in his "Drawing-Book" this is well exemplified.

When he was developing the suggestions of other artists he either ignored the authors to whom he was indebted or busied himself in casting obloquy on their achievements. When he ventured into pastures new he displayed ignorance and self-assertiveness to a pathetic extent. Possessed of but a smattering of knowledge, poor Sheraton became more arrogant, blatant, and dictatorial as he floundered deeper in the mire. The refining influence which he had wielded became sterilised by unbalanced and ambitious yearnings, and all traces of the *master* passed away. He wrote concerning one of his designs : " To shew in as pleasing a way as I could, the stability of this Performance, and the subject of the book in general, I have, by the figure on the right hand, represented Geometry standing on a rock, with a scroll of diagrams in his hand, conversing with Perspective, the next figure to him, who is attentive to the principles of Geometry as the ground of his art; which art is represented by the frame on which he rests his hand. On the left, seated near the window, is an Artist busy in designing; at whose right hand is the Genius of Drawing, presenting the Artist with various patterns. The back figure is Architecture, measuring the shaft of a Tuscan column; and on the back ground is the Temple of Fame, to which a knowledge of these arts directly leads."

It is difficult to picture the Sheraton of early days, with his mastery over tapered leg-work and serpentine swells, identifying himself with ludicrous and involved compositions such as this, and we can only imagine that his head had been turned as he gained ascendency in the craft.

There was a wide difference between Chippendale's "Director" and Sheraton's "Drawing-Book," yet Sheraton, to judge by his utterances, failed to grasp this. Chippendale wrote for finished cabinet-makers and the gentry who patronised them. Sheraton, absorbed in the study of perspective, produced a work more suitable for the education and advancement of apprentices. Chippendale started with the supposition that he had before him a skilled and trained workman, and forthwith tried to convert the craftsman into an artist. Sheraton, on the other hand, assumed that his readers were composed of

An exquisite little Bottle Cabinet in hairwood, the sides and interior of which are decorated with floral marquetry. Sheraton; circa 1780. Author's Collection.

Sheraton.

workmen who needed sound but elementary grounding in the rudiments of their calling

Sheraton sold a large number of his "Drawing-Books," but they seem nearly all to have been absorbed by the trade. Chippendale, on the other hand, found quite half of his readers outside the cabinet-maker's

Inlaid Side-table of Sheraton's period.

profession. He styled his book "The Gentleman and Cabinet-Maker's Director," and it proved to be what its author intended it to be—of assistance to the artistic *lay* mind.

Picking up the "Director," one is so impressed with the versatility of the author and interested in the freedom of his designs that, even if we have to condemn some of his wilder suggestions, we feel interested from cover to cover. It was this power of holding the sympathy of his patrons which secured such an influential subscription for the earlier master's work. How different is the case with the reader who has Sheraton's "Drawing-Book" placed in his hands! He will have to wade through voluminous dissertations on Perspective—spelt with a big P—through folio upon folio of reiterated constructional detail, and the probability is that he will have flung the volume aside with a sigh of boredom long before he has gathered the valuable information which it undoubtedly possesses for those patient enough to extract it.

Curvilinear Treatment.

Guided by the precepts of Shearer and of the Louis Seize school, Sheraton was a master of straight lines, and had a rooted objection to unsupported curves, such as those at times affected by his predecessor Chippendale. Yet the curvilinear was not absent from all the designs of his best period, as the illustrations on page 572 will prove. In later years, although he had spoken and written against the use of the misplaced curve, he was constantly employing it, just as poor General Colley at Majuba selected a position whose characteristics were those which in his Staff College lectures he had warned all officers to avoid.

In broad matters of commonsense and principle connected with cabinet-making our master was, as a rule, sound. Thus he wrote: "The general style of furnishing a dining-parlour should be in substantial and ordinary things, avoiding all trifling ornaments and unnecessary decorations," this, of course, in apposition to the garnishing of a boudoir or a drawing-room. When, however, he designed a chair-back he would occasionally insert detail

A, Sheraton Clock in mahogany, on stand, circa 1785, compared with an old Marquetry one (B), both coming from Mr. D. A. F. Wetherfield's beautiful collection. It will be noticed that the Sheraton outline is the less graceful of the two. Sheraton inlaid work on Grandfathers is more stereotyped than is that which we find on the earlier examples with floral, arabesque, or geometrical decoration—dating 1670-1720.

in an unwarrantable and interlaced profusion, though it is fair to add that this failing was chiefly noticeable during the later phases of his career.

Again, Sheraton would furnish a room (in design), and give a promise of meritorious harmony, yet mar the whole by a scheme of execrable window-drapery. Was it a false note in the designer's taste which failed to discriminate between good and bad, or did the overweening conceit of the man gloss over the shortcomings of what he may have regarded as "the latest mode" ordained by Sheraton—correctness guaranteed?

Position as a Tradesman.

There is a general and very widespread error amongst collectors and dealers as to Sheraton's position during the latter years of the eighteenth century. The usual idea is that Sheraton had a large factory or a workshop wherein he manufactured chairs, sofas, cabinets, &c., after his own designs or adaptations. There is no evidence in support of this, and the probability is that he was never a master cabinet-maker on an important scale.

We have no data as to his movements when first he came to London from Stockton-on-Tees, where he had been earning his living as a journeyman, but this can scarcely be wondered at seeing that the advent of one new hand from the provinces would scarcely have attracted notice amongst an artistic community as numerous as it was talented. Frugal, steady, and gifted, Sheraton was doubtless ambitious as a youth, and, like his predecessors the Gillows, Chippendale, and Heppelwhite, decided on "an adventure" to London. We know that in 1791 he published his first and best work, "The Cabinet-Maker and Upholsterer's Drawing-Book," now usually alluded to as the "Drawing-Book," and we may thus infer that he had already risen high in the craft.

It has been lately stated that our designer came to London about 1790, but this date is probably incorrect. Sheraton's claims to recognition as a genius are based on his successes of Louis Seize Anglaise type over the period leading up to 1800 or a year or two later. Assuming therefore for a moment that he came to London as late as 1790, his useful phase of work commenced with his fortieth year and terminated just after he was fifty. His "school," in the common acceptance of the term, only came into being when it was supplied with a text-book, *i.e.*, his "Drawing-Book" of 1791. To digest this work and to benefit by its principles would have entailed time, application, and experiment; thus if Sheraton had not a personal following independent of that attracted by his book, we can only allow the *school* ten years of useful work at most before its efforts became decadent.

To suggest that all models bearing strong resemblance to the popularly-conceived notions of Sheraton style must be of a date subsequent to 1790 would be to impose on the credulity of the reader. Sheraton owned in 1791 that he had borrowed and appropriated models and designs for his book, and the very patterns which he has so utilised had been tested and found successful in the 'eighties. The writer believes that Sheraton won the nucleus of his following in the 'eighties, that he watched the development and possibilities of other vogues over the same period before venturing into print.

Sheraton's book undoubtedly represented years and years of hard work in its compilation. It shows more than traces of a knowledge at first hand of the work of his

Typical Sheraton Sideboard of the period 1785. In the possession of Robert Dalby Reeve, Esq.

London rivals, and could not have been compiled at Stockton, where facilities for its preparation must have been limited to the study of such books as the London cabinet-makers had issued. It is improbable that Sheraton could have afforded to purchase some of these works; it is not likely that he could have obtained access to all of those outside the limit of his purse. Without these advantages it would have been next to impossible for Sheraton to have gleaned so much from Heppelwhite and Shearer, for instance, as he undoubtedly did. But if we are to accept 1790 as the date of Sheraton's advent in London, we have the picture of a poor journeyman cabinet-maker arriving in London to join the cabinet-making fraternity—a fraternity which we must remember consisted of a race of giants in the arts and crafts. We should then have to imagine Sheraton at once attaining such a position as would command respect amongst jealous and talented rivals. Further, the measure of superiority displayed would have had to be very marked to warrant the lately-arrived journeyman's posing as author and designer *with reasonable chances of success.*

Then comes the question of the "Drawing-Book." Was this compiled during 1790 and 1791? Was it so brilliant that publishers consented to launch it for a new man forthwith, and could it have been written, edited, and printed in the stated time? Assuredly not. It must be remembered that all this time Sheraton would have had to be earning his living day by day, and it must also be remembered that the book was large and expensive to produce, whilst its price was small; consequently it would have been imperative that a quick and ready sale for it should be assured. And to whom was it to be sold? The master cabinet-makers and designers of London and the provinces. Had these craftsmen the requisite confidence in, and respect for, a country journeyman arrived from Stockton the year before? Yet they supported Sheraton almost to a man at the time when they had before them the work of such recognised masters of the later vogues as Shearer, Heppelwhite, and the Adam brothers, not to mention many others. If we were to accept so late a date as 1790 for Sheraton's arrival in London, those writers who have taken up the cudgels on his behalf would have the ground cut from under their feet, for it would be obvious that the Stockton craftsman could have contributed nothing towards the *earlier* and better designs of the Adams, Heppelwhite, and Shearer. The utmost credit we could attach to Sheraton would arise from help accorded to the Adelphi *after 1790* and influence on the firm of A. Heppelwhite and Co., as witnessed in the last and decadent publication of that combine.

It has been held that the Adams, Heppelwhite, and Sheraton were all to a certain extent indebted to one another, and the writer would like to add to this body the names of the Gillows, and Seddon, Sons, and Shackleton. Of these five firms Sheraton was probably the last to contribute any material share—that which he brought being rather the fruits of the skilled craftsman and draughtsman than of the originator or scholar.

We must revert to precedents. Chippendale came to London from Worcester and published his "Director," not to signalise his advent, but after many years of effort, and when his reputation was established; Robert Adam came to town from Kirkcaldy, and, settling down after years of Continental travel, published his works some fifteen years subsequently; Heppelwhite came to the

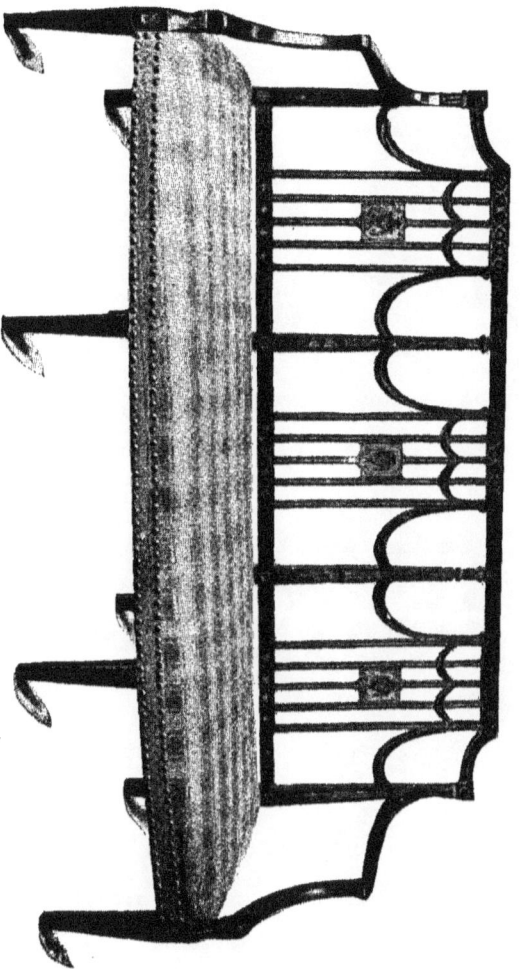

Painted Sheraton Settee with typical back and arm shaping. Circa 1790

metropolis from Durham, but the "Guide" which his widow brought out only gave a *posthumous* and imperfect exposition of his style.

Earlier designers had not rushed into print until they had earned their laurels and become recognised authorities in their calling. They had possessed capital, and could have borne the losses which unsuccessful publications would have entailed. Sheraton was poor, and if he arrived in London so late as 1790 could have had no clientèle by 1790-1, when he was filling his subscription list. On the other hand, one can conjure up a picture of young Sheraton, with his talent, thriftiness, and ambition, early realising that continued residence in Stockton promised only the limited scope of a provincial horizon, with restricted opportunities to even its most successful citizens, and meagre facilities for advancement in the paths of art. Then, after due consideration, the removal to London, in which centre we can picture him conscientiously working as a journeyman for this master or for that, whilst he broadened his knowledge of technique. In the 'eighties he would have come into touch with Louis Seize, Adam, Heppelwhite, and Shearer designs, and his "Drawing-Book" of 1791 shows that these were the styles upon which he modelled his most successful productions.

Presently, as might have been expected, we find that the journeyman has been taken at his true worth, and been made the "head" of a shop, where, too, the master, recognising his genius, has welcomed the assistance of a pencil probably more skilled than his own; and then one step further, and we have our designer in embryo executing work for this master or that, and very possibly receiving specific commissions from patrons inside or outside "the profession." We follow him supervising the cabinet-maker or craftsman who prepared the carcase of the model, at times assisting in its construction, and then giving hints to the artist or inlayer as to the scheme of painted or inlaid decoration supplying the complement to his work.

Grounded in his profession, conversant with all those steps through which the craftsman rises, we find him in an assured position, confident in his own powers, recognised as a success amongst his compeers, and then—the wish of his life—the opening up of a possibility of leadership in his craft, the inception of his book, its completion, and the substantial support of a profession that freely subscribed for it prior to its issue because of the reputation that Sheraton was winning.

Of profit there can have been little, to either author or publisher, and we know that the former was disappointed and financially on the down-grade shortly after the issue of the work. This disappointment, and the consequent bitterness which it engendered, owed their existence to natural causes. If there was no designer of the last decade in the eighteenth century who could be classed as a dangerous rival to Sheraton, there were many skilled craftsmen capable of interpreting clever designs. Similarly, there must have been a large section of the community who remained wedded, or at any rate fairly loyal, to the Adam, Shearer, Heppelwhite, or Gillow tradition.

With a public only partially won over to his way of thinking, there would still have been a fortune ready to fall into Sheraton's lap had he been able to control the output of the new order or style of furniture; but his book had placed a weapon in the hands of his friends

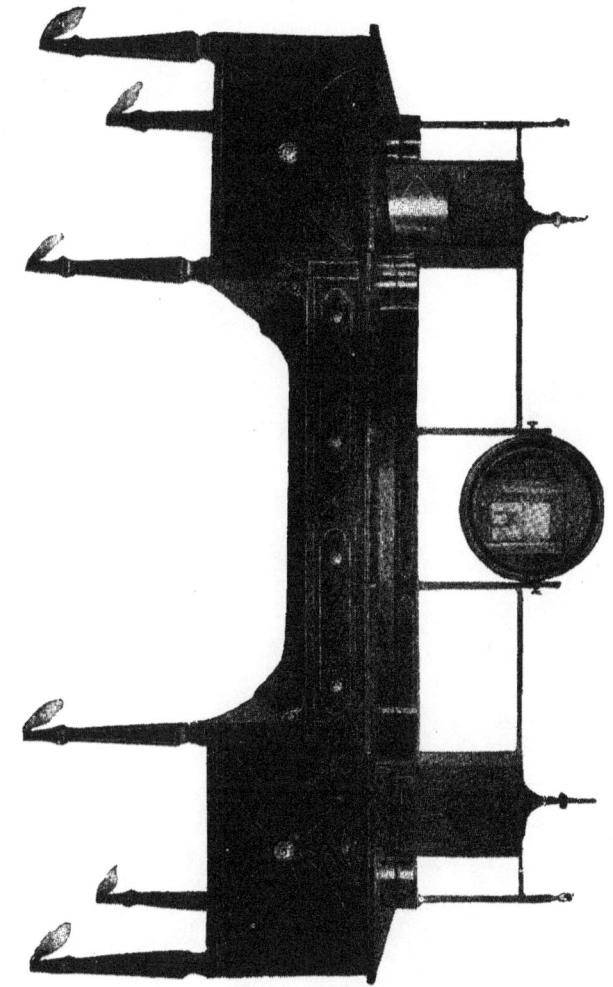

Sheraton Sideboard of about 1795. Though styled Sheraton, this in reality may have been the work of a member of either the Sheraton, Shearer, or another kindred School.

Sheraton. 561

and rivals, and many unimportant workmen successfully picked his brains at an initial cost of something like 20s. laid out in the purchase of the book. Sheraton was, in fact, from a business point of view, somewhat of a Frankenstein, for he had cleverly raised up a force whose power of bringing grist to the mill he was unable to control. Many were the country craftsmen who made more profit in their districts out of Sheraton's brain

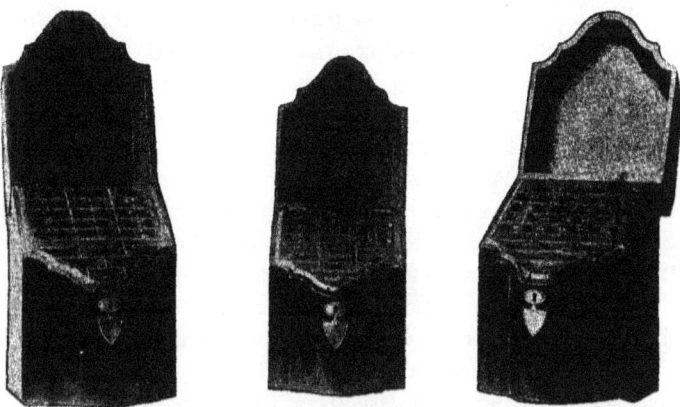

A Set of Three very fine Knife-boxes, beautifully inlaid; circa 1780.
Author's Collection.

and pencil than did Sheraton himself out of the whole nation; and here we notice the gulf which separated Sheraton from Chippendale.

Chippendale weaned the country from Queen Anne decoration; he initiated such brilliant and meteoric work that few could translate and scarce anyone emulate it when unassisted by his guiding eye and hand. Nor was this all. He charged three times the price for his book that Sheraton obtained, and sold the bulk of each of his editions to private individuals, who would not plagiarise his efforts; whilst he came on the scene to find no school of craftsmen trained to cope with mahogany relief-carving satisfactorily, and so fitted to poach materially on his preserves. Sheraton found the schools of many a powerful rival trained and quite capable of duplicating his creations (which lent themselves readily to reproduction), and it was to this class—now known as the Sheraton school—that his book was sold.

We know that Sheraton made a study of the works of his predecessors, taking whatever seemed to him to be good, acknowledging nothing so appropriated, but, on the contrary, trying to throw dust in the eyes of his patrons by disparaging the sources of his various adaptations. Was this a spontaneous manœuvre, or was it part of a carefully-prepared plan of campaign? Surely the latter. Intended to enhance his own reputation, this merely reflected the meanness of his character; but it is certainly a point in favour of that careful deliberation which is the keynote of the " Drawing-Book," a deliberation which would scarcely be apparent had the book been written and issued in the spare moments of 1790-91 at Sheraton's disposal.

Early Examples.

The writer has concerned himself very closely with the study of early " Sheraton " furniture in the generally accepted use of that term, and he has traced many examples back to the 'eighties, but one example is of peculiar interest, namely, a clock. The works are those of the period 1780, the decoration the recognised Sheraton type, and the maker's name Crow, of

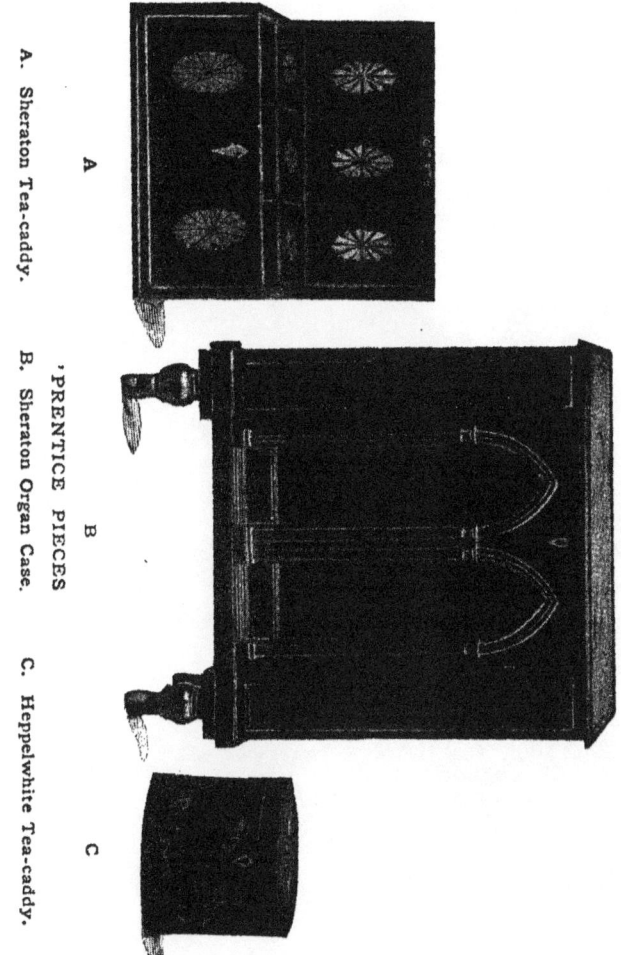

'PRENTICE PIECES

A. Sheraton Tea-caddy.   B. Sheraton Organ Case.   C. Heppelwhite Tea-caddy.

Feversham. Faversham was spelt Feversham by Lambarde in his 1596 "History of Kent," and by Harris, the historian, in 1718. In 1727 Lewis, in his history of the town, gave it the name of Favresham, whilst in Seymour's "Kent" of 1776 the author tells us that the name is commonly written Faversham, and he is confirmed in this by Hasted and Ireland, two succeeding historians who confine themselves to the style of Faver·sham. It is therefore reasonable to place this clock as being of the period 1775-1780 (when the old style of "Feversham" still survived fitfully), and incidentally the writer has seen an inlaid Sheraton barometer of the period 1785 by Crow of *Faversham*.

Having regard to the popularly-conceived notions as to the characteristics of his outline and decoration, not one collector in five hundred would fail to ascribe this clock-case to Sheraton, and if this idea were correct and Sheraton only came to London in 1790, Crow of Feversham must have commissioned a clock-case from Stockton! Imagine the cost under the head of carriage! The writer has adduced these points for a two-fold purpose, for he fails to accept the late date of Sheraton's arrival in Town, and he cannot in any way agree that that master was directly or indirectly responsible for the line, banded, or fancy inlaid decoration generally associated with that designer's name.

By setting back the date of Sheraton's arrival in London to 1780 we allow him a decade in which he could have established himself before wooing the public with his "Drawing-Book," and in that decade he doubtless became a recognised force in the craft, able to stand independently of those who had hitherto acted as steps in his upward progress.

We know that the period 1770-1780 led to the very general substitution of fancy woods for the hard dark plain mahogany which had obtained under Chippendale and of painted, japanned, gilt, or inlaid decoration in place of chisel work. All the great masters, with their disciples and the rank and file of the craft, conformed to the new taste, and Sheraton has fewer claims to the origination of the inlay in question than such masters or designers as the Chippendales, Adams, Gillows, Heppelwhites, Shearer, Seddon, Sons, and Shackleton, and a host of others. Sheraton merely fell in with the fashion of the day, and one has to be conversant with his cold and correct style of outline and decoration before one can speak with any degree of certainty when asked to diagnose late eighteenth-century furniture.

It is easy to describe chairs and cabinet-work as "Sheraton" if we merely indicate by this use of the word that the models under discussion are of the Sheraton period, but it must be clearly understood that Sheraton had nothing whatever to do with the vast majority of examples coming within the loosely-used term of "Sheraton," and which are merely so called because they bear more or less resemblance to the types which that master is popularly supposed to have affected.

Painted Furniture.

Painted decoration was an inferior substitute for carving, and many craftsmen who could not carve a shell with dignity or freedom were able to compass mechanical and lifeless brushwork. With the exception of a few examples, such as the Seddon cabinet painted by William Hamilton and owned by Mr. R. W. Partridge, the paintings on cabinet-work were mediocre,

Sheraton.

and their artistic claims would scarcely have been deemed worthy of consideration had they been executed on paper or canvas.

Festoons of roses, tulips, convolvuli, &c., were applied to chair- and settee-backs, table-tops, commode-

Sheraton Chair in painted satinwood, being one of a set owned by R. W. Partridge, Esq. Circa 1795. Note the drapery at the top of the back—this is beautifully painted in the originals.

tops and fronts, often in conjunction with medallions. Strings of painted flowers were applied to the outer faces of square tapered legs in pendent fashion or encircled rounded leg-work spiral-wise. Bands of floral matter followed the course of borders, and garlands enclosed the central schemes with a flowery setting or framework. The ribbon which Chippendale had introduced in carved mahogany on chair- and settee-backs now came to be painted in fancy shades such as turquoise-blue, and art *per se*, as represented by this particular vogue, savoured too often of the Christmas card.

For some reason difficult to explain and impossible to justify, Sheraton's reputation as a designer rests largely on the painted furniture for which he drew the carcase-outline. The last quarter of the eighteenth century found practically every cabinet-maker, large or small, building commodes, cabinets, side-tables, settees, chairs, &c., which were destined to receive painted embellishment at the hands of Italian artists, their pupils, disciples, or private purchasers more or less skilful with the brush. If these models come on the market and are not typical of Adam or Heppelwhite outline they are very generally attributed to Sheraton, although it is safe to say that that designer had nothing to do with the majority of such pieces. The value which lies in painted satinwood depends on the volume and quality of the brushwork rather than on any achievement of the cabinet-maker, and the prevailing custom of attaching the whole honour and glory of painted satinwood to any craftsman, at the expense of the artist who produced the main decorative scheme, is to be deprecated.

Seeing that the addition of a limited volume of painted garnishment added so greatly to the appearance of a model, and to-day gives it a high market value, it is not surprising that the faker is busy in our midst. Plain pieces of satinwood are painted up and sparsely decorated examples have their schemes amplified, so that the would-be purchaser needs to have expert knowledge. One watering place on the South Coast has earned an unenviable reputation for these treatments of so-called Sheraton furniture, and practice has made the culprits so perfect that many London dealers have been taken in.

At one time these "treated" examples were sold

Sheraton Chair in painted satinwood, being one of a set owned by R. W. Partridge, Esq. Circa 1795-1800.

openly in the district of their origin, but they are now sometimes placed in obscure and distant centres to await discovery by some enterprising collector or "runner." *Punch's* advice to those about to marry—" Don't "— applies with greater force to the inexperienced collector who would purchase painted satinwood. In no field are the chances less in favour of the amateur, and in no other class of furniture are so many pitfalls for the unwary presented.

Belts of classic matter and isolated detail, such as pateræ, vases, or urns, were freely introduced, but sadly caricatured the lights and shades, the verve, and dignity which had characterised the preceding chiselwork.

Inlaid Decoration.

The inlaid decoration of the day was often mechanical. The craftsman who could not carve brilliantly could yet insert shells or pateræ at so much a dozen. Work came to be done at so much per foot. Ovals were charged for on the hard-and-fast basis of their diameters, and work became stilted and lacked freedom in consequence. A given model had a standard carcase price, and upon this the intending purchaser could expend as much extra money as he liked, bearing in mind that so many yards of tulipwood banding would cost so much, and so many ovals of amboyna would involve such and such an additional outlay. Under this unfortunate system, Brown, Jones, and Robinson could each acquire identical models, save that Jones would go one better than Brown in the selection of more complicated inlays, to be in turn eclipsed by Robinson.

The taste for bright decoration which had called into existence so many pieces of painted, gilded, japanned, or inlaid furniture was largely assisted by the advent on the market of fine and fancy woods. Satinwood, hairwood, amboyna, &c., possessed handsome figure, but they were expensive, and cabinet-makers, as a rule, had their planks cut into veneers with the object of making timber go as far as possible. In these circumstances we seldom find these media carved, because there was no substance for the craftsman to work upon. Chair-backs, settee-backs, arms, and leg-work generally were carried out in solid satinwood, but in cabinet-work veneering was resorted to whenever possible.

All' the great masters, from Chippendale to Sheraton, favoured veneered work, using, as a rule, a lighter and more showily-grained mahogany than the " old Spanish " for this purpose. Fortunately, too, the best designers all gave us carved mahogany models with no fancy accessories, and so it is possible to form a collection of representative pieces *in mahogany*. The tyro is apt to be attracted by the brilliancy and variety of which the fancy woods permit, but, with experience, one learns to appreciate the unobtrusive dignity of the plainer medium and to look for the effects of light and shade which it presents when sharply carved.

There is a strange lack of consistency in the criticism of some writers on English eighteenth-century furniture. Thus one condemns Chippendale's ribbon-back chairs as belonging to the " pretty-pretty " school. He complains, moreover, that the ribbon does not decorate construction; it is construction itself. With the former contention we will now deal. The latter is mere hairsplitting, seeing that the ribbon chairs are strong constructionally, comfortable in use, and, withal, pleasing to gaze upon.

It is questionable whether ribbons, drapery, festoons of flowers, and similar detail are happily situated on the back of a chair, as part of the scheme of decoration, if we go into a theoretical examination of the subject. A peach beautifully painted at the bottom of a soup-plate may seem out of place when covered with pea-soup, whilst flowers would ill stand the pressure caused by a person leaning up against the chair-back. We have to consider rather the soundness of work, comfort afforded, and artistic results achieved under a treatment where *all* the masters took some little licence—if one cares to press the point.

The relief-carving of Chippendale, Adam, Heppelwhite, and Sheraton on the backs of chairs was sufficiently deep to give good effect and borrow from light and

Table and Tripod showing Sheraton style of the curvilinear.
Circa 1790.

Sheraton.

shade, but it in no way interfered with the comfort of the sitter's back. Now, Sheraton elected to paint the ribbon in bright colours in the form of knots and bunches, adding flesh-coloured cupids, festoons of flowers, and medallions of the Wedgwood order on the bright surface which satinwood afforded, yet it has been stated by a recent authority that Sheraton never wearied in well-doing. Shall we acquiesce in this the while we condemn Chippendale for a ribbon carved in a self-coloured and deep-toned mahogany? The reader will surely form a fairly shrewd idea as to which of these two methods erred on the "pretty-pretty" side.

Many writers have indicated that Sheraton was a cabinet-maker in a large way of business, but this can scarcely have been the case. The "Drawing-Book" expressly tells us that Sheraton passed from one "shop" to another, absorbing the details of their special models and contrivances with a view to their explanation and exploitation in his book of designs. In this compilation of widely-culled ideas Sheraton differed from preceding designers, who had one and all endeavoured more or less honestly to present their own suggestions. Our designer did not dissemble in this matter, for he frankly acknowledged the extraneous assistance of *cabinet-makers*, and we can only assume that he was not in direct competition with his collaborators. Had Sheraton been a trade rival he would scarcely have had the *entrée* of all these workshops, and he certainly would have been debarred from studying their several specialities. Sheraton gave a list of 252 master cabinet-makers, chair-makers, and upholsterers then practising in London with whom he was conversant, so that he had a wide field to draw upon. If he had been producing furniture he would scarcely have busied himself in puffing other people's wares; neither would it have paid him to publish secrets which he had gleaned as the result of the special facilities which were vouchsafed to him.

If one may hazard a suggestion, Sheraton probably undertook to give prominence to the wares of certain firms in return for assistance rendered him, but the bait was not uniformly successful, for he wrote: " I have made it my business to apply to the best workmen in different shops, to obtain their assistance in the explanation of such pieces as they have been most acquainted with," adding, " and, *in general*, my request has been complied with." That there were numerous abstentions is obvious, for the author, piqued that facilities were denied him, went on to say that the " Drawing-Book " " will not meet with the approbation of those who wish to hoard up their own knowledge to themselves lest any should share in the advantage arising from it." Sheraton then devotes half a page of abuse to these recusants, and winds up by asserting that he will leave them " to themselves as unworthy of notice, who only live to love themselves, but not to assist others."

Doubtless the bulk of so-called Sheraton designs were appropriated direct from the obliging craftsmen who assisted in the compilation, but as all shops followed the same outlines in construction more or less closely, the collated plates were not incongruous. It is probable that those cabinet-makers who held aloof from Sheraton's overtures were the most independent and well-established, yet their productions, in default of proper pedigrees, go to swell the volume of work incorrectly associated with the author of the " Drawing-Book."

One often hears that the stability of early English

Sheraton Side-table, based on a Gillows design, circa 1800; with set of Sheraton Knife-boxes, period 1790.

cabinet-work was due to the employment of fine, seasoned timbers, as much as to sterling workmanship, and this contention is always on the tongue of apologists of latter-day craftsmanship. That this was not the invariable case is obvious when one has studied the "Drawing-Book," where Sheraton points out that panels "*should stand to shrink as much as possible*" when they had been tongued and fitted; and later, again, that tops "should stand for some time at a moderate distance from a fire. If these methods are not pursued the panels will shrink and their joints will draw down," &c., &c. It would, therefore, appear that cabinet-makers were not more favoured then than now, but that in pursuance of their conscientious and thorough methods the old-time craftsmen were at pains to counteract the immaturity of their media.

We find Sheraton (and so-called Sheraton) furniture decorated with the same patterns in the different processes of carving, inlaying, and painting. Friction and wear-and-tear have improved the appearance of the carved models, but they have often annihilated the skin-deep beauties of painted specimens. The inlay in use at the close of the eighteenth century was much shallower than that in favour one hundred years earlier, and it often requires to be relaid, having buckled or blistered with exposure to changes of temperature. The units in a scheme, such as oval paterae or shells, were held together by a backing of paper in order that the component pieces or segments might retain their proper positions. Fakers have even gone so far as to employ old news-sheets of the late eighteenth century as a foundation whereon to build up their spurious marquetry.

False drawers, doors, and so on, were commonly

emplaced on late eighteenth-century furniture, the process being known as "shamming." For this work cabinet-makers were allowed from 2d. to 4d. for doors ranging from 8in. to 4ft. on straight-front models, from $2\frac{1}{4}$d. to 5d. on round models, and from $2\frac{1}{2}$d. to $5\frac{3}{4}$d. on serpentine models, with an approximate increase of 120 per cent. if the drawers were marked out by a cock-beading.

To "sham" was legitimate, of course, for the treatment was necessary to preserve the balance of decoration; but the early craftsmen were not always above suspicion, for the author has seen one account wherein an extra allowance was made to a workman for veneering a softwood with satinwood "so as to make it appear of solid satinwood."

During the latter half of the eighteenth century leaf-work became extremely popular, leaves being arranged in small sheaves, noticeably as crowns to leg-work or chair-splats (or chair-*splads*, as Sheraton had it). Chippendale had been content with variations on the classic acanthus *as a rule*, varying this at times with an acorn and oak-leaf, &c. The Adam brothers, Heppelwhite, the Gillows, Sheraton, and other masters affected laurel, bay, endive, thistle, oak, parsley, rose, or fancy leaves in addition to classic foliations of the acanthus or laurelled banded type. Where these leaves were carved the effect was pleasing, although in theory they were commonly misplaced, if we are disposed to be hypercritical.

As a Chair-Designer.

Sheraton successively executed the most correct, the most mediocre, and the worst of all old English chair-designs—the best when he was varying and modifying the types for which the Adam brothers, Gillows, Heppelwhite, and the Louis Seize School were responsible, and the worst when he was endeavouring to anglicise the pernicious Empire vogue. Early Sheraton patterns were often so true and pleasing that no fault could be found with them; decoration was chastened and leg-work savoured of Shearer at his best. When critically examined, the better-class chairs by this designer show a wonderful grasp of proportion set out by the cleverest of pencils, and one wonders how their creator can have lost power so suddenly as he did.

Following on this useful and meritorious phase of work came one at the close of the century wherein Sheraton, forsaking well-proved patterns, was seeking to originate new ones. Reminiscent at times of the happier designs he was discarding, this second stage also foreshadowed the dark days that were to come. Mastery over line became less apparent, decoration became inconsequent, and Sheraton's chair-work, as in the case of his general designs for cabinet-work, lacked cohesion and failed to convince. One can almost picture the master searching for novelty but loth to draw up an anchor on which he had relied lest he should drift on shoals hitherto avoided. There is always an element of sadness in the passing of genius, and soon the qualms of those who had wondered at Sheraton's decadence must have turned to dread certainty, for the new century found him lost to all sense of outline, grace, and general seemliness.

It is interesting to note that Sheraton scored his main successes in connection with Louis Seize types and perpetrated his most aggressive blunders when plagiarising the succeeding Empire vogue. Although the credit of the so-called Louis Seize Anglaise is usually laid at Sheraton's door, he only put on the final touches to work inaugurated by the Adams, Shearer, Gillows, and others. Similarly Sheraton is unduly blamed for Empire travesties such as Ackermann and Hope produced, and with which he should not be charged.

Sheraton always favoured a lower chair-back than Chippendale's standard patterns possessed, but he followed an inverse rule when his designs come to be compared with those of Heppelwhite. Heppelwhite commenced with very low-backed models, increasing their height gradually until he evolved the models which the "Guide" exhibited. Sheraton at his best gave us chairs very similar in pitch to Heppelwhite's later productions, but as his work deteriorated, the tendency was for his models to grow lower and lower. The general elevation of Sheraton's chair-designs was rectangular in form, a little relief being afforded at times by the introduction of curvilinear treatment of the top- or cresting-rail. It is worthy of note that sideboard-fronts designed or adapted by Sheraton display—of course on a larger scale—just such breaks, sweeps, swells, and curves as we find applied to the tops of this master's chair-backs. In the case of eighteen chairs designed by Sheraton, showing variations of this shaping, seventeen present contours practically identical with those on sideboards which the writer has at one time or other possessed.

In his last phases Sheraton became more partial to the curvilinear, but his translations of it were often abominations pure and simple. One outstanding feature of the Sheraton chair is the bottom rail of the back, which, running horizontally between the back uprights, supports the central splat and side rails built up on it at right angles. The rail in question serves a useful purpose constructionally, knitting the framework together and keeping the back rigid. Incidentally, when Sheraton chairs are re-upholstered, this rail should be left clear, as the proportions of the chair demand that it should show plainly above the level of the seat. One often comes across chairs which have been heavily stuffed *up to the top* of this bar, the upholsterer seeming to have considered that it was intended as a sort of level for him to work up to. A glance at the illustration on page 537 will show this typical bar, with daylight showing between it and the seat, *as it invariably should do.*

The Sheraton chair-leg was far lighter than the Chippendale leg, and it was almost invariably tapered. It may be found square or round, occasionally hexagonal to octagonal. Many of the early varieties show tasteful turning, some of them a combination of turning and carving, whilst reeding was also commonly resorted to at a late date. The hexagonal-octagonal class are to be met with inlaid with fine woods down each face; the square varieties are often found fluted, moulded, or carved with pendent strings of husk-nuts or bell-flowers, whilst the finer examples may show an inlaid pendant of husks or bell-flowers, sometimes suspended from a looped knot of ribbon. In the plainer varieties of the square-face tapered leg a holly stringing, usually mis-described as satinwood, was inserted just within the two edges and running down the course of the leg-face. All types of legs were treated to painted decoration, but the round varieties lent themselves best to the spiral wreaths of flowers so frequently used for columnar work in Sheraton's day.

As in the case of fine cabriole or claw-and-ball Chippendale chairs, Sheraton seldom favoured stretcher-work on his best models, though many of these have had under-framing added when the pieces became rickety. In shape there were three varieties of square leg-work which were commonly employed — one of the type seen on page 537, known as the Marlboro', another known as the "thimble-toe" or "spade," as seen on page 551, and a third in which a band of ebony or other dark wood encircled the ankle of the tapered extremity.

Between 1795 and 1800 complications of the square-legged order similar to that seen on page 559 gained popularity, but from 1795 onwards turned leg-work began to oust square tapered varieties. The turned legs on pages 569 and 575 show an early and pleasing type of swell resembling that to be seen on the back uprights of the chair on page 567. This particular type of turnery is reminiscent of Heppelwhite lines, and the Gillows also affected it. A reference to the chair on page 569 will show this work in conjunction with a pronouncedly late back of the period 1800-1805, whilst on page 567 the positions are reversed, for there we find the earlier style of turned work in the back overlying an altogether later order of leg-work. In this last-mentioned illustration the front feet are of the incipient pegtop kind which became popular during the early nineteenth century and may be classed as being a decadent variety of the older spade or thimble type.

Early Sheraton chairs usually contained three or five perpendicular splats within the back-uprights, and of these the central or main splat was larger and more freely decorated. The outer splats were generally plain in comparison with the inner and detached, but when we meet with five-splat backs the three inner ones are commonly woven together by one central theme of drapery, festoons,

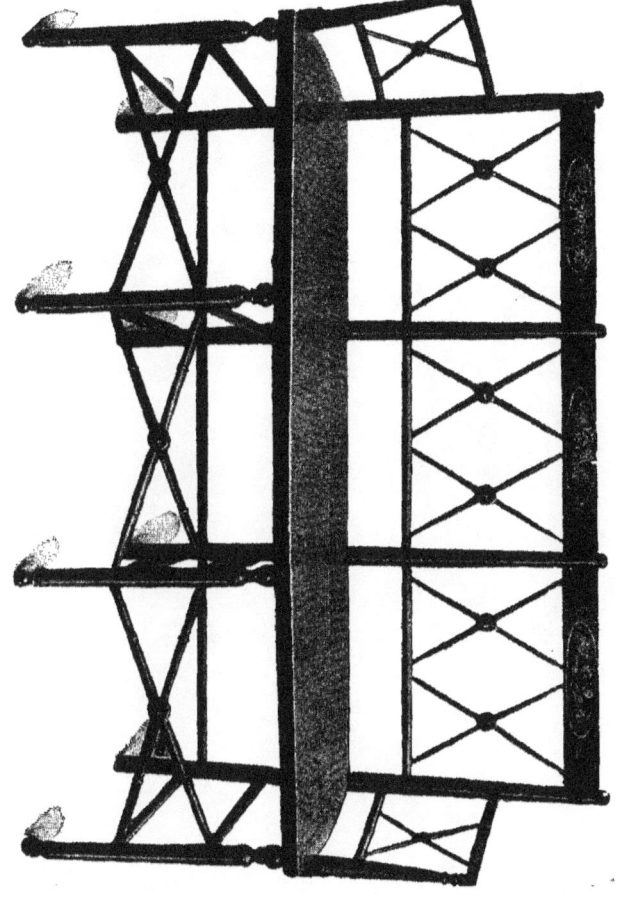

Painted Sheraton Settee, with the deep cresting-rail characteristic of the 1805 period.

or dainty detail in the earlier varieties and by a lattice pattern in the later ones.

The bases of the Sheraton splats frequently widened out, and the tops commonly showed a swell just below their junction with the cresting-rail, as seen in the chair illustrated on page 537. The wider surface so obtained was nearly always decorated, however plain the rest of the splat might be. Occasionally the designer broke the centres of his splat-work by oval swells similar to those seen on the Gillow chair on page 525.

Chippendale arm-supports used to rise, as a rule, from the side of the seat-frame, except in the case of large easy-chairs. The finest Heppelwhite arms swept back from the front legs, which they capped, the curve commencing at the plane of the seat (*vide* central chair on page 493), but Sheraton generally affected perpendicular arm-supports, rising at the front corners of the chair-seat and generally repeating the outline and decoration of the underlying leg-work (*vide* pages 569 and 583). In many of the early chairs which Sheraton designed the arm-uprights were a continuation of the underlying legs to all intents and purposes.

Taking a leaf out of the Adelphi's book, Sheraton favoured festoons of flowers or drapery, pateræ, medallions, leaf-work, lyres, rainçeaux of acanthus, just as he adopted and adapted the vase or urn of Adam and Gillow, or the Prince of Wales's feathers of Heppelwhite, though Sheraton's use of the feathers lacked the political significance usually attaching to their introduction on Heppelwhite models.

At times we find Sheraton inserting an inlaid shell on the top-rail or back-splat of his chairs, where the other decoration was furnished by clever relief-carving—

a jarring note where otherwise harmony would have existed.

Sheraton's shield-back chairs were not, as a rule, successful; they are commonly classed as Heppelwhite when met with, or, if the diagnosis is carried one step further, they may be put down as Sheraton *after Heppelwhite*.

Some Features of the Sheraton School.

One feature of the late eighteenth-century cabinet-making which was prevalent in the Sheraton school was the straight-winged model with a concave or a convex centre linking its extremities. Chippendale, the Adams, Heppelwhite, and Shearer rightly eschewed this somewhat abrupt union of the rectangular and curvilinear, holding it to be inferior to the serpentine swell for instance. Sheraton, too, affected satinwood, or "sattinwood" as it was then spoken of, more freely than did any of his contemporaries.

Satinwood coming from the East Indies showed a better figure and was richer and harder than any of its rivals, though it came in smaller planks. This variety was used for the finest work, and was very highly prized. West Indian satinwood, coarser and larger, did not possess such decorative properties of surface or grain, consequently it was employed for veneering the sides of large models or was sawn up into narrow strips or bands where fine figure was not an essential. The tree from which satinwood proper comes is very delicate and shy-growing, consequently supplies of this timber are somewhat limited.

Towards the end of the 'nineties Sheraton, with recurring frequency, began to complicate his chair- and settee-splats by the addition of diagonal strips of wood, and on many occasions he promulgated this idea to the exclusion of all other motives. X-shaped or diamond-shaped panes of lattice-work were so arrived at, but the consummated pattern which obtained from 1800 onwards took the form of a bold X contained within a square back, the cresting-rail to which was unduly heavy. Our illustrations on pages 569 and 583 show these diamond- and X-shaped backs in their best aspect, the settee on page 583 being especially interesting as displaying the extension of the X-shaping to the enclosed wings and to the stretcher-work.

The Sheraton two-, three-, or four-chair-backed settee was often a pleasing model, but, unlike the earlier types evolved by Chippendale and others, it was seldom carried out in carved mahogany. The finer models were executed in solid satinwood and the more ordinary specimens in japanned beech or other inferior woods. Upon the satinwood, as on the japanning, artists painted floral festoons or other typical detail, but this decoration has for the most part fared badly at the hands of Time. Painted and japanned settees were fitted, as a general rule, with cane seats, and, upon these, squabs, or long flat cushions, were placed for comfort's sake.

That Sheraton himself looked with scant favour on the process of japanning is evident from his observations in the "Drawing-Book." Writing of some fine models he tells us: "Sometimes they are finished in white and gold, and sometimes all gold, to suit the other furniture. *In inferior drawing-rooms they are japanned* answerable to the furniture."

Sheraton sofas **or** couches were not so satisfactory because the upholstery they carried too often dominated the woodwork. The contour of these models was often admirable, but the narrow belt of wood which framed the back-work, even in the better-class specimens, did not admit of a sufficient body of decoration being applied, and one finds oneself wishing that the upholder had been less to the fore and the cabinet-maker more strongly in evidence.

In his large pieces of cabinet-work Sheraton's designs do not show to advantage, for they very frequently lacked character, and, although imposing in proportion, they can scarcely be styled dignified. No master was more at home when making suggestions for models such as that illustrated on page 533, but when Sheraton essayed a large bookcase on architectural lines he was, as a rule, unconvincing. Some of his break-fronted models, with broken or swan-necked pediments overlying cornices relieved by pendent peardrops and dentil-work, possessed features of merit, but they were seldom masterpieces. A past-master in the use of the serpentine swell, Sheraton almost attained greatness in some of his more important designs wherein he introduced this outline feature, but his happiest expositions of it are seen in the commodes, sideboards, and side-tables which he gave us.

The bulk of Sheraton's commodes followed somewhat closely on the earlier designs of the brothers Adam, and were intended for use in boudoir, salon, or drawing-room, where they rested under pier-glasses, &c.; but he also evolved dressing-commodes with a glass under the lid, powder-boxes, and a writing-tray or slab which pulled out. A reference to the little cabinet on page 530 will give the reader a good idea as to the decoration with which these important commodes were treated.

Although Sheraton devoted much attention to four-poster and State bedsteads, giving his customers a great

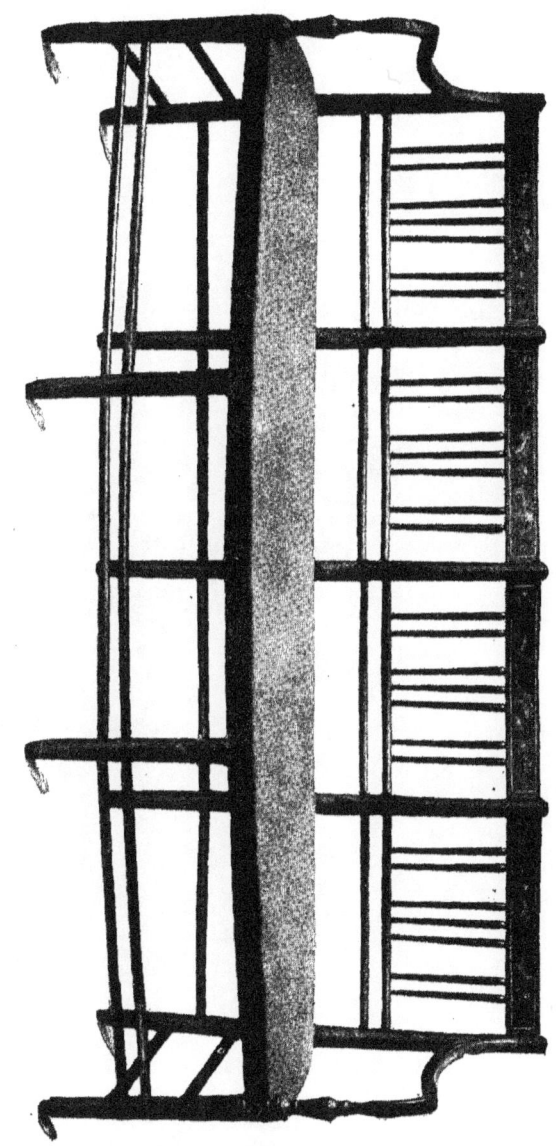

A painted Four-chair-back Settee by a country cabinet-maker, showing strong Sheraton straight-line influence, relieved by a soupçon of the curvilinear at the bend of the arm, the supports of which are typical; period 1805.

variety of models to choose from, his efforts in this field were seldom successful. It was not that his pillars or poles were unsatisfactory, for these were often refined and pleasing, but his cornices and schemes of drapery were too often laboured or ridiculous. Drapery was ever a rock in Sheraton's pathway, a fact of which our designer remained to the end sublimely unconscious; whilst when figures emblematic of Justice, Clemency, and Mercy, supplemented by others "expressive of the different branches of the British Government," were introduced on a State bedstead, the effect must have made for nightmare rather than repose.

In addition to the ordinary types of four-poster and State beds, Sheraton designed sofa, alcove, summer, and Duchesse bedsteads, the two former of which were merely glorified sofas or couches. Fitted with a dome, whence hangings issued, these models could be shut in by drapery, and they must have proved both unwholesome and uncomfortable. The summer bed consisted of two small or single beds under one broad canopy. The Duchesse bed was practically a chaise-longue, with a dome whence the draped curtains were suspended, for it was nothing more than two bergère chairs turned towards one another and linked by a connecting stool, with the addition of four movable posts which could be screwed on to the corner legs to carry the tester. The Duchesse was, therefore, a convertible model used as a bedstead on an emergency.

When writing of pier-tables, Sheraton said that "stretching-rails have of late been introduced," obviously overlooking Batty Langley's designs of 1739 and the similar efforts of such masters as Chippendale and Ince and Mayhew. This misstatement has led at least one writer to credit Sheraton with the introduction of a peculiar type which the Gillows had already exploited. In the humbler field of work Sheraton achieved well-deserved successes with his plainer tables, but when, in pursuit of ornate effects, he broke up the simple lines he drew so well, he was apt largely to stultify the artistic value of his work, and so we have it that many elaborately turned, gilt, carved, and painted legs possess inferior decorative properties when compared with the finely-proportioned and delicately-tapered extremities which he affected in common with Shearer.

Sheraton has, rightly or wrongly, reaped much kudos from his frieze compositions, but it is more than doubtful whether he should be credited with any great achievements in this direction. He built up cold schemes based on those of the Adam school where he did not resort to abject plagiarism. In a design which he uttered as his own on 18th Oct., 1791, he practically reproduced an earlier one drawn by Robert Adam in 1773 for the Earl of Derby, and page upon page of the " Drawing-Book " bears witness to this unfortunate propensity on the part of its author.

Of the many novelties with the introduction of which Sheraton's name has at one time or another been associated, few, if any, owe their origin to his inventive genius. There are many models belonging to the Sheraton period of which the ordinary collector has but little experience on account of their rarity, and some at least call for a passing notice. The harlequin table in no way resembled the butterfly of the pantomime, but owed its description to the fact that, like the stage fittings in the harlequinade, it embodied numerous mechanical devices. By the agency of these jack-in-the-box mechanisms and springs, nests of drawers, &c., rose and disappeared at the owner's will. It is interesting to note that Sheraton expressly disclaimed any credit in connection with the introduction of this model, the ideas for which he gleaned from a friend.

The Universal table was a rectangular model whose area could be increased from a breakfast- to a dinner-table size by the insertion of an extra leaf, and whose carcase contained a drawer divided into compartments for tea, sugar, or stationery, with a slider to write upon when this was pulled out.

Screen-tables were adapted for ladies' use, the protection rising from the back of the writing-table to shield the fair one from the glare of the fire (*vide* page 253). The combined library steps and table was taken by Sheraton from one Campbell, upholsterer to the Prince of Wales. In this instance a square table with roomy carcase enclosed two short flights of steps and a handrail, which, almost automatically, rose when the table-top was lifted. By the aid of this device people could mount and inspect the upper shelves of their library bookcases. Campbell in turn had appropriated the idea from old combined stools and shelves in fashion under Chippendale, but his development was an improvement because it enabled the user to ascend to a greater height and with greater security.

Sheraton's conversation chairs were the antithesis of the Tudor cacqueteuse varieties, being built low in the back and with a broad, flat padded cresting-rail, so that the sitter, who sat the reverse way to the ordinary, could rest his arms thereon. The seats were ballooned, with the narrow portion behind, so that the seat could be the more readily straddled.

The Sheraton "horse" dressing-glass resembled in outline the horse-screen shown in our Heppelwhite chapter, only that it was taller, and in place of the needlework panel between the uprights there was at the top a mirror, and underneath this an enclosed dressing-case box, which lifted up at right angles to the uprights whilst the user was shaving or engaged on his or her toilette. Similar devices were in favour for writing- and work-tables on the horse principle.

These " horse " models must not be confounded with the horse-chairs or chamber-horses of the period, pieces of furniture in the shape of arm-chairs or stools fitted with deep leather-covered seats, wherein were contained a series of boards connected with tiers of springs. These " horses " were for exercise, the sitter bumping up and down to stimulate a liver quite possibly disordered by overnight libations.

In closing this list of rather unusual examples, mention should be made of one rather curious device which Sheraton described as follows : " Within this ottoman are two grand tripod stands, with heating urns at the top, that the seat may be kept in a proper temperature in cold weather. On the front of the ottoman are two censers containing perfumes, by which an agreeable smell may be diffused to every part of the room, preventing that of a contrary nature which is the consequence of lighting a number of candles."

In addition to the processes of decoration common to the late eighteenth-century cabinet-makers, Sheraton models may frequently be found with engravings applied to them, these being framed with painted or inlaid embellishment. These pictures were heavily coated with translucent varnish as a protective treatment, but they are generally very much stained or rubbed when we happen on them. It is best when one comes across damaged specimens of this class to take the advice of a picture-restorer before interfering with them, as the ordinary cabinet-maker finds the task of repairing quite beyond his powers, but naturally wants a job, and will run the risk joyfully.

In addition to the legitimate use of brass in the form of back-rails to sideboards, candelabra, finials, &c., Sheraton grew more and more attached to brass inlay and galleries. As his work followed the Empire feeling and became decadent, he relied more and more on this metal to the displacement of wood, with deplorable results.

There is one passage in Sheraton's book which seems to have escaped notice hitherto, and yet it is pregnant with interest. When writing of the centaurs, sphinxes, griffons, &c., which played so large a part in the decorative compositions of the day, Sheraton tells us : " It will be proper that the learner should study to compose these if he intends being a proficient in ornaments . . . *and particularly to see the painted walls in noblemen's houses*, in many of which the art is exhibited to its utmost perfection."

The houses which carried this special style of decoration were those erected and garnished by the Adam brothers, their collaborators or disciples, and though Sheraton pointedly withheld from the Adams their meed of praise, he inadvertently placed on record the sources upon which he had drawn—in other words, he let the cat out of the bag.

It is interesting to picture Sheraton's attitude with regard to rival designers. Chippendale and Haig he could almost disregard, because, with the second Thomas Chippendale dead and the new management posing as cabinet-makers to other people's designs, no serious rivalry was to be feared. Of the " Director " designs he wrote : " They are now wholly antiquated and laid aside, though possessed of great merit, according to the times." He was bitterly and pointedly hostile to the Heppelwhites, because they were actual contemporaries and competitors, who so far from putting anything in his way would perhaps have taken food out of his mouth. Of the Adams he said nothing, possibly because he received commissions from them, and so had to keep his mouth closed; or it may be that he realised that their knowledge, power, and assured position were so immeasurably superior to his own that any snarls on his part would have been ill-advised. Policy seems to have prevented positive injustice, and the pettiness of his spirit led him merely to withhold the tribute which should have been gracefully paid to his benefactors.

Reverting for a moment to Sheraton's study of the decorations in the houses of the nobility, and of its bearing on the date of his arrival in Town, the collector who has studied Sheraton and Adam designs side by side will have found numerous plagiarisms by the former spread over a wide area. The glaring case to which attention was drawn earlier in the chapter, in which Sheraton published a practical fascimile of an early Adam design as his own, was no isolated example. Sheraton had studied Adam creations thoroughly, as he intimated indirectly. When were these studies made? To what sort of a man were the facilities necessary for these studies vouchsafed?

If for a moment we assume that his advent in London took place so late as 1790, Sheraton must at once have been welcomed to the homes of the aristocracy and State apartments must have been set aside for his study and convenience. Admitting for a moment this most unlikely supposition, months and months of patience and research on the young designer's part alone could account for his conversancy with Adam suggestions and technique, and as the influence of the Adelphi is apparent in Sheraton's *early* designs, we can only assume that the "Drawing-Book" followed after Sheraton had imbibed the Adam tradition. In these circumstances Sheraton would have had *less than a year* wherein to gain his reputation, captivate the craft in London, prepare a voluminous book, secure a large trade *forward subscription*, and see the "Drawing-Book" published and launched, in addition to earning his daily bread. Any reasonable person perusing the "Drawing-Book" will realise that it would have entailed years of solid and uninterrupted labour in the evenings and spare time likely to have been at Sheraton's disposal.

If, on the other hand, Sheraton began as a craftsman in 1780, his calling would have taken him into those mansions to which he was contributing his quota, and this advantage, together with such facilities as art-loving patrons extended to a talented and rising man, would have smoothed away difficulties, fostered his powers, and enabled him to press forward steadily to the goal he aimed at and ultimately reached. There are few traces of hurry in the arrangement of the "Drawing-Book," which speaks rather of deliberate work.

As this book seeks to call attention to the beauties of old English furniture, it is best to draw a veil over the latter phases of Sheraton's career. At the close of the eighteenth century the master began to favour the style now known as English Empire, which rapidly developed into a travesty of art. In this field Sheraton had as rivals

Ackermann, Thomas Hope, and others. Furniture was still finely constructed, ingenious contrivances and fittings continued to be introduced, but the simple beauties of outline were forgotten and decoration ran to seed. From this phase the descent to the Trafalgar and Waterloo types was but a step in the downward course of English craftsmanship.

Sheraton furniture of early date was usually veneered as to its carcase-work, and the legs, when in satin- or hair-wood, were similarly dealt with as a general rule. Mahogany legs far oftener than not were cut out of the solid plank, as the timber was cheap and the alternative process would have involved greater expense than the saving of material would have warranted.

Although some early models were fitted with rounded leg-work, the vast majority stand on square tapered legs, and to such an extent is this marked that round extremities carry with them presumptive evidence of the comparatively late origin of the pieces they support. Such rounded members as we find of the period leading up to 1790 are usually pleasing, whilst we seldom find intrinsically bad designs of the decade 1790-1800. After 1800 until the close of the so-called Sheraton period rounded leg-work was generally decadent and frequently obnoxious.

To those who are not conversant with the evolution of Sheraton types it is well to recall that the growth of turnery, the free use of brass, the deepening of cresting-rails, and the decrease in the height of backwork all make for lateness in the model under examination, whilst reeding, especially in leg-work over the pegtop foot, indicates the latest work produced under the direction of Sheraton.

Sheraton was wont to favour the *lavish* use of satinwood more than any other great master, with the possible exception of the Seddons, and it suited admirably the chaste and delicate models characteristic of his earlier work. Later, when Sheraton's art was on the wane, this beautiful wood served to mitigate to a certain extent the unfortunate points which began to assert themselves with increasing force. Kingwood and tulipwood, the favourite media for banding, were put on in cross-grained manner, *i.e.*, at right angles to the model's edge. Hairwood models were occasionally made, and the writer owns a cabinet, the bulk of the veneer on which is in amboyna, but as a golden rule the low-priced pieces were veneered in mahogany, with fine-wood bandings, and the high-priced ones in satinwood. From 1795 onwards rosewood largely took the place of mahogany, with which it is not uncommonly confounded.

Sheraton's decline was not without its element of pathos, for although the man was unlovable to a degree, the craftsman in him was at one time inimitable. Had this designer died at the age of forty or forty-five he might have been considered our greatest master, and we should have forgotten to cavil at his various plagiarisms of the Adams, Shearer, the Gillows, Heppelwhites, or of the school of Louis Seize. As it is, we have to weigh his inferior work and to appraise the value of his suggestions in other directions and of later date.

The story of his imperfect education was told in many an ill-balanced theme or design of the post-1795 period, and ambition, instead of ensuring continued progress towards the goal he originally aimed at with such promise of success, seems to have expended its stimulus in diverting the energies of a tasteful designer and draughtsman into experimental fields of Divinity, Science, and Letters.

His career opened with promise of the best; it closed with failure, bitterness, and disappointment, which came as an aftermath of his pettiness and overweening self-confidence. In her " English Furniture Designers of the Eighteenth Century" Miss Constance Simon tells us that " on 22nd October, 1806, he died of overwork "; but to this cause, if the truth were known, we should probably have to add those of privation and a broken spirit.

CHAPTER XXI.
The Seddons.

Status in the Art-crafts.

MOST writers on old English furniture have entirely overlooked the achievements of those sterling cabinet-makers and designers, the Seddons. This is all the more noticeable when we come to consider the fact that these craftsmen were contemporaries, in succession, of the great Chippendale, of R. and J. Adam, the Gillows, Heppelwhites, Shearer and Sheraton, not to mention the many other designers who, for convenience' sake, are usually set down as disciples of one or other of these masters in the art-craft of designing or cabinet-making. The Seddons largely followed the general trend of public taste, and therefore, with the Gillows, mainly helped to swell the volume of furniture erroneously ascribed to the better-known craftsmen of the day, to whose products their own work for the time being most closely approximated.

Family History.

The family possessed two businesses, for they were cabinet-makers and designers and also silk-mercers and threadmen. George Seddon was one of the principal cabinet-makers to subscribe in 1754 to the first edition of Chippendale's " Director," and the business was still vested in him in 1770, according to Kent's " London Directory " of that date, when his address was given as at 151, Aldersgate Street. Baldwin's "Guide" of the same year speaks of him as occupying premises at 158, Aldersgate Street, but Kent continues to describe him as of 151 in the directories of 1771—1780. In 1754 Robert Seddon was the proprietor of the silkmen's branch, which he carried on from Paternoster Row, the threadmen's business being run by William Seddon at Bishopsgate Street Without.

Shortly after 1780 George Seddon took his sons into partnership, the firm being known as G. Seddon and Sons, but in 1789 one Thomas Shackleton, an upholsterer of 115, Long Acre, was assisting the partnership in his branch of the craft. According to Loundes' "Directory" for 1789, George Seddon and Sons were then carrying on their business at 150, Aldersgate Street, and if we are to believe the same authority, Shackleton had not been admitted into the firm in 1790.

In 1791 Kent's "Directory," and also that by Loundes, show that Shackleton had cast in his lot with the Seddons, for these two publications record the new style of the firm as Seddon, Sons, and *Shacleton* (*sic*), Cabinet-makers and *Upholsterers*, of 150, Aldersgate Street.

It will have been noticed that there is a discrepancy between Kent and Baldwin as to Seddon's address in 1770, but this is easily accounted for. In his inimitable "History of English Furniture," Mr. McQuoid has stated "it is probable that Seddon was making a great deal of fashionable furniture as early as 1770," and he proceeds to quote the "Annual Register" for 1768 as follows :—" A dreadful fire burnt down London House, formerly the residence of the Bishops of London, in Aldersgate Street, now occupied by Mr. Seddon, one of

Painted Panels by William Hamilton, R.A., on a Satinwood Cabinet, by Seddon, Sons, and Shackleton, finished in 1793. The property of R. W. Partridge, Esq., and exhibited at the Franco-British Exhibition.

the most eminent cabinet-makers in London. The damage is computed at £20,000." After this disaster the business was doubtless moved to temporary premises, and one directory would seem to have adhered to the old style of address, whilst the other located the place provisionally utilised by Seddon. George Seddon probably retired from active participation in the firm about 1790, his place being taken by his sons Thomas and George. Seddon furniture can therefore be definitely traced back to the middle of the eighteenth century, whilst Seddon, Sons, and Shackleton's productions may be dated as from 1791.

G. Seddon had two grandsons who attained celebrity in later years, the one as a pre-Raphaelite painter, the other as an architect. The founder of the firm may be put down as one of the cabinet-makers whom the Adam brothers doubtless favoured with commissions, and in the ordinary loose interpretation of the day he probably created many thousand pounds' worth of "Chippendale," "Heppelwhite," "Adam," and "Sheraton" furniture. In addition to possessing a fine private connection, the Seddons were patronised by Royalty, much of the fine furniture in Windsor Castle having come from their shop.

A Notable Cabinet.

Mr. R. W. Partridge owns a cabinet by the Seddons which is at once the finest example of their work extant and the most important piece of English eighteenth-century cabinet-work known to this generation. It was built to the order of the King of Spain (Charles IV.), and was completed on 28th June, 1793. Designed by Seddon, the cabinet-making was entrusted to R. Newham, the foreman cabinet-maker to the firm. The panels were subsequently painted by William Hamilton, R.A., and are to-day held to be some of the best examples of that great artist's handiwork. Hamilton was born in 1751, and studied in Italy under our old friend Antonio Zucchi, the future husband of Angelica Kauffmann and the brilliant collaborator of the Adams. Bryan spoke most highly of Hamilton, recording that "his politeness covered no insincerity, nor his emulation envy." His coloured drawing, as the same authority tells us, "may be placed among the most tasteful and effective efforts of the art."

The subjects which Hamilton depicted on this fine cabinet represented the insignia of the Spanish Orders of Knighthood, the Golden Fleece, and the Immaculate Conception, together with Spring, Summer, Autumn, and Winter, Fire and Water, Night and Morning, Juno in a car drawn by peacocks, Ceres in a car drawn by lions, with cupids and other detail. The paintings, exquisitely refined, are still fresh and brilliant.

The extreme height of the piece is 9ft., greatest length 6ft., and depth 3ft. The inlaid work on it is superlative, whilst the ormolu mounts which it carries are unequalled in other English work. Inside, the carcase is fitted as a dressing-table, bureau, and jewel-case in cunning fashion. In outline, a majestic dome rises from the centre, flanked by two square wings. Imperial eagles guard the top, whilst for feet the piece rests on six lions couchant. Classic, draped figures, cherubs, and fauns' heads, in the finest carving, further set off this remarkable example, which, too magnificent for the ordinary mansion, might well be purchased for the nation and rest in South Kensington.

The Seddons.

It is evident that the Seddons were the cabinet-makers and designers, and Shacleton or Shackleton only the upholsterer who supplied the finishing touches to his partners' masterpieces. There is no inferior work which can be associated with these craftsmen, whilst on the other hand the Royal patronage which they enjoyed at home and abroad points to their having been very leaders in the craft. The firm did not subscribe to Sheraton's " Drawing Book," neither did it contribute ideas to Sheraton when he was compiling the work in question, and it would thus appear that the Seddons' was one of those establishments which, secure in its strength, pointedly held aloof when approached, and so attracted Sheraton's censure and abuse.

Constitution of the Firm.

Seddon, Sons, and Shackleton continued to push their business as cabinet-makers and upholsterers throughout the 'nineties, although they were once described as *Seddons*, Sons, and Shackleton, and undue prominence was given from time to time to the upholstery branch of the concern. In 1802 or early in 1803 Shackleton seems to have retired from the firm, which then, according to the Post Office New Annual Directory, became known as T. and G. Seddons, upholsterers and cabinet-makers, of 150, Aldersgate Street. At the commencement of the nineteenth century a branch establishment, or offshoot from the parent stock, was founded at 24, Dover-street, under the style of Seddon and Co., upholsterers and cabinet-makers.

In the new rendering or description of the partnership at Aldersgate Street we first ascertain the name of old George Seddon's second son, for we find Thomas and

George Seddon freely mentioned thenceforward. If the "George" had related to the originator of the business, the firm would have been " George and Thomas Seddon," so that we may assume that the two sons—who, according to Loundes, were the junior partners in 1789—were Thomas and George Seddon, jun.

In 1810 the "Post Office Annual Directory" reverted to the old style of George Seddon, upholsterer, &c., 150, Aldersgate Street; but it also showed that a man named Blease had been taken into partnership at the Dover Street business, which then came to be known as " Seddon and Blease, upholsterers and cabinet-makers, 24, Dover Street."

Kent's and the Post Office Directories of 1811-1816 continued the original title of " George Seddon, of 150, Aldersgate Street "; but in 1817 this appears to have been changed to Thomas Seddon, for the latter of these publications gives the firm from 1817-1819 as " Thomas Seddon, upholsterer, of 150, Aldersgate Street." From 1820 the business was conducted from the same address under the style of " Thos. and Geo. Seddon, upholsterers, &c."; but in 1826 these two sons of the original owner of the concern added new premises at 16, Lower Grosvenor Street, and described themselves as " cabinet manufacturers " at both addresses.

Thomas Seddon, junior, the pre-Raphaelite painter to whom we have already referred, was born in 1821, and studied in Paris in 1841. Bryan tells us that " in 1852 he exhibited his first work, ' Penelope,' " and " in 1853 and 1854 he travelled with Mr. Holman Hunt in the East, and, setting out again two years later, he was taken ill at Cairo, where he died in 1856." The history of the Seddons is therefore traceable from 1754 to 1856.

CHAPTER XXII.
The "Lesser" English Cabinet-makers.

Their Position in the Craft.

THE cabinet-makers and joiners of the eighteenth century may almost be likened to sheep or their shepherds, for there were those who quietly followed the lead of others or drifted with the general trend of somewhat fickle fashions, whilst others were engaged in attracting the sheep within the folds which they prepared for the reception of their less enterprising brethren. It would not be correct to lay this down as a hard-and-fast rule, for to do so would be to ignore the power of such firms as the Seddons or Gillows, who, owing to the fact that they unostentatiously pursued their businesses, might be classed with the sheep; and, on the other hand, we might be led to attach undue importance to such craftsmen as William Jones, Abraham Swan, and Thomas Hope, who posed more or less humbly as leaders of contemporary taste.

It has been the custom to divide cabinet-makers into broad groups or schools, called after the particular designer to whose style their own efforts most nearly approximated, and in pursuance of this practice Edwards and Darly, W. and J. Halfpenny, Johnson, Robert Manwaring, and Ince and Mayhew have been classed as disciples of Chippendale, just as Richardson, J. Carter, J. Crunden, and Pergolesi have stood under the ægis of the Adelphi, or Ackermann and Thomas Hope under that of Thomas Sheraton. This convention affords the collector a bird's-eye view of the ground he has to cover, but it will not prove infallible when analytically examined. Citing three cases only, one from each of the schools just mentioned, Johnson *led* Chippendale on the downward path of Chinese extravagances and eccentricities; the Adams owed more to Pergolesi than he owed to them; whilst the salient point of Ackermann's work, namely, his exploitation of " English Empire," was distinct from Thomas Sheraton's performances in the same direction.

Literature.

Notice has already been taken of the books setting forth the styles of the better-known designers. We have discussed Langley's " Treasury," Chippendale's " Director," Heppelwhite's " Guide," and Sheraton's " Drawing-Book "; but it is desirable that we should turn for a moment to some of the less well-known works and note the goals at which their several authors aimed.

In many instances the date of issue was not given with the various books of designs, and, if one may hazard a reason for the omission, this was probably held back in order that the suggestions given might not be stamped as otherwise than fresh in an age when fashions became obsolete within a decade. The following works are of considerable interest, and are rarely to be met with for reference purposes. Parenthetically, we must remember that their basic suggestions seldom reflect originality of thought on the part of their authors :—

William Jones.

The Gentlemen's or Builder's Companion, containing variety of usefull Designs for Doors, Gateways, Peers, Pavilions, Temples, Chimney Pieces, Slab Tables, Pier Glasses, or Tabernacle Frames, Ceiling Pieces, etc. Explained on Copper Plates.

Published 1739.

Printed for the Author, and sold, at his house, near the Chapple, in King St., Golden Square.

(*Mainly Early Georgian or pseudo-Classic ideas.*)

Abraham Swan.

The British Architect; or the Builder's Treasury of Stair Cases. The Whole Illustrated with upwards of 100 Designs and Examples curiously engraved by the best Hands on 60 fol. copper plates.

London. Printed for and sold by the Author, near the George, in Portland St., Cavendish Square.

MDCCLVIII.

(*Many of Swan's interiors harmonise admirably with Chippendale furniture.*)

William Halfpenny, *Carpenter and Architect.*

Practical Architecture. 5th edit., dated 1736. 12°.

William and John Halfpenny.

The Country Gentleman's Pocket Companion and Builder's Assistant for Decorative Architecture. Also The Modern Builder's Assistant. Chinese and Gothic Architecture properly ornamented. 12 copper plates, with instructions to workmen. 1752. 4°.

(*Nearly akin to Chippendale's "Director" style.*)

Thomas Johnson.

Designs for picture-frames, candelabra, chimney-pieces, &c. Dedication to the Right Honble. Lord Blakeney, etc. 56 Engs. by B. Clowes and T. Kirk.

Westminster, 1758. 4to.

Also, One Hundred and Fifty New Designs by Thomas Johnson, Carver. 1761.

George Edwards and Matthew Darly.

A new book of Chinese Designs, calculated to improve the present Taste, consisting of Figures, Buildings and Furniture, Landskips, Birds, Beasts, Flowers and Ornaments, etc.

London. 1754. Quarto.

Sold by the Authors, first house on the right North Ct., Strand.

Ince and Mayhew (1762).

The Universal System of Houshold Furniture, consisting of above 300 Designs in the most elegant Taste, both useful and ornamental, Finely engraved, in which the nature of Ornament and Perspective is accurately exemplified. The Whole made convenient to the Nobility and Gentry in their choice, and comprehensive to the Workman, by directions for executing the several Designs, with specimens of Ornament for young Practitioners in Drawing.

By Ince and Mayhew, Cabinet-Makers and Upholders in Broad St., Golden Sq., London.

Robert Manwaring.

The Cabinet and Chair-Maker's Real Friend and Companion, or The Whole System of Chair making made plain and easy, containing upwards of 100 new and useful designs for all sorts of chairs in the Chinese and Gothic taste. Also some very beautiful designs supposed to be executed with the Limbs of Yew, Apple, or Pear Trees, ornamented with Leaves and Blossoms, which, if properly painted, will appear like Nature. These are the only designs that ever were published. 6sh. sewed, 7s. 6d. bound.

Invented and drawn by Rob. Manwaring, Cab. Maker. 1765.

(*The author possesses a very beautiful hall table showing the carved yew decoration of which Manwaring wrote.*)

Matthias Lock and H. Copeland (or Copland).

A new book of Ornaments, consisting of Tables, Chimnies, Sconces, Spandles, Clock-Cases, Candle-Stands, Chandeliers, Girandoles, &c.

Published according to Act of Parliament Jany. 1st, 1768, by Robt. Sayer, at No. 53 in Fleet St., London. Price 5sh.

The "Lesser" English Cabinet-makers. 613

Matthias Lock *(1740-1770)*.
    A new Drawing Book of Ornaments, Shields, Compartments, Masks, etc. 6 plates. (? 1768.)
    A new book of Pier-Frames, Ovals, Gerandoles, Tables, etc. Imp. 8vo. London. 1769.

Darly, M. *(or Darley)*.
    Sixty Vases by English, French, and Italian Masters.
        Obl. 4to. London : 1767.
  Also :—
    Book of Ornaments, Stucco, Carving, Ceilings, Picture Frames, &c. 1769.
(Herein Darly trenches on the Classic, as expounded by the Adams.)

John Crunden.
    The Joyner and Cabinet-Maker's Darling or Pocket Directory, containing 60 different designs, entirely New and Useful. Forty of which are Gothic, Chinese, Mosaic, and Ornamental Frets, proper for Friezes, Imposts, Architraves, Tabernacle Frames, Book-Cases, Teatables, Tea-stands, Trays, Stoves, and Fenders. And 20 new and beautiful Designs for Gothic, Modern, and Ornamental Fan-lights for Over-doors in the most elegant Taste, calculated for the Universal Use of Carpenters, Joyners, Cabinet-Makers, Masons, Plaisterers, Smiths, &c.
  London.   Printed for and sold by A. Webley, Holborn.
        MDCCLXX. 3sh.

J. H. Morris, *Carpenter, and* **J. Crunden.**
    The Carpenter's Companion for Chinese Railing and Gates, a work for Carpenters, Joyners, &c.
        MDCCLXX. 2sh. sewed.

N. Wallis.
    The Complete Modern Joiner, or a Collection of Original Designs in the present Taste for Chimney-Pieces and Door-Cases with their Mouldings and Enrichments at Large, Frizes, Tablets, Ornaments for Pilasters, Bases, Sub-bases, and Cornices for Rooms, &c., with a Table shewing the Proportion of Chimneys with their entablatures to Rooms of any size. By N. Wallis, Architect.
        London. 1772. Obl. 4to. 8sh.
  Also :—
    A book of Ornaments in the Palmyrene Taste. London. 1771. 4s. 6d.

Placido Columbani.

A new book of Ornaments, containing a variety of elegant designs for modern pannels, commonly executed in stucco, wood, or painting, and used in decorating principal rooms. Drawn and Etched by Placido Columbani. 1775. 4to. Sewed, 7s. 6d.

Also :—

A Variety of Capitals, Freezes, and Corniches, and how to increase or decrease them, still retaining the same proportion as the original. Likewise 12 Designs for Chimney-Pieces, the whole consisting of 12 plates. 1776.

(*In the so-called "Adam" style approximately.*)

Michele Angelo Pergolesi.

Designs for various Ornaments, on 70 plates. London. 1777-1801. Fol.

(*In the so-called "Adam" style approximately.*)

William Pain.

The Practical Builder. 1776.
The Carpenter and Joiner's Repository. 1805.

T. Shearer.

Designs of Household Furniture. 19 plates. On each plate, Published according to Act of Parliament. 1788.

(*From this work we learn the source of many of Sheraton's finest "inspirations."*)

Thomas Hope.

Household Furniture and Interior Decoration. Executed from Designs by Thomas Hope. Fol. 1807.

G. Smith.

A collection of Designs for Household Furniture and Interior Decoration, in the most approved and Elegant Taste. 1808. London. 4to.

Also :—

A collection of Ornamental Designs after the manner of the Antique. Engraved on 53 plates with descriptions. London. 1812. 4to.

Also :—

The Cabinet-Maker and Upholsterer's Guide. London. 1826. 4to

John Taylor.

> The Upholsterer's and Cabinet-Maker's Pocket Assistant. Being a Collection of Designs for Fashionable Upholstery and Cabinet Work. On 100 plates. Coloured. In 2 vols. 8vo. £2 2s. 1810-1820.

A Trade Enumeration.

Although Batty Langley's "Treasury" possesses less intrinsic value from an artistic point of view than many other eighteenth-century works, it has this merit in common with Chippendale's "Director" and Sheraton's "Drawing-Book," that it affords a good insight into contemporary craftsmanship, and shows the names of those in the profession who were attracted by the teachings or suggestions of the author.

The following lists are mainly built up from the names given in the "Treasury," "Director," and "Drawing-Book," and so may be relied upon as being authentic. There were, of course, many other craftsmen of whom no record has been preserved; but, as it so happens, we are able to glean reliable data at three of the most important periods in the eighteenth century.

Cabinet-makers and Joiners of the pre-"Director" period.

NOTE.—Where not otherwise stated it may be generally accepted that these were London craftsmen.

CABINET-MAKERS.

ALMOND, THOMAS	BELL, WILLIAM
ARMITSTAD, JOHN	BOWMAN, JAMES
ASH, JOHN, at Malton	BROWN, THOMAS
ASHLEY, JOHN	BUTTON, JOHN
BARRAS, JOSEPH	CHETTNAM, JOHN

Cabinet-makers of the pre-"Director" period (continued).

EDWARDS

FLINTHAM, ROBERT

GARDINER, JOHN
GRAHAM, DAVID, St. Paul's Churchyard
GRENDEY, GILES

HODSON, JAMES

JONES, JAMES

KINDT, GEORGE

LEISTEL, JOSEPH
L'RESSEM, RIMNAUS

MASON, JOSEPH
MEDSENER, JOHN
MILLER, JOHN
MORLEY, JAMES

NICHOLS, ROBERT

PAXTON, JOHN
PERRIN, HENRY
PETERS, JOHN

RUSH, THOMAS
RYLEY, THOMAS

SHATFORD, SAMUEL
SPENCE, ROBERT
STEEL, DAVID,
STEVENS, EDWARD
STEVENS, NATHANIEL

TYLER, JOSEPH

ULMAN, CHARLES

WILKS, WILLIAM
WOOD, WILLIAM

JOINERS.

ASHBY, SAMUEL

BAEN, WILLIAM
BADCOCK, JOHN
BADCOCK
BARE
BARKER, THOMAS
BARTON, WILLIAM
BAXTER, ROBERT
BENNET, DAVID
BINFIELD, GILBERT
BOOTH, ROGER
BOSSWELL, RICHARD
BRALSFORD, JOSEPH
BROOKS, LEWIS

CAMERON, WALTER
CHIPPENDELL, JAMES
CHURCHOUSE, THOMAS
CLINCH, MATTHEW
COWARD, ADAM
COX, SAMUEL,

DANIEL, THOMAS
DARLING, ROBERT
DAVIS, DANIEL
DAVIS, SAMUEL
DAVIS, WILLIAM
DAWKINS, CHARLES
DIBDON
DISHINGTON, GEORGE

The "Lesser" English Cabinet-makers.

Joiners of the pre-"Director" period (continued).

DORREY, DANIEL
DOUGLAS, JOHN

EASON, RICHARD
EDINGTON, JOHN
ELLIOT, JOHN
EMMES, JOSEPH

FINCH, JOHN
FOSTER, JOHN
FOWLE, THOMAS
FRANCIS, HENRY
FRETWELL, ALLEN
FREW, ROBERT
FRITH, ROBERT
FRITH, THOMAS
FURNEAUX

GILL, WILLIAM
GIVER, WILLIAM
GOLDING, JOSEPH
GOODMAN, WILLIAM
GOODRIDGE, JAMES
GRAHAM, DAVID
GRAVENER
GRAY, JOHN

HAINES, JAMES
HALL, JOHN
HARPHAM, FRANCIS
HARRIS, ROWLAND
HARVEY
HARVEY, EDMUND
HAYES, WILLIAM
HINKS, JOHN
HINTON, THOMAS
HITCHCOCK, ROBERT
HOLROIDE, JOHN
HORN, JAMES
HOWEL, THOMAS

JACKSON, THOMAS
JAGGAR, NATHANIEL
JOHNSON, RICHARD, at Wickham
JOHNSON, ROBERT, at Aylesbury

KELL, WILLIAM
KEYS, WILLIAM

LANCASTER, ROBERT
LEAF, JOHN
LEWIS, ROGER
LEWIS, THOMAS
LIGHT, JOHN
LONGMAN, RICHARD

MACBETH, WILLIAM
MARR, ARCHIBALD
MARTIN, RICHARD
MAXSUEL, JOHN
MERRIOT, RICHARD
MILSON, THOMAS, at Menithorp
MILLER, JOHN
MINTON, RICHARD
MOUNT

NOYCE, FRANCIS

PAGE, GEORGE
PAIN, EDWARD
PASCOE, JOSEPH
PATERSON, GEORGE
POPE, JAMES
POULTER, JOHN

RANKIN, ANDREW
RATCLIFF, RICHARD,
REYNOLDS, JAMES, at Epsom

Joiners of the pre-"Director" period (continued).

REYNOLDS, JOSEPH, at Oxford
REYNOLDS, PHILIP
RICE, JOHN
RIDDLE, THOMAS
RIDEWAY, RALPH
RINGROSE
ROBARDS, JOHN
ROBERTS, RICHARD
ROBINSON, JEREMIAH
ROWLAND, THOMAS

SAY, HUMPHRY
SCOTFORD, JAMES
SHARP, WILLIAM
SHAW, JOHN
SINCLAIR, WILLIAM, at Burnby
SLATER, HENRY
SMITH, JAMES
SMITH, MICHAEL

STEAD, JACOB
STOCKMAN, HENRY
SUTTON, JOHN, of Congleton

THRIFT, THOMAS
TILDSEY, HANDSON
TRINGHAM, FRANCIS

VINCENT, RICHES

WALLER, RICHARD
WALLIS, WILLIAM
WATERS, DAVID
WEBB, DANIEL
WESTMORE, GEORGE
WHITCOMB, WILLIAM
WILDON, ANDREW
WILLIAMS, JOHN
WOOD, WILLIAM
WRIGHT, DANIEL
WYAT, PETER

List of Cabinet-makers, Upholders, and Joiners of Chippendale's "Director" Period.

CABINET-MAKERS.

AFFLECK, JAMES
ANDERSON, JAMES
ATKINSON, THOMAS

BARBER, JOHN
BELCHIER, THOMAS
BROWN, JOSEPH
BROWN, ROBERT
BURBY, JAMES
BUTLER, WILLIAM

CANTY, ROBINSON
CHANNON, CHARLES (senior)
CHANNON, CHARLES (junior)

CLAIR, JOHN
CONYEARS, JOSEPH
COOPER, JOSEPH
CROSBY, JOHN

DALE, JOHN
DAVISON, WILL.
DAWSON, THOMAS
DEAN, THOMAS
DICKSON, GEORGE
DINGWALL, ALEX.

FAIRWEATHER, GEORGE
FARMBOROUGH, WILL.

The "Lesser" English Cabinet-makers.

Cabinet-makers of Chippendale's "Director" period (continued).

Fox, Benjamin
Foy, Henry

Gaffield, Ambrose
Goodeyre, John
Gordon, Will.

Hall, Pearce
Halse, Will.
Hobson, Nath.
Hopkins, David
Hopper, Thomas
Hudson, James
Hudson, Robert

Ince, William

Jackson, Joseph
Jeacock, Caleb
Jellings, Thomas
Jennings, Leonard
Jersier
Jones, Owen

Kaygill, Will.
Kier, John
Kincaid, Alex.

Lee

Malton, Thom., of Nottingham.
Marsh, George
Martindale, Nath.
Mathison, Jos.
Melvill, Rob.
Milldew
Miller, Will.

Newman, Isaac
Newman, John

Parran, Benj.
Paterson, John
Platts
Preston, John

Ranken, John
Rannie, James
Ridge, John
Reed, Andrew
Reynolds, George
Roberts, John
Roberts, Timothy

Seddon, George (afterwards G. Seddon and Sons, then Seddon, Sons, and Shackleton)
Shatford, Sam.
Spark, John
Spear, Hugh
Spence, Rob.
Stevenson, Dav.

Trewin, Will.
Trotter, John
Troughton, John
Tuttop, Charles

Underwood, Hugh, of Scarborough

Walkinton, John
Ware, James
Waters, David
Waters, John
West, George
White, James
White, John
Williams, Will.

UPHOLDERS.

AFFLECK, JAMES

BARKER, ROB., of York
BLADWELL, JOHN

CADDELL, JAMES
COLLINS, CH.
CONSTABLE, HENRY

DARK, RICH.

ELWICK, CH.

FARRER, RICH., of York

GOOD, EDW.
GOOD, JAMES

HARDMAN, ANTH.
HUNTER, WILL.

JEFFRIES, JOHN

KILPIN

MAINLOVE
MILLER, WILL.

REYNOLDSON, G., of York

SACKAM
SAUNDERS, PAUL.
SAY, FRANCIS
SHAVE

WRIGHT, RICH.

JOINERS.

ALLAN, THOMAS

BURGESS, JOHN
BUTTER, JOHN

COOK, CH.

DADE, THOM.
DAVIS, THOM.
DINGLE, SOLOMON

FOTHERGILL, JOHN

HARDCASTLE, AARON

MOSS, JAMES

PIT, JAMES

RAISIN, JOHN

WARRELL, CH.
WEBSTER, WILL.

List of Master Cabinet-makers of Sheraton's Period, with Addresses.

ADAMS, Strand, London
ANGUS, Shug Lane, London

BADGER, Batterly Moor, Lancashire

BAGSTER, J., Piccadilly London
BALLY, 10, Milsom Street, Bath
BEALE, J., 7, Rose Street, Soho, London

The "Lesser" English Cabinet-makers.

Master Cabinet-makers of Sheraton's period (continued).

BINNS, ED., 1, Burden Street, Berkley Square, London

BISHOP, Houndsditch, London

BLACKLOCK, 79, Park Street, London

BLACKSTOCK, P., Castle Street, Long Acre, London

BOUCH, WILL., Wells Street, London

BOWER, 12, Round Court, Strand, London

BROMRIDGE, George Yard, Hatton Garden, London

CAMPBELL AND SON, Marylebone Street, London

CHEATHAM, J., Eagle Court, Clerkenwell, London

CHISHOLME, T., 7, Great Pultney Street, London

CHOWLES, 21, North Audley Street, London

CLELAND, A., St. Anne's Court, Peter Street, London

COOK, ED., Cow Cross, near Smithfield, London

COOPER, Bishopsgate, London

COTTER, W., 24, Burn Street, London

CROSS, Blackfriars Road, London.

DAWS, THOM., 27, Dean Street, Soho, London

DENT, HENRY, 27, Little Castle Street, London

DODS, JAMES, 34, Broad Street, Carnaby Market, London

DONALD, ROB., Grosvenor Street, London

DUNCOMB, JAMES, Gt. Garden Street, Whitechapel

ENGLEHEART, P., 40 Castle Street, Oxford Market

FLEMING, W., Chandois Street, London

FLETCHER, Rose Street, Soho, London

FOLGHAM AND SON, 81, Fleet Street, London.

FRANCE, St. Martin's Lane, London

FREEMAN, Oxford

GILLOCK, THOS., 10, Worship Street, Moorfields, London

GILNEY, Castle Meadows, Norwich

GRAHAM, St. Paul's Churchyard, London

GREGSON, Preeson's Row, Liverpool

GRIMES, Bolton, Lincolnshire

GROUPNER, PETER, 43, Greek Street, Soho, London

HARGRAVES, Cloth Hall, Leeds

HENLEY, Newton Abbot, Devonshire

HOUGHTON, 96, Holborn, London

HOWE, Strand, London

Master Cabinet-makers of Sheraton's period (continued).

HUDSON AND CORNEY, 1, Broad Street, Soho, London

JENKINS, JOHN, Long Acre, London

KELLEY, WILL., Catharine Wheel Alley, London
KERR, Pall Mall, London
KILOH, 18, Air Street, Golden Square, London
KING, Chapel Street, Mayfair, London
KIRK, THOM., 8, Rose Street, London

LIVESAY, Church Row, Limehouse, London
LONSDALE, WILL., Broad Street, London

MARSHALL, G., Mount Street, London
MARSHALL, J., Gerard Street, Soho, London
McEWEN, JONAH, 13, Castle Street, Oxford Market, London
McKENZIE AND BLISSETT, Mary-le-bone Street, London
MEDHURST, St. John Street, London

NASH, Brewer Street, London

ODGE, Uphill, Malmesbury, Wiltshire

OLLIVE, Aldersgate Street, London

PAUL, PETER, 4, Silver Street, London
PETTIT, Brewer Street, London
POTTS, Compton Street, London
POWELL, 180, St. John Street, London
PRENTICE, Wild Street, London
PRICKETT, Foster Lane, London
PRINGLE, Wardour Street, London

REEDER, Oxford Street, London
RILAND, Oxford Street, London
ROBINS, J., Chancery Lane, London

SALMON, Chapel Street, London
SEDDON AND CO., 24, Dover Street, London
SEDDON, SONS, AND SHACKLETON, 150, Aldersgate Street, London
SEMPLE, Margaret Street, Newcastle
SHAW, WILL., 11, George's Court, Clerkenwell, London
SIMPSON, St. Paul's Churchyard, London
SMALL, Piccadilly, London

The "Lesser" English Cabinet-makers.

Master Cabinet-makers of Sheraton's period (continued).

SMITH, WILL., 10, Beak Street, London
STONE, Houndsditch, London
TARN, WM., AND SON, 28, London Wall, London
TAYLOR, East Smithfield, London
THOMAS, Carpenter Street, near Berkley Square, London
TOLPUTT, Long Acre, London
TURNER, New Bond Street, London
WARROCK, 5, Jermyn Street, London
WEIGHT, Savoy Stairs, London
WILKIE, JAMES, Hamilton, Scotland
WILLIAMSON, Bedford Court, London
WRIGHT, FRANCIS, 410, Oxford Street, London
WRIGHT, WILL., 410, Oxford Street, London
WRIGHT, Clerkenwell, London

List of Master-Upholders of 1793, with Addresses.

BARNARD, Leather Lane, London
BLADES, THOM., 114, Jermyn Street, London
BRUCE, 307, Holborn, London

EDMUNDS, 6, Compton Street, London
ELLIOTT, CH., New Bond Street, London
EYER, near the Pantheon, Oxford Road, London

FLETCHER, 8, Houndsditch, London
FLINT, H., 17, Greek Street, Soho, London
FRASER, J., Charles Street, Mary-le-bone, London

GIBBONS, 3, Goldsmith Street, Cheapside, London
GLOVER, C., Piccadilly, London

GUEST AND SON, Bury St. Edmunds

OKELEY, St. Paul's Churchyard, London

PEARCE, Ludgate Street, London
PERSON, THOM., Clement's Lane, Lombard Street, London

SEDDON, THOM., 24, Dover Street, London
SMITH, J., Eastcheap, London
STOVELL, G., Grosvenor Street, London

THOMPSON, WM., Saville Row, London

WALDRON, THOM., Catharine Street, London

List of Minor Cabinet-makers of Sheraton's Period, with General Addresses.

AHAIR, Bristol
ALDERSON, Newcastle
ALDERTON, Brighton
ALLEN, London
ALLISON, ROBT., London
ANDERSON, ALEX., London
ANDERSON, H., London
ANDREWS, Ipswich
ANGEL, ED., Brighton
APPLEBY, Stockton
APPLETON, C., Halifax
ATKINSON, THOM., London
ATKINSON, WILL., Rippon

BAISTON AND HARGILL, Leeds
BAKER, Islington, London
BALES, SIMON, Norwich
BALLS, THOS., London
BANKS, THOM., London
BARRY, London
BASSICK, A., Scarborough
BATTER, London
BEAL, London
BEALE, THOM., York
BECKWITH, Stockton
BELCHAR, Bristol
BELFOUR, ALEX., London
BELLARD, London
BENSON, London
BENWELL, C., Reading
BINGS, JOHN, Sheffield
BLAND, Halifax
BLACK, ALGERNON, London
BLACK, J., London
BLACK, R., London
BORE, Norwich
BOROUGH, London
BOTCHERBY, R., Darlington

BOWMAN, JOHN, London
BOWMAN, WILL., London
BRAILSFORD, T., Sheffield
BRAILSFORD, W., Sheffield
BRASH, JOHN, Leeds
BREAM, SAM., Yarmouth
BROADLEY, S., London
BRUMMELL, Newcastle
BRUNTON, J., London
BRYTAM, S., London
BROWN, London
BROWN, JAMES, London
BROWN, MICH., London
BULLOCK, RICH., London
BULLOCK, WILL., London
BULMER, Newcastle
BURBURY, London
BURN, JAMES, Hadington
BURNET AND PANTER, Bristol
BURNIS, CH., London
BURNS, Glasgow

CAMPBELL, A., London
CAMPBELL, JOHN, London
CARTWRIGHT, Ipwich
CASEMENT, W., London
CHAMBERLAIN, Ipswich
CHRISTIE, London
CLARK, W., Stockton
COATS, J., London
COCK, Bristol
COLBORN, W., London
CONYER, G., London
COOK, WILL., London
COOPER, London
COOPER, JOS., Derby
CORLETT, ED., London
COURT, Bristol

The "Lesser" English Cabinet-makers.

Minor Cabinet-makers of Sheraton's period (continued).

COWIN, J., London
COWLEY, Liverpool
COX, ED., Northampton
CROCKETT, CH., London
CROFT, Leeds
CRAGG, JAMES, London
CRAGG, LEONARD, London
CRASTAY, London
CROSS, AUBERY, London
CROSS, JOS., London
CROW, CH., London
CROWTHER, Halifax
CRYSTALL, WILL., London
CUBITT, London
CUDBERT, JOHN, Whitby
CURTIS, Wisbich

DANIEL, SAM., London
DAVIES AND WILSON, York
DAVISON, W., London
DICK, London
DIGBY, JAMES, York
DILLON, Russia
DIXON, London
DIXON, G., London
DOBSON, CHRIST., London
DODSON, Colchester
DODMAN, W., London
DREWELL, London
DUESCAN, Bristol
DUNCOMB, M., London
DUNN, JOHN, Newcastle
DUTTON, THOS., London

EBDITCH, London
EDIE, JAMES, London
EDMUNDSON, Liverpool
EDON, Newcastle
ELDEN, EARL W., London

ELEXANDER, WILL., Edinburgh
ELLERBECK, JOHN, London
ELLIOT, London
ELLIOTT, London
ELLIS, CH., London
ELWICH AND ROBERTSON, Wakefield
EUSTICE, London,

FAIR, W., Berwick
FAIRCHILD, ROWLAND, London
FARLOW, RICH., London
FARNES, MARTIN, London
FERGUSON, THOM., London
FIELD, JOS., London
FINN, ROB., London
FOWLER, GILES, London
FRASER, JAM., London
FREEMAN, London

GIBBONS, JOS., London
GIBSON, THOM., Darlington
GIRLING, London
GOADILL, Ipswich
GOODMAN, London
GOZNA, JOHN, London
GRAINGER, Bristol
GRANT, W., London
GREEN, Ipswich
GREEN, T., London
GREENFIELD, ALEX., Edinburgh
GREY, Edinburgh
GROATERS, JOHN, London

HALFORD, J., London

2 S

Minor Cabinet-makers of Sheraton's period (continued).

HALL, JOHN, Stockton
HALL, R., London
HALLA, W., London
HALLUM AND PIDCOCK, Nottingham
HARDING, J., London
HARFORD, J., London
HARKER, ANTH., London
HARRISON, London
HARRISON, Norwich
HARRISON, W., London
HARRON, C., London
HASTIE, B. M., Glasgow
HASTIE, THOM., Glasgow
HATCH, WILL., Norwich
HAWKINS, Norwich
HAWKINS, WILL., York
HAY, THOM., London
HEAD, W., London
HENDERSON, Newcastle
HENDERSON, CH., Newcastle
HENDERSON, WILL., London
HEWETT AND JEFFERSON, Sunderland
HEWITT, JOHN, London
HICKS, London
HIGGS, London
HILDEBRANT, W., London
HILL, THOM., London
HIND, J., Gainsborough
HOBSON, G., London
HODGELAND, Bristol
HODGES, HENRY, London
HOGG, ROB., London
HOLMES, London
HOLT, WILL., London
HORN, ANDR., London
HOUSE, London
HOWARTH, Halifax
HOWELL, Bristol

HUGHES, JAM., London
JAPPS, Montrose
JENKINSON, J., Sheffield
JILLIWE, London
JOHNSTON, London
JOHNSTON, W., London
JONES, London
JONES, JOHN, London
JONES, THOM., London
JONSTONES, Barton
JORDAN, JAM., London

KAYE, ROB., London
KING, Norwich
KING, Whitehaven,
KNIGHT, London

LANG, M., London
LANGSHAW, W., Bristol
LAMBERT, Hull
LAMBERT, PH., London
LARGE, W., London
LEDGEWOOD, Greenlaw
LEVETT, Hull
LEWIS, London
LINCETT, ASH., Malton
LISLE, Newcastle
LIST, Ipswich
LISTON, ED., Edinburgh
LOWE, WILL., Liverpool
LUCAS, RICH., London
LUMBLEY, JOHN, London
LUNSDALL, Newcastle
LYALL, JAM., London

MACKAY, G., London
MACKEY, JAM., London
MAITLAND, ROB.
MALTMAN, JAM., London
MANN, BAILLIE, Glasgow

The "Lesser" English Cabinet-makers.

Minor Cabinet-makers of Sheraton's period (continued).

MARSHALL, ALEX.
MARSHALL, ROB.
MARTIN, WILL., jun., Glasgow
MARTINDALE, JOHN, Stockton
MATHEON, ROB., London
MAUNDER, London
MCDONALD, W., London
MCEWEN, ALEX., London
MCFARLANE, London
MEEKE, G., London
MEIN, JAM., London
METCALF, FOSTER, London
METCALF, JOHN, Stockton
MILES, JAM., London
MILLER, HUMPH., London
MOFFAT, HENRY, London
MORCHIRD, JAM.
MORRIS, THOM., London
MORSELY, Doncaster
MORTON, JOHN, London
MOWER, J. WILL., London
MUIR, DAVID,

NEWTON, WILL., London
NORRIS, J., London

ORANGE, G., London
ORPWOOD, JOHN, London

PARK, Halifax
PARLBY, London
PARTRIDGE, London
PAULTON, CH., Reading
PECK, W., London
PEDDIESON, London
PENDRILL, RICH., London
PERKINSON, JOHN, Halifax
PETERS, G., London
PHELPS, W., London

PICKERING, London
PILKINGTON, Derby
POQUET, London
POTTER, JAM., London
POTTER, ROB., London
POTTER, W., Lincoln
PRESTON, T., Lincoln
PRICE, London
PRICE, RICH., London
PRINGLE, T., Edinburgh
PROUD, W., London

QUICK, Tiverton

REDFORD, London
REID, H. AND J., Glasgow
RICHARDSON, London
RICHERLEY, T., Durham
ROBERTSON, ISAAC, London
ROBINSON, THOM., London
ROBSON, THOM., London
ROSS, JOHN, London
ROTHERY, London
RUTHERFORD, Hull

SANDERS, London
SCHOLEFIELD, RICH., Newcastle
SCHURREY, W., Wakefield
SCOTT, Glasgow
SCOTT, ALEX., Aberdeen
SCOTT, JAM., London
SCOTT, JOHN, London
SCOTT, JOHN, Newcastle
SCOTT, W., Wakefield
SCREENS, WORTLY, Stamford
SERSONS, Stamford
SHALLIS, JOHN, London
SHARATH, LAWRENCE, London
SHARP, London

Minor Cabinet-makers of Sheraton's period (continued).

SHAW, JAM., London
SHEERWOOD, Newcastle
SHELTON AND ELEY, Nottingham
SHEPHERD, BEACHNOFT, London
SHEPHERD, G., London
SHEPHERD, THOM., London
SHERATON, N., Newcastle
SHEREN, ROB., Newcastle
SHERIFF AND OATES, Edinburgh
SHLESCHA, PAUL, London
SIMPSON, RICH., Bristol
SIMPSON, W., London
SMILES, JOHN, London
SMITH, Newcastle
SMITH, jun., Norwich
SMITH, DAN., Windsor
SMITH, JAM., London
SMITH, THOM., London
SOPWITH, Newcastle
STAFFORD, Bristol
STANDAGE, JOHN, London
STANDING, London
STARK, W., London
STENSON, MATTHEW, London
STEWART, Bengal
STEWART, CH., London
STILES, Cambridge
STONEY, BENJ., Nottingham

STOOKS, T., Leeds
STRANGEWAYS, CHRIST., London
STRIBLAND, Bristol
SUMMERS, London

TATAM, H., Stamford
TATE, London
TATE, JOHN, Newcastle
TAYLOR, G., London
TAYLOR, JOHN, London
TAYLOR, ROB., Exeter
THARRAT, THOM., London
THOMAS, Bristol
THOMPSON, Whitehaven
THOMPSON, JAM., London
THOMPSON, JOHN, Durham
THOMPSON, WM., Beverly
TOWNLEY, London
TUBBY, Norwich

WADDLE, Glasgow
WALLACE, London
WALLING, London
WATTS, London
WENTWORTH, D., Cambridge
WILLIAMS, London
WILLS, Montrose

YOUNG, TROTTER, AND HAMILTON, Edinburgh

List of Minor Upholsterers of Sheraton's Period, with General Addresses.

ARCHER, WILL., London

BIGGER, WILL., London
BLACKBURN, WILL., London

BROWN, Newcastle
BUNNELL, Colchester

CALVERT, MATTHEW, London

The "Lesser" English Cabinet-makers.

Minor Upholsterers of Sheraton's period (continued).

CERR, J., Glasgow
CHAPMAN, Ipswich
CHALLIS, JOHN, London
CHILD, London
CHRISTIAN, JAM., London
CLARK, J., London
CLIFF, London
COOK, Colchester
COUNSEL, London
CROMER, JAM., Edinburgh

DOBSON, Newcastle

FACEY, London
FEMAISTER, G., London
FORREST, ROB., London
FRANCIS, W., London

GRAY, J., London

HALFPENNY, York
HARRISON, W., London
HILL, J., London
HIXON, THOM., London

IRON AND SON, Ipswich

KEENE, R., London
KING, London

KNIGHT, London

LAMB, W., Edinburgh
LANGDON, London
LUFF, London

MAKIN, JOHN, Alford
McBEAN, Windsor

NOON, JOHN, London

OLIPHANT, T., London
OLIVER, London

PERRY, London
PILKINGTON, London
PLAYSTED, London

ROBINSON, G., London

SMITH, London
SMITH, JAM., London
SMITH, T., London
STEEL, J., London
STEVENS, London

TALBOT, R., Edinburgh
TODD, H., Edinburgh

WHITE
WRIGHT

List of Minor Joiners of 1793.

NICHOLSON, WILL., London
NORTH, Bristol

STEVENSON, RICH., London
THORNE, WILL., London

The author would be very grateful to any collector sending him information relative to the foregoing craftsmen.

CHAPTER XXIII.
Bracket Clocks and Musical Instruments.

Bracket Clocks.

WHILST mutability was the characteristic of most eighteenth century design, the contour of the bracket clock until 1780 was so little subject to radical alteration that it forms one of the few exceptions to the rule. Looking at the centre specimen of the first three bracket clocks shown we notice an exquisite example of the William and Mary period. It is a pull quarter repeater by John Martin, and is decorated with a scheme of arabesque marquetry on its face, back, and sides.

To left and right we have Queen Anne and George I. varieties, the left-hand specimen being a pull quarter repeater by Charles Gretton, the right-hand example a six-bells chimer by Daniel Quare. These two latter clocks are not decorated, being in ebony, and their outline is suggestive of the models of the period 1700-1750. Collectors rightly prefer the cases showing embellishment, and, as a result, the ebony case has to a certain extent to stand in the background, although it usually encloses works of exceptional quality.

Passing on to the second series of clocks (page 635), we find on the left a handsome variety by John Farley, of Southwark, which we may style " Mid-Georgian." The frame is in finely-figured mahogany, with pierced fretwork

Bracket Clocks of the William and Mary, Queen Anne, and George I. periods, from the fine collection of D. A. F. Wetherfield, Esq.

sides, and the excellent mounts are in chased brasswork; like its predecessor, it is a repeater, and owns a first-class movement.

The little timepiece in the centre marks a new departure in case decoration, for it is typically Sheraton of an early date. The inlaid work on it is very fine, and the dial is in beautiful enamel.

A comparison of the first five clocks shows us that, even if size and proportion vary, they possess a strong family likeness, since outline varied very little between the years 1690 and 1780. The variations in dial shaping and handling correspond in the main with the evolution of the "grandfather" face already dealt with.

In passing to our last clock, we come to a fine specimen by Brockbank in mahogany inlaid with satin and other fancy woods. This model is typical of the Shearer-Sheraton school, and held the public fancy until well into the nineteenth century.

The novice perusing Chippendale's "Director" may expect to unearth ornate specimens characteristic of the great master's work in other fields, but his quest will prove fruitless almost without exception. The probability is that Chippendale was seldom called upon to embody any of his rather pretentious suggestions in this direction. The Clockmakers Guild was very close, and its members doubtless employed regular case "hands" who made a speciality of this particular work. Owing to absence of competition, it would seem that these craftsmen got into somewhat of a groove at the expense of originality.

In the case of London-made clocks the brasswork decorating the dial affords circumstantial evidence as to period. Small mannerisms in the rococo scroll-work supervened one on top of another, and the best makers kept abreast of the times by coming into line. When we turn to the productions of the leading provincial makers, this test is not reliable, for, on the rare occasions when they visited London, they laid in a store of parts and fitments according to their estimated requirements for a considerable period *in advance*. It is probable that in the remoter parts of the country clockmakers were happy in the acquisition of obsolete adjuncts to decoration; very possibly, too, they were put off with movement parts not of the latest. In these circumstances the country districts were fully twenty years behind the times on occasions. An interesting example of this slow development is noticeable in Sandwich churchyard, where Charles II. embellishment and that of Adam exist side by side on tombstones erected over worthies laid to rest *after* 1785. The bulk of eminent clockmakers found their way sooner or later to London, and collectors to-day make a special point of acquiring specimens made in the metropolis.

One word as to the age of clocks. It is often asserted that the age of a clock, failing direct evidence on the point, can be fixed if the " works maker " was a registered member of the Clockmakers Company or other registered guild. This is not the case, for Jones may have made clocks from 1740 and have been admitted a member of the chief society as late as 1770. Brown, on the other hand, working over the same period, owing to good fortune, or perhaps to merit in having invented an improved movement, may have been welcomed into the fold in 1741, or, as was often the case, Brown or Jones may have deferred adopting for a considerable period some distinctive development in the works which, if it had been

Bracket Clocks—Second half of the Eighteenth Century. Author's Collection.

universally adopted, would have definitely marked an era in clock-making.

Musical Instruments.

Musical instrument frames were usually built by special case hands, and examples such as the harpsichord which Robert Adam designed for the Empress of Russia were seldom taken in hand by our best-known cabinet-makers. At an early date clavichords and virginals, though sometimes embellished, were in movable cases or frames which were placed upon tables, and they did not possess their own especial stands as complementary fittings. As such they fail to come within the compass of decorative furniture. The virginal displaced the clavichord, and with the spinet, harpsichord, and early piano may be classed as of the greatest interest from our point of view. From the days of Charles II. clavichords, virginals, and spinets were generally mounted upon stands, and the under-framing usually reflected the fashion of its day pretty accurately. Thus we may happen on early spinets mounted on legs in spiral turnery, with stretcher-work to match, of the period 1670, just as we may find late supports savouring of Shearer or Sheraton. Claw-and-ball under-framing is of the greatest rarity, the writer having only seen one really fine and genuine example of this work.

Inlaying was the favourite style of decoration on these models, but we find much painted embellishment on specimens dating from 1780-1820, usually in conjunction with a modicum of inlay. The painted and inlaid decoration which these old instruments carried very frequently led to their dismantlement. Such woodwork as was cleverly set off by brushwork or inlay was carefully removed and then built into plain but more saleable furniture. Square tapered legs were detached and then refitted to late Sheraton models previously resting on round or turned members, indicative of the lateness of their period.

The majority of collectors leave these models alone when they acquire them, though extremists have gone to the length of having their " works " restored. This latter process entails great cost, and seldom yields satisfactory results. Unless, then, the model is of exceptional beauty or the buyer is a student of old-time music, interested in experimenting with the scope and tone of a given instrument, he may at first sight seem to be acquiring a white elephant when he purchases an example. All these models, however, possess latent possibilities, for they may be acquired reasonably, and lend themselves readily to adaptation for a variety of uses. In shape there are two main varieties, namely, those whose tops are, roughly speaking, triangular (often resembling a recumbent harp), and those whose cases are oblong; of these, the latter are by far the more useful.

Either type may be adapted for the display of china, enamels, old silver and curios, if the carcase be cleared out and the interior lined with velvet, satin, or some material to the taste of the owner, the lid of course being made to rise and fall or stay partly open at the collector's will. Both make excellent bookcases if the carcases are cleared out and partitioned off so as to admit of books being inserted in rows with their backs looking upwards.

The oblong varieties may be converted into dressers, side-tables, sideboards, or dressing-tables at a small cost and with practically no disturbance of their original outline and condition. It was a general custom for the casemaker to decorate the upright surface of woodwork rising above the keyboard, and this garnishment, generally the most important on the instrument, was hidden when the piece was closed. This section of inner work is often removed nowadays and projected into the facework of the model, and, under this treatment, *if the carcase is to be hollowed out*, the whole of the decoration shows to advantage. The face of the descending lid was usually plain, and it will just receive the interior strip of garnishment whether this be of a painted or an inlaid description. Generally speaking, these old instruments go very reasonably at auctions, and the collector whose purse is limited may, by the exercise of a little taste and ingenuity, obtain useful and decorative adjuncts to his home at small cost.

The piano is generally the *bête-noire* of the collector; its case is usually so aggressively hideous, and, in the light of this, it is well to bear in mind that some few old cases exist enclosing upright or cottage pianos of the late Sheraton period which are not only distinctly decorative, but can be refitted with up-to-date works in a satisfactory manner.

Old harps are very decorative in a drawing-room, and, placed in the corner of an interior carried out or furnished in the style of the Adam brothers, Heppelwhites, Gillows, Seddons, or Sheraton, they show to especial advantage.

CHAPTER XXIV.
Notes Concerning Mirrors.

Progress of the Mirror.

THE collector who has access to a representative collection of our old mirrors will be able to gather from their frames the decorative styles and processes evolved by English designers and cabinet-makers in the whole field of their art, and the illustrations which accompany this chapter afford a glimpse, in a condensed form, of the striking differences which marked a century of progress. The glass contained within these old frames is generally the worse for wear, the silvering at the back has been rubbed, scratched, rust-pitted, or corroded, and yet we instinctively insist on this old glass because it is old and possesses features of merit in the eyes of the collector. The process of resilvering and reparation is costly and uncertain as to the results which it will yield, and the individual who fancies a fine specimen with faulty reflecting power had far better remove and store the old field of glass and insert a new one than interfere with the original.

If the mirror is intended for a decorative adjunct to a room, leave its old glass severely alone; if it is to be purchased as a dressing-glass the collector *may* find that he has purchased a white elephant.

Glass was a great source of revenue to the country from the close of the seventeenth century, when duties

Late Stuart Mirror, with beadwork frame. The property of Gill and Reigate, Ltd.

were first imposed upon it, and Mr. Henniker Heaton, of postal fame, has furnished the writer with some interesting figures relative to these charges. Duties were first imposed in 1695, to be repealed in 1698; they were again introduced in 1745, reduced in 1819, modified further in 1825, increased in 1840, and abolished in 1845. From 5th July, 1819, the duty on plate glass, which had stood at £4 18s. per cwt., was lowered to £3 per cwt., but even this was a crushing impost. From 5th July, 1825, the duty of £4 18s. per cwt. on flint glass was repealed in favour of another charge of a drastic nature. From 15th May, 1840, the duties on all glass rose by 5 per cent., and the duty on broad glass was raised to £3 13s. 6d. per cwt.

Owing to Protection we had built up a fair business despite the home taxes on glass, and so late as 1843 the foreigner was mulcted for crown or window glass £8 6s. 8d. per cwt.; German sheet glass, £10 per cwt.; plate glass, 6s. per foot; silver or polished glass, 4s. per foot; and, whereas we were still thriving, the national revenue from foreign glass duties then reached £563,437, figures which serve to indicate that many people still believed that foreign glass was the best. For some reason the taxes on English glass were not equally levied. Thus, when the approximate duty on Vauxhall wares rose at one time as high as 50 per cent., the impost at Black Fryers appears to have been 10 per cent. lower. The duties on glass increased the price of that commodity very considerably, but they were not solely responsible for the heavy cost to the public. Olden methods were primitive, and we learn from " The Plate-Glass Book " of 1757 that " the Exceeding Brittleness of glass, as well as the many unavoidable Hazards and accidents it is liable to in the working, Silvering, Framing, Packing, &c., is so considerable an affair that it is usual to

William and Mary Mirror. The property of Frank Partridge, Esq.

allow the workmen, on that account, a Profit of 5s. or 6s. in the £. But in things that are very curious, this

Notes Concerning Mirrors.

Allowance is by no means sufficient." Thus, in order to make provision for accidental breakages, an extra minimum cost of 25 per cent. had to be tacked on to quotations to cover the vendors against contingent risks.

In addition to the duty and the insurance against breakages yet another risk had to be faced, for glass when finished might not come out the right hue, thickness, or quality. The best glass was that of a watery hue, and the anonymous author of " The Plate-Glass Book " writes: " Thus all glass looks like frozen water, which made a modern author merrily say that ' it made wine smile to see itself cherished in the bosom of its most Mortal Enemy.' " But all glass would not come out the right watery hue, for this little book cites how, owing to defects in manipulation by the teaser (who spread out the molten glass in the height of the founding) some plates came out " (1) of a reddish colour (which is much coveted by pale-faced People), (2) of a greenish colour, (3) of a yellowish colour, (4) of a blackish colour, which is the worst of all."

The inferior-hued glasses were cast out and sold for coach glass or other ordinary uses at a heavy discount, but some were purchased and by careful treatment were improved so that they would pass muster amongst the more unsophisticated of purchasers, the Glasshouse clerk going on to explain, " and when this can be effected it is productive of a very extraord^y Profit."

Hints to Collectors.

Collectors should look to the quality of the glass they buy, for the best plates were carefully tended, and we generally find them contained in frames of surpassing merit. Inversely, the glass which showed the greatest deviation from the true water-colour, towards black or green especially, were usually framed in an inferior manner, as they would not have appealed to purchasers of means and discrimination. We learn from the same source that " to distinguish the Colour of the best glass, as well as all the inferior sorts, you need only put a Piece of clean writing paper under the Plate, and the colour will shew itself." Although this proved an excellent test, it is seldom applicable to-day, when the glass has the old silvering behind it and the example is backed up and sealed; the collector therefore has to learn the range of hues which are referred to and also to make allowance for a smoky and dingy appearance, which may present itself on the best of glasses but owes its existence to the defective condition of the old silvering.

So much for the question of colour, which we may liken to different water qualities in diamonds; but the best plates would sometimes emerge too thin for adequate grinding, with a tendency to warp, and with flaws or uneven surfaces, and these failures had to be relegated to inferior uses or sacrificed to speculative buyers from the scrap heap.

Factors Affecting Prices.

There were thus many factors which all tended to raise the price of glass to a prohibitive figure, and we can understand how a sheet 36in. by 24in. fetched £4 5s. 9d., or about £12 of our money. The same piece broken into five fragments would have been measured up and sold for from 30s. to £2; glass was so expensive that the smallest bits had their value, and in the number of small mirrors, noticeably of the Queen Anne period, which show a small piece of glass at the top within the hooping

Late Queen Anne Mirror. Owned by Messrs. Gill and Reigate, Ltd.

over a larger plate, we see how our craftsmen used up small areas to avoid cutting into and wasting larger ones.

One disastrous effect of the exorbitant price of glass was that people who purchased old engravings were tempted to cut away all the margins and plate mark, thereby reducing the glass area necessary for the framing and protection of their prints. Those who collect mezzotints must rue the cause which led their forefathers thus to mutilate early states, an ill-judged parsimony which has to-day reduced the value of such engravings quite possibly by some hundreds of pounds apiece.

Grinding.

The processes of grinding, polishing, and silvering are all set out in the little book already referred to. When grinding " a Plate of glass is fixed to a horizontal table and to another lesser table is fixed another Plate, over the hind part of which is added a box loaded with stones and other weights. Over the first Plate is sprinkled fine sand and water, in a sufficient Quantity, for the Grinding, and the 2nd, or less Plate, is laid on it, and thus worked this and that way, till each has planed the other's surface. As they begin to grow smoother, finer sand is used, and at last Powder of Smalt.

Polishing.

" The plate being thus fitted for polishing, it is bedded in Plaster of Paris, and a small oblong Piece of wood, having another lesser Piece let in across its Top, which serves for a Handle to each Side, has a Notch cut in the top if it, and this they call a Block; this Block is lined on the under-side with a Piece of coarse

Blanketing, milled very thick, which they call a Lap; The Block being thus lined, is properly charg'd with Emery, Tripple or Putty, and laid upon the Plate, and a strong Stick, which they call a Bow, is then bent, and one end of it fix'd to the Top of the Room and the other End into the Notch at the Top of the Block; and then the Block is worked to and fro again, till the glass has got a perfect Politure."

" The Ingredients for polishing are these; Emery to take out the scratches, Stobs and Bloaches; Then Tripple (which is rust of old Iron) for clearing the Grinder's Ground; this is called Black lapping; afterwards white Putty is used, which is the Polisher's Finishing, and this is called White lapping.

Silvering.

" The Plates being polished, a thin blotting Paper is spread on a Table, and sprinkled with fine Chalk; and this done, over the Paper is laid a thin Lamina, or Leaf of Foil, on which is poured Quicksilver, which is to be equally distributed over the Leaf, with a Hare's Foot or Cotton. Over the Leaf is laid a clean Paper, and over that the Glass Plate. With the left Hand the Glass plate is pressed down, and with the Right the paper is gently drawn out; which done the Plate is covered with a thicker Paper, and loaden with a greater Weight, that the superfluous Quicksilver may be driven out, and the Foil adhere more closely to the Glass. When it is dried, the Weight is removed, and the Looking-glass is complete."

Our glass-workers, until the end of the great Chippendale's active days, were not clever at handling larger kinds of mirror glasses, and for anything like big

Carved Chippendale Mirror. Circa 1755. Author's Collection.

fields their prices seem to us to have been exorbitant Thus for a mirror ready to frame 52in. long by 39½in. broad the charge worked out at £63 5s. 6d., or about £180 of our money. Of this sum £5 12s. 8d., or, say, £16 of our money, was allocated to the silvering.

Oval, round, or shaped glasses were an expensive luxury, as they could only be cut from larger square fields, a process involving great waste at the corners or edges. In addition to flat-faced mirrors our workers also produced concave and convex glasses, the latter being especially popular at the end of the eighteenth and at the commencement of the nineteenth centuries. The plates in both these styles were bent and then ground, silvered, and polished, and they were not cast in their curved shape, as they have been of late, or gouged out from the solid, as people at one time imagined. The concave mirror magnified the objects which it reflected, whereas the convex diminished them.

The Glasshouse clerk thus wrote of the properties of concave and convex mirrors: "A concave Mirror reflects the Rays which follow it, so as to make them converge, or approach nearer to each other. . . . Hence, Concave Mirrors magnify Objects presented to them. A Convex Mirror represents its Images smaller than the Objects; as a Concave One represents them larger; a Convex Mirror reflects the Rays from it diverging; and therefore disperses and weakens their Effect."

It is not perhaps necessary to go further into the question of glass-making, but should the reader wish to enter into the minutiæ of the craft the subject may be followed in many old works, perhaps the most succinct of which is "Ure's Dictionary" of 1867 (Longmans, Green, and Co.).

In that most admirable work we learn that glass, "a solid and transparent body formed by the fusion of siliceous and alkaline matter," was known to the Egyptians and Phœnicians of old, and that glass orna-

Early and very fine Convex Mirror. Circa 1780. Owned by Messrs. Gill and Reigate.

ments have been recovered from the old Egyptian burying-places. The secret, we are told, was "learnt by the Crusaders and brought to Venice in the thirteenth century."

From Venice the art passed on to Germany, France, and finally to England, where factories were established at Vauxhall, Lambeth, Black Fryers, and elsewhere. Ure tells us that "window glass manufacture was first begun in England in 1557 in Crutched Friars, London," and that "fine articles were afterwards made in the Savoy House, Strand." In a further passage we learn that "the Venetians were the first who attained excellence in the art of working glass, but the French became eventually so jealous of rivalling them, particularly in the construction of mirrors, that a decree was issued by the Court of France declaring not only that the manufacture of glass should not derogate from the dignity of a nobleman, but that nobles alone should be masters of glass works." This is most interesting, for we in England tacitly followed on similar lines. The nobility and gentry of this country were attracted to the glasshouses, and Ure records how "in 1635 *the art* received a great improvement from Sir Robert Mansell, by the use of coal fuel instead of wood. The first sheets of blown glass for looking glasses .... were made in 1673 at Lambeth by Venetian artizans employed under the patronage of the Duke of Buckingham."

Colbert had pushed this process in France, and in this latter country the secret of casting mirror plates was discovered by one Abraham Thevart in 1688 (Ure). France and Venice distanced England in the production of large mirrors until the Adam period, when we were able to hold our own; but the excellence of our polishing and grinding not only satisfied our own requirements for small glasses, but led to our obtaining orders from America so early as in 1720, when Judge Sewall sent for " A True Looking Glass of Black Walnut Frame of the

Newest Fashion (if the Fashion be good), as good as can be bought for five or six pounds " (Frances Clary Morse).

The joined plates which we meet with in English glasses are usually of early date, when the fashion of

Heppelwhite Looking-Glass. Circa 1775.

arching or hooping the top of the frame obtained very generally. At times the glass was cut and joined plain, but in the more elaborate glasses the lower edge of the top or super-imposed glass and the upper edge of the lower plate were both bevelled so that the reflecting surface was cut into two fields and its usefulness thereby curtailed. Bevelled borders were, of course, useless for reflecting, but they set off the models to which they were appended. Many small looking-glasses were in reality little better than ornaments owing to the minute size of the *useful* fields which they presented.

That many of the small mirrors were intended as ornaments and light-reflectors rather than as looking-glasses is proved by the fact that at the end of the Stuart period many specimens were engraved at the back of their glass fields. A design was cut or engraved intaglio fashion on the mirror from behind, and the decoration so achieved of course interfered with the usefulness of the field so treated—from a looking-glass point of view. The engraving was often applied to the upper section of a two-plate mirror, the lower plate being left plain for the owner's use.

Over and above the tone which helps us to distinguish original glasses from their brighter, more regular, and mechanical-looking successors, bevelling proves a most invaluable guide. The old bevels were irregular; that is to say, their inner edges did not lie evenly between their extreme points. Latter-day bevels are coldly correct, and run in straight horizontal and perpendicular lines. The old glass-workers, too, possessed the faculty of imparting life to their bevels with the minimum of departure from a flush surface; the modern bevel, with no improved appearance, runs away at a much acuter angle. When running the finger over an old bevel one can only just detect the reduction at the edge, whilst in the modern work it is comparatively pronounced. The old idea was that the bevels were obtained by grinding away the edges of the glass until the right angle of inclination had been obtained, and to this contention the irregularity of the old edges lends colour. It has been suggested of late that the glass was pressed into the requisite shape when in a molten condition, a contention which the author does not endorse.

John Hungerford Pollen, when commenting on the superiority of the old over the modern bevels, wrote that the mirrors "had the plates finished by an edge *gently bevelled of an inch in width*, following the form of the frame, whether square or shaped in curves. This gives preciousness and prismatic light to the whole glass. It is of great difficulty in execution, the plate being held by the workman over his head and the edge cut by grinding. The feats of skill of this kind in the form of interrupted curves and short lines and angles are rarely accomplished by modern workmen, and the angle of the bevel itself is generally too acute, whereby the prismatic light produced by this portion of the mirror is in violent and too showy contrast to the remainder."

The old bevels, as a matter of fact, were frequently *less than an inch in width*, and they were never so aggressive as the modern ones.

Early mirror frames were executed in numerous mediums, of which beadwork, ebony, olivewood, walnut, lacquer, gilt pine, and mahogany were the most striking. They bear witness to the Stuart, William and Mary, Grinling Gibbons, Queen Anne, Architectural, Rococo, Chinese, Gothic, and many later styles of the second half of the eighteenth century. Of the pre-Adam glasses some of the most effective were those in the architectural or classic fashions of early Georgian days, such as the one shown on page 647; whilst the least defensible of all patterns were those which the Johnson, Chippendale,

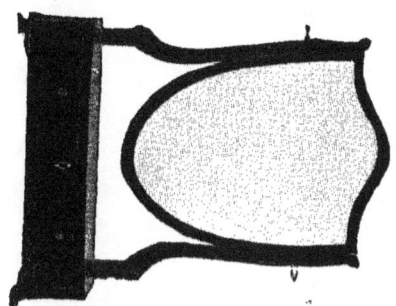

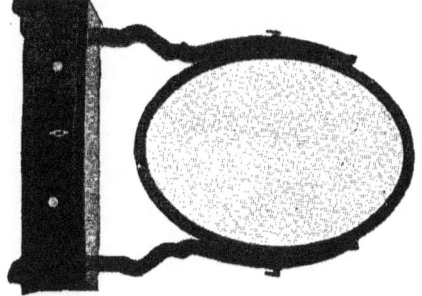

A and C. Shearer or Sheraton Glasses, 1780-1790. B. Queen Anne Glass.

Edwards and Darly, Lock, and Ince and Mayhew schools produced during the 'fifties when blending rococo and Chinese matter in weird and exaggerated manner. Girandoles intended for decoration or as light-reflectors followed much the same course as these larger mirrors, and, with them, were usually carried out in gilt over carved pine.

Chippendale and his disciples often produced mirrors for overmantel use, building them in three compartments, the partitions between which were in decorated gilt woodwork en suite with the rest of the model. These large pieces were usually treated in a rococo or Chinese vein.

The Adams were noted for their long upright pier-glasses as well as for their smaller mirrors, and towards the close of the century our designers were responsible for a new type of oval glass. An oval was enclosed by a larger oval, the two ellipses being joined by strips of decoration which divided the marginal space between them into fan-shaped segments. These were very plain and graceful, with their dainty decoration of beadings, &c., and they are very useful in that they suit narrow or broad wall spaces, looking equally well when hung upright or horizontally.

CHAPTER XXV.
Upholstery.

What to Select, and Why.

ONE is constantly being asked such questions as "How ought I to have these chairs re-covered?" or "Would you help me choose a material for an old settee which needs re-upholstering?" and in view of these everyday inquiries a few notes on old fashions may prove of some assistance.

In Tudor days, whilst our forefathers were content with rushes strewn upon the floors, they commonly decorated their walls with priceless hangings, which naturally dominated such limited upholstery schemes as then obtained. The love of panelling, which grew from Elizabethan times and was very marked in the seventeenth century, curtailed the governing properties of the walls, whilst at the same time the carpet or rug came into greater prominence. During the sixteenth century few sitting-rooms boasted more than one or two pieces of upholstered furniture, but with the advent of James I. the interest in covered models, which had awakened under Elizabeth, rose very rapidly. Chairs, stools, sofas, and settees were set off by rich materials, and people studied Turkey carpets and curtains when arranging their decorative plans. To these general rules there were exceptions, for we know that here and there Persian rugs had found their way into English homes of the fifteenth century, whilst panelling was introduced at an early date, work at Haddon, by no means the oldest known, dating back to 1490 A.D. In some districts panelling in oak was still resorted to during the first half of the eighteenth century, after it had become obsolete in other centres.

With the dawn of the eighteenth century the Queen Anne style of mural decoration had replaced Jacobean *oak* panelling, and interiors presented features more closely resembling our own, French carpets came in more commonly, a wider range of materials was made in England, and tapestry or oak panelling no longer constituted setpieces in mural treatment. The brothers Adam, who left nothing to chance, introduced into their stuffs the same *motifs* that we find on their ceilings or models; thus a covering to a chair or settee became as distinctly Adamesque as the lines of the furniture to which it was applied. But if the range of stuffs and materials increased with time, the quality very generally showed a retrograde tendency. The eighteenth-century velvets and so on lacked that richness which had characterised earlier productions, whilst needlework became less effective as time wore on. Many late Stuart, Queen Anne, and early eighteenth-century pieces owed half their glories to the needlework with which they were bedecked, whilst we seldom find *late* eighteenth-century chairs, sofas, couches, or settees greatly indebted to the fingers of some painstaking needlewoman.

The little silk and wool pictures and fire-screens of the period 1780-1810 bear witness to the diligent application of the needle, but they compared badly with the stump needlework of Stuart days. Figures of men, women, cupids, &c., which played so important a part in early compositions for upholstery proper, became crude and sank almost into desuetude after the Queen Anne vogue had had its day. The decorative floral needlework in the *petit-point* on a Chippendale chair made the coarser bouquets of later date look third-rate, whilst the conventional peacock tail on a Queen Anne wing-chair quite eclipsed the stereotyped patterns in woolwork to be found on a Sheraton stool.

This decadence was only natural, for, as the facilities for obtaining materials increased, the incentive to self-reliance in the home passed away. Once upon a time the ladies of a house set to work to prepare coverings for the models commissioned for their use, but the Adams, to quote one instance only, sent home their chairs, stools, window-seats, sofas, settees, or confidentes complete as to their upholstery, having watched over the selection of materials as carefully as they gave their instructions to the craftsmen entrusted with the preparation and decoration of the framework.

In 1575 only the richest and most noble called for any volume of upholstered furniture, and that which they obtained was excellent. By 1675 the upper and middle classes used it freely, whilst in 1775 its use was practically universal. As the demand for cheaper materials arose, quality, of course, fell, and we seldom find late eighteenth-century coverings which will compare with those of earlier days.

The following list of materials may prove of interest, but the reader must not *expect* to find old coverings prior to Jacobean days, and all pre-Commonwealth materials when met with will be found to be much the worse for wear. We must remember, in parenthesis, that though stump and bead work are highly prized by collectors, tent-stitch or *petit-point* is the more useful type of needlework, in that it can be effectively employed for upholstery:

Upholstery.

Late Tudor.

Velvets—Continental. Embroideries or needlework, applied to a linen foundation on many occasions. Leather. Gold or silver cloth, threading and tasselling.

James I. to Commonwealth.

Damasks, cloths, crewelwork, satins, taffeta silks, tapestries, Turkey work. Velvets—Genoese, Venetian, Norwich, &c. Silver threads, tasselling; rarely gold threads. Colours—reds; crimsons, scarlets, or claret carmines predominating.

Cromwellian.

Leathers—first natural, cowhide, pigskins, &c.; afterwards showing colouring *on occasions*. Sombre-hued stuffs.

Restoration and Onwards.

Cloths, crewelwork, embroideries (often applied), leathers, mohair, needlework (silk or wool, sometimes compounded), plushes, satins or sateens, silks, tapestries, and velvets. Colour-schemes bright.

NOTE.—English silks and velvets were freely used towards the close of the seventeenth century. Protestant refugee weavers settling in England. Damasks and chintzes, especially under Queen Anne.

Queen Anne Period to 1765.

Brocades, chintzes (especially on loose or squab cushions), damasks, horsehair, moroccos, &c., tent-stitch or *petit-point* and coarser needlework, satins, silks, velvets (plain or figured).

1765 Onwards.

Printed cottons and linens, coloured cottons and linens, painted or printed silks, dimity, morine or moreen, taberray.

NOTE.—" Manchester stuffs," mainly cottons, became very popular towards the close of the century. French trimmings, too, were greatly in favour.

These lists must not be construed in a hard-and-fast manner, as it would be incorrect, for example, to assume that horsehair was popular in Queen Anne times, that brocades might not come under the headings of the earlier silks on occasion, or that taffeta was not used until after 1765.

There was a strong similarity between many of the earlier woven materials and their successors as we know them to-day, and this guide is compiled from experience of the old-time coverings, hangings, and draperies, and from the recommendations of writers who spoke of the fashions of their day.

A few words of comment are called for in order that the collector may be saved some little trouble when applying the process of exhaustion to get at what he or she may require.

A rich old red velvet nearly always looks well on early Jacobean chairs. Velvets, although perhaps permissible, never seem to suit Chippendale.

Needlework is par excellence *the* covering for late Stuart, Queen Anne, and Chippendale models. A clever restorer will frequently be able to give new life to an apparently hopeless piece of work. The writer is indebted for some skilled work in this direction to the Royal School of Art Needlework, South Kensington.

Cowhide or pigskin invariably looks well on Cromwellian furniture, and both gain tone with age and wear. Horsehair usually goes well with stuff-over, saddle-shaped Chippendale seats and with stuff-over mahogany Heppelwhite or Sheraton models. It may not be striking, but it will never be offensive—to look at. For Chippendale, morocco may be in a bright—almost to sealing-wax—red, in a soft sage to myrtle green, or in blue. The old masters used to recommend the scarlet or daring colour. The green is safe, and the writer favours it, whilst blue leather is of questionable value. Some collectors have satisfied themselves with pigskin. Roans may be substituted for morocco at a slight saving where the seats are wide and demand the largest skins; their wear, however, is hardly so satisfactory.

In the soft materials a rich old-rose colour is the best, and when this is not obtainable a soft, mellow green will prove satisfactory.

Satinwood demands delicate hues, the most favoured of which are soft green, rose, or light blue shades. Adam models should be re-upholstered with Adam patterns, which are now readily obtainable in the form of clever reproductions. Sheraton models look well in striped materials, and may be covered in materials of Adam type.

Heppelwhite chairs, settees, &c., may be treated as though they belonged to either of the two foregoing and kindred styles.

Many of the light French reproductions of the Louis Seize order show off Adam, Heppelwhite, or Sheraton furniture to advantage.

For berdroom furniture, chintzes with festoons of flowers, &c., look bright and clean, and these, together with cottons or linens, may *correctly* be used on late eighteenth-century models. Chintz covers look well on most easy chairs from the Queen Anne " grandfather " (or wing) chairs onwards.

The late eighteenth-century masters laid particular stress on the desirability of obtaining complete sympathy between curtains and chair-coverings, &c., frequently advocating that seats and curtains should be from the same material. Many collectors purchase old damask or brocade curtains for the express purpose of having correct coverings in hand against the day of need.

Seats should not be too heavily padded, a point which many upholsterers overlook in an effort to achieve comfort. A reference to the chair shown on page 525 shows this mistaken treatment, and the consequent loss in effect which a model may suffer when over-seated. The specimens shown on pages 488 and 537 have been correctly treated, with the result that the woodwork is not interfered with or hidden from sight.

In rooms which face south, and where the light is strong, neutral tints are often desirable. Such shades are not hot and aggressive, neither do they clash with the coloured porcelains, engravings, pictures, or rich-hued furniture which the collector intends to introduce. Grey carpets or felts show off eighteenth-century furniture to especial advantage, and grey or plain brown papers with woodwork painted in stippled white are safe backgrounds for the display of one's treasures.

Mr. J. D. Phillips, our greatest judge of English Gothic furniture, recently made an important find in the shape of a series of original coloured designs for the decoration of Chippendale interiors. Devotees to our greatest master's work will now be able to have their curtains, wallpapers, and colour-schemes reproduced on true lines.

CHAPTER XXVI.
Spindle and Turned-Leg Furniture.

TURNERY has always played an important part in connection with English cabinet and chair work, though its progress met with a somewhat serious check when once the Queen Anne vogue ceased to appeal to Englishmen, and that intractable medium mahogany had come into use but was not yet thoroughly understood. During Tudor and Elizabethan days the productions of the primitive lathes then in use were generally said to have been "thrown," but from the seventeenth century onwards this term was less frequently used, and we generally find lathe work defined as turned work nowadays.

In the eighteenth century very light and attenuated models, such as those illustrated on pages 671-2-4-5-7, enjoyed a considerable vogue, and for purposes of differentiation this light and graceful class is commonly spoken of as spindle-work, spindle-leg, spider-leg, &c.

King's College, Cambridge, possesses some of the finest of this early turned work in the balustered columns which grace the Provost's and adjoining stalls in its beautiful chapel, and the Elizabethan, Jacobean, Cromwellian, Restoration, and Queen Anne vogues all brought excellent types in their train, the apogee of the turner's art occurring between 1690-1715.

Turned members were intended either to stand as an integral part of the cabinet-maker's ultimate scheme, as in the legwork to the chair on page 117, or to provide a rounded surface for the carver or inlayer to work upon, as in the case of the bulbous swells to the buffet on page 45, or in that of the knife-urns shown on page 540. They

Oak Gate-table, showing action subsequently favoured by the Mahogany School. Circa 1670.

were thus of primary or secondary importance, as they fulfilled decorative and constructional duties at once, or merely afforded a surface for subsequent decoration. Knife-urns were first of all glued up in sections by the cabinet-hand, then passed on to the turner, who handed them on to the inlayer or carver.

In the case of the legwork shown on page 117 the

Spindle and Turned-Leg Furniture.

whole credit of the scheme goes to the turner, but in that of the swells shown on page 45 so much chisel work has been brought into play that they have passed from the province of the turner to that of the carver. In the case

Early Spindle Writing-table surmounted by two Globe-stands.

of the knife-urns, though credit is due to the cabinet-maker who built up the frames and subsequently fitted them so cleverly, and to the inlayer who decorated them, the main triumph belongs to the turner under whose guiding hand the models assumed such graceful form.

After the Queen Anne vogue had had its day turnery languished for awhile, for our great eighteenth-century masters did not display a liking for it. Chippendale

Lady's Writing-table surmounted by bowl and candlestands.

favoured the process for a bedpost or for a tripod column, but even then the carver hid the efforts of the turner pretty frequently. The Adams eschewed the practice as a rule, though plain-turned pateræ or rounded legwork

Spindle and Turned-Leg Furniture.

savouring of the lathe may, of course, be found on their designs. Heppelwhite was by far the most successful user of turnery when we judge results under the law of average, for he gave us many pleasing suggestions with but few indefensible ones. Sheraton was the least happy of all, for though he produced some few admirable types, his later work was wrapped up with execrable patterns.

Spindle furniture is a genus perfectly distinct from the *recognised* production of our great designers, and with it we only get a faint indication here and there of any given influence. Tables, the commonest of all models in this work, show that there was continuity of purpose in matters constructional as between the years 1650 and 1800. A reference to the illustrations on pages 670-1-2-4-7 will make it evident that the principles which governed the gate action of the first piece in oak were applied to the succeeding types in mahogany, and that the proportions of the eighteenth-century pieces were uniformly light and graceful.

Spindle-ware is delicate and commendably simple. Its delicacy has contributed to its rarity, whilst its simplicity has, unfortunately, led to its being neglected by that large body of collectors preferring ornate to unpretentious furniture. For many years the market has been flooded with reproductions, a fact which has militated against a due appreciation of the genuine pieces, and which renders the closest scrutiny necessary when purchases are being made.

Original and untouched surface condition must be a *sine qua non* with intending buyers. Genuine bits which have been mended and repolished may be put out of court by this precautionary standard, but it is the only wise step to enforce on one's judgment if mistakes are to be avoided.

Spindle-work was introduced into most light articles of furniture; it figured freely in many of the old-time chairs, even in settee-backs; but it is oftenest met with in old tables, fire-screens, towel-rails, and basin-stands. Strictly speaking, it was rectilinear as to outline, though in some instances curvilinear treatment shows its influence, notice-

Exceptionally fine Cluster Table, with veneered top and moulded edges. Nearly all specimens in mahogany have plain, solid tops. Circa 1780.

ably in such dainty little specimens as the tripod wig-stands which Chippendale created. The usual finish to the column was formed by a light astragal, above which rose a plain capital exactly similar to those which appear in Cassington Church, Oxon. (dating from 1120). Any influence which the English masters asserted is apparent in (1) the foot, (2) the shape of the column, and, to a

Spindle and Turned-Leg Furniture.

lesser degree, in the finials which grace the uprights of such pieces as we see represented by the towel-rail here illustrated.

Beautiful Towel-rail, the square facets to which are finely inlaid after the manner of Shearer or Sheraton. Circa 1780.

Many readers may not realise the difficulties which beset the workmen of 1720 or thereabouts when confronted with the task of manipulating dainty models in the new medium—mahogany. These conscientious craftsmen would only work in thoroughly seasoned timber, and hard old Spanish wood of the quality used in the second quarter of the eighteenth century more than taxed the tools of men used to handling walnut, chestnut, and softer timbers only, with now and then a piece of oak. If anyone should doubt, let him endeavour to cleave one or two plain pieces of the wood and watch the vagaries of the grain. He will note it flying off at a tangent right or left handed, with no indication on its surface to enable him safely to gauge its intentions.

Rarity of the Work.

The rarity of genuine examples is attributable to two causes : (1) the ravages of Time on models necessarily fragile; (2) the disfavour into which they fell during the crazes for ornate decoration which passed over the country 1750-1820, and later during the Victorian era. Now and then we find a card-table in spindle-work surviving, but it is generally in a rickety and unsound condition. The delicate maze of under-framing could not stand the kicks which players' feet imposed, nor was the bed of the table of sufficient body to carry the hinge soundly, or to resist its tendency to warp when standing in the sun or near a blazing fire. More rarely still we meet with little hanging shelves which were meant to house books or display china. The only genuine successes, when judged by resistance to fair, if hard, wear-and-tear, are the basin-stands, towel-horses, screens, and small occasional tables.

Many are the terms used to describe this class of work : butterfly, spider-leg, spindle-leg, cluster-leg, eight-

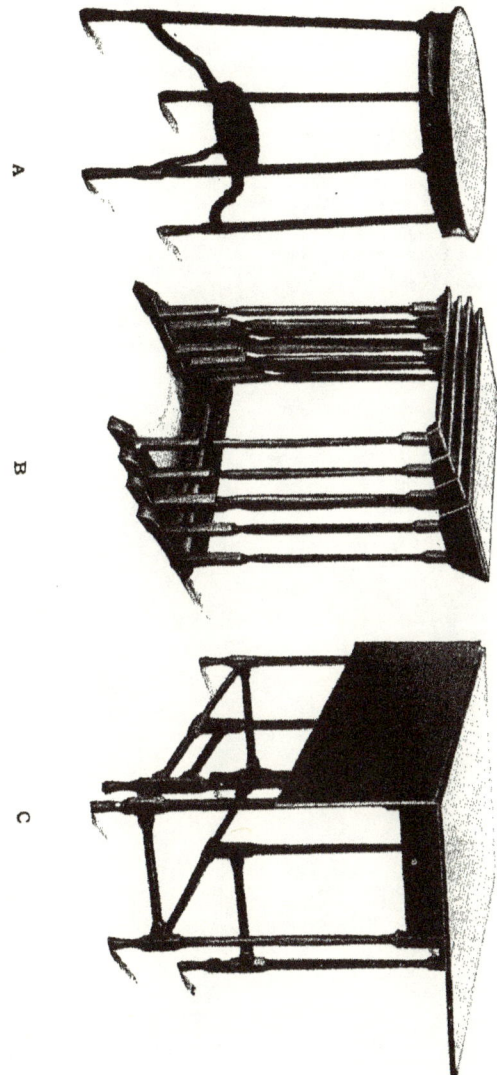

A. Oval Urn Table suggestive of Heppelwhite influence.
B. Nest of Tables, sometimes known as "Hen and Chickens" or as a "Set of Coffee Tables."
C. Large Table, probably country-made.

leg, or gate-leg would possibly be applied to the same tea-table by six collectors selected at haphazard.

When 1800 arrived, cabinet-makers began to employ rosewood in lieu of mahogany, and from this time forward models began to show decadence. By 1810 designs had become stilted and ungraceful. Collectors should eschew all models save those in mahogany, other fine woods having been so rarely employed as to represent practically a negligible quantity.

The first indications of outline decadence are to be found in the feet platforms which carried the little columns on models following the idea shown in the " hen and chickens " type, B on page 677. In the early essays these were plain, and they were subordinated to the columns they supported. As the Trafalgar and Waterloo phases arrived these platforms were raised to admit of the addition of the weak and unfortunate foot outline characteristic of the times.

It is questionable whether any elaboration was called for, but the ugly concave sweeps which came into favour by 1810 were ill calculated to set off these dainty pieces, and these false curves only served to distract the eye from the fine lines of the superstructures above them.

Late types of these sets of tables are to be met with in lacquer of Oriental pattern, occasionally burdened with brass mounts in sympathy with Empire teachings.

Spindle and turned pieces were produced by the old pole lathe, which, when compared with our modern appliances, was very hard to manipulate, and demanded much greater skill and finesse in its management.

CHAPTER XXVII.
Miscellanea.

Gilt Furniture.

It may have been noticed that, with the possible exception of mirrors, little has been said on the question of gilded furniture. The omission has not been an oversight, but as the vogue in question was not truly artistic, the writer has deliberately passed it over with the minimum of comment and emphasis. Less characteristic of British craftsmanship at its best than any other treatment, gilding frequently conferred a bizarre and ornate effect on the models to which it was applied. We find gilt furniture from the seventeenth century in comparative profusion, but it made for nothing good or new in applied art, and we see our early craftsmen in a happier light when examining early examples wherein the process was eschewed or, at any rate, sparingly employed. Old gilding was cleverly applied and only good materials were utilised. When contrasted with later work the old, which has mellowed with time, appears to be singularly unaggressive, and it blends better with various coloured schemes.

For half a century, dating from the days of Charles II., we find models, such as cabinet-stands or high-backed chairs, gilded all over, even to the cane in the seat and back-splats of the latter. In the days of Queen Anne gilding seems to have reached its climax, and it would be comparatively easy to furnish rooms entirely with this particular work. The gilt was applied over soft and inferior woods, and was of such good quality that we find it in good order to-day where it has been fairly used. We also meet with gilding in conjunction with walnut. Perhaps the best examples of this particular phase are the small hanging mirrors with a gilt eagle crowning them which we all know so well.

During the early days of mahogany we still find this picking-out of detail in gold; but the beautiful wood, although it served as an excellent background or foil to gilded decoration, certainly lost caste as the result of what can only be considered to have been an unfortunate scheme. Pedestals of Louis Quatorze character were fairly often subjected to this treatment. Chippendale favoured gilding for some particular models, such as side-tables and mirrors, but he seldom prostituted mahogany in the process. During the last quarter of the eighteenth century all our masters resorted to gilding, but the models so embellished during this latter phase did not, as a rule, carry the same volume of gilding as did those of the Queen Anne era, if we except such models as mirrors, girandoles, torchères, &c.

The fashion beloved by exponents of the Sheraton and late Adam school gave purchasers cabinets, chairs, side-tables, &c., &c., with detail and legs picked out in gold over pine or composition. During this phase garish results were achieved in a blind and slavish effort after Italian, French, or other alien effects.

Stained and Ivory Furniture.

Staining soft and inferior woods in imitation of mahogany was a common feature of eighteenth-century work, but it seems to have been chiefly resorted to by the smaller craftsmen of the period. Mahogany was obtainable after 1725, and the inferior woods (which were of a more perishable character) were used because they were cheaper in the first place and then easier to carve.

We meet with ivory furniture of the English school on rare occasions; sometimes the ivory is solid, at others it is veneered over wood. Small models of late seventeenth-century make are happened on now and then, and these usually carry engraved embellishment. Typical Chippendale and Sheraton chairs in ivory or ivory-veneer also exist, and as some of the earliest noted of the former *came back from India*, it was at first thought that plain chairs had been experimentally decorated in that country after their receipt from England. Although this treatment of ivory veneering may on occasion have been meted out to consigned chairs, it is obvious that some English craftsmen made a speciality of such furniture, for specimens of undoubted character and authenticity exist which have never left these shores. Although English pieces in ivory often exhibit the cleverest of turnery and the most delicate of engraving, they confer a somewhat chilly appearance on the room in which they are placed. Genuine examples show the deepened tone which the medium assumes with age.

Retrospect.

When glancing back over the work of the eighteenth-century masters, one very strange fact presents itself, viz., that all the better-known men came originally from the provinces; thus the Chippendales hailed from Worcester, the Adams from Kirkcaldy, Heppelwhite probably from Durham, and Sheraton from Stockton-on-Tees.

Now it will be noticed that all these homes were distant from London, and it may be more than a coincidence which brought these great craftsmen to the head of their profession. Living, as they originally did, in the remoter corners of the kingdom, they were less under Continental influence as youths, and therefore thrown, perhaps, more on their own resources at the early and all-important period when they were embracing their profession.

It will be said that the great Chippendale enjoyed no provincial training, since his eyes were opened to the rudiments of his profession in London. Still, he was brought up under the guidance of his parent, a carver born and trained in Worcestershire. Be this as it may, each one of these masters preserved throughout his career a distinctly British method of handling alien or extraneous matter. Classic, French, Chinese, or Gothic outline or detail was materially anglicised under the pencil or chisel of our greater craftsmen, and it would seem that the seeds of a sound and thoroughly English grounding in their craft came happily to fruition in after-years. But if this contention be somewhat hypothetical, there is another feature of this school of English craftsmanship which is incontrovertible yet far more strange. All of our master-craftsmen gave England the best of their work when developing the style with which they were *primarily* identified, and each showed a serious falling-off when he was off with the old love and on with the new.

One would have expected to find mannerisms smoothed down, greater breadth of treatment, and increasing discrimination combined with enhanced purity of purpose following in the wake of experience, but all our designers seem to have been imbued with one great purpose, to which they gave happy expression, and then to have descended to less pleasing types.

To this somewhat sweeping statement exception might be taken in the case of George Heppelwhite, who was successful alike in the Louis Quinze and Louis Seize, but even his decadence became marked when he endeavoured to conform more closely to the rectilinear handling of the latter school.

Whilst we are on the general subject of eighteenth-century craftsmanship, there is one point which the writer would especially like to press home. One frequently hears such pernicious expressions as " a splendid example, carved all over, covered with painting or smothered in inlay," and far too many collectors bow the knee to over-decorated specimens which would come within one or other of the foregoing categories.

Were taste of high order the rule rather than the exception, such recommendations would not carry force in their train, but so long as the demand is loud for ornate work, *because it is ornate*, the merits of purer and less pretentious specimens will too often be overlooked.

The discriminating collector will welcome the handiwork of all our great craftsmen conceived in either simple or complex vein, and no collection can be thoroughly complete or interesting when its owner, making a fetish of over-elaboration, has neglected the triumphs of refinement and simplicity in a quest for redundancy of detail.

More about the " Worm."

Since the earlier passages on the " worm " pest were written, Mr. Alfred Hardcastle has concluded an exhaustive series of experiments having for their object the discovery of the safest and most efficient manner of

Miscellanea.

dealing with the scourge. With his kind permission these recipes are now given with a few comments as to the manner of application. *For worm in oak*: Petrol, 1 pint; naphthaline, 2 oz.; crush and dissolve. Dress thoroughly two or three times, avoiding naked lights or propinquity to fires during and immediately after operations. *Worm in mahogany veneers*—sappy mahogany—and all *polished* fine woods (including walnut): Paraffin, 1 pint; thymol, ½oz.; dissolve thoroughly. Dress once or twice, allowing an interval of twenty-four hours. Formalin—40 per cent. formic aldehyde solution—applied as in the case of the paraffin-thymol mixture, is also of use, but is rather more expensive as an alternative.

Where the mischief is confined to surfaces which are not exposed to view, either of these dressings would be effective on worm-eaten specimens. It is, however, difficult to avoid running the solution over the exposed surfaces of the models under treatment, and in the light of this Mr. Hardcastle enjoins:

1. Paraffin and thymol should not be used on oak, owing to the fact that the wood may be rendered too dark by the soaking in of oil.

2. Petrol and naphthaline should not be applied to polished pieces, as gum or lac varnishes, &c., are very susceptible to the attacks of spirit.

3. To make assurance doubly sure, it is advisable to give a further dressing after an interval of a fortnight, with a view to annihilating larvæ, &c., undestroyed by the initial dressing or dressings.

Paint Removal.

Mr. Hardcastle considers that the best method for removing paint from *flat* surfaces is to cover the portion needing treatment with American potash, avoiding the lime which is so generally used. The potash should be mixed up into a poultice with sawdust, and it is also a good plan to melt soft soap and stir it up with a strong potash solution. This alternative mixture should be of the consistence of paint, and should be thickly applied where necessary.

Once the paint has been removed, the properties of the alkali necessitate a corrective, and the wood should be wiped dry and then rubbed over with vinegar. The acid will neutralise the possible ill-effects of the potash and the virtues of the wood may be restored to something like their original state by assiduous hand-polishing (and the use of a little oil in the case of mahogany). If potash or soda is used without the corrective referred to, the wood turns to a grey or ashen hue.

Mr. Hardcastle points out that when carved work is being cleaned, potash or any wash containing water should not be employed. The use of such cleansers swells the grain of the wood, disturbs the softened edges of the relief work, and quite modernises the appearance of all embellishment. There are several restoratives and washes on the market which possess value, and the best of these would seem to be built up on a basis of ether. Adams Polish is said to have excellent results on walnut and mahogany.

CHAPTER XXVIII.
On Prices.

Collectors and Collecting.

THOSE who appreciate old English furniture may be divided into two classes to commence with, namely, those who collect it and those who from utilitarian motives realise that it may well be employed to furnish their homes. The collector is always a collector, but of his class there are many grades. The furnisher usually becomes a collector sooner or later. It is quite possible for the individual with slender means but who is possessed of taste, application, energy, and patience to form a most interesting and valuable collection: it is more than probable that the man who allows the strength of his purse to do duty for the other virtues will get together an accumulation of pieces rather than a collection proper.

It has been said that the intelligent pursuer of the arts and crafts is born and not made, but application and study will improve the powers and develop the capacity for enjoyment in every devotee of the antique. Some persons collect, or pose as collectors, because they consider it the right thing to do; but their case is hopeless unless they are guided in their work by some friend who possesses knowledge and taste. Yet again there are many who lack enterprise or doubt their own judgment, and who consequently let many a chance of filling a gap in their collection slip through their fingers. Dealing first of all with the case as it presents itself to those who elect to purchase old furniture for use in the home, one may premise that there are always plenty of models to be acquired at bargain prices, such as old chests of drawers, bureaus, &c., which are practically as good as new. The initial cost of these, when we consider the different value of money then obtaining, approximated to the prices now ruling for them, whilst their reproduction to-day would involve far greater expense than that at which they may now be purchased.

In order that this may be understood, lists of prices for late eighteenth-century work are appended, and the reader must remember that the sovereign then represented between £2 and £3 of our twentieth-century money.

The prices for carcase work are shown first of all, and then the supplementary charges, but to these items have to be added the cost of timber, handles, locks, hinges, and fine woods for inlaying purposes, and it must be remembered that the list of complementary extras, handed in by the craftsman, often trebled the cost of the framework in the case of good but not extravagantly-finished furniture.

To the sum total thus arrived at must be added the cost of designing in the case of out-of-the-way pieces, and always a proportion of establishment charges, together with the vendor's trade profit. When everything has been reckoned up and due allowance made for the excellence of the outer timbers and linings, and for the soundness of construction, it will be apparent to the furnisher that his purchases, if intelligently made, have been amply justified and constitute the best of value.

A perusal of these old scales discloses the reason for the rarity of serpentine models, which always entailed a heavy expenditure on carcase work and garnishment. They were, if anything, less useful than those in simpler shapes, and this fact, coupled with their great cost, evidently led to their being considered somewhat in the light of luxuries. Their rarity as compared with rectilinear, bow-fronted, or break-fronted specimens, and their incomparable charm of outline, have endeared them to collectors, and the mere furnisher may consequently find them beyond his means.

Furniture of the period under consideration was built to last, and apologists for modern work fail to appreciate that secrets and devices were once passed on from father to son, from generation to generation, and that sterling work came naturally to the apprentices, who were surrounded by an atmosphere of conscientious talent. Nowadays the workman who wished to supply the best of work would have to begin to teach himself at a time when his forbears had mastered the rudiments of their calling, as ducks take to water, and he would be further discouraged by the competition of machinery and of showy goods made with the express purpose of catching the public eye.

These prices were the standard ones for *plain* carcase work in mahogany, all decorations extra, and were, of course, exclusive of *all materials*. When the models were executed in satinwood 2s. 6d. extra in the £ was charged, and where the medium was king, tulip, rose, snake, zebra, yew, or maple the cost was 20 per cent. higher than the foregoing quotations.

The author has been so frequently asked questions as to the original net cost of English furniture that he has deemed it advisable to set out some of the standard prices paid for work handed in by London craftsmen at the close of the eighteenth century :—

Prices for making Carcases only.

	£	s.	d.
A Dressing Chest, 3ft. long, four drawers	0	18	0
A Round-front Dressing Chest, 3ft. long	1	6	0
A Serpentine Dressing Chest, 3ft. long	1	17	0
A Serpentine-fronted Dressing Chest, 4ft. long	3	11	0
A Serpentine-fronted Dressing Chest, 4ft. long, but with shaped ends	4	10	0
A Kneehole Dressing Chest, 3ft. long, six short drawers	1	10	0
A Round-front Dressing Chest, 3ft. long, six short drawers	2	0	0
A Serpentine Dressing Chest, 3ft. long, six short drawers	2	12	0
A Secretary, 3ft. 6in. long, six small drawers	2	2	0
A Round-front Secretary, 3ft. 6in. long, six small drawers	2	16	6
A Serpentine Secretary, 3ft. 6in. long, six small drawers	3	11	0
A Bureau, 2ft. 8in. long, four front drawers and inside fittings	1	12	0
A Tallboy, 3ft. 6in. long, 6ft. 4in. high, eight drawers	2	4	0
A Round-front Tallboy, 3ft. 6in. long, 6ft. 4in. high, eight drawers	3	5	0
A Low Clothes Press, 4ft. long, two doors	1	14	0
A Round-front Low Clothes Press, 4ft. long, two doors	3	15	0
A Straight-front Library Bookcase, 5ft. long, 8ft. high	3	12	0
Another, 6ft. long, 8ft. high, more elaborate	5	15	0
A Serpentine-front Cabinet, 4ft. long, 5ft. high	4	16	0
A Cylinder-fall Writing Table, 3ft. long, £2 11s. and	2	18	0
A Tambour Writing Table, 3ft. long, 2ft. 2in. deep	1	10	6
A Tambour Desk, 3ft. long, three drawers	2	8	0
A Library Writing Table, 3ft. 6in. by 2ft. 6in.	3	12	0
A Kneehole Library Writing Table, 4ft. by 2ft.	2	8	0
A Serpentine Library Writing Table	3	15	0
A Circular Library Writing Table, 3ft. 6in. diam.	1	15	6
A Kidney Library Writing Table	5	2	0

On Prices.

	£	s.	d.
A Gentleman's Library Writing Table, 4ft. 6in. by 2ft. 6in.	8	0	0
A Lady's Writing Fire Screen	0	16	0
A Gentleman's Writing Fire Screen	2	8	0
A Harlequin Table, 2ft. 9in. long, 3ft. high ...	3	6	0
A Pembroke Table, 2ft. 3in. by 3ft. when open ...	0	10	6
Card Tables, square, 7s. 6d.; round, 10s. 6d.; with Ovolo corners...	0	15	0
A Square-fronted Pier Table, 3ft. by 1ft. 6in. ...	1	5	0
An Enclosed Pier Table, 3ft. 6in. by 1ft. 6in. ...	2	10	0
A Straight-fronted Celleret Sideboard, 5ft. by 2ft. 6in.	1	9	0
A Round-fronted Celleret Sideboard, 5ft. by 2ft. 6in.	2	2	0
A Serpentine-fronted Celleret Sideboard, 5ft. by 2ft. 6in.	2	6	0
A Circular Celleret Sideboard, 5ft. long	2	16	0
A Straight-front Sideboard Table, 4ft. 6in. by 2ft. 6in.	0	10	0
A Round-front Sideboard Table, 4ft. 6in. by 2ft. 6in.	0	15	0
A Serpentine-front Sideboard table, 4ft. 6in. by 2ft. 6in.	0	17	0
An Elliptical-front Sideboard Table, 4ft. 6in. by 2ft. 6in.	1	9	0
An Elliptical Sideboard, 5ft. by 2ft. 6in.	3	0	0
An Elliptical Sideboard, ogee ends, 5ft. by 2ft. 6in.	3	6	0
A Pedestal, 3ft. high, 1ft. 4in. square	0	12	0
A Vase for same (glued up for the turner)	0	6	0
A Half-round Dining Table, 4ft. long	0	11	0
A Horseshoe Dining Table, 7ft. long, 2ft. 6in. wide	2	5	0
A Lady's Dressing Table, 2ft. 6in. long, 1ft. 6in. wide	1	5	6
A Lady's Dressing Table, 2ft. 9in. long, 1ft. 8in. wide	3	3	0
A Rudd Dressing Table, 3ft. 4in. long, 2ft. wide	3	3	0
A Bason Stand, 1ft. square	0	4	4
A Bason Stand, enclosed, 1ft. 2in. square	0	14	0
A Corner Bason Stand	0	13	0
A Corner enclosed Bason Stand	1	10	0
A Cylinder-fall Wash-hand Table	2	10	0

	£	s.	d.
A Shaving Stand, as shaping, &c., became more complicated, £1 1s., £1 7s., £1 11s., £2 5s., and	2	6	0
A Counting-house Desk, 3ft. 6in. by 2ft. 4in. ...	1	0	0
An Oval Work Table ...	0	6	6
A Square Urn Stand ...	0	4	3
An Oval Urn Stand ...	0	8	0
A Serpentine Urn Stand ...	0	10	6
A Square Celleret ...	0	7	6
An Oblong Octagonal Celleret ...	1	0	0
An Oval Celleret, £1 2s. or, larger ...	1	18	0
Plain Oval Trays, 3s. and ...	0	7	6
Towel and Clothes Horses, from 2s. 6d. to ...	0	10	0
A Horse Fire Screen ...	0	8	0
A Screen Dressing Glass Frame ...	1	1	0
A Butler's Tray, 2ft. by 1ft. 8in. ...	0	2	6
A Gentleman's Portable Desk ...	1	10	0
A Vase Knife Case, £1 9s., £1 18s., £2 1s. 6d, and	2	4	0
Tea Caddies, square, 2s. 3d.; double square, 3s. 3d.; hexagon, 2s. 9d.; double hexagon, 3s. 3d.; octagon, 3s.; double octagon, 4s.; oval, 4s. 3d.			
An Oval Tea Chest, 8½in. by 5½in., fitted ...	1	4	0
A Tambour Inkstand, 7s., 10s., or ...	0	10	6
A Tambour Inkstand, combined with Dressing Case	0	16	6
Dispensaries (to hold drugs), 13s. 6d., 15s., 17s. 6d., 21s., 23s., 27s. 6d. and ...	2	7	0
(These small pieces make good coin or egg cabinets.)			
A Dumb Waiter ...	0	4	0
A Plate Carrier, 12in. deep, 13in. diameter ...	0	13	0
A Lady's Workstand, 2ft. 6in. high ...	0	3	3
A Lady's Writing Box, 10in. by 6in. ...	0	3	6
A Canted Corner Work Table, 1ft. by 1ft. 4in. ...	0	7	0
A Sliding Fire Screen, 4ft. 4in. high by 1ft. 10in.	1	1	0
A Moving Library or Bookstand, 2ft. 6in. long, 3ft. high ...	0	16	0

Mouldings.

Cornice mouldings cost for labour from 6d. to 1s. on straight work, from 1s. 2d. to 1s. 8d. on circular work,

On Prices.

or from 1s. 6d. to 2s. when this was hollow, and from 1s. 4d. to 1s. 9d. on serpentine work *per foot* on plain models, with heavy extras for base, surbase and top mouldings, ogees, block eye or fret dentils, and applied pear-drop decoration. From 7d. to 1s. 1d. per foot was allowed for the cutting of Gothic fret embellishment.

The scales of remuneration were worked out minutely. Thus we read of items of 1s. $6\frac{1}{4}$d. per foot for the working of a "toadback moulding" with beads, and of $8\frac{1}{4}$d. per foot for a moulding consisting of two beads and a hollow, the former of which rose to 1s. $8\frac{1}{2}$d. in the case of light models such as flower or candle stands.

The two beads and hollows peculiar to Marlborough legs rose from $1\frac{1}{4}$d. to 4d., according to the size of the model, and the reeding from $1\frac{1}{2}$d. to 5d.; but when working to a taper the scale ran from $2\frac{1}{4}$d. to 7d. For veneering these extremities lengthwise and crossway the cost varied from 1d. to $2\frac{1}{2}$d. and from $1\frac{1}{2}$d. to 4d. respectively.

From 5d. to 2s. 6d. apiece was allowed for forming a single string panel, and for the therming of legs the piece ranged from 4d. to 1s. 8d. apiece as the pattern became more complex.

Banding and Stringing.

For forming small ovals or circles by the insertion of strings (as in the case of Sheraton models) the scale worked out at from $3\frac{1}{2}$d. to 8d. for small work, and $1\frac{1}{2}$d. to $3\frac{1}{2}$d. per foot for large examples. Threepence per foot was sanctioned for crossbanding, with an allowance of from $\frac{1}{2}$d. to $\frac{3}{4}$d. for each mitre. The lowest scale charge for this banding appears to have worked out at $1\frac{3}{4}$d. per foot, and the highest at $6\frac{3}{4}$d.

Square panels were marked out with a single string at a cost of 4d. with an extra charge of ½d. for each foot after the first; the charge for a double string was 5d., with ¾d. for each extra foot; and treble stringed panels were 6d., with 1d. for each additional foot.

Cross or Long Banding Oval or Circle Panels.

On flat surfaces an oval 4in. long with a single stringing cost 9d., and one between 4in. and 6in. in length 11d.; larger types cost from 4½d. to 7d. per foot with the banding ½in. or less in width; from 5d. to 7½d. when the band was from ½in. to 1in. wide; from 5½d. to 8d. when the band gauged 1in. to 1½in.; and from 6d. to 8½d. when the banding measured over 1½in.

On hollow or round surfaces the prices ranged from 8½d. to 11d., from 9d. to 11½d., from 9½d. to 1s., or from 10d. to 1s. 0½d., according to whether the diameter of the inlaid band was ½in., 1in., 1½in., or 2in., with a single string at each side.

Fluting.

Small common flutes were paid for at the rate of 4d. per dozen cross-ways, or 5d. per dozen long-ways, when they measured 1½in. or under, 5d. or 6d. similarly when they were over 1½in. and up to 3in., 6d. or 7d. when between 3in. and 4½in., and 7d. or 8d. when their length went from 4½in. to 6in.

Long flutes were settled for at so much per flute, 1d. being allowed for one under 10in. but over 6in., 1¾d. for one between 18in. and 22in., 2¾d. when the length exceeded 34in. but did not exceed 38in., and so on.

(These flutes were commonly inserted on cornice or table friezes, on pilaster or legwork, &c.)

Inlaid Flutes.

These were inserted at 10d., 1s., 1s. 2d., or 1s. 4d. per dozen, according to whether the flutes measured 1½in., 3in., 4in., or 6in. or under, 2d. extra per dozen being allowed when they were in any way tapered. Long flutes of 6in. or over involved an outlay of from 2d. to 8½d. apiece, according to their size; and where legwork was turned and so presented swells which the inlayer had to negotiate, the scale of charges was proportionately increased.

Veneering.

For preparing and laying the veneer for a panel on a flat surface, the cost was 2d., 4d., 6½d., 9d., 11d., 1s., 1s. 3d., or 1s. 5d., as the length varied from 6in. to 1ft., 1ft. 6in., 2ft., 2ft. 6in., 3ft., 3ft. 6in., or 4ft., similar sized panels on faintly curved surfaces costing 3d., 6d., 10d., 1s. 2d., 1s. 4d., 1s. 6d., 1s. 8d., or 1s. 11d.; and on bold swells 5d., 8½d., 1s. 1d., 1s. 5d., 1s. 7d., 1s. 9d., 1s. 11d., or 2s. 2d. In the case of serpentine surfaces 8d., 11½d., 1s. 4d., 1s. 8d., 1s. 10d., 2s., 2s. 2d., and 2s. 5d. were the standard prices. These quotations were for the plainest of work only, as when the panels were quartered up, as in the case of best work, a 5d. fee would rise to 1s. 6d., with substantial though not proportionate advances for larger work.

Inlaid Ovals.

The collector will have noticed that the fashion for inlaid ovals was very strongly marked during the closing phases of the eighteenth century, since this decoration appears on nearly all the cabinet-work of that period.

For shaping and laying an oval panel on a flat surface the charge was 4d., 7d., 10d., 1s. 1d., 1s. 4½d., 1s. 7d.,

1s. 10½d., or 2s. 2d. according as its extreme length was 6in., 12in., 18in., 24in., 30in., 36in., 42in., or 48in., with an approximate rise of 50 per cent. if the oval was quartered; on a faint curve the prices for similar-sized inlay were 6d., 9d., 1s., 1s. 1½d., 1s. 4d., 1s. 9½d., 2s., 2s. 3½d., or 2s. 8d., with an extra charge of about 25 per cent. for quartered work; on a full, circular or hollow sweep the scale was 8d., 11½d., 1s. 4½d., 1s. 7d., 2s. 0½d., 2s. 3d., 2s. 6½d., or 2s. 11d., with heavy advances for quartering; and on all kinds of serpentine work 9d., 1s. 0½d., 1s. 5½d., 1s. 8d., 2s. 1½d., 2s. 4d., 2s. 7d., or 3s., with extras in some cases amounting to 100 per cent. for quartering.

Astragals.

On plain surfaces 5d., 7d., 9d., 10d., 11d., 1s., 1s. 1d., or 1s. 2d. were the recognised prices for astragals ranging from 1ft. to 4½ft. When the member was hollowed or with round corners the fees rose to 1s. 1d.—1s. 10d. for similar lengths. On circular or hollow sweeps the scale started at 8d. and rose to 2s. 2d.; and on serpentine work with square corners 10d. to 2s. 8d. was allowed. There was a heavy advance for serpentine models where the shaping was with hollow or round corners, for the remuneration was then from 1s. 10d. to 3s. 8d. Oval astragals were the most expensive of all, for they ranged on the plainest surfaces from 1s. 4d. to 3s. 5d.; on circular or hollow sweeps from 1s. 10d. to 6s. 5d.; and on serpentine pieces from 2s. 1d. to 7s. 4d.

Doors to Bookcases, &c.

The cost of the completion of these was a serious item, £2 2s., £2 2s. 6d., £2 7s., £2 13s. 4d. being recognised rates for pairs of lattice doors with crossbanding on each edge, without the astragal work, which often involved an additional outlay of over 10s.

For shamming drawer fronts 2d. to 1s. 3d. apiece was allowed in the plainest work (most Pembroke tables have one real and one shammed drawer front), and the scale rose rapidly when complicated decoration was called for.

Mitreing Mouldings.

For a mitred moulding to a panel 4in. long the workman was allowed from $2\frac{1}{2}$d. to 4d.; for the mitreing of an octagon, $6\frac{1}{2}$d. to 8d., rising to 1s. $7\frac{1}{2}$d. when the work became complicated. Diamond panels ran from 4d. to $5\frac{1}{2}$d. under this heading, and the charge for each 6in. of moulding scaled from $\frac{1}{2}$d. to 1d., with an extra 1d. per foot when these were in ebony, rosewood, satinwood, or other hard wood.

Oiling and Polishing.

The charges herein were most reasonable, and it is almost impossible to imagine how such excellent work was done for so little money. A sum of 2s. would have covered the outlay on the largest of ordinary models, and many pieces were treated for a few pence.

Brass Fittings.

One penny each was the allowance for common caster fittings, with $2\frac{1}{2}$d. to 3d. when these were let into tableclaws. Handles and rings were let in at $1\frac{1}{4}$d., but lifting handles (at sides of heavy models) were charged for at the rate of 6d. per pair. Pendent rings were let in at $\frac{1}{2}$d. apiece, and escutcheons were affixed at 1d. each.

Auction Prices.

There are several channels through which old furniture may be acquired, but it is doubtful whether the young collector can do better than place himself in the hands of an honest dealer, assuming that he has not the advice of a friend who is an expert to fall back upon. When buying at auctions many collectors allow their feelings to run away with them, with the result that they pay prices far in excess of those which they would give in their saner moments for the self-same articles.

The collector should *not* go by auction prices always, for there are forces at work which render these anything but reliable guides. The "knock-out" has a very depressing influence on bidding, and it has to be reckoned with at almost every country sale; on the other hand, it pays owners of certain stock to *make* prices for isolated pieces of the wares which they are for the time being interested in exploiting. Under these circumstances chairs may be controlled and knocked down to the ring of dealers at £10 apiece which all in the know are aware will command £25 each at the ensuing knock-out, whilst, on the other hand, some Wedgwood vase, which might have been obtained for £10, may be carried up to a considerably higher figure by Brown and Jones because it has been deemed advisable to inflate and call attention to the value of similar specimens already in the possession of those worthies.

The young collector must examine "lots" carefully before the sale commences, seeing that the conditions of the auction very probably leave him with no redress if he bids unwisely. At the sale the tyro should take no notice whatsoever of disparaging remarks dropped by strangers *sotto voce* concerning the "lots" he is interested in. If the collector has, after careful examination, or on the guidance of an experienced judge, decided to bid £10 for a chair and he overhears something to its disadvantage which is obviously thrown out to be heard, he should feel inclined to bid £12 rather than £8. London dealers do *not* go down to the country to stop fools and their money from being parted; they can hardly be styled philanthropists, and they have neither time nor incentive for instituting manœuvres over unimportant "lots" with no margin for profit attaching to them.

If the would-be purchaser *has* knowledge and experience he should fix his limit in cold blood before the auction starts or his "lot" comes up, otherwise he should place his commission with a straightforward dealer, for, despite what has been said, this class of man is to be found. The honest professional may stop his client from making a mistake in the first place, whilst he will provoke less competition from "the trade" and act as a drag on the wheel of amateur excitement. When once you have made up your mind and entrusted your bid do not give indications of your plans by hovering round your agent; leave him to do his duty in his own way, and do not invite the room to run you up, as they assuredly will do if they consider you to be an over-anxious greenhorn.

Some Prices for Collectors' Pieces.

Elizabethan.

Armchair,
Oak, the back being carved with foliage and an arch, with inlaid chequer ornaments. 16 guineas.

Bedstead,
Oak, with carved terminal figures, arches, and floral ornaments, the panels decorated with marquetry. 64 guineas.

Elizabethan (continued).

Buffet,
> Oak, 7ft. 6in. by 6ft. 2in., having carved canopy top and gallery shelf, with lions rampant as supporters. £60.

Chest,
> Oak, having inlaid panels, under arches, with figures of caryatides carved in boxwood. £40.

Jacobean.

Cabinet,
> William III., English marquetry, walnut ground, with folding doors, beautifully inlaid with flowers in vases, birds, and insects; sixteen drawers and cupboard; height 5ft. 9in., width 3ft. 11in. 100 guineas.

Chairs.
> Pair of Charles II. armchairs, oak, having carved foliage and amorini supporting crown, spiral side-rails; legs and stretchers carved. 70 guineas.

> Six Charles II. (from the Anglesey collection), oak, with high backs carved with rosettes, flowers, and foliage; scroll legs, having thereon conventional scrolls; carved stretchers and claw feet. 235 guineas.

> Charles II., oak, back having shaped canework panels; borders and stretchers carved with scroll foliage. 20 guineas.

> James II., oak, carved, with back and seat covered in leather, and studded with brass nails; pierced and carved baluster legs, and carved X-shaped stretcher. 57 guineas.

> Pair of James II., in chestnut, with high backs slightly carved, and having two cane panels; carved cabriole legs and shaped stretchers. 35 guineas.

> Four William and Mary, oak, having open backs and carved with shells and gadroon ornament; carved cabriole legs, hoof feet, and stretchers. 100 guineas.

> Six William and Mary walnut chairs, with high open backs carved with foliage, and inlaid with marquetry in centre; carved cabriole legs, and eagle's-claw feet. 300 guineas.

Jacobean (continued).

Clock.
William III. marquetry long-case clock, by C. Gould, London; chased metal-gilt dial showing day of the month; case inlaid with terminal figures, flowers in vases, birds, and arabesque foliage; height 7ft. 9in. 70 guineas.

Coffer,
Charles II., in carved oak, dated 1681. 18 guineas.

Couch,
Charles II., oak, 5ft. 6in. long, with canework end panels; carved with amorini supporting crowns, flowers, and foliage. £73 10s.

Mirror,
William III., in English marquetry frame, with flowers and foliage beautifully inlaid in coloured woods and ivory on a walnut ground. £43.

Stools.
Pair of Charles II., carved oak, having scroll-top legs and stretchers carved with foliage. 60 guineas.

Pair James II., carved oak, the top embroidery-covered; scroll legs and X-shaped stretcher. 27 guineas.

Queen Anne and Georgian.

Cabinet,
Marquetry, with ten drawers, and a cupboard having one drawer, in a stand having two drawers with scroll-shaped supports, inlaid all over with arabesque foliage; brass drop handles; height 5ft. 5in., width 3ft. 5in. 340 guineas.

Chairs,
Set of twelve, in walnut, on cabriole legs, and with ball-and-claw feet. £1102 10s.

Six singles and two arms, in walnut, lyre-shaped backs, nicely carved with shells and foliage, and with scale-pattern panels; cabriole legs, also carved with foliage, ball-and-claw feet; arms having eagles' heads at their termination. 170 guineas.

Six, in walnut, with carved foliage, cabriole legs, with shell carving and ball-and-claw feet. £173.

Queen Anne and Georgian (continued).

Chair.
Arm-chair, walnut, with carved foliage, the arms having masks as terminals; cabriole legs and lion's-claw feet. £50.

Clock.
Walnut grandfather clock, by P. Wise, London (1693-1726), enriched with marquetry, finely embossed brass dial. £24 13s.

NOTE.—Though this price was actually paid at auction for the piece specified, yet it by no means represents the value of a typical piece, which may realise £50 to £100.

Mirror,
Oblong-shaped, gilt frame, with elegantly carved foliage and gadrooning. £26.

Chippendale.

Bedstead,
Mahogany, having fluted columns as supports and lion's-claw feet. £27.

NOTE.—Fine and representative pieces with decorated cornices may realise several hundreds of pounds.

Bureau-Bookcase,
Mahogany, 7ft. 6in. by 3ft. 6in. and 1ft. 9in. deep; upper portion having carved folding doors; drawers beneath. £33.

Cabinet,
Show, mahogany, 5ft. 10in. by 3ft. 2½in., glazed sides and folding doors, with carved lattice-work borders; legs of the cluster-column type. 72 guineas.

Chairs.
Two, arm, mahogany, having open backs with pierced vase-shaped centres, elegantly carved with scrolls, foliage, flowers, shell and gadroon ornament; carved cabriole legs. 1000 guineas.

Eight, arm, mahogany, in the style of Louis Quinze; boldly carved fluted and scroll arms; cabriole legs and scroll feet. 210 guineas.

Ten, eight singles and two arm, mahogany; backs carved with foliage; carved cabriole legs and ball-and-claw feet. 220 guineas.

Chippendale (continued).

Chairs.

Six singles and one arm, ladder-pattern backs, mahogany, on straight legs with stretchers. 39 guineas.

One, mahogany, with high open back and vase-shaped centre, the top being carved with eagles' heads and shell and scroll ornament; arms having eagles' heads at their termination; cabriole legs, with shell carving. 32 guineas.

Two singles and one arm, mahogany; vase-shaped pierced backs, having carved drapery, tassels, and festoons; cabriole legs, ball-and-claw feet. 32 guineas.

One, mahogany, with elegantly carved drapery, tassels, and foliage; cabriole legs, carved, and ball-and-claw feet. 86 guineas.

Four, arm, mahogany, having interlaced foliage-carved backs; cabriole legs and ball-and-claw feet. £28 7s.

Chest of Drawers.

Tallboy or hautbois set (3ft. 10in. wide, 7ft. high), eight drawers, the whole surmounted by an arched pediment having a carved lattice border. 13 guineas.

Settees.

Mahogany, triple back, 66in. wide; carved with foliage; carved cabriole legs and ball-and-claw feet. 200 guineas.

Two-chair-back, 54in. wide, having scroll top, carved with handsome foliage; arms terminating in masks; legs carved with lions' masks, and terminating in claw feet. 265 guineas.

Tables.

Four-legged, mahogany, with shaped front and ends, marble top, 6ft. 3in. long by 2ft. 9in. wide; massive cabriole legs, boldly carved, and ball-and-claw feet. £195.

Mahogany, having lattice and wave border, with elegantly carved fruit and flowers above the rectangular pierced legs. £262.

Gallery, mahogany, oblong form, 36in. in width, on pierced latticed legs and stretcher similarly treated. 115 guineas.

Tripod, mahogany, circular, with open balustrades; legs carved, on claw feet. 56 guineas.

Chippendale (continued).

Tables.

Gallery, eight-legged, mahogany, 45in. in width, oblong shape, with carved lattice-work frieze and wavy border; legs rectangular, on pierced feet. £257.

Square, mahogany, having folding ends, openwork Gothic border, and latticed corners; legs of cluster-column type. 68 guineas.

Gallery, mahogany, 32in. in width, straight legs, having pierced X-shaped stretcher. 26 guineas.

Gallery (two), mahogany, 27in. long, with lattice borders and legs. 60 guineas.

Tray top, mahogany, 24in. by 21in., with pierced lattice-work sides and square legs also similarly pierced. 55 guineas.

Tripod, mahogany, square tray top, nicely carved with foliage, on openwork pillar. £112.

Card, mahogany, 31in. in width, cabriole legs, carved, on ball-and-claw feet. 18 guineas.

Tripod, gallery, mahogany, 32in. across, with carved border; legs carved with foliage, on claw feet. £60 18s.

Side, mahogany, 2ft. 10in. wide, surmounted by veined-white marble slab; carved with trellis-pattern, rosettes, foliage, &c., cabriole legs, with ball-and-claw feet. £320.

Console, mahogany, 63in. wide, with grey marble top; frieze boldly carved with flowers, scrolls, &c., and with terminal masks at the corners; legs carved, and having eagle's-claw feet. 190 guineas.

Kneehole writing, 5ft. 4in. wide, elaborately carved with flowers and foliage, and with gold decoration; metal-gilt handles; on feet. £210.

Side, mahogany, 4ft. 6in. wide; sides and front carved with masks, roses, acorns, shells, &c.; shaped legs, with claw feet. £100.

Pedestal, writing, mahogany, 5ft. wide, eighteen drawers, with fine ormolu mounts. £550.

On Prices.

Chippendale (continued).

Tables.

Writing, mahogany, with nicely carved shell ornament, gadrooned; cabriole legs and claw feet. £37 16s.

Console, mahogany, with frieze boldly carved with oak leaves and fruits, birds, and a basket of fruit; carved cabriole legs and lion's-claw feet. 145 guineas.

Tea-Caddy.

Mahogany, 10in. square, with four divisions, the borders beautifully carved with ribands and rosettes; at sides, oblong Worcester plaques painted with exotic birds, flowers, insects, &c. £52 10s.

Wine-Cooler.

Oval, bound with brass and having handles of a similar metal; on stand with square legs. 7 guineas.

Chinese Chippendale.

Chairs.

Pair arm-chairs, mahogany, backs carved with foliage and having pagoda-formed tops; borders carved with interlaced ribands and rosettes. 80 guineas.

Mahogany, scroll top, square, open back, with interlaced key-pattern centre. 17 guineas.

Pair of arm-chairs, mahogany; backs of rectangular form, having trellis-work centres; arms also rectangular; tops slightly carved. 32 guineas.

Pair of arm-chairs with pierced backs, lacquered in black and gold; arms having eagles' heads at their terminations; legs resembling bamboo. £189.

Settees.

Triple-back, mahogany, with centres of architectural design carved in Chinese taste; scroll arms; carved cabriole legs having claw-and-ball feet. 190 guineas.

Two, mahogany, carved with small arms and having pagoda-shaped backs; from the Murthly Castle collection. £252.

The Brothers Adam.

Various Examples.

Fine examples of Adam furniture come on the market at rare intervals only, and there is always keen competition for them at Christie's. Adam glasses and side-tables when compared with other models by these designers appear pretty frequently. The former fetch from £10 to over £100, according to their quality, and exceptional specimens would realise even more. The tables command anything from £15 to £300, according to their importance and the volume and merit of the decoration which they display. In pairs, both mirrors and side-tables are distinctly rare, and they elicit proportionately higher prices.

When the sideboard-table is accompanied by its attendant pair of pedestals and arms in mahogany the collector will have to pay from £300 and upwards for fine examples, and it is worth remembering that these sets have ere now reached from £900 to £1000. Sofas by the Adams, when they display a good field of woodwork, are promptly snapped up; but chairs and sofas with the minimum of woodwork and a heavy scheme of upholstery may be picked up at very moderate rates. Painted or inlaid cabinet commodes with any pretensions go from £100 to £300 or so. Bookcases when fine, as in the illustration on page 445, run into hundreds of pounds.

Heppelwhite.

Bookcases.

Mahogany, 7ft. high, 8ft. wide, with anthemion (honeysuckle) ornament to mouldings, folding glazed doors above, with fluted Corinthian columns in high relief; cupboard below. 130 guineas.

Mahogany, inlaid, 4ft. 8in., with shelves and drawers enclosed by doors. £44.

Chairs.

Six single, two arms, mahogany, with rectangular backs, carved with foliage and drapery. 50 guineas.

Pair, mahogany, shield-shaped, with fluted rail-centres, ornamented with foliage; legs fluted, tapering. £35 14s.

On Prices.

Heppelwhite (continued).

Chairs.
One mahogany arm, with flutings on arms and legs, carved with foliage. 15 guineas.

Six singles, mahogany, partly gilt, with shield-shape backs, and honeysuckle, rosettes, and laurel festoons carved thereon. £35.

Knife-boxes,
Three, mahogany, inlaid, vase-shape, on square plinths. £25.

Settee,
Mahogany, cane-seated; back and arms with pierced trellis panels, the former having four panels containing cupids painted *en grisaille*. £67.

Suite,
Mahogany, ten arm-chairs and a settee; open shield-shape backs, having vase-shaped centres and classic foliage and ornament; backs, arms, and legs fluted. 310 guineas.

Window-seat,
Mahogany, the ends terminating in open shield-shaped backs, decorated with Prince of Wales' feathers, drapery, and rosettes; legs carved and fluted. 32 guineas.

Sheraton.

Bookcase,
Mahogany, 8ft. high, 8ft. 9in. wide, winged, with glazed folding doors, fluted side columns. 56 guineas.

Cabinets,
Satinwood, painted with baskets of flowers; 7ft. 9in. high, 3ft. 5in. wide; glazed folding doors enclosing shelves; central drawer, forming secretaire, and folding doors below. 180 guineas.

Small (2ft. wide), from the Huth collection; folding doors above enclosing drawers, with tulip-wood inlay in the form of bands and zig-zags; fall-down front and drawers at end. 100 guineas.

Chairs.
Ten singles and two arm, mahogany, shield-shaped backs, with rail centres, and on fluted legs. 80 guineas.

Sheraton (continued).

Chairs.
Two mahogany, shield-shaped backs, and wheat-ear ornament. 52 guineas.

Two, arm, shield-shaped backs, having Prince of Wales's feathers painted thereon, and pearl ornament on a black ground. 27 guineas.

Commode.
Satinwood, door-panels lacquered in black and gold and ornamented with birds, flowers, &c.; satinwood and hairwood chequered borders; grey marble slab. 50 guineas.

Cupboard.
Mahogany, inlaid satinwood, 2ft. wide, from the Huth collection. 32 guineas.

Knife-box.
Satinwood, banded with tulipwood, showing curvilinear treatment; silver escutcheon-plate and handles. £4 14s.

Sideboards.
Mahogany, 5ft. 2in. wide, semicircular, inlaid with satin and hair woods; three drawers, cellaret and cupboards; with brass handles and escutcheon-plates; square, tapering legs. 300 guineas.

Mahogany, 5ft. 7in. wide, shaped front, with central drawer and cupboards at sides; ornamented with satinwood and inlay of Prince of Wales's feathers, &c.; lion-mask handles. 23 guineas.

Tables.
Side, 6ft. wide, satinwood, with flower and ribbon border and fan ornament in the form of inlay; on painted and gilt stand, with festooned cords as border. 42 guineas.

Satinwood, oval, 3ft. 8in. wide, with scrolls, friezes, &c., inlaid. 62 guineas.

Pembroke, satinwood, inlaid with flowers, &c. 38 guineas.

Wardrobe.
Mahogany, banded with satinwood, 7ft. high, 8ft. wide; folding doors above and below; five central drawers. 58 guineas.

Bracket Clocks.

Flower and bird marquetry cased example, 15½in. high, by Peter Garron (also called Garon), a well-known maker in London in 1694; nicely chased metal-gilt dial, showing days of the month; pierced sides. 100 guineas.

20in. chiming clock, by J. Roberts, in ebonised case; metal-gilt dial and pierced fretwork side-panels. 19 guineas.

Eight-day mahogany-cased clock, by Thomas Oliver, of Fleet Street and Hanover Square, London (1780-1800); silvered dial, showing days of month; brass pine cones at top and brass feet. 13 guineas.

Mirrors, &c.

Mirrors.

Pair, oval, by Adam brothers, in carved and gilt frame. £46.
Pair, Chippendale, 8ft. long, 3ft. 6in. wide, with Vauxhall plates in two divisions; scroll and floral carved frame, surmounted with masks. £79.

Chippendale, carved and gilt, 7ft. 4in. long, 4ft. 2in. wide. 90 guineas.

Chippendale, bevel-edged, 7ft. high by 3ft. wide; upright black frame, with festoons of flowers, foliage, rosettes, acorns, and arabesques in relief. 38 guineas.

Chippendale, gilt, three-light, 5ft. 6in. high, 4ft. wide; scroll outline frame having floral borders. £89.

Pair, Georgian, carved and gilt, of rectangular form and in three divisions. 50 guineas.

Girandoles.

Pair, Chippendale, 4ft. 5in. high, 1ft. 5in. wide; gilt and carved in Gothic design. £27.

A GLOSSARY OF TERMS
Used in Cabinet-making, etc., with some Explanation as to their Derivation.

Acanthus Leaf.

This classic detail reached us in common with other Renaissance matter, and may be met with beautifully carved on eighteenth-century examples. Early oak pieces from Elizabethan days show the acanthus carving rather crudely executed, and late eighteenth-century specimens frequently exhibit it in moulded composition. It was introduced in the capitals of the Corinthian, then of the Composite, Orders. Chippendale excelled all others in its reproduction, applying it with equal success to table, chair, bookcase, &c.

Adelphi.

A term applied to the brothers Robert and James Adam.

Anthemion, or *Grecian (Classic) Honeysuckle.*

This was very popular in England between 1765-1810 for frieze and chair-back decoration, &c. It was used by such masters as the Adelphi, Gillows, Seddons, Heppelwhite, and Sheraton, whilst late Chippendale patterns also display it. The Adam brothers are generally credited with its introduction. A reference to the illustration on page 530 shows the feature at the centre and to the extreme right of the frieze.

Arabesques. See Grotesques.

Architrave.

The lowest moulding of an entablature, *i.e.,* immediately under the frieze.

Astragal.

A small semicircular moulding or bead used to encircle classic columns. All the English masters employed it as a finish to door and drawer edges; it was freely used to enclose and set off shaped panels or panes, and was prevalent in turned spindle- or spider-legged furniture, where it capped the delicate little legs just before their junction with the entablature they supported. It would overlap at the edge of door or drawer, and so exclude dust and dirt. The word is derived from the Greek *astragalos*, the ball of the ankle-joint.

Baluster *(corruptly Banister or Bailister).*

A small pillar, usually round (though often with a square base), showing one or more swells at the middle or towards the bottom. The oak tables of the seventeenth century have legs based on the revival of this Classic detail. The hoods of bread-and-cheese cupboards are found resting on an adapted baluster; the arcading of Yorkshire chairs, &c., is built upon these supports, as also are the stalls round the Vice-Provost's seat in King's College Chapel, Cambridge, though in these latter cases the work is generally stated to rest on balustrades. Later, again, the legs of Queen Anne furniture (other than those of the cabriole order) are free interpretations of the same idea. Spindle-work, too, may be traced to a similar source, although it is a very toned-down edition of it.

Banding.

Bands of inlay, sometimes doubled on the herringbone pattern. Late eighteenth-century models often show kingwood, tulipwood, satinwood, and, at the turn of the century, rosewood, so employed.

Bartizan.

This was a round turret, projecting at the angle of a building, and gave the idea for the round columnar excrescences common to sideboard and chest-of-drawers fronts of the late Sheraton and Waterloo periods.

Bead, *or, as it is commonly known,* **Cock-beading.**

A small rounded moulding frequently employed by English cabinet-makers.

Beakhead.

As the term denotes, this was a head with pendent beak, and was applied to decorate Norman doorways of the more richly ornamented kind; it was closely akin to the "catshead," another form of head with protruding tongue similarly employed. The "beakhead" gave rise to the eagle's head or vulture's head and beak which found such favour here during the whole of the first half of the eighteenth century as an item of carved relief decoration for the backs and arms of chairs or sofa-settees. The "catshead" was the forerunner of our lions' heads, sometimes with tongue exposed, commonly met with in cabinet-work and interior *fixed* decoration. The lion's head in brass work was generally used as a handle or door-knocker.

Bevel.

An old architectural term now freely applied to furniture. It signifies the sloping away of the edges, so that the main surface is left in relief but reduced in area. Old English glass such as that employed for mirrors at Vauxhall was bevelled. Panels in bookcases, wardrobes, or bureau-bookcases of the eighteenth century were sometimes similarly treated.

Boss.

A small split oval or round (usually) ornament applied in relief to furniture. It was commonly affixed in conjunction with split mace or baluster work on seventeenth-century oak, but it was generally superseded by the patera, as favoured by the Adams, in the succeeding century.

Braces.

Wooden rails binding the legs of cabinet-stands, chairs, tables, &c. These braces were often shaped and decorated, whilst in late eighteenth-century work we find them supporting small shelves or platforms.

Bracket.

We find the bracket freely employed in church architecture, where it was usually introduced to support images or figures. Chippendale had no rival to challenge his productions in this field. In contour his early brackets conformed very closely to their ecclesiastical forerunners, but the decoration he favoured was generally unorthodox. After 1755, for some ten years or so, English brackets very generally partook of Chinese or Gothic character.

Cabochon.

A small plain, reserved, and polished convex surface, usually of oval or kidney shape, which was enclosed within a decorated frame. The cabochon is frequently found on the knees of Chippendale legs designed in the style of the Louis Quinze.

Cabriole.
A curved leg showing a knee with convex and an ankle with concave sweep.

Capital.
The head of a column or pilaster, which may be decorated in any one of the Classic or other vogues. The pilasters guarding each side of the grandfather-clock door, and supporting the entablature, show various capitals in their more or less pure and primary interpretation. It is common to find these capitals on " grandfathers " decorated in chased brass, surmounting wooden columns, adaptations of the Corinthian style being commonest. Spindle-work legs are frequently met with crowned by a plain Norman capital, such as those seen in Cassington Church, Oxon.

Caryatides.
In ancient times the more or less draped figure of a woman was employed by the Greeks to support architectural entablatures. The word is derived from the Greek *Karuatides* (women of Carya). The legend is that when Carya was conquered by the Greeks the women were taken as captives, and to perpetuate their slavery were represented on buildings as bearing burdens. In Egypt the figure of a man was introduced supporting table-tops, &c., as detail symbolical of servitude.

Figures so employed are styled caryatides, and the English craftsmen in Elizabethan times freely introduced this treatment. Later, Batty and Thomas Langley, Abraham Swan, Chippendale, Adam, and many other eighteenth-century craftsmen availed themselves of the same idea, employing it chiefly for such examples as chimney-pieces and pier-tables.

Casement.
In addition to its relation to a window, this term is sometimes employed to signify a deep hollow moulding in early doors and cornices, which *may* be found freely decorated with running schemes of foliage.

Cavetto.
A concave moulding freely used by our old masters for such positions as the top of a cornice to a tallboy or a cabinet.

Chamfering.
This signifies the paring-off of an angle edge, with the consequent provision of an added face at each angle so chamfered.

Sometimes the chamfer face was left plain; more often, in English eighteenth-century work, it was covered by a scheme of appliqué fretwork.

Clubfoot.

A shaped and thickened foot under a plain rounded leg, commonly met with from 1695 to 1800 in the less pretentious specimens of English furniture. Sometimes known as a "pad" foot.

Console.

A term, borrowed from the French, to describe a piece of furniture supported bracket fashion ((Fr. *console,* a bracket); hence it will be seen that the console partakes somewhat of a corbel in architecture in its English interpretation. We are thus enabled to distinguish between a bracket proper and something which is of the nature of a bracket, or fulfils a similar function in its relation to some object of which it forms a part. All our master cabinet-makers made console tables, and these pieces were intended to be fastened to walls on the "lean-to" principle; they look best under large mirrors, in corners, or in niches.

Corbel.

Architecturally this is used of a projecting stone or timber whose duty it is to support a superimposed weight. During Queen Anne's reign and Chippendale's days the lion's head may frequently be found playing the part of the corbel; whilst the brothers Robert and James Adam constantly affected its use, substituting, as a rule, the heads of goats, rams, or fauns for the lion's mask. The corbel is oftenest found at the top of a table-leg, under mantel-shelves, brackets, or "overdoors."

Cornice.

The horizontal moulded projection crowning cabinets, wardrobes, or tallboys, &c., the term being derived from the Greek *korone,* a crown. All the great eighteenth-century masters paid careful attention to their cornice decorations, and they produced much exquisite work in this decoration. Some very effective mouldings based on the Norman, Early English, Decorated, and Perpendicular styles were used by Thomas Chippendale, who was obviously conversant with all these vogues. The succeeding cabinet-makers and designers adapted, modified, or amplified Chippendale's translations, but it is doubtful whether any of them improved upon his work.

Below these cornice mouldings *dentil* work was almost invariably affixed (the term "dentil" comes from the Latin *denticulus,* and signifies a small tooth). This work, which was originally employed on the bed-mouldings of Ionic, Corinthian, and Composite cornices, consisted of a row of small tooth-like blocks laid on in relief, with small spaces in between them to strengthen the effects of light and shade. By degrees the work became more elaborate, the little blocks had their centres removed so that only the outer edges at the sides and bottom of each tooth were left, and so a continuous chain of hollow, square, tooth-like formation was presented. Heppelwhite now and again carried this elaboration even further, undercutting each tooth from its base so that it became only a hollow shell. The last-mentioned treatment involved such delicate handling that it was seldom employed, and then only by the most skilled workmen.

Below the dentil line came the *frieze,* and this gave our great craftsmen plenty of scope for their ingenuity; they seem one and all to have eschewed the examples of the Tuscan and Doric schools, which made for chaste simplicity in this direction, and to have succumbed to the allurements of the Corinthian and Composite Orders, which included free ornamentation.

Broadly speaking, the frieze was decorated in two different ways. It may be found with a belt of fretwork running round it, which may be Chinese, Gothic, or composite in character, or we may find classic matter, such as acanthus work, a volute, fluting, or a key design. The majority of friezes show fretwork embellishment *when the model is a tall one, such as a bookcase or tallboy,* and classic detail becomes commoner in friezes placed lower, such as those running along table-framing.

Crockets.

These are typical of the relief carving of Chippendale and Heppelwhite in the Louis Quinze. Architecturally, crockets (from the French *crochet,* a little hook) were used in the form of bunches of foliage in hook-shape to decorate spires, pinnacles, gables, &c., and those in Hereford Cathedral, dating from A.D. 1250, are almost identical with the adaptations made by the two cabinet-makers above mentioned. The crocket was used at the top of a chair- or table-leg, on the knee of a tripod stand, on the upper foliated scroll of a foot, or upon a sofa-arm, and was exceedingly decorative. (*Vide the knees of tripod table shown on page 266.*)

Cusps.

The projecting points which sprang from the under-surface of Gothic archways. The term is derived from the Latin *cuspis*, a point. If we imagine that the space within an Early English or a Decorated archway is a sea, the cusps form a series of little promontories eating into it, and the spaces between them, resembling minute bays, are known as *foils*. The cusp may be found in Early English Gothic oak, and it is commonly met with in English eighteenth-century furniture. Perhaps the finest examples are those appearing in the lancet-shaped tracery of Chippendale's Gothic chair-backs. Sheraton also employed this detail on some of his models of the last decade of the century. Occasionally the cusp would figure in the tracery of a cabinet-front, or, of course in conjunction with the trefoil or the quatrefoil, at any position on the model showing Gothic *motif*.

Cyma.

An undulated or waved moulding, of which there are two varieties. *Cyma recta*, the first, is found to be round in the lower part and hollow in the upper. The term, which is derived from the Greek *kuma*, a wave, was employed on Classic entablatures (excepting those of the Tuscan and Doric Orders). It was used in a horizontal position as a crowning moulding by our eighteenth-century masters, and appears chiefly on tall pieces, such as wardrobes, &c., where there is a flat, level top with no pediment. The second kind of *cyma* is known as the *reversa*, and here the moulding is hollow as to its lower part and rounded above. When in this latter form it is generally known as the ogee. The ogee, as we have seen, was the standard and effective foot favoured by Chippendale for massive chests, bureaus, cabinets, &c., and it may be found on many other eighteenth-century pieces. The *cyma recta* crowns old models, then, whilst the *cyma reversa* supports them.

Echinus.

A strip (generally horizontal) of carving, consisting of alternate eggs and tongues, darts, or anchors. Originally carved on old Classic ovolos, it was greatly favoured by Chippendale and other English masters for all models where bands of carving could be effectively introduced. The echinus is sometimes misdescribed as an ovolo moulding.

A Glossary of Terms. 717

Empire.

Napoleon loved display, yet hesitated to reintroduce the earlier and grand styles identified with the dynasty which he had swept aside. As an alternative a vogue based on that of the Roman Empire, and emblematic of a second and similar, if not superior, dominion which he hoped to found, was evolved in consonance with the Corsican's aspirations. In France, therefore, the Empire fashion had a certain meaning, though it was inferior in artistic value to the earlier fashions which had then lapsed into desuetude. Unfortunately Englishmen sought to establish it here, where it had no *raison d'être* save in the case of those unnatural households which favoured Napoleon's pretensions. Hope, who, with Sheraton and Ackermann, exploited the style in this country, wrote: "The French Revolution commenced in 1792; Freedom, now consolidated in France, has restored the pure taste of the antique reproduction of ancient Greek forms for chairs, &c. The mouldings represent antique Roman fasces, with an axe in the centres; trophies of lances, surmounted by a Phrygian "Cap of Liberty"; winged figures emblematical of Freedom; and antique heads of helmeted warriors arranged with cameo medallions." Pompous, heavy, emblematical, and chimerical, the vogue was a concession to the revolutionary forces of the day, and was intended to symbolise a new autocracy without chafing the susceptibilities of those called upon to submit to it. The Empire style also favoured the Egyptian side of Roman decoration, doubtless in consonance with Napoleon's designs on the land of the Pharaohs.

Escutcheon.

There are two uses of this word—one common, one rare. The first application is in connection with the little decorated brass shield-like guards to keyholes, and if we asked for escutcheons in a shop, these are what we should find placed before us. Our forefathers took great care over the selection of these fittings, and some beautiful craftsmanship was accordingly developed.

The escutcheon proper was a small shield intended to set off crests or armorial bearings, and greatly favoured in Gothic architecture. During Queen Anne's reign many of the large hall- or side-tables had these "escutcheons" fitted to them at the centre of the architrave in front. Chair-backs, too, were similarly decorated as to their centre splats. Upon these escutcheons the family crest gave way at times to the mask of some diabolical-looking man or beast. Chippendale very seldom used the escutcheon for heraldic devices, but in his early work it is fairly often found in strong relief, enclosing one of the masks referred to. The later masters discarded the raised escutcheon as a rule, simply carving a coat-of-arms in a reserved panel, on a chair-back, for instance, whilst now and then the device was painted or inlaid, the latter process being exceedingly rare. (Term dropping out of use.)

Fascia.

This is a broad fillet which used to grace the architraves in Classic architecture. Sometimes the top of an eighteenth-century cabinet, wardrobe, or bookcase is found showing two or three fascias (from the Latin *fascia,* a band or fillet), rising like steps, one above the other, towards the top, and each projecting slightly over the one below it. This detail was effective, as it threw up lights and shades into strong relief. At the same time is was rather mechanical, and therefore seldom relied on for any but the plainer designs.

Fillet.

There are keel fillets and wing fillets. The former are little flat faces in relief on the fronts of round or oval mouldings, having somewhat of the same appearance thereon as the keel has on the bottom of a ship. The wing fillets stand out at each side where the moulding joins the body of the piece, and serve the purpose of separating the different mouldings or other items of decoration. These fillets were used by all our great eighteenth-century masters, and figure freely on the faces of important upright models. The idea seems to have come from the Early English and Decorated styles, since these show this detail in profusion.

Finial.

This term is applied to the decoration which caps a "pinnacle" appearing on some model. Thus the flame-shaped carving crowning the pole of a tripod fire-screen is correctly known as a "finial" (a word coined from the Latin *finis,* the end). Again, the little brass or gilt wood bulbs culminating in a point which crown the hood of an old grandfather clock would come under the same heading. In architecture, especially in the Decorated style, the finial consisted of a bunch of foliated work rising to a point, and somewhat resembling the crocket. Our great designers, however, were very free in their adaptations, and so we find that an acorn, a flame, a bird, an urn-shaped vase, a pineapple, torch, or other detail was frequently pressed into service to fulfil this duty.

Flamboyant.

A term of reproach used to describe ornate and over-decorated work. (The French decadent "Decorated" in architecture was so styled because the tracery then favoured somewhat resembled the flame of a torch in outline.)

Flatings or Flutes.

These consist of grooves or channels running parallel with one another, such as might be cut out with a chisel. The Doric column used to show twenty flutes in its circumference, whilst the Ionic, Corinthian, and Composite Orders employed twenty-four.

Chippendale brought the "flute" into use on his wine-cooler stands in its perpendicular application; spirally he would use it for decorating the column of a tripod table—to quote two instances. The later designers employed it freely on cabinet cornices, the entablatures of side-tables, chairs, table-legs, and so on.

Sometimes the lower portion of the fluting is blocked up with a round convex bead or moulding, and we then talk of "cabled" or "stopped" fluting. This latter treatment was freely meted out to chair-backs from 1760 onwards.

Fly-Brackets.

The small pivot supports which swung out to carry the side-flaps of Pembroke tables, &c.

Fret.

Although it is the fashion to put fret designs down as Chinese whenever they are met with, it is demonstrably wrong to do so. Many of the eighteenth-century frets are based purely on their Classic forerunners. The Renaissance brought to life again the key and interlaced key frets, with certain modifications, and these only took the place of the Gothic frets, which were peculiarly charming. Chippendale used the Classic, Gothic, and

Chinese fret at his own sweet will, and sometimes evolved a composite fret breathing something of the spirit of all three.

Grotesques and Arabesques.

Terms applied to networks of conventional ornaments which were imported from Italy to be introduced on English furniture from Elizabethan times down to the end of the eighteenth century. Thus the marquetry on an Elizabethan bedstead, a Jacobean coffer, a William and Mary grandfather clock, a Queen Anne cabinet, or the painting on an Adam ceiling may one and all be found showing this detail typically handled. Robert Adam, the last of our great designers to use this kind of decoration successfully, thus defined matters : " By grotesque is meant that beautiful light stile of ornament used by the ancient Romans in the decoration of their palaces, baths, and villas. It is also to be seen in some of their amphitheatres, temples and tombs, the greatest part of which, being vaulted and covered with ruins, have been dug up and cleared by the Italians, who, for these reasons, give them the name of *grotte*. . . . The French . . . have branded those ornaments with the vague and fantastical appellation of arabesque."

Arabesque work may best be seen in our marquetry of the 1690-1720 period, where amidst birds, beasts, flowers, and fruit the interstices are filled in with carved sprays of this quaint and fanciful detail in stereotyped profusion. Adam suggestions in this direction were usually graceful, if somewhat thin. Grotesque work is now generally held to signify a coarser rendering of this Italian detail, with which, incidentally, ugly masks. &c., are often incorporated.

Guilloche.

A belt or band of classic detail, usually applied horizontally, which was especially popular during the Elizabethan and succeeding style. The central decoration to the buffet shown on page 45 is a true presentment of the guilloche. Usually carved, this pattern may be found inlaid and, during the late eighteenth century, in brushwork.

Herringbone.

During the last quarter of the seventeenth century the marquetry bands round various models were "herringboned," just as in the eleventh century bricks, tiles, or stones were laid aslant. Under this treatment two courses of inlay met, one pointing

A Glossary of Terms.

downwards, the other upwards, at a corresponding angle, so that the whole pattern made by the figure in the grain resembled a succession of blunt arrow-heads. Pointing horizontally, the grain generally slanted away at an inclination of 45deg. In later years the grain commonly stood at right angles to the carcases in which it was inlaid.

Mitre.

The line formed by the meeting of a succession of mouldings, fillets, astragals, &c., which intersect or intercept one another at the angle so formed. Nearly all good-class chests or decorated upstanding pieces were mitred, and a good price was allowed to the workman for accomplishing this delicate junction work.

Moulding.

Everybody knows what a moulding is, but some may not know that the orthodox varieties include the fillet or list, the astragal with pearl-and-bead variations, the cyma, the cavetto, the ogee, the ovolo, the Scotia, and the torus, and that all these were employed by our eighteenth-century masters in one form or another, the astragal and ogee being the commonest varieties.

Patera.

Architecturally this was a round decorated ornament, somewhat resembling a "boss," which appeared in relief on Classic friezes. Our cabinet-makers, but above all the brothers R. and J. Adam, availed themselves of this decoration, using it chiefly in oval or round formation, now and then even in diamond shapes, or at times as a square. Long, narrow leaves used to converge on the centre of the patera as a rule, and it was sometimes further embellished by bands of beading round the centre "button" and on its outside edge.

Paterae, as they are generally styled, appeared on all manner of fixed or movable interior garnishments from 1765 to the close of the century; they usually crowned a leg or graced some frieze, and may be seen on decadent nineteenth-century work.

Pediment.

A triangular-shaped decoration crowning the cornices of bookcases, cabinets, &c. The term *broken* pediment is applied when the projection of the sides of the triangle is stopped short of the completion of what would otherwise be the apex. (*Vide illustrations in Georgian chapter.*)

Rabbet or Rebate.

A groove made in the edge or side of a piece of wood, into which another body has to be welded. The lattice tracery of most old cabinets was subjected to rabbeting.

Rainçeau.

A graceful form of decoration, mainly used by the Adam brothers, consisting of winding and twisting stalks of acanthus or other foliage. Sometimes introduced *per se,* sometimes with arabesques, &c.

Spandrels.

These are the triangular spaces in the corners of a rectangular space which a circle or an archway contained in the said space leaves. There would, of course, be two spandrels to an archway, one over each side of the arch; whilst if we insert a circle of inlay within a square there would be four spandrels —one at each inner corner of the square.

The spandrel is most commonly found over the sides of the arch in the centre of the sideboard. The Adams, Heppelwhite, Shearer, and Sheraton all favoured it, and they elected to decorate it with inlaid work or with relief-carving.

The plain sideboard has its spandrels, as a rule, picked out with a narrow band of inlay; but the finer specimens show effective fan or shell inlay, covering the spandrels practically all over.

Very rarely we come across carved spandrels on such pieces as kneehole writing-cabinets, &c., and where these are found they will be closely akin to their old architectural prototypes both in design and execution.

Therming.

A process of conferring a delicate taper, especially applied to the feet of chairs, sideboards, and tables of the Sheraton order treated with rectilinear legwork.

Volute, or Vitruvian Scroll (sometimes known as the " Wave " pattern).

A band of classic decoration very popular in England. (*Vide the upper of the two horizontal belts shown on the side table, page 333.*)

INDEX.

INDEX.

A.

Acanthus decoration, 264, 389, 465
Ackermann, 610
ADAM BROTHERS, 400
  acanthus decoration, 465
  "Adelphi," the, 400
  animal creations, 466
  appropriations, 431, 440
  arabesques, 466
  architectural designs, 400
  biography, 400
  bookcases, 445
  cabinets, 427, 436
  candlestands, 436
  "carton-pierre," 412
  caryatides, 466
  ceiling decorations, 432, 433
  chairs, 462
  Chippendale style fused with, 470
  claims to originality, 407
  classic decoration, 408, 410, 435, 449, 455
  Clerisseau, C. L., collaborates with, 443
  Clouston, R. S., on, 407
  collaboration with Italian artists, 409
  Columbani influence, 431
  commissions for, 462
  commodes, 436
  "compositions," 412
  curtain-holders, 19 and Plates
  curvilinear treatment, 469
  decoration schemes, 410

ADAM BROTHERS (cont.):
  Derby's (Earl) commission, 456
  descriptions of executed work, 472
  designs, 429
  doors, 441
  doorways, 413, 417
  dressing-cabinets, 437
  early work, 424, 453
  English and French styles contrasted, 419
  Etruscan art development, 455
  fine woods introduced, 470
  firegrates, 403
  Flaxman plaques, 436, 437
  followers of, 610
  French influence on, 440
  gilt work, 459
  girandoles, 459
  grotesques, 466
  handles, 19 and Plates
  hanging lights, 460, 461
  harpsichords, 436
  Heppelwhite influence on, 482
  hints for buyers, 463
  inlaid decoration, 423, 470
  interiors, 411
  Italian influence, 408
  japanned furniture, 459
  Kauffmann, Angelica, 432, 436, 439, 441
  Kenwood commission, 401
  late work, 424
  "Liardet," 411
  Louis Seize influence, 454

ADAM BROTHERS (cont.):
  lyre-backed chairs, 487
  Manocchi inspirations, 431
  mantelpieces, 410, 421, 423, 435, 436,
  military trophies, 466
  mirrors, 429, 459, 468
  mythological subjects, 466-7
  notes and designs, 449
  ormolu employed by, 458
  painted work by, 419, 422, 457
  papier-mâché used by, 416
  pateræ treatment, 454
  pediments discarded by, 469
  Pergolesi influence, 435
  Piranesi influence, 425, 430, 431
  prices, 706
  R. and J. Adam, 221
  rainçeaux employed, 435, 465
  serpentine swell, 468
  shield-backed chairs, 487
  sideboards, 420
  sideboard-tables, 420
  side-tables, 405, 451, 464, 471
  Sion House designs, 429
  sofas, 463
  spiral volute, 466
  stucco treatment, 453
  tables, 454
  teachings, 404, 449
  Trafalgar period, 459, 472
  tripods, 262
  veneer, 423
  Vitruvian scroll, 466
  wall-lights, 416, 459
  wall-mirrors, 468
  Waterloo period, 459, 472
  Wedgwoods commissioned, 436
  wood employed, 416
  work executed by other cabinet-makers, 407
  writing-tables, 436
  Zucchi, 432, 439
Adam, James, 400, 401, 430, 473
  literary efforts, 430
Adam, John, 400

Adam, R. and J., sideboards, 307
Adam, Robert, 57, 400, 401, 444, 473
  Admiralty commission, 402
  anthemion ornament, 300
  Classic revival, 403
  criticisms on furniture-designers of the period, 404
  death of, 476
  quoted, 194
  services of Italian artists enlisted, 409
  Sion House work, 402
  sojourn in Italy, 409
Adam, William, 400, 401, 474
  associated in partnership with the Robertsons, 476
  furniture attributed to, 477
Adaptations, 10
"Adelphi," the, 400
Age, determining, 26
Amboyna wood, 14
Angelo, Michael, 55
Animal creations, Adam, 466
Anthemion ornament, 299, 300, 486, 492
Antique style, 58
Applied art in cabinet-making, 121
Appliqué decoration, Jacobean, 66
  fret decoration to Chinese Chippendale, 277
Apprentices' pieces, Sheraton, 562
  work, 14
Arabesques, Adam, 466
Architectural designs, Adam Bros.', 400
  influence on craftsmen, 176, 217
Armchairs, faked, 12, 17
Armoires, Elizabethan, 48, 49
Armorial decoration in Queen Anne furniture, 175
Arm-supports, Chippendale, 585
Astragals, prices, 696
Auction prices, 698

Index.

B.

Banding and stringing, prices, 693
Barjiers, 513
Barometers, Sheraton, 565
Basin-stands, Chippendale, 249, 379
    spindle-leg, 674
Beakhead garnishment applied to furniture, 355
Bedroom furniture, Chippendale, 375
    Heppelwhite, 514
Bedstead drapery, Chippendale, 373
Bedsteads, Charles II., 111
    Chippendale, 373 and Plate
    Elizabethan, 49, 51
    faked, 10
    Heppelwhite, 518
    Sheraton, 588, 591
Belcher and Macartney quoted, 203
Bell-flowers as decoration, 486, 488
Benches, 36
Benn quoted, 531
Bergère chairs, Heppelwhite, 513
Bergères, 313, 513
Bevelling mirrors, 657
Bird-and-bouquet marquetry, 125, 127
Birdcage clocks, William and Mary, 126
Black, Adam, on Sheraton, 528, 532
"Blistered" inlay, 15, 577
Bone inlay, 111
Bone-polishing, 25
Bookcase doors, prices, 696
    writing-cabinet, Irish Chippendale, 386
BOOKCASES, Adam, 445
    bureau-, 169, 171, 208, 343, 346, 347, 349, 351
    Chippendale, 383
    closed-in, 173
    faked, 12
    Georgian, 208, 211, **213**

BOOKCASES, glazed Chippendale, 366
    Heppelwhite, 514
    Queen Anne, 171, **173**
    Sheraton, 588
Bookshelf, hanging Chippendale, 353
Bottle-cabinets, Sheraton, 543
Bowl-stands, spindle-leg, 672
    revolving Chippendale, 251
Box-chairs, 37, 76
Bracket clocks, 630, 631
    Georgian, 631
    prices, 709
    Sheraton, 633
Brackets, Chinese Chippendale, 275, 284
Brass employed by Sheraton, 595
    fittings, prices for, 697
    furniture, 19, 20, 21, and Plates
Brockbank, clock-maker, 635
Broken pediment, the, 175, 208, 366
"Buckled-up" inlay, 15, 577
Buffet, the, 36
    Elizabethan, 45, 48
Bulbous swell affected by Chippendale, 260
    characteristic of Elizabethan furniture, 47
Bureau-bookcases, 343
    Chippendale, 343, 346, 347, 351
    Georgian, 208
    Queen Anne, 169, 171
Bureau fittings to tallboy chest, 539
Bureaus, Chippendale, 345
    Queen Anne, 169, 171
Burjars, 313
Butterfly-leg furniture, 676
Buying furniture, 1, 2
Byzantine style, 38, 55

C.

C-scroll, 108, 165
C- and S-scrolls, Chippendale, 270, 271

Cabinet-making, advance of, in Britain, 32
   Eastern influence, 30
   evolution of, in Britain, 29
   Western influence, 30
Cabinets, Adam, 427, 436
   bottle, 543
   china, 171
   china-, Irish Chippendale, 397
   corner, 535
   dressing-, 436
   glass-fronted, 18
   Heppelwhite, 509, 514
   lacquered, 111, 147
   Queen Anne, 156
   Seddons, 603
   writing, 533
Cabinet-work, heavy, made by Chippendale, 383, 384
Cabriole chairs, 513
Cabriole, derivation of, 151
Cabriole-leg, 154, 159
   evolution traced, 160
   extended popularity of, 159
   superiority of British work, 159
Cacqueteuse chairs, 53
Caffieri, 30
Camel-back chairs, 488
Candlestands, Adam, 436
   Chippendale, 342
   spindle-leg, 672
Candlesticks, Chippendale, 341
Carcase-work, prices, 689
CARD-TABLES, abundance of, 296
   broken-fronted, 298
   candlestick stands, 294
   Chinese Chippendale, 287
   Chinese influence on, 298
   Chippendale, 293-299
   claw-and-ball feet, 240, 262, 294, 357
   complicated fitments in, 295
   concertina action of framework, 296
   dragon's-claw feet, 297
   egg-and-anchor decoration, 298

CARD-TABLES (*cont.*):
   egg-and-dart decoration, 298
   egg-and-tongue decoration, 297
   guinea-wells, 294
   Heppelwhite, 485, 506
   leg-terminals, 297
   lion's-claw feet, 297
   Louis Quinze handling, 298
   oval, 298
   pearl-and-lozenge moulding, 298
   Queen Anne, 169, 170, 297
   Queen Anne and Chippendale, contrasted, 297
   re-covering, hints on, 295
   rose-and-ribbon border, 298
   round, 298
   serpentine, 298
   square, 298
   William and Mary, 119
Carter, J., 610
Carton-pierre, introduced by the Adams, 412
Carving, 8
   Elizabethan, 44
   faked, 8
   Irish Chippendale, compared, 389
   Jacobean, 65
   "picked-out," 11
   ribbon, 264
Carving-tables, Chippendale, 332, 333, 334
Caryatides, animals used as, by the Adams, 466
Ceiling decorations, 432
Ceilings, Adam, 433
Cellarets, Chippendale, 337
   Heppelwhite, rarity of, 513
CHAIRS, Adam, 462
   barjiers, 513
   bergère, 513
   box, 37, 76
   burjars, 313
   cabriole, 513
   cacqueteuse, 53
   camel-back, 488
   Charles I., 81
   Charles II., 97

Index.

CHAIRS (*cont.*):
  Chinese Chippendale, 277, 280, 281
  Chippendale, 218, 223, 245, 246, 247, 248, 309, 313, 315
  cluster-leg, Ince and Mayhew, 289
  conversational, 53, 594
  conversions, 17
  corner, 38
  crested, 80
  Cromwellian, 97
  Derbyshire, 77
  double-panelled, 98
  drop-in-seats, 314
  drunkards', 313, 314
  easy, 174
  Elizabethan, 50
  Flemish, 117
  grandfather, 169, 314
  Heppelwhite, 482, 488, 493, 495, 503
  Hogarth, 166, 203
  hooped-back, 165
  Jacobean, 63, 75, 79
  ladder-back, 247, 299, 301, 317, 490, 501
  lyre-back, 462, 487
  oval-back, 495
  padded-back, 313
  Queen Anne, 166, 167
  relief-carving on backs of, 572
  ribbon, criticised, 571
  saddle-back, 491
  shepherdess's, 314
  Sheraton, 537, 547, 567, 569
  shield-back, 412, 487, 491, 524, 525
  spindle-leg, 674
  spoon-backed, 156, 167
  stuff-over seats, 314
  upholstered, 496
  wheel-back, 484, 489, 490, 492
  William and Mary, 117
  wing, 170, 314
  wing-ear, 169
  writing, 169

CHAIRS (*cont.*):
  X-shape, 37
  Yeoman quality Chippendale, 248
  Yorkshire, 77
Chair-back decorations, Chippendale, 308
  Sheraton, compared with Chippendale, 580
  William and Mary, compared with Heppelwhite, 484
Chair-designs, Sheraton, 578, 580
Chair-legs, Sheraton, 581
Chaises-longues, 313, 328
Chambers, Sir William, 30, 364
Charles II. adaptations, 111
  arts and crafts considered, 89
  bedsteads, 111
  chairs, 95, 97
  chestnut used, 94
  claw-and-ball used as leg-terminal, 105
  couches, 103
  day-beds, 97, 103
  dining-tables, 107
  draw-tables, 107
  Evelyn quoted, 112
  grandfather clocks, 94
  lacquered cabinets, 111
  marquetry, 110
  oak supplanted by walnut, 94
  panelled chairs, 98
  Restoration period, 85
  salient points, 93
  scroll-forms used on, 105, 108
  serving-tables, 107
  side-tables, 107
  spiral turning on, 95, 106
  stoles, 97, 105
  stretcher-work, 109
  tables, 106
  tabletops, 106
  upholstery, 112
  walnut supersedes oak, 94, 113
  woods used, 94, 113

Chestnut used in Charles II. furniture, 94
Chests, double, 539
    faked, 10
    Gothic, 35
    Jacobean, 5
    leather-, 37
    of drawers, 173, 378
China-cabinets, Georgian, 208
    Irish Chippendale, 397
    Queen Anne, 169, 171
China show-case, Chippendale, 359
Chinese influence, 248, 309, 310, 331, 333, 334, 339, 341, 346, 353, 362, 365, 367, 369, 377, 378
Chinese-cum-Gothic, 286
Chinese-cum-Louis Quinze designs, 362, 363, 366
CHINESE CHIPPENDALE, 239, 273
    appliqué fret decoration, 277
    brackets, 275, 284
    candlestands, 284
    card-tables, 287
    chairs, 277, 280
    Chambers, Sir William, connection with, 272, 279
    Chambers and Chippendale compared, 283
    Chippendale as an exponent of, 291
    Clouston, R. S., 283
    cluster-leg chairs, 289
    combinations of, 278
    competitors of Chippendale, 283
    condition of, 281
    console tables, 284
    Edwards and Darly, 279, 283, 285
    fretwork imitated, 282
    fretwork tables, 284
    hints to purchasers, 282
    hybrid Gothic style, 277
    Ince and Mayhew, 280, 286

CHINESE CHIPPENDALE (cont.):
    Johnson, T., 279, 283, 284, 285
    Langley, Batty, designs, 279
    lanthorns, 284
    Louis Quinze influence, 270
    mirrors, 284
    origin, 272
    pierced fret decoration, 280
    pier-tables, 284
    prices, 705
    résumé, 291
    rococo-cum-Oriental, 283
    surface-condition often lacking, 282
Chippendale and Co., 232
Chippendale and Haig, 232
Chippendale the Elder, 227
    picture-frames, 227, 229
CHIPPENDALE, THOMAS, THE GREAT, 217
    acanthus and wheel decoration, 264
    anglicises Dutch element, 222
    anthemion as ornament, 299, 300
    architectural feeling the dominant factor, 217, 342
    arm-supports, 585
    artist-craftsman, 236
    artistic renderings of other vogues, 231
    basin-stands, 249, 379
    bedroom furniture, 375
    bedsteads, 373 and Plate
    bookcases, 366, 383
    bowl-stands, revolving, 251
    brackets, 222
    broken pediment used by, 366
    bureau-bookcases, 346, 347, 351
    bureaus, 345
    " C's " as centre work in chairs, 309
    C- and S-scrolls, 270, 271
    candlestands, 341, 342

Index.

CHIPPENDALE, THOMAS, THE GREAT (*cont.*):
card-tables, 293-299
carving-tables, 332, 334
cellarets, 337
chair-back decorations, 308
chairs, 223, 245, 246, 247, 309, 313, 315
chaises-longues, 313, 328
"Chambers" (*see* Chinese Chippendale)
Chambers craze, 364
characteristics of cabinet-work supports, 385
chests of drawers, 378
Chinese (*see* Chinese Chippendale)
Chinese influence, 248, 309, 310, 331, 333, 334, 339, 341, 346, 362, 365, 367, 369, 377, 378
Chinese-cum-Louis Quinze designs, 362, 363
classic and Renaissance detail, 217
claw-and-ball feet, 240, 262, 294, 357
clock-cases, 349
clothes-presses, 378
Clouston, R. S., quoted, 227, 233
commodes, 368, 383
comprehensiveness of his work, 307
concertina principle employed for tables, 357
console-tables, 341
constructive skill, 235
contour of line *v.* luxury, 311
couches, 313
cresting-rails, 223
curtain-holders, 19 and Plates
decadent period, 232
dining-tables, 355, 357
"Director" considered, 220, 236, 301, 302, 308
disciples of, 610
dish-top tables, 263

CHIPPENDALE, THOMAS, THE GREAT (*cont.*):
drapery to bedsteads, 373
drawing-tables, 256
dressing-tables, 379
dumb-waiters, 260
Early English and Perpendicular styles, 256
early status, 233
Eastern and Western styles combined, 278
Eastern school favoured, 361
enumeration of pieces, 308
faked settees, 328
family history, 226
fire-screens, 369, 371
fixed garnishments, 379
flamboyant tracery, 310
footwork, 382
French influence a retrograde factor, 219
fusion of style with the Adams', 470
gadroon edge, 334
galleries as fashionable rendezvous, 236
gallery-tables, 237, 243, 264, 266
gilt furniture, 221
Gothic influence, 248, 258, 309, 331, 334, 340, 341, 345, 353, 364, 367, 369, 375, 377, 378
Gothic-cum-Louis Quinze, 378
gouty-stools, 268, 270
handles, 19, 21
hanging-bookshelf, 353
hangings to bedsteads, 373
heavy cabinet-work, 383, 384
Heppelwhite compared with, 483
hints for collectors, 226
honeysuckle, Grecian, as ornament, 299
influences in the cabinet-maker's art,
inlaid, 381

CHIPPENDALE, THOMAS, THE
  GREAT (cont.):
 Irish Chippendale, 385, 399
 "ironing-up" tables, 263
 Jack-in-the-box vogue, 258
 ladder-back chairs, 299
 leg-work, 382, 384
 Louis Quatorze, 116, 266, 342
 Louis Quinze and Chinese, 379
 Louis Quinze, Chinese, and Gothic styles blended, 278
 Louis Quinze influence, 242, 245, 252, 266, 331, 333, 334, 337, 340, 341, 342, 346, 353, 362, 367, 369, 375, 376, 379
 lovers' seats, 313
 mirrors, 651
 multum-in-parvo furniture, 256
 on Chinese chair-designs, 239
 organ-cases, 340
 padded-back chairs, 313
 pagoda-shaped dome used by, 365
 parrot's-beak garnishment, 355
 péché-mortel, 338
 pedestal tables, 331
 "peg-top" tables, 266
 picture-frames, 350
 pie-crust tables, 263
 pier tables, 341
 plain-top tables, 267
 Portuguese, 389
 prices, 702
 Queen Anne vogue, 259, 332
 raised-ribbon tables, 263
 range of subjects, 220
 Rannie, his partner, 231
 Redgrave quoted, 233
 résumé, 380
 rococo decoration, 333, 337, 374
 serving-boards, 335
 serving-tables, 331
 settees, 313, 318, 319, 327
 shell ornament, 334

CHIPPENDALE, THOMAS, THE
  GREAT (cont.):
 show-case for china, 359
 show-shelf, 353
 sideboards, 307
 side-tables, 296
 sofas, 313
 square-leg, use of, 354
 Simon, Miss Constance, quoted, 228, 231, 232, 236, 357
 stools, 339
 supports to various pieces, 383, 384, 385
 swan-necked pediment, 208
 tea-caddies, 367
 torchères, 341
 tripod tables, 224, 225, 238, 240, 243, 251, 259, 261, 263, 264, 266, 267, 269
 tulip-shaped bulbous swell, 260
 turned work, 251
 Vernis-Martin, 368
 versatility of, 545
 Vitruvian scroll employed, 333
 wardrobes, 375
 washstands, 379
 whorled feet, French, used in tables, 267
 wig-stands, 249, 379
 wine-coolers, 337
 wine-tables, 268, 269
 writing-tables, 252, 299, 329, 331, 383
 X-chairs, 312
Chippendale, Thomas, the Younger, 232
Classic and Renaissance detail employed by Chippendale, 217
Classic style, 58, 408, 435, 449, 455
Classification of Heppelwhite furniture, 482
Claw-and-ball feet, 105, 158, 173, 297, 357
Clerisseau, C. L., an Adam collaborator, 443

Index.

Clock-cases, Chippendale, 349
CLOCKS, age of, 634
    birdcage, William and Mary, 126
    bracket, 630, 631, 635
    grandfather (*see* Grandfather Clocks)
    grandmother, 133
    lantern, William and Mary, 126
    marquetry, 547
    Queen Anne, 131, 631
    Wetherfield collection, 515, 547
    William and Mary, 631
Clothes-presses, 378
    Irish Chippendale, 397
Clouston, R. S., quoted, 227, 283, 407, 479, 521, 522, 524, 531
Cluster-leg furniture, 287, 676
Cluster-tables, spindle-leg, 674
Cobweb marquetry, 131
Coffee-stools, Elizabethan, 49
    Jacobean, 78
Colouring furniture, 15
Columbani and the Adams, 431
    quoted, 614
Commodes, Adam, 368, 383, 436, 530, 588
Commonwealth upholstery, 665
Composite furniture, Adam, 422
"Compositions," Adam, 412
Concertina action employed by Chippendale, 357
"Condition," 2
Confidantes, Heppelwhite, 513
Console-tables, Chinese Chippendale, 284, 341
Conversational chairs, 53, 593
Convex mirrors, 654
Copeland, H., 612
Corner-cabinets, Sheraton, 535
Corner-chairs, 38
Couches, Charles II., 103
    Chippendale, 63, 79, 313, 314
Court-cupboards, 48, 49
    Elizabethan, 48
    Jacobean, 61, 83

Crested chairs, 80
Cresting-rails, Chippendale, 223
CROMWELLIAN FURNITURE, 85
    chairs, 97
    tables, 106
    upholstery, 665
Crossbanding, prices, 694
Crow, of Feversham, quoted, 565
Crunden, J., 613
Cupboards, Court, 48, 49, 61, 83
    short, 49
Curtain-holders, Adam, 19 and Plate
    Chippendale, 19 and Plate
Curvilinear treatment, Adams', 469
    adopted by Sheraton, 580
    Sheraton's, 546

D.

Darly, Matthew, 612, 613
Day-beds, Charles II., 97, 103
    Jacobean, 63
Dealers' guarantee, 1
Decoration, additions to, 9
    schemes, Adam, 410
Derbyshire chairs, 77
Dining-tables, 354
    Charles II., 107
    Chippendale, 357
    early, 36
    telescopic, Gillows, 524
Dinner-wagons, Elizabethan, 45
Dish-top tables, 263
Doors, Adam, 441
    false, 577
Doorways, Adam, 413, 417
    Corinthian, 190
    Georgian, 196
Dragons' claws as feet, 297
Drapery festoons as decoration, 492
Drawers, false, 577
    free running of, 18
Draw-tables, Charles II., 107
    Elizabethan, 50

"Drawing-Book," Sheraton, 545, 550, 553
Drawing-tables, Chippendale, 256
Dressing-cabinets, Adam, 437
Dressing-tables, Chippendale, reflecting, 517
Drop-in seats to chairs, 314
Drunkards' chairs, 313, 314
Duchesse, Heppelwhite's, 513
Dull-polishing, 25
Dumb-waiters, Chippendale, 260
Dutch influence and Chippendale, 222

E.

Early Georgian work, 185, 189
East, Edward, clockmaker, 123
Eastern school of work favoured by Chippendale, 361
Easy-chairs, Queen Anne, 174
Edwards and Darly, 279, 283, 285, 291, 364, 609
Edwards, G., 612
Egg-and-anchor decoration, 298
Egg-and-dart decoration, 298
Egg-and-tongue decoration, 297
Eighteenth-century upholstery, 665
Eight-leg furniture, 676
ELIZABETHAN FURNITURE:
  armoires, 48, 49
  bedsteads, 49, 51
  buffets, 45, 48
  bulbous swell characteristic, 47
  carving, 44
  chairs, 50
  characteristics, 43
  coffin-stools, 49
  Court cupboards, 48
  dinner-wagons, 45
  double hutches, 48
  draw-tables, 50
  furniture, 40
  joint-stools, 49
  partiality for marquetry, 43

ELIZABETHAN FURNITURE (cont.):
  prices, 699
  sideboards, 45
  strapwork, 44
  style, 34
  tables, 48, 50
  three-deckers, 49
  tridarns, 49
  woods employed, 44
  writing-cabinets, 53
Embellishments, Jacobean, 67
English Empire period, 501, 507, 579, 597
"English Furniture Designers of the Eighteenth Century," 228, 231, 232, 357, 479, 600
Engraving furniture, 15
Engravings, transference of, to faked pieces, 11
Escutcheons, 19 and Plate
Etruscan art as developed by the Adams, 455
Evelyn quoted, 112, 140, 178, 179, 180

F.

FAKED FURNITURE, 1, 568, 577
  adaptations, 10
  additions, 9
  armchairs, 12, 17
  bedsteads, 10
  bookcases, 12
  brass furniture, 20
  bureaus, 345
  bureau-bookcases, 349
  card-tables, 299
  carving, 8
  chairs, 17
  chests, 10
  colouring, 15
  condition as guide, 2
  dated oak, 11
  decoration additions, 9
  doors, 577
  drawers, 18, 22, 577
  embellishments, 19
  engravings transferred to, 11, 15

Index.

FAKED FURNITURE (*cont.*):
  escutcheons, 19
  evidences of wear, 13
  fire-screens, 370
  fretwork imitated, 282
  fronts, 18
  furniture-improvers, 9
  gilding, 27
  glass-fronted cabinets, 18
  glue, 13
  hairwood, 14
  handles, 19
  inlaid design, 11, 13, 15
  Jacobean panelling, 107
  joinery evidences, 15
  joints, 18
  made-up pieces, 10
  marquetry, 15, 577
  paintings used on, 11, 17
  panelling, 10
  patina, 4, 464
  picked-out carving, 11
  putty, 18
  re-carving, 9
  relaid inlay, 15
  replicas, 12
  re-veneering, 11
  sand-burning 15
  satinwood, 14
  settees, 12, 318, 322, 328
  sideboards, 499
  sub-surface exploration, 26
  table-tops, 267
  under-framing to inlaid cabinets, 111
  wood-grain as guide, 7
  wormholes, 8, 23, 24, 140, 500, 684
Fakers, methods of, 1, 26
False doors, 577
False drawers, 577
Fireplaces, Adam, 403
  Georgian, 205
Fire-screens, Chippendale, 369, 371
  conversions, 370
  faked, 370
  folding, 372
  Heppelwhite, 517, 518
  horse, 372

Fire-screens, spindle-leg, 674
  tripod, 372
Flamboyant tracery in Chippendale designs, 310
Flaxman, John, and the Adams, 436, 437
Flemish chairs, 117
Fleureau, George, clockmaker, 131
Flower-festoons as decoration, 486
Fluting, prices, 694
Folding screens, Chippendale, 372
  Heppelwhite, 518
Footwork, Chippendale, 382
Frames, mirror, 658
  tabernacle, 208
French-polishing, 3
Fretwork, Chinese or Gothic, 353, 283
  tables, Chinese Chippendale, 284
Frieze compositions, Sheraton, 592
Furnishing, Sheraton on, 546
Furniture improvers, 9

G.

Gadroon edge, 334
Gallery - tables, Chippendale, 243, 264, 266
Gardes-de-vin, Heppelwhite, 513
Garnishments, fixed, Chippendale, 379
Gate-tables, spindle-legged, 670
GEORGIAN FURNITURE, 184
  architectural influence on, 193
  Belcher and Macartney quoted, 203
  bookcases, 208, 211, 213
  bracket clocks, 631
  broken pediment a feature, 208
  bureau-bookcases, 208
  china-cabinets, 208
  classic treatment, 194
  Corinthian doorways, 191

GEORGIAN FURNITURE (*cont.*):
  decorations at Godmersham, 207
  doorway, 196
  Evelyn quoted, 183
  fireplaces, 205
  frieze handling, 208
  governing motifs, 190
  grotesqueries, 217
  Hogarth chairs, 253
  interiors, 205, 209
  Kent, William, quoted, 200
  literature of the subject, 212
  meaning of the term, 185
  mirrors at Godmersham, 201
  mural and ceiling decorations, 182
  overmantels, 205
  partiality for gilt work, 189
  periodically divided, 185, 186
  prices, 701
  stools, 220
  Strange, F. H., quoted, 200
  tabernacle frames, 187
  wardrobes, 208
GIBBONS, GRINLING, 177
  all-round craftsman, 180
  association with Wren, 179
  birthplace, 178
  carvings by, 180
  Evelyn quoted, 178, 179, 180
  influence of, 208
  master-carver to George I., 183
  parentage, 178
  plaster-work, 182
  position as a craftsman, 177
  prices for his work, 183
Gibbs quoted, 193
Gilding, 27
Gill and Reigate, 647, 654
GILLOWS, 519
  characteristics of the vogue, 519
  Clouston, R. S., quoted, 521, 523
  influences of other craftsmen on their work, 526

GILLOWS (*cont.*):
  interlaced heart model, 525
  origin of the firm, 521
  reconstitution of the firm, 523
  shield-back chairs, 487, 524, 525
Gillow, Richard, 523, 524
  Robert, 521, 523
  Thomas, 523
Gillow and Barton, 522
Gilt furniture, 155, 189, 221, 680
Gilt-work, Adam, 459
Girandoles, 459, 661
Glass, duties on, 643
  making, art of, 655
  Vauxhall, 643
Globe-stands, spindle-leg, 671
Glossary of terms, 710-722
Glue, suspicious use of, 13
Godmersham, Georgian decoration schemes at, 207
Gothic chest, 35
  influence, 32, 39, 248, 258, 286, 309, 331, 334, 340, 341, 345, 353, 364, 367, 369, 377, 378
Gothic-cum-Louis Quinze, 378
Grades in furniture, 242
Grandfather chairs, 169, 314
GRANDFATHER CLOCKS, 94, 123, 133, 515
  bijou specimens, 133
  lacquered, 152
  marquetry, 547
  pre-Chippendale, 129
  Queen Anne, 131
  Sheraton, 547
  warning to purchasers of, 130
  Wetherfield collection, 122
  William and Mary, 120
  wood used in early specimens, 133
Grecian honeysuckle as decoration, 492
Gretton, Charles, clockmaker, 125, 127
Grinding mirrors, 649

Index.

Grotesqueries in Georgian furniture, 217
Grotesques, Adam, 466
   Irish Chippendale, 397
Grylls, Mr., 118

H.

Haig and Chippendale, 232
Hairwood, 14
Halfpenny, W. J., 609, 611
Hamilton, William, R.A., 603
Handles, 19 and Plate
   Adam, 19 and Plate
   Chippendale, 19, 21, and Plate
   Heppelwhite, 19, 21, and Plate
   ivory, 22
   Queen Anne, 21
   reproductions, 22
   Sheraton, 19, 21, and Plate
Hanging-lights, 460, 461
Hardcastle, Mr. A., quoted, 684
Harlequin-table, Sheraton, 592
Harmony between house and furniture, 196
Harpsichords, Adam, 436
Hautbois, 539
Hawksmoor quoted, 193
Heaton, Mr. Henniker, quoted, 643
Henry VII., 32
HENRY VIII. FURNITURE, 32, 33
   benches, 36
   box-chairs, 37
   buffets, 36
   corner-chairs, 38
   decoration, 39
   dining-tables, 36
   Gothic influence, 39
   hutches, 36
   leather-chests, 37
   occasional tables, 36
   turned-wood chairs, 38
   X-shaped chairs, 37
HEPPELWHITE, 221, 479
   Adam influence in, 482
   aims declared, 501

HEPPELWHITE (*cont.*):
   anthemion decoration, fondness for, 486
   armchair, 481
   arms, 585
   barjiers chairs, 513
   bedroom furniture, 514
   bedsteads, 518
   bergère chairs, 513
   bookcases, 514
   brass furniture, 19 and Plate
   cabinets, 509, 514
   cabriole chairs, 513
   card-tables, 485, 506
   cellarets, 513
   chair-arms, 496
   chairs, 482, 486, 503
   characteristics of his work, 491
   classification into periods, 482
   compared with his compeers, 505
   confidantes, 513
   connection with the Gillows, 479
   Duchesse, 513
   early examples, 480
   employed by the Adams, 497
   fire-screens, 517, 518
   folding-screens, 518
   gardes-de-vin, 513
   grandfather clocks, 515
   "Guide," 480, 511
   handles, 19, 21
   horse-screens, 518
   japanning methods, 499
   knife-boxes, 497
   knife-urns, 497
   ladder-backs, 501
   looking-glasses, 656
   Louis Quinze style, 481, 485
   Louis Seize influence, 487, 491, 492
   oval-backs, 495
   Pembroke tables, 509
   points of differentiation from Chippendale, 483
   pole-screens, 518

3 B

HEPPELWHITE (cont.):
  political convictions influence his work, 507
  position as designer, 479
  prices, 706
  Prince of Wales's feathers as decoration, 518
  reflecting dressing-table, 517
  rococo decoration, 491
  roll-over pieces, 514
  Rudd's table, 514
  saddle-backs, 491
  "school," 508
  secretaires, 514
  shield-back chairs, 487, 491
  sideboards, 307, 420, 496, 497, 513
  sideboard-tables, 497
  Simon, Miss Constance, quoted, 479
  simplicity of style a characteristic, 486
  sofa-arms, 496
  tables, 514
  tea-caddies, 563
  transitional style, 482
  tripods, 262
  upholstered chairs, 496
  urn-stands, 514
  wheatears as decoration, 518
  wheel-back chairs, 484, 489, 490, 492
  window-seats, 483, 513
  wing-cupboards, 496
Heppelwhite and Co., 480, 508
Hepplewhite (see Heppelwhite)
High-backed chairs, Queen Anne, 169
Hinges, cabinet, 21
Hogarth chair, 166
Honeysuckle, Grecian, 299, 492
Hope, Thos., 609, 610, 614
"Horse" dressing-glass, Sheraton, 593
  fire-screens, Chippendale, 372
House-decorations, Sheraton, 595
Husks as decoration, 488
Hutches, 36
  double, 48

I.

INCE AND MAYHEW, 279, 286, 291, 359, 609, 612
  C-scrolls, 288
  compared with Chippendale, 287, 288
  pierced and cluster-leg work, 288
  styles in Chinese Chippendale, 286
INLAY, 15
  Adam, 423, 470
  blistered, 15, 577
  bone, 111
  buckled-up, 15, 577
  Chippendale, 381
  Elizabethan, 13
  ironing, 25
  Jacobean, 66
  ovals, prices, 695
  pateræ as decoration, 491
  relaid, 15
  shell, 585
  Sheraton, 570
  started, 15
Interiors, Adam, 411
IRISH CHIPPENDALE, 386
  acanthus decoration, 389
  bookcase writing-cabinet, 386
  carving compared with English, 389
  china-cabinets, 397
  clothes-presses, 397
  decoration scheme, 390
  design, 390
  frauds in, 395
  grotesque masks on, 397
  Jones, Thomas, quoted, 398
  Kauffmann (Angelica) influence, 398
  Louis Quinze influence, 389
  mahogany used in, 393
  origin, 394
  Pembroke tables, 399
  side-table, 391
  staple pieces, 393
Ironing inlay, 25
"Ironing-up" tables, 263

Index.

Italian influence on the Adams, 408
Ivory furniture, 681
  handles, 22
  inlay, 111

J.

Jack-in-the-box vogue, Chippendale's, 258
JACOBEAN FURNITURE, 59
  appliqué decoration, 66
  carving, 65
  chairs, 63, 75, 77, 79, 81
  Charles I., 80
  Charles II. furniture, 89
  chests, 5
  coffin-stools, 78
  couches, 79
  Court cupboards, 61
  Court cupboards, Welsh, 82, 83
  Cromwellian furniture, 85
  day-beds, 63
  influence of Continental schools, 60
  inlay, 66
  James I., 59
  joint-stools, 78
  lovers'-seats, 79
  meaning of the term, 60
  minor embellishments, 67
  panelling, 64, 107
  piquet-tables, 293
  prices, 700
  products of carpenter and joiner differentiated, 65
  progression of, 72
  Restoration, 85
  settees, 63, 79
  stools, 63, 79
  table-benches, 74
  table-chairs, 73
  tabourets, 79
  Ueberhangs-Schrank, 69
  upholstered furniture, evolution of, 63
  William and Mary, 115
  woodwork, 105

James I. furniture, 59
  upholstery, 665
Japanned furniture, Adam, 459
  warning to buyers, 500
Japanning, claims of, urged by Heppelwhite, 499
Jasper-ware plaques, 436
Johnson, Thos., 279, 281, 285, 609, 611
Joint-stools, Elizabethan, 49
  Jacobean, 78
Joints, 18
Jones, Inigo, 57, 177, 193
Jones, William, 609, 611

K.

Kauffmann, Angelica, and the Adams, 432, 433, 436, 439
  mural paintings by, 209
  quoted, 398, 409, 413, 441, 453, 457
Kent, William, 57, 193, 200, 203
Kneehole-tables, Queen Anne, 169, 170
Knife-boxes, Heppelwhite, 497
  Sheraton, 561
Knife-urns, Heppelwhite, 497
  Sheraton, 540

L.

Lacquer, Oriental, 30
LACQUERED FURNITURE, abundance of, 152
  cabinets, 14, 147
  Chambers's teachings, 134
  colours most prized, 152
  decorative schemes, 134
  difficulty in repairing, 140
  Dutch work, 136
  Eastern and Western products compared, 141
  Eastern ideas, 134
  England's contribution to, 138
  Europeans contributing, 135
  Evelyn quoted, 140

LACQUERED FURNITURE (*cont.*):
grandfather clocks, 152
lacquering process described, 142
Louis Quatorze influence, 147
monopoly in, 138
periods of popularity, 134
stands for cabinets, 150
"worm," liability to, 140
Lacquering, antiquity of, 141
description of, 142
evolution of, 151
Ladder-back chairs, 490
Chippendale, 247, 301, 317
Heppelwhite, 501
Langley, Batty, 279, 363
on cabinet-makers of the time, 234
Lanthorns, Chinese Chippendale, 284
Late Georgian work, 187
Late Tudor upholstery, 665
Leafwork, popularity of, on Sheraton furniture, 578
Leather chests, 37
Legwork, Chippendale, 382, 384
LESSER ENGLISH CABINET-MAKERS, 609
Ackermann, 610
Adam Brothers' disciples, 610
Carter, J., 610
Chippendale disciples, 610
Columbani, P., 614
Copeland, H., 612
Crunden, J., 610, 613
Darly, Matthew, 612, 613
"Director" period, 618
Edwards and Darly, 279, 283, 285, 291, 364, 609
Edwards, G., 612
enumerated, 615
Halfpenny, W., 611
Halfpenny, W. and J., 609
Hope, Thos., 609, 610, 614
Ince and Mayhew, 279, 286, 291, 359, 609, 612
Johnson, Thos., 609, 611
Jones, William, 609, 611

LESSER ENGLISH CABINET-MAKERS (*cont.*):
literature of, 610
Lock, Matthias, 612, 613
Manwaring, Robt., 609, 612
Morris, J. II., 613
Pain, W., 613
Pergolesi, M. A., 610, 614
pre-"Director" period, 615
Richardson, 610
Shearer, T., 614
Sheraton period, 620
Smith, G., 614
Swan, Abraham, 609, 611
Taylor, J., 615
Wallis, N., 613
Letter-scrolls, 109
"Liardet," an Adam introduction, 411
Library-steps and table combined, Sheraton, 593
Linacre, Thomas, quoted, 31
Lion's-claw feet, 297
Literary work of eighteenth century masters analysed, 221
Literature, Georgian, 212
Lock, Matthias, 612, 613
Long-banding, prices, 694
Looking-glasses, Heppelwhite, 656
Queen Anne, 659
Shearer, 659
Louis Quatorze, 118, 147, 291
Louis Quinze, 19, 242, 245, 252, 266, 283, 286, 291, 292, 298, 309, 319, 331, 333, 334, 337, 340, 341, 342, 346, 353, 362, 367, 369, 375, 376, 379, 481, 487, 491
Louis Quinze-cum-Chinese, 286, 379
Louis Quinze, Chinese, and Gothic compounded, 286
Louis Seize Anglaise type, 550, 579
Louis Seize influence, 421, 454, 467, 487, 491, 492, 532, 541, 579

Index.

Louis Treize style, 80
Lovers'-seats, Jacobean, 79, 313, 314
Lowndes, Jonathan, clockmaker, 131
Lyre-back chairs, Adam, 487
  originators of, 462

M.

Macquoid, Mr. Percy, quoted, 141, 602
Made-up pieces, 10
Mahogany, grain of, 7
  used by the Adams, 419
  used in Irish Chippendale, 393
Manocchi and the Adams, 431
Mantelpieces, Adam, 410, 421, 423, 435, 436
Manwaring, Robt., 609, 612
"Marlboro" leg, Sheraton, 582
Marquetry, 15, 43
  bird-and-bouquet, 125, 127
  cabinets, 171
  Charles II., 110
  cobweb, 125, 131
  English, 122
  floral, 172
  seaweed, 125, 131, 172
  spider-web, 172
  spurious, used in Sheraton furniture, 577
  writing-cabinet, 53
Mayhew and Ince quoted, 283
Medallions as decoration, 492
Michelangelo, 55
Mid-Georgian work, 186
Mirrors, 640
  Adam, 429, 459
  bevelling, 657
  Chinese Chippendale, 284
  Chippendale, 651
  collectors' hints, 645
  convex, 654
  duties on glass, 643
  early Georgian, 201
  factors affecting prices, 646
  frames for, 658

Mirrors (*cont.*):
  Gill and Reigate quoted, 654
  girandoles, 661
  glass-making, evolution of, 655
  grinding, 649
  Heaton, Mr. Henniker, quoted, 643
  Partridge, F., 644
  polishing, 649
  pre-Adam, 658
  prices, 709
  progress of, 640
  Queen Anne, 163, 647
  silvering, 650
  Stuart, 641
  William and Mary, 644
  wall, Adam, 468
Mirror-frames, Queen Anne, 169
Miscellanea, 680
Mitreing mouldings, 697
Monastic period, 35
Morris, J. H., 613
Morse, Frances Clary, quoted, 129, 322
Mouldings, prices for, 692
Multum-in-parvo furniture, 256
Musical instruments, 630, 637
Mythological subjects used by the Adams, 466-7

N.

Needlework, stump, 137

O.

Oak, collectors of, 199
Occasional tables, 36
Oiling, 2
  and polishing, 697
Orders in architecture, influence of, 57, 58
Organ-cases, adapting, 340
  Chippendale, 340
  Sheraton, 563
Ormolu used by the Adams, 458
Oval-back chairs, 495
Overmantels, Georgian, 205

P.

Pagoda-shaped dome used by Chippendale, 365
Pain, W., 614
PAINTED FURNITURE, Adam, 419, 422, 457
  condition of, 577
  Sheraton, 555, 566
Paintings, use of, in fakes, 17
Paint-removers, 685
Palladio, 55
Panelling, faked, 10
  Jacobean, 64
  Jacobean, used in reproductions, 107
Papier-mâché used by the Adams, 416
Parrot's-beak knee-garnishment, 355
Partridge, F., quoted, 644
  R. W., quoted, 567, 569, 605
Pateræ as decoration, 486
  inlaid, as decoration, 491
"Patina," 4, 464
Pearl-and-lozenge moulding, 298
Péché-mortel, Chippendale, 338
Pedestal tables, 331
Pediment, swan-necked, 208
Pediments discarded by the Adams, 469
Peg-top tables, Chippendale, 266
Pembroke tables, Heppelwhite, 512
  Irish Chippendale, 399
Pergolesi, M. A., 409, 610, 614
  and the Adams, 431, 435
Phillips, J. D., quoted, 668
Picture-frames Chippendale, 350
Pie-crust tables, 263
Pierced fret decoration in Chinese Chippendale, 280
Pier-tables, Chinese Chippendale, 284
  Chippendale, 341
  Sheraton, 591
Piquet-tables, Charles II., 293
Piranesi, 409
  and the Adams, 425, 430, 431

Plain-top tables, Chippendale, 267
Plaques, Flaxman's jasper-ware, used by Adams, 437
Pole-screens, Heppelwhite, 518
Polishing, 2
  mirrors, 649
Porcelains, famille-rose, 249
  famille-verte, 249
Portuguese Chippendale, 389
PRICES, 687
  Adam brothers, 706
  astragals, 696
  auction, 698
  banding and stringing, 693
  bookcase doors, 696
  bracket clocks, 709
  brass fittings, 697
  carcase-work, 689
  Chinese Chippendale, 705
  Chippendale, 702
  crossbanding, 694
  Elizabethan, 699
  fluting, 694
  Heppelwhite, 706
  inlaid ovals, 695
  Jacobean, 700
  long-banding, 694
  mirrors, 709
  mitreing mouldings, 697
  mouldings, 692
  oiling and polishing, 697
  Queen Anne and Georgian, 701
  Sheraton, 707
  veneering, 695
Prince of Wales's feathers as decoration, 492, 495, 518
Pure-state furniture, 10
Putty, colouring, to give age, 15

Q.

Quarrelling, 18
QUEEN ANNE FURNITURE, 154
  architectural influences, 176
  armorial decoration, 175
  bookcases, 171, 173
  bracket clocks, 631

QUEEN ANNE FURNITURE (cont.):
  brasswork, 19 and Plate
  broken pediment in, 175
  bureaus, 169, 171
  bureau-bookcases, 169, 171, 173
  C-scroll, 165
  cabinets, 156
  cabriole-leg considered, 154
  card-tables, 169, 170, 297
  chairs, 156, 165, 166, 167, 169, 174
  characteristics of, 154
  chests of drawers, 173
  china-cabinets, 169, 171
  claw-and-ball extremities, 158, 173
  doming, 175
  Dutch weakness in, 176
  escallop-shell decoration, 165
  gilding introduced, 155
  handles, 21
  kneehole-tables, 169, 170
  looking-glasses, 659
  marquetry, 171
  mirrors, 163, 173, 647
  mirror-frames, 169
  plain period of, 172
  prices, 701
  settee, two-chair-back, 159
  settees, 166, 169
  tea-caddies, 173
  toilet-glasses, 173
  upholstered, 168
  walnut the popular wood, 155
  wing-chairs, 170
  writing-tables, 169

R.

Rainçeaux used by the Adams, 435, 465
"Raised" grain, 8
  ribbon tables, 263
Rannie, James, 231
Raphael, 55
Redgrave quoted, 233
Reeve, Robert Dalby, quoted, 551
Reflecting dressing-table, 517
Relief-carving on chair-backs, 572
Renaissance, Early English, 56, 193
  Italian, 54
Replicas, 12
Restoration furniture, 85
Restoring furniture, 85
  upholstery, 665
Retrospect, a, 683
Re-veneering, 11
Rhus vernicifera, 143
Ribbon carving, 264
  chairs criticised, 571
Richardson, 610
Ripley quoted, 193
Rococo blended with Oriental work, 283
  decoration, 333, 374, 491
Roll-over pieces, Heppelwhite, 514
Rose-and-ribbon border, 298
Rosewood supplants mahogany, 599
Rudd's table, 514

S.

S-scroll, 108
Saddle-back chairs, Heppelwhite, 491
Sand-burning furniture, 15
Satinwood, 14
  lavish use of, by Sheraton, 599
Scent-diffusers, Sheraton, 594
Scratch-carving, 65
Screen-tables, Sheraton, 593
Screens, fire-, 518
Scroll-work, Charles II., 105
Scrolls, C- and S-, 108, 165, 270, 271
Seaweed marquetry, 125, 131, 172
Secretaires, Heppelwhite, 514
SEDDONS, THE, 601
  cabinets, 603
  constitution of the firm, 607
  family history, 601
  George, 601
  McQuoid, Mr., quoted, 602

SEDDONS, THE (*cont.*):
   Partridge, Mr. R. W., quoted, 605
   quality of work, 607
   Robert, 602
   Sons, and Shackleton, 602
   status in the art-crafts, 601
   Thomas, jun., pre-Raphaelite painter, 608
   William, 602
Serpentine swell, Adam, 468
   Sheraton, 588
Serving-boards, Chippendale, 335
Serving-tables, Charles II., 107
   Chippendale, 331, 332, 333
Settees, Chippendale, 313, 318
   "conversions," 322
   Dutch, 325
   faked, 12
   foreign, 322, 323, 325
   Jacobean, 63, 79
   Portuguese, 323, 327
   Queen Anne, 159, 166, 169
   Sheraton, 555, 583, 588
   three-chair-back, 318, 321
   two-chair-back, 318, 321
Settee-backs, spindle-leg, 674
Shackleton, Thomas, a partner with the Seddons, 602
"Shamming," 578
SHEARER, T., 614
   influence on Sheraton, 533
   looking-glasses, 659
   sideboards, 307, 420
Shell-border, down-turned, 238
   embellishment, 334
   inlay, Sheraton, 585
SHERATON, 221, 528
   barometers, 565
   bedsteads, 588, 591
   Adam Black on, 528, 532
   Adams' influence, 539, 541
   ambition and aims, 536
   arrival in London, 528
   Benn quoted, 531
   birthplace, 531
   bookcases, 588
   bottle-cabinets, 543
   bracket clocks, 633
   brass utilised by, 595

SHERATON (*cont.*):
   business capacity considered, 561
   capabilities as a draughtsman, 529
   chairs, 537, 567, 569
   chair-backs, 546
   chair-designs, 578, 580
   chair-legs, 581
   Clouston, R. S., quoted, 531
   combination library-steps and table, 593
   commodes, 530, 588
   commonsense hints on furnishing, 546
   conversation chairs, 593
   corner-cabinets, 535
   curvilinear treatment, 546, 580
   decadent period, 597
   decoration, 577, 585
   designs, origin of, 574
   "Drawing-Book," 529, 536, 545, 550, 553
   "Drawing-Book" and "Director" compared, 542
   early examples, 562, 598
   Empire vogue, 579, 597
   fancy woods replace mahogany, 566
   fondness for satin-wood, 599
   frieze compositions, 592
   genius recognised, 557
   grandfather clocks, 547
   handles, 19, 21
   harlequin-table, 592
   "horse" dressing-glasses, 593
   house decorations, 595
   indebtedness to other makers, 554
   inlaid decoration, 570
   involved compositions, 542
   knife-boxes, 561
   knife-urns, 540
   leafwork, 578
   looking-glasses, 659
   looseness of the term, 566

Index.

SHERATON (*cont.*) :
Louis Seize Anglaise types, 550, 579
Louis Seize influence, 532, 541, 579
"Marlboro'" leg, 582
multum-in-parvo furniture criticised, 538
organ-cases, 563
painted furniture, 555, 566
Partridge, Mr. R. W., quoted, 567, 569
pier-tables, 591
position as a craftsman, 528
position as a tradesman, 549
'prentice pieces, 563
prices, 708
rainçeaux, 585
reviews Heppelwhite's Guide, 501
rivals, 562
rosewood ousts mahogany, 599
scent-diffusers, 594
"school," 550, 586
screen-tables, 593
serpentine swell, 588
settees, 555, 583, 589
Shearer influence, 533, 540, 541
shell inlay, 585
sideboards, 307, 551, 559, 588
side-tables, 545, 575, 588
Simon, Miss Constance, quoted, 600
"spade "-toe, 582
splats, 582
spurious marquetry, 577
straight-line influence, 589
stretcher-work, 581
tables, 572
tea-caddies, 563
technique, mastery of, 541
"thimble-toe," 582
tract-writer, the, 531
trade followers, 610
trays, 540
tripods, 262, 572
vindictiveness, 529
window-drapery, 549

SHERATON (*cont.*) :
writing-cabinets, 533
X-shaping, 587
Shield-back chairs, 487
Adam, 487
Heppelwhite, 491
Gillows, 487, 524, 525
originators of, 462
Short cupboards, 49
Show-case, china, Chippendale, 359
Show-shelf, Chippendale, 353
Sideboards, Adam, 307, 420
Chippendale, 307
Elizabethan, 45
faked, 499
Heppelwhite, 307, 420, 496, 497, 513
Heppelwhite's, compared with Shearer's, 498
painted, Heppelwhite, 498
Shearer, 420
Sheraton, 307, 551, 559, 588
Sideboard-tables, 420
Heppelwhite, 496, 497
Side-tables, 464
Adam, 405, 451, 471
Charles II., 107
Chippendale, rarity of, as compared with card-tables, 296
Irish Chippendale, 391
Sheraton, 545, 575, 588
Silvering mirrors, 650
Simon, Miss Constance, quoted, 228, 231, 232, 236, 357, 479, 600
Smith, G., 614
Sofas, Adam, 463
Chippendale, 313
"Spade "-toe, Sheraton, 582
Spider-leg Furniture (*see* Spindle-leg Furniture)
Spider-web marquetry, 172
SPINDLE-LEG FURNITURE, 669, 676
basin-stands, 674
bowl-stands, 672
candlestands, 672
chairs, 674
cluster-tables, 674

SPINDLE-LEG FURNITURE (*cont.*):
  fire-screens, 674
  gate-tables, 670
  globe-stands, 671
  method of production, 679
  outline decadence, 679
  rarity of the work, 676
  tables, 677
  towel-rails, 674, 675
  turnery employed for, 669
  wood used in, 676
  writing-tables, 671, 672
Spiral turning, 95
  volute used by the Adams, 466
Spoon-back chairs, 167
Square-leg, use of, by Chippendale, 354
Stained furniture, 681
Stained-wood inlay, 111
"Started" inlay, 15
Stools, Charles II., 97, 105
  Chippendale, 339
  Chippendale's X-shaped, 339
  Georgian, 220
  Jacobean, 63, 79
Straight-line influence, Sheraton, 589
Strange, T. A., quoted, 200
Strap-work, Elizabethan, 44
Stretcher-work, Charles II., 109
  eschewed by Sheraton, 581
  William and Mary, 118
Stuart mirrors, 641
Stucco treatment, Adam, 453
Stump-needlework, 137
Supports to cabinet-work, Chippendale, 385
  used by Chippendale, 383, 384
Swan, Abraham, 609, 611

T.

Tabernacle frames, 187, 208
Table-benches, 74
Table-chairs, Jacobean, 73
Tables. (*See* under the various periods, makers, and specific headings)

Table-tops, Charles II., 106
  faked, 267
Tabourets, 79
Tallboys, 539
Taylor, J., 615
Tea-caddies, Chippendale, 367
  Heppelwhite, 563
  Queen Anne, 173
  Sheraton, 563
Telescopic dining-table, Gillows, 524
Thimble-toe, Sheraton, 582
"Three-deckers," Elizabethan, 49
Tied-work, William and Mary, 118
Toilet-glasses, 173
Tompion, Thomas, clockmaker, 123
Toning recipe for new cane on chairs, 98
Torchères, Chippendale, 341
Towel-rails, 675
  spindle-leg, 674
Trafalgar period, 459, 472, 501
Trays, Sheraton, 540
Tridarn, Welsh, 49
Tripod, application of the term, 260
  fire-screens, Chippendale, 371
  tables, Chippendale, 224, 225, 238, 240, 243, 251, 259, 261, 263, 264, 266, 267, 269
Tripods, 260
  Sheraton, 572
Trophies, military and other, used by the Adams, 466
Tudor style, 34
Turned-leg furniture, 669
Turned-wood chairs, 38
Turned work, Chippendale, 251
Turning, spiral, 95, 106

U.

Ueberhangs-Schrank, 69
Universal table, Sheraton, 593

Index.

Upholstered chairs, Heppelwhite, 496
  furniture evolved, 63
  Charles II., 113
UPHOLSTERY, 662
  Cromwellian, 665
  eighteenth-century, 665
  James I. to Commonwealth, 665
  late Tudor, 665
  materials for, 662, 667
  Phillips, J. D., quoted, 668
  Restoration, 665
  Royal School of Art Needlework, 666
Urn-stands, Heppelwhite, 514
Urns as decoration, 492

V.

Vanbrugh, Sir John, quoted, 193, 194
Varnish, 24
Vases as decoration, 486
Vauxhall glass, 643
Veneer, mahogany, used by Adam, 423
Veneering, prices, 695
Vernis-Martin, 368
Vitruvian scroll, 333, 466

W.

Wall-lights, Adam, 416, 459
Wall-mirrors, Adam, 468
Wallis, N., 613
Walnut supplants oak for furniture-making, 94
  used in Charles II. furniture, 113
Wardrobes, Chippendale, 375
  Georgian, 208
"Washing-off," 8
Washstands, Chippendale, 379
Waterloo period, 459, 472, 501
Waxing, 2
Wear, evidences of, 13
Webb and Carter quoted, 193
Wedgwoods and the Adams, 436

Welsh Court cupboard, 83
Wetherfield collection of clocks, 515, 547
Wheat-ears as decoration, 518
Wheel-back chairs, 489
  Heppelwhite, 484, 490, 492
Whorled feet used by Chippendale, 267
Wig-stands, Chippendale, 249, 379
WILLIAM AND MARY FURNITURE, 115
  applied art in cabinet-making, 121
  birdcage clocks, 126
  bracket clocks, 631
  brass furniture, 19 and Plate
  card-tables, 119
  chairbacks compared with Heppelwhite, 484
  chairs, 117, 118
  cobweb marquetry, 131
  Flemish influence, 117
  grandfather clocks, 120, 127, 131
  lantern clocks, 126
  Louis Quatorze influence, 116
  mirrors, 644
  seaweed marquetry, 131
  stretcher-work, 118
  tied-work, 118
Wincklem, J. J., quoted, 436
Window-drapery, Sheraton, 549
Window-seats, Heppelwhite, 483, 513
Wine-cooler, Chippendale, 337
Wine-tables, Chippendale, 268, 269
Wing-chairs, 169, 170, 314
Wood, quoted, 193
Woods, grain of, as guide when purchasing, 7
  allowed apprentices, 14
  employed, 44, 94, 114
  used by the Adams, 416
Woodwork, Jacobean, 105
  of fire-screens in relation to date, 371

"Worm," exterminating, 8, 23, 24, 140, 500, 684
"Wormer," the, 9
Wren, Sir Christopher, 57, 190
Writing-cabinet bookcase, Irish Chippendale, 386
    marquetry, 53
    Sheraton, 533
Writing-tables, 383
    Adam, 436
    Chippendale, 252, 299, 329, 331, 383
    Queen Anne, 169
    spindle-leg, 671, 672

X.

X-shaped chairs, 37, 53
    Chippendale, 312
    stools, Chippendale, 339
X-shaping, Sheraton, 587

Y.

Yorkshire chairs, 77

Z.

Zucchi, Antonio, 409
    and the Adams, 422, 439

www.ingramcontent.com/pod-product-compliance
Lightning Source LLC
Chambersburg PA
CBHW021411300426
44114CB00010B/460